PEOPLE AND ISSUES IN
LATIN AMERICAN HISTORY

PEOPLE AND ISSUES IN LATIN AMERICAN HISTORY:
FROM INDEPENDENCE TO THE PRESENT

Sources and Interpretations

Edited by
LEWIS HANKE and
JANE M. RAUSCH
University of Massachusetts, Amherst

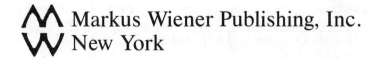 Markus Wiener Publishing, Inc.
New York

For information write to: Markus Wiener Publishing, Inc. 225 Lafayette Street, New York, NY 10012.

Library of Congress Cataloging-in-Publication Data

People and issues in Latin American history : from independence to the
   present / edited by Louis [i.e. Lewis] Hanke and Jane M. Rausch.
      Rev. ed. of: History of Latin American Civilization. Sources and
      Interpretations, vol. 2. 2d ed., 1973.
      Includes bibliographical references.
      ISBN 1-55876-018-0 :
      1. Latin America—History—1830–   I. Hanke, Lewis.   II. Rausch,
   Jane M., 1940– .   III. Hanke, Lewis. History of Latin America.
   F1413.P457 1989
   980.03—dc20   89-27946
                                                                    CIP

The photographs in the text are reproduced courtesy of the following sources: Jane Rausch, Amherst, Cuban Interest Section, Washington, Helen Wiener, Munich, Germany, and Fritz and Inge Neske, Munich.

Printed in the United States of America

CONTENTS

PREFACE

In 1969 Lewis Hanke published HISTORY OF LATIN AMERICAN CIVI-LIZATION: SOURCES AND INTERPRETATIONS, a two-volume reader designed to serve as the principal text for survey courses on Latin American history. Hanke's purpose was "to present a reasonable selection of sources on and interpretations of some of the important events and topics in the history of Latin America." The book was an instant success. Scores of professors adopted it for their classes and continued to rely on the second edition when it was published by Little, Brown and Company in 1973.

This reader is an attempt to salvage a portion of Hanke's valuable text which has been out of print for more than ten years. Sections II, III, IV, and V are slightly abridged units that appeared in the second edition of Volume II of SOURCES AND INTERPRETATIONS, subtitled THE MODERN AGE. Sections I, VI, VII, and VIII are new units which include some excerpts from the original reader. Wherever possible I have retained Hanke's introductions to the units and individual selections. I am grateful to Professor Hanke who has generously permitted me to reprint sections of his book.

In its new form, this reader is not intended to replace the textbooks normally assigned in a course but to supplement them by providing a range of materials that will enable students to debate the historical significance of individuals and issues in their class discussion sections. An effort has been made to include primary as well as secondary sources, and to incorporate selections from the works of outstanding Latin Americans as well as prominent British and North American scholars. For each unit I have appended suggestions for additional reading and the titles of some readily available 16 mm. films and videotapes that will add visual dimension to the printed word. It is my hope that a careful examination of these materials will initiate undergraduates into the fascinating complexities of historical analysis and enhance their understanding of some of the memorable men and women who have helped to shape the destinies of the Latin American nations.

Jane M. Rausch
Amherst

Bolívar in 1819

SECTION I

Simón Bolívar—
The Liberator

Simón Bolívar was the most extraordinary figure to emerge from the era of independence in Latin America. In his relatively short lifetime (1783–1830), he played the varied roles of Jacobin conspirator, military hero, state-builder, nationalist and hemisphere leader. Indeed, as historian David Bushnell has pointed out, "Bolívar justly occupies a significant place not only in Latin American annals as a founder of independent nations, but in the broader history of Western Civilization as one of the most gifted leaders of the cluster of revolutionary movements that marked the last quarter of the eighteenth century and the beginning of the nineteenth." [1]

The first three readings are taken from the two-volume *Selected Writings of Bolívar* (New York: Bolivarian Society of Venezuela, 1951) compiled by Vicente Lecuna, translated by Lewis Bertrand and edited by Harold A. Bierck, Jr. Reading 1 is a biographical sketch of the Liberator (the title that Bolívar preferred). Readings 2 and 3 are two important documents composed by Bolívar. Reading 4 is an excerpt from a biography written by British historian J.B. Trend. It recounts the last two years of Bolívar's career, during which he survived a humiliating attempt on his life and witnessed the dissolution of Gran Colombia. On December 17, 1830, on his way into exile, Bolívar died of tuberculosis at Santa Marta on the Colombian coast. In one of his last letters to General Juan José Flores, he poured out his despair with the words, "He who serves a revolution ploughs the sea."

[1] David Bushnell, *The Liberator, Simon Bolívar: Man and Image* (New York: Knopf) 1970, xiii

1

1. Simón Bolívar: The Life, The Man

HAROLD A. BIERCK, JR.

I—THE LIFE

Simón José Antonio de la Santisima Trinidad Bolívar was born on July 24, 1783, in Caracas, Venezuela; he died on December 17, 1830, at the Villa San Pedro Alejandrino near Santa Marta, Colombia. Proclaimed "Liberator" by his own people, he was a world-renowned figure in his day. His prophetic vision of hemispheric solidarity lives today, and his political thinking serves dictator and democrat alike in contemporary Latin America. Bolívar has no parallel among the leaders of the United States. The military prowess of Washington, the political views of Jefferson, the humaneness of Lincoln—all can be found in varying measure in the heart, the writings, and the deeds of the Liberator.

Courageous, indeed, will be the author of the definitive life of Bolívar. Although such a work has yet to be written either in Spanish or in English, there are many available "lives" from which the reader of English can learn the main facts about his career. Glorifying rather than analyzing, such works as *The Passionate Warrior, He Wouldn't Be King,* the *Dauntless Liberator,* the *Idealist,* the *Man of Glory* are to be found in university and public libraries. For the most part these biographies, as well as those cited below, portray the man himself, while minimizing the powerful influences—social, economic, and political—of the time in which Bolívar fought and lived.

The Bolívarian era was fraught with greed and stained with blood. Cries for justice and liberty resounded over a land confused by social and economic inequalities born of a colonial existence that favored birth over initiative. In 1810 a minority group of propertied white men, obsessed by the magic of independence, began their struggle to break a pattern of life that had been molded by more than three centuries of political restrictions, economic handicaps, and social barriers. These men of property, of whom Bolívar was

From: *Selected Writings of Bolívar,* compiled by Vicente Lecuna, edited by Harold A. Bierck, Jr. (New York: Bolivarian Society of Venezuela. 1951). 1, pp. xiii–xxx. Reprinted by permission.

one, attempted the impossible. The life, liberty, and happiness that they sought to gain through the adoption of a political structure similar to that of the United States had become, by 1830, more a fantasy than a reality. The ideal of freedom was never relinquished, yet realism was the true victor. Lack of experience in democratic government, illiteracy, ill-chosen foreign debts, a temperament that made compromise difficult, the continuance of social inequalities based on birth and property—all combined, as Bolívar prophesied, to prolong the disrupting force of revolution. From this vortex, nevertheless, there emerged a personal dignity, a state of mind, a conviction, a driving force that can only be termed democracy—Latin American democracy. This democracy is epitomized in the writings of Bolívar. Its comprehension by the people of the United States will be the reasoned answer to Latin American political disturbances.

Within the framework of colonial restriction and revolutionary ferment Bolívar was born, raised, and honored. His life, prior to the beginning of his public career in 1810, was somewhat typical of the wealthy young white of his day. Although he was orphaned at the age of nine (his father died when he was three) his maternal uncle Esteban Palacios cared for his extensive properties and provided him with tutors. Among the latter was Simón Rodríguez. This eccentric disciple of the eighteenth century Enlightenment schooled the young Bolívar in the precepts of Locks, Hobbes, and the French *philosophes*, particularly Rousseau. The concepts and principles that were reborn in the Age of Reason were never to be abandoned by Bolívar. Indeed, in his writings the political philosophy of the Enlightenment frequently outweighs his praise of British parliamentarianism and his criticism of United States federalism.

At the age of sixteen Bolívar went to Spain. In Madrid his wealth procured for him the finest clothes and further education, but his American birth was a handicap to success in the court life of the Spanish capital. Intrigue, a supposed insult to the Prince of Asturias, later King Ferdinand VII, and a love affair that was soon to culminate in marriage highlighted his first three years in Spain. After spending several months in Paris the nineteen-year-old Bolívar, deeply in love, returned to Madrid in 1802 and married María Teresa Rodríguez del Toro, daughter of a Caracas-born nobleman. In the summer of that year he brought his bride to Caracas, resigned, apparently, to assume the life of a landed gentleman. But within six months María Teresa died, leaving him childless. Vowing never to remarry, Bolívar returned to Europe, determined to live life to the full.

After a brief visit in Madrid, Bolívar journeyed to Paris, where, with an intensity that characterized his every effort, he gambled, loved, and studied. The charming and adventurous Madame Fanny Dervieu du Villars became his friend and, some say, his mistress. Through her Bolívar became acquainted with the social life of imperial France. But the glamour of the Napoleonic capital appeared tarnished to the young man of Caracas, and he came to regard the Emperor Napoleon as a dishonored tyrant who had betrayed the principles of French republicanism. His mind, filled with ideas of freedom, liberty, and human rights gained from an avid reading of the works of Montesquieu, Voltaire, Rousseau, Locke, Condillac, Buffon, D'Alembert, Helvitius, Hobbes, and Spinoza, found monarchy and its trappings repugnant; hence, he turned to his former tutor, Rodríguez, for advice and intellectual stimulation.

Under the guidance of Rodríguez, or Robinson as he occasionally called himself, Bolívar became a republican in spirit and purpose. "You molded my heart for liberty, justice, greatness, and beauty. . . . You cannot imagine how deeply engraved upon my heart are the lessons you taught me. Never could I delete so much as a comma from the great precepts that you set before me," Bolívar wrote his mentor in later life. In 1805 master and pupil journeyed to southern France and then to Italy. In Rome, on the Monte Sacro, Bolívar vowed that he would liberate his native land. Whether or not this was but an impulse of the moment or the result of mature reasoning cannot be determined from the evidence at hand. It cannot be denied, however, that the remainder of his life was devoted to the fulfillment of that vow. Leaving Rodríguez in Italy, Bolívar returned to Paris, confided his hopes to Fanny du Villars, and then set sail for the United States. Early in 1807, he visited Boston, New York, Philadelphia, and Charleston. By February of that year he had arrived in Caracas.

The years 1807–1810 saw the initiation of the Spanish-American Independence movement. Its birthplace was Caracas; one of its children was Bolívar. Aroused by the inequalities of the colonial system, incited by revolutionists like Francisco de Miranda, and angered by the Napoleonic invasion of Spain in 1808, a determined, republican-minded group in Caracas began a series of revolts that ultimately resulted in independence. In 1808, the people and the colonial authorities of Caracas rejected Joseph Bonaparte as King of Spain, and in April, 1810, the colonial governor was deposed and a *junta* independent of Cádiz was established.

Bolívar secretly, and in 1809 publicly, participated in these developments. Meetings with other spirited young men were held at his home in Caracas in 1808 when agitation for revolution and independence was rife. After the arrest of some of the conspirators Bolívar withdrew to his country estate, but in April, 1810, he and his only brother Juan Vicente openly supported the extremists who were insisting on the expulsion of the colonial rulers. Two months later Bolívar was promoted to the rank of colonel in the militia and appointed head of a diplomatic mission to London.

The London mission marked the inception of Bolívar's career as a public servant. For twenty years his pen and sword were plied in behalf of the cause of freedom and independence. His achievements were many, his errors numerous, and, perhaps of greater significance, his enemies, both foreign and domestic, were energetic and jealous. But towering ominously over all personal factors was the inevitable conflict between a socio-economic heritage born of monarchism and a democratic-republican ideal made complex through factors of race, unbalanced economy, lack of educational opportunities, and ignorance of governmental procedures. In the final analysis, Bolívar's career is a study in adversities. He was aware of his own personal problems as well as those of all Spanish America, and during his lifetime he endeavored to find two basic solutions—one for the difficulties of his day and another for the inevitable catastrophes that he predicted for the future.

From the standpoint of events and accomplishments, Bolívar's life from 1810 to 1830 falls into eight periods, namely, (1) service in the army of the first Venezuelan Republic under General Francisco Miranda from January, 1811, to the fall of that Republic in July, 1812, following his return from London; (2) the campaign to liberate Caracas, starting at Cartagena, Colombia, late in 1812 and ending with the Spanish reoccupation of Venezuela in 1814; (3) military participation in the New Granadan Confederation and failure, after a civil war, to secure arms from the patriots in Cartagena in July, 1815; (4) self-exile to Haiti, highlighted by two naval expeditions against the Spanish in Venezuela in 1816 and 1817 and the establishment of headquarters at Angostura, present-day Ciudad Bolívar; (5) military success in the Orinoco River region of Venezuela and in New Granada and the creation of the Republic of Colombia during the years 1818 to 1821; (6) liberation of Ecuador and negotiations with General José de San Martín and the Peruvian government from 1821 to 1823; (7) defeat of the Spanish armies in Perú and the establishment of independent governments in Perú and Bolivia, 1824 to 1826; and (8) return to Venezuela and New Granada, dictatorship, and resignation, 1827 to 1830.

Bolívar's activities through these years can be grouped into three principal categories—military, political, and international. His progress as a military leader stemmed in large measure from his hatred of the royalists and from his tenacity and perseverance. No small part of his own success was due to the activities of his subordinates, yet full credit must be accorded him for his ability to choose leaders as well as to lead and inspire the rank and file. Secondhand muskets purchased in England and the United States, few and small bore cannon, and cavalry equipped principally with lances constituted the only matériel of war with which he worked. A small corps of Venezuelans and New Granadans and an even smaller group of English and Irish volunteers formed the nucleus of his army. Lack of time and money prevented the adequate equipping of the bulk of his forces. Combat was largely of a hand to hand nature, and casualties were frequently greater than in modern warfare.

The War for Independence in northern South America involved a maze of minor actions, attacks and counterattacks, raids, and lootings, culminating in major battles in which one to ten thousand men were engaged on each side. Bolívar, as a general, is remembered today chiefly because of his victories in battle, although his writings graphically describe the minutae of the warfare of his day. From the standpoint of success, Bolívar's military achievements from 1810 to 1818 were temporary only. Lacking organization and equipment, his troops could not maintain the momentary advantages obtained over a combination of regular Spanish troops, royalist sympathizers, and the fierce *llaneros,* or Venezuelan plainsmen. This period was highlighted by his daring expedition from New Granada to Caracas in 1813— an undertaking which brought him fame as a leader of men. But lack of supplies, coupled with strong royalist and *llanero* opposition, forced his retreat from the Venezuelan capital in 1814 and eventual exile. Given command of the army of the New Granadan Confederation in 1814–15, he forced the city of Bogotá to recognize the government of the Confederation; yet he failed in his efforts to subdue the rebellious officials of the city of Cartagena. At this point the entire movement for independence virtually collapsed with the arrival of General Pablo Morillo and a Spanish expeditionary force of some ten thousand troops. Bolívar spent eighteen months in Jamaica and Haiti seeking and obtaining aid from President Alexander Pétion of Haiti and Luis Brión, a wealthy Dutch merchant-adventurer from Curaço. The ships, equipment, and money so procured enabled him to establish headquarters in the Orinoco River region. At Angostura, during 1817 and 1818, he directed minor attacks against the Spanish to the north, won the respect of José Antonio Páez, leader of the *llaneros,* received numerous British and Irish volunteers, and gathered about him a small but extremely faithful group of commanders—all preparatory to his first major campaign.

In 1819, convinced of the futility of ousting the enemy from their Venezuelan strongholds, Bolívar and his aides conceived the audacious plan of crossing the Andes into New Granada, and, so to speak, attacking the Spanish from the rear. The wisdom of this plan was proved with the defeat of the royalist army at Boyacá, on August 7, 1819. The victory was the catalyst needed to stir the populace which had been suffering under the Spanish yoke. After taking Bogotá, Bolívar returned to free his native land for the third time. During a period of truce, he mapped out several campaigns and personally directed the one which culminated in victory at Carabobo on June 24, 1821, and in the reoccupation of Caracas four days later. Meanwhile,

Páez, Carlos Soublette, Mariano Montilla, and others were freeing numerous regions and cities in Venezuela and New Granada.

With the establishment of the Republic of Grand Colombia in October, 1821, the Liberator initiated a series of military undertakings which, by 1826, resulted in the freeing of Ecuador, Perú, and Bolivia. On April 7, 1822, at Bomboná in western Colombia, Bolívar was again victorious; his ablest lieutenant, General Antonio José de Sucre, enjoyed a like success at Pichincha on May 24 of the same year. These victories liberated Ecuador, and Bolívar entered Guayaquil on July 11, 1822. Fifteen days later he met General José de San Martín, the liberator of Chile and the Protector of Perú. This meeting has, in all probability, resulted in Latin America's greatest historical controversy. In view of this fact, Doctor Lecuna has written, especially for this volume, a *précis* on the meeting, to which have been appended various pertinent documents. Regardless of the exact nature of the conversations of San Martín and Bolívar, it is apparent that San Martín did not ask the Liberator for troops. On the contrary, San Martín expressed complete satisfaction with his army in Perú as he was confident that it would defeat the Spaniards in that area. Bolívar, however, viewed the Peruvian situation in a different light. On September 9, 1822, he dispatched a communication to the governments of Perú and Chile in which he mentioned San Martín's optimism but expressed his own fears for the fate of Perú. He concluded the communication by offering to send 4,000 troops to the aid of Perú. Time justified Bolívar's views respecting the fate of Perú, for the army left by San Martín on his retirement was decisively defeated. Following this defeat Bolívar proceeded to Perú to free that region which San Martín and his aids had failed to accomplish.

Faced with divided loyalties among the Peruvian leaders and compelled to rely largely upon Colombia for troops and supplies, Bolívar undertook the defeat of the Spanish royalists in Perú and Upper Perú, present-day Bolivia. On August 4, 1824, he won his first major victory in that area at Junín. A second and final victory was gained by Sucre at Ayacucho on December 9, 1824. Except for the war between Colombia and Perú in 1829, Bolívar's military career came to an end in 1825. Persistence, untiring zeal, and a depth of purpose coupled with an openly admitted desire for glory enabled him to free five nations. The glory was his, but for this he sacrificed his health, made many enemies, and failed to carry out his plans respecting government.

Bolívar's views on politics and government are to be found in three major tracts: the so-called Jamaica Letter of September, 1815; his Address to the Congress of Angostura, 1819; and his Constitution for Bolivia, 1825. These documents, together with the noteworthy work of the Peruvian scholar Victor Belaunde, entitled *Bolívar and the Political Thought of the Spanish*

American Revolution, render superfluous any but the briefest remarks respecting the Liberator's political views.

Bolívar fervently believed in democracy, yet more in the Hamiltonian sense than the Jeffersonian. He, like many other statesmen of Colombia, pleaded for recognition of the lack of political experience on the part of the people. Few, too few, were even acquainted with parliamentary procedure; and virtually none possessed an appreciation for compromise, so vital to the operation of the United States and English systems of democracy. A constitution could not, in his opinion, change political concepts and practices molded by three centuries of royal government. His political system was primarily one of paternalism. He envisioned a transitional period during which the people would be educated for complete democracy. History has proved the validity of his views. But many of his contemporaries claimed he sought a crown—a charge unwarranted by the evidence at hand.

Failure rather than success marked Bolívar's efforts in the realm of governmental structures. Bolivia and Perú alone adopted his life-term constitution. This plan of government was rejected in his own country in 1826 and again in 1828 as were many of his political innovations, such as a hereditary senate and a board of censors which he recommended to the Congresses of Angostura (1819) and Cúcuta (1821). Viewed in the historical perspective, his greatest political opponent was the United States Constitution of 1787. Bolívar's own words are proof of this statement. Time and time again he pleaded with congressional delegates and friends not to adopt many of the features of that instrument of government. The colonial political experience of the United States citizen, he repeated, was utterly different from that of the Spanish-American of the day. Time and time alone together with a truly patriotic guidance could prepare the people of Colombia for full participation in their government.

Bolívar was not above dictatorship. In 1827, compelled by circumstances compounded of national debt, civil war, and personal animosities, he assumed dictatorial powers in keeping with the Constitution of 1821. This move, born of a break between the Liberator and Francisco de Paula Santander, Vice President of Colombia, is more to be regretted than debated. Their parting, in 1827, led to a political schism that caused much bloodshed in the years that followed. Perhaps, if the times had not been so turbulent, Bolívar's insistence on a highly centralized government could have been reconciled with Santander's concept of a national state. The failure of these two leaders to agree was responsible for the dictatorship of 1827, an attack on Bolívar's life, exile for Santander, and the creation of two parties in New Granada that were to battle many times subsequent to 1829. Such is the stuff of revolutions.

Failure, however, is not always synonymous with defeat. Time, aided by many a historian, has rendered a different verdict in regard to Bolívar's political achievements, for few will deny that his thoughts and plans of government form the basis of contemporary Spanish-American political thought. The sum total of his theories—their practicality, their eclecticism, yes, even their inconsistencies—stand out today as a tower of wisdom midst the woeful political ignorance of his era. In spite of his faults, he was a political martyr engendered of colonial adolescence in the field of government and enraptured by the paeans to the United States, English, and French democratic-republican systems. At the close of his career he wrote:

> I do not expect well-being for the country. This feeling, or rather this inner conviction, quenches my desire and drags me to the most miserable depths of desperation. I believe all lost forever and the country and my friends submerged in a tempest of calamities. If there were only one more sacrifice that I could make, if it were of my life, my happiness, and my honor, be sure that I would not hesitate. But I am convinced that the sacrifice would be in vain, because one poor man can do nothing against a whole world, and because I am unable to bring about the happiness of my country, I deny myself its command. There is yet more, the tyrants of my country have deprived me of it and I am an exile; so that I do not even have a fatherland for which to make the sacrifice.

The third major undertaking of Bolívar during the years 1815–1830 belongs in the realm of international affairs. Therein he advocated a Hispanic-American league of states the council or assembly of which would serve as an arbiter of disputes, provide for military coöperation among those states in order to defend the continent, and negotiate an alliance with Great Britain. He also wrote of the desirability of creating a world organization dedicated to the maintenance of peace. For the greater part, Bolívar provided the inspiration for these schemes, leaving to others their realization. He did, however, personally endeavor to bring about military coöperation among all the Spanish-American states during the years 1822 to 1824.

The grandeur of Bolívar's plans is vividly reflected in the present-day Organization of American States. Terms such as Inter-American Coöperation, Continental Solidarity, Non-Intervention, and Continental Defense have real meaning today. They were born of necessity created by a fear that the continental European nations of the 1820's, leagued under the Holy Alliance, would seek to eradicate republicanism in the Spanish New World. Under the practical direction of Santander and Pedro Gual, Colombian Minister of Foreign Affairs, offensive and defensive treaties of alliance were negotiated with Perú, Mexico, Central America (then one nation) and Chile. All but the latter ratified these treaties. The United Provinces of the Río de la Plata signed a defensive treaty with Colombia. In December, 1824, Bolívar issued an invitation to these nations, seeking to make operative that article in the treaties calling for a general congress designed to erect the American system of states. Invitations were also sent to Great Britain, the United States, the Netherlands, Brazil, and France. Only Colombia, Perú, Central America, and Mexico dispatched official delegates to Panamá in 1826. Great Britain and the Netherlands sent unofficial observers; one United States delegate died while en route; the other received news of the closing of the Congress prior to his departure.

In essence Bolívar sought a defensive-offensive league backed by the military might of Great Britain. He did not favor United States participation for fear that this would anger England. Coupled with the military aspects of the proposed league was that stressing the peaceful settlement of disputes by a council. Yet, despite the effort and time expended, the lofty principles involved, the Congress of Panamá came to naught. Even Bolívar forsook it midst the reverberations of internecine revolt that swept through the former Spanish colonies in the late 1820's. Pan-Americanism, the child of the Spanish-American Wars of Independence, was destined to grow slowly during times of peace, rapidly when the continent was threatened. In the post-World War II era Bolívar's dream of military coöperation and a council for the maintenance of peace have become realities, at least on paper.

The career of Simón Bolívar ended on a note of disillusionment. Twenty full years of active service had, in his opinion, achieved little but independence from Spain. His message to the Congress of Ocaña in 1828 and his Panoramic View of Spanish America reveal his anguish. In fact, at the time of his death he was preparing to seek exile in a foreign land. But the personal reward which he cherished most—*glory*—has been lavishly and sincerely accorded him. Moreover, his spirit permeates the Spanish-American contemporary scene in a far more productive manner than did his presence in his own day.

II—THE MAN

"Sentiment, idealism, drama, flamboyance, sensuality, eloquence, egotism, realism, brutality, mercy, compromise, courage, generalship, vision, and statesmanship," Professor William Whatley Pierson has written, "all were there in the new Don Quijote, who was also the Liberator." Small wonder, then, that the contemporaries and latter-day critics of a man so complex in character should differ in their opinions of him! The aura of prejudice that settles about every major historical figure clouds even the thinking of those who adhere to the tenets of historical criticism. One cannot, it seems, view Simón Bolívar dispassionately. He is either loved and revered or hated and damned. Heretofore, Bolívar has been able to speak personally only to the reader of Spanish; now, it is hoped, those who read only English can converse, so to speak, with him directly and thereby form their opinion from the documents included herein. What follows, therefore, is merely a sketch of some of the main facets of the man and his character that he himself could not or did not clearly reveal in his writings.

General Daniel F. O'Leary, aide-de-camp, intimate friend, and author of a life of Bolívar, wrote the most widely accepted description of the Liberator:

> Bolívar had a high but not extremely wide forehead, which was wrinkled from an early age—the mark of a thinker. Heavy and well-formed eyebrows; black eyes, alert and penetrating. His nose was long and perfect, but it had a small wart which preoccupied him greatly until it disappeared in 1820, leaving an almost imperceptible scar. His cheek bones were prominent, but the cheeks were hollow after 1818, when I first knew him. His mouth was ugly and his lips rather thick. The distance from his nose to his mouth was notable. His teeth were white, uniform, and beautiful; he took excellent care of them. His ears were large, but evenly placed. His hair was black, fine, and curly. He wore it long from 1818 to 1821, when it began to turn gray, and then he wore it short. The side-burns and mustache were reddish, but he shaved them off for the first time at Potosí in 1825. He was five feet, six inches in height. His chest was narrow, and his body slender, especially the legs. His skin was dark and somewhat rough. His hands and feet were small and well-developed—a woman might have envied them.

"I am like the sun; I cast my rays in all directions." This simile, written by Bolívar in 1823 to describe his varied activities, might well describe the effect of his character and personality; for, despite an irascible temper, he exuded a personal charm that overcame opposition and won for him many friends. "With all the calumnies and distrust that different partizans have raised against him," wrote a United States representative in Bogotá, "there is an intrinsick [sic] moral force in the man, that awes the disaffected and inspires courage in the patriot."   This personal charm or "moral force" was in large measure compounded of the many complexities in his mental and physical makeup. A man of tireless energy, he seemingly was inured to fatigue, and he shared the same foods, hardships, and terrain as did the common foot-soldier. Unlike the latter, however, he was not given to hard liquors, preferring champagne and claret, which, according to O'Leary, he drank in moderation. His ability as a horseman, although not exceptional for the day, provoked wonderment on the part of many of his companions. His tremendous store of physical energy and his willingness to endure the hardships of campaigning won for him the respect and admiration of troops that knew little of discipline. Subsequent to 1826 his health began to fail him, necessitating a lessening of those feats of agility of which he was so proud and which, through the nervous energy expended, undoubtedly shortened his life. His small frame withstood occasional waning fevers, and even though he was aware of his condition he continued to drive himself until his death of tuberculosis at the age of forty-seven.

Bolívar was a leader of great personal courage. Examples of his daring on the field of battle are numerous, yet he was not given to comment respecting these feats. Being extremely sensitive to unfavorable criticism, however, he took great care in 1812, 1814, and 1815 to explain why he had abandoned his country. In 1829 he asserted: "In war I took no step dictated by prudence or reason that can be attributed to cowardice. My every action was guided by calculation, and, more, by daring." In the same document he defended his flight from Ocumare in 1816, stating that he had been left ashore by foreign seamen in the midst of the enemy. This defense was occasioned by the violent personal attacks to which he was subjected during the last two years of his life, for Bolívar was not without enemies who sought to lessen his popular appeal by slandering his character.

Bolívar's ability as a speaker, both public and private, served him well. His manner of address was usually amiable, although, when the occasion demanded, he was capable of employing harsh language filled with bitter invectives. In the easy camaraderie of the camp, he often amused his companions with personal anecdotes concerning the fair sex, while his short, pithy statements prior to giving battle were sources of inspiration. His public discourses and messages to Congress were delivered in a clear-cut, forceful manner free of hesitation and delay. Much of his amiability, regrettably, depended upon his mood, although he was well able to restrain his feelings when he so desired.

Personal gain in the form of wealth was the least of Bolívar's desires. He died virtually a pauper. His inheritance—an entailed estate at San Mateo near Caracas, mines at Aroa, and dwellings in Caracas—did not provide him with funds and subsequently was given to his sisters. A friend in need was rarely turned away. He set aside a considerable portion of his salary as commander in chief and president to provide pensions and gifts for those close to his heart. Pecuniary rewards were distasteful to him, and he rejected several, including an offer of one million *pesos* from Perú. Poverty and illness, nevertheless, forced him to accept a pension granted by the Colombian Congress in 1830. Plagued constantly by the lack of government funds, he grew more and more sparing of their use and insistent upon any and all means of taxation and forced loans. Such a policy sprang from urgent necessity resulting from the collapse of the colonial system of revenue following the decrease in the production of basic agricultural and pastoral crops. He also wholeheartedly approved the distribution among his officers and men of public lands and various properties sequestered from the royalists.

Not unlike many another leader of his day, Bolívar was very fond of festive occasions of every type. He particularly liked to dance. O'Leary recorded: "Following a journey which would have exhausted the strongest, I have seen him work five or six hours or dance as long because of that passion he possessed for a ball." On entering cities and towns, he was usually greeted by a deputation composed of young ladies, the most attractive of whom presented him with flowers. The ladies of Lima, in August, 1826, on learning of his intention to return to Colombia (and unquestionably prompted by the gentlemen of Lima) "were invited to meet at the palace at seven in the evening . . . to entreat the Liberator not to abandon Peru. Three young girls delivered him short addresses on this occasion. . . . To these he answered that he regretted he could not remain, that he was sensibly affected by their kindness, but that his duty called him to Colombia. On this answer . . . a general cry was raised, 'he must not go': those nearest to him caught him in their arms, insisted that he should promise to stay, and with the exception of a very few, about seventy ladies being present, the whole went forward to embrace him. He said it was impossible to resist so much beauty and attraction. . . ." William Tudor, United States Consul at Lima, the author of this description, added: "Every mode of adulation has been so exhausted here, that it is difficult to practice any that does not appear to him insipid: this however was sufficiently high seasoned to be relished, and it put him in the most extraordinary spirits. He went round in the most courteous manner and addressed all the ladies. . . ." Similar scenes were repeated on innumerable occasions. Indeed, Bolívar was perhaps a greater hero to the ladies than to the stronger sex.

Of the numerous mistresses credited to Bolívar only Josefina Machado and Manuela Sáenz de Thorne captured his fancy for any length of time. The former died in 1820. Manuela, age twenty-two, wife of an English doctor, became enamored of the Liberator in Quito in 1822. Of a fiery nature, she possessed a healthy distaste for the conventional and a great desire for love and adventure; but, contrary to legend, she did not dress in men's clothes or uniforms and ride among the troops. In Lima in 1823, Manuela left her older husband for Bolívar. Her temperament—a mixture of passion, jealousy, and keenness of mind—endeared her to the Liberator, for, except when duty separated them, she was always at his side. Their correspondence was typical of lovers. Bolívar would write: "I think of you and your situation every moment. Yes, I adore you. . . . You beg me to tell you that I do not love anyone but you. No, I do not love anyone else, nor shall I ever love another." On learning of his death Manuela is reputed to have said: "I loved the Liberator when he was alive, but, now that he is dead, I worship him."

That she shared his thoughts, consoled him, and encouraged him to fight for his beliefs cannot be denied. In many respects she was, as many called her, *La Libertadora*. Driven from Bogotá following his death, she eked out an existence in the small Peruvian port of Paita, selling sweets until her death.

Many of the social problems of the day were of vital concern to Bolívar. Although he was enmeshed in war and politics, his prophetic vision made him conscious of the changing times and customs respecting the religious and educational aspects of the society around him. "Religion," he stated in 1823, "has lost much of its power, which, perhaps, it will not regain for a long time, since customs now differ from the sacred doctrines." At least as far as Venezuela is concerned his comments are true today, for in that country "the institution has no political power, in spite of the fact that it is still established; and outside a few centers . . . its social effectiveness is slight." In present-day Colombia, however, the church plays a much greater political and social rôle. Bolívar, in part, was responsible for the origin of these conflicting developments.

The fall of the first and second Venezuelan republics was attributed in large measure to the clergy. That body, royalist in its sympathies, so employed its powers, Bolívar wrote in 1814, that the people were "led astray by religious fanaticism." In 1812, the churchmen preached that the March earthquake was an act of God designed to punish the people of Venezuela for their support of the Patriot cause. Convinced that the pro-royalist activities of the priests constituted a danger to the Republic, Bolívar, in August, 1813, dispatched a strong letter of remonstrance to Narciso Coll y Prat, Archbishop of Venezuela, suggesting that the clergy "expound each week the just principles of American emancipation, and explain the obligation to embrace and defend them at the sacrifice of personal interests and life itself." The abuse of the confessional, Bolívar continued, "would be most effectively prevented if any who, in administering confession, should seek to undermine political opinion that favors the present government, were to be suspended from their duties. . . ."

During these early years of the rebellion, Bolívar was convinced that the church sought only to maintain its privileged position. He questioned the integrity of its members, and he was of the opinion that the principles of liberty and democracy constituted a threat to the church which caused it to fear that it would lose its hold upon the populace. He ordered money to be collected from the church and funds confiscated from the brotherhoods, and he did not object to governmental control (patronage) of the church as decreed by the Congresses of 1821 and 1824. Nevertheless, he was not averse to obtaining and exploiting church support for his cause. "A bishop," he wrote Santander, "can be a useful person." And as the bishops of Popayán and Mérida agreed to take an oath to support the new government, they were retained in their posts. Further, subsequent to 1827, during his dictatorship, he supported the church in New Granada and appointed an archbishop to his Council of Government. All this was in keeping with his desire to reëstablish order order. Ever practical, he encouraged the clergy publicly and privately to exert their influence in the struggle against internal anarchy.

Bolívar's use or misuse of the church must be viewed as the actions of a statesman, but his personal opinions mark him as a deist. "Religion," he wrote, "governs man in his home, within his own walls, within himself," and he was convinced that "a political constitution should not prescribe any particular religion." To him religion was the law of conscience, and man based his morality upon revealed truths acquired through personal experience. He would give the church a place in the community but would have that body stand alone and apart from the laws and the body politic.

Ignorance and its remedy, education, concerned Bolívar greatly. His letters and public addresses make frequent mention of the illiteracy of the masses to which he attributed their lack of interest in democratic government. His own educational experience enabled him to evaluate the shortcomings of public education as it existed during his day. This is not to say that his education was meagre or neglected, for he defended his boyhood tutors and was proud of his mastery of the philosophic thought of the Enlightenment. He did admit on one occasion that he had not studied the philosophy of Aristotle or the works of those men who wrote on law. "Although I have very little learning," he confessed, "the fact remains that I was educated as well as any child of good family in America could possibly have been under Spanish rule."

Bolívar recorded his philosophy of education in two tracts, "Essay on Public Education" and "On the Education of Fernando Bolívar." For his nephew he recommended the study of civil engineering, following the mastery of more basic disciplines. Included among the latter was history, which in his opinion "should begin with a study of the present day, going back by degrees to the remote ages of the fable." But he also suggested that Fernando should be imbued with "the love of cultivated society where the fair sex exerts its benign influence." As to methods, he favored those designed to oblige the child to think as well as memorize. For the nation as a whole he recommended an organized system of free public education, for he could not envision a great nation devoid of a great educational program—"a people whose principles of education are wisdom, virtue, and discipline will be wise, virtuous, and war-like in character. A nation will be superstitious, effeminate, and fanatical if its educational system develops these attitudes." Vital to the success of the system was the teacher—"a man of ability, who understands the human heart and can guide it skilfully, and a simple system [of instruction] with a clear and natural curriculum are the effective means by which a community may make extraordinary and brilliant progress in a short time." It is this reasoning and attention to the welfare of the masses that raises Bolívar the man above the level of a mere warrior. Unfortunately, he was able to accomplish little in furthering pedagogy. The political unrest, the financial distress, and the reluctance of many to aid the masses made impossible the initiation of any large scale educational movement. Yet certainly history should record that Bolívar the Liberator saw and pleaded for the correction of the greatest social evil—ignorance.

In the realm of culture Bolívar made few outright contributions, yet today he is invariably listed as a man of letters in works relating to the literature of Latin America. He is credited with a forceful, limpid, and brilliant style—a brilliance difficult to capture in translation. Bolívar himself, however, was not of this opinion, for he specifically requested of Santander in 1825—"do not have my letters published, either during my lifetime or after my death, as they have been written in a style far too free and disorganized." He denied the charge that he was wordy but admitted that he was "careless through impetuosity, negligence, and impatience." This carelessness, stemming, perhaps from rapid dictating—on occasion as many as three letters at once—resulted in frequent obscurities, changes in tense, subject, and object. Clarity has been the goal in this translation, but the limitations of the English language are such that many of Bolívar's stylisms have been lost in translation. To be fully appreciated, the writings of Bolívar must be read in the Spanish.

Bolívar, the man of many and varied interests, was truly a man of destiny, but far and above his accomplishments he personally wished to be remembered for what he symbolized—liberty and freedom. "History will say," he opined, that " 'Bolívar took the command in order to free his fellow-citizens, and, when they were free, he permitted them to govern themselves by laws, and not by his will.' " During his lifetime he repeatedly endeavored to make the popular will his will. His frequent resignations, although considered by some to have been a device with which to secure greater power, may have been prompted by an inner force that drove him to seek approval for his actions. He was fully aware that many of these actions circumvented the law and that he had been "roundly criticised for doing what was right in defiance" of his duty. "I make my general confession daily, or, rather," he admitted, "I tremble for the sins that I have committed against my will for the sake of the cause and because of the guilt of the *godos*."*

Bolívar's great yearning for glory made him ever conscious of his duty. This consciousness apparently rankled deep when he was forced by the times and enemies to overstep the limits set by his philosophy of government. "Who knows," he mused prior to his departure for Perú, "but that one day I shall

---

*Literally Goths, an epithet for Spaniards.

be made to suffer extreme penance for my misguided patriotism?" The failure of many of his contemporaries to recognize this patriotic motivation embittered him. The Bolívar of 1830 was a far different man from the Liberator of an earlier decade. But time has softened the bitterness, and history records his achievements rather than his failures. Nevertheless, history will never cease to evaluate Simón Bolívar, the Liberator. Each generation must and will reflect upon his worth, his character, his thoughts, his interests, his hopes, and his failures, for Bolívar is a veritable symbol of liberty, of liberty triumphant over despotism.

2. *The Jamaica Letter*

SIMÓN BOLÍVAR

Bolívar wrote the Jamaica Letter in September 1815 while he was in exile. It presents in detail his view of the concrete difficulties that stood in the way of liberal and republican institutions in Spanish America and his consequent insistence on a strong, centralized government as the only means of assuring even a modicum of liberal republicanism in practice. The letter indulges in some shrewd speculation concerning the future of Spanish America; and in typically Bolivarian fashion it reasserts unshaken confidence in final victory.

REPLY OF A SOUTH AMERICAN TO A GENTLEMAN OF THIS ISLAND [JAMAICA]

Kingston, Jamaica, September 6, 1815.

My dear Sir:

I hasten to reply to the letter of the 29th ultimo which you had the honor of sending me and which I received with the greatest satisfaction.

Sensible though I am of the interest you desire to take in the fate of my country, and of your commiseration with her for the tortures she has suffered from the time of her discovery until the present at the hands of her destroy-

From: *Selected Writings of Bolívar* compiled by Vicente Lecuna, edited by Harold A. Bierck, Jr. (New York: Bolivarian Society of Venezuela, 1951), 1, pp. 103–122. Reprinted by permission.

ers, the Spaniards, I am no less sensible of the obligation which your solicitous inquiries about the principal objects of American policy place upon me. Thus, I find myself in conflict between the desire to reciprocate your confidence, which honors me, and the difficulty of rewarding it, for lack of documents and books and because of my own limited knowledge of a land so vast, so varied, and so little known as the New World. . . . Every conjecture relative to America's future is, I feel, pure speculation. When mankind was in its infancy, steeped in uncertainty, ignorance, and error, was it possible to foresee what system it would adopt for its preservation? Who could venture to say that a certain nation would be a republic or a monarchy; this nation great, that nation small? To my way of thinking, such is our own situation. We are a young people. We inhabit a world apart, separated by broad seas. We are young in the ways of almost all the arts and sciences, although, in a certain manner, we are old in the ways of civilized society. I look upon the present state of America as similar to that of Rome after its fall. Each part of Rome adopted a political system conforming to its interest and situation or was led by the individual ambitions of certain chiefs, dynasties, or associations. But this important difference exists: those dispersed parts later reestablished their ancient nations, subject to the changes imposed by circumstances or events. But we scarcely retain a vestige of what once was; we are, moreover, neither Indian nor European, but a species midway between the legitimate proprietors of this country and the Spanish usurpers. In short, though Americans by birth we derive our rights from Europe, and we have to assert these rights against the rights of the natives, and at the same time we must defend ourselves against the invaders. This places us in a most extraordinary and involved situation. Notwithstanding that it is a type of divination to predict the result of the political course which America is pursuing, I shall venture some conjectures which, of course, are colored by my enthusiasm and dictated by rational desires rather than by reasoned calculations.

The rôle of the inhabitants of the American hemisphere has for centuries been purely passive. Politically they were non-existent. We are still in a position lower than slavery, and therefore it is more difficult for us to rise to the enjoyment of freedom. Permit me these transgressions in order to establish the issue. States are slaves because of either the nature or the misuse of their constitutions; a people is therefore enslaved when the government, by its nature or its vices, infringes on and usurps the rights of the citizen or subject. Applying these principles, we find that America was denied not only its freedom but even an active and effective tyranny. Let me explain. Under absolutism there are no recognized limits to the exercise of governmental powers. The will of the great sultan, khan, bey, and other despotic rulers is the supreme law, carried out more or less arbitrarily by the lesser pashas, khans, and satraps of Turkey and Persia, who have an organized system of oppression in which inferiors participate according to the authority vested in them. To them is entrusted the administration of civil, military, political, religious, and tax matters. But, after all is said and done, the rulers of Ispahan are Persians; the viziers of the Grand Turk are Turks; and the sultans of Tartary are Tartars. China does not bring its military leaders and scholars from the land of Genghis Khan, her conqueror, notwithstanding that the Chinese of today are the lineal descendants of those who were reduced to subjection by the ancestors of the present-day Tartars.

How different is our situation! We have been harassed by a conduct which has not only deprived us of our rights but has kept us in a sort of permanent infancy with regard to public affairs. If we could at least have managed our domestic affairs and our internal administration, we could have acquainted ourselves with the processes and mechanics of public affairs. We should also have enjoyed a personal consideration, thereby commanding a certain unconscious respect from the people, which is so necessary to preserve amidst revolutions. That is why I say we have even been deprived of an active tyranny, since we have not been permitted to exercise its functions.

Americans today, and perhaps to a greater extent than ever before, who live within the Spanish system occupy a position in society no better than that of serfs destined for labor, or at best they have no more status than that of mere consumers. Yet even this status is surrounded with galling restrictions, such as being forbidden to grow European crops, or to store products which are royal monopolies, or to establish factories of a type the Peninsula itself does not possess. To this add the exclusive trading privileges, even in articles of prime necessity, and the barriers between American provinces, designed to prevent all exchange of trade, traffic, and understanding. In short, do you wish to know what our future held?—simply the cultivation of the fields of indigo, grain, coffee, sugar cane, cacao, and cotton; cattle raising on the broad plains; hunting wild game in the jungles; digging in the earth to mine its gold—but even these limitations could never satisfy the greed of Spain.

So negative was our existence that I can find nothing comparable in any other civilized society, examine as I may the entire history of time and the politics of all nations. Is it not an outrage and a violation of human rights to expect a land so splendidly endowed, so vast, rich, and populous, to remain merely passive?

As I have just explained, we were cut off and, as it were, removed from the world in relation to the science of government and administration of the state. We were never viceroys or governors, save in the rarest of instances; seldom archbishops and bishops; diplomats never; as military men, only subordinates; as nobles, without royal privileges. In brief, we were neither magistrates nor financiers and seldom merchants—all in flagrant contradiction to our institutions.

Emperor Charles V made a pact with the discoverers, conquerors, and settlers of America, and this, as Guerra puts it, is our social contract. The monarchs of Spain made a solemn agreement with them, to be carried out on their own account and at their own risk, experessly prohibiting them from drawing on the royal treasury. In return, they were made the lords of the land, entitled to organize the public administration and act as the court of last appeal, together with many other exemptions and privileges that are too numerous to mention. The King committed himself never to alienate the American provinces, inasmuch as he had no jurisdiction but that of sovereign domain. Thus, for themselves and their descendants, the *conquistadores* possessed what were tantamount to feudal holdings. Yet there are explicit laws respecting employment in civil, ecclesiastical, and tax-raising establishments. These laws favor, almost exclusively, the natives of the country who are of Spanish extraction. Thus, by an outright violation of the laws and the existing agreements, those born in America have been despoiled of their constitutional rights as embodied in the code. . . .

The Americans have risen rapidly without previous knowledge of, and, what is more regrettable, without previous experience in public affairs, to enact upon the world stage the eminent rôles of legislator, magistrate, minister of the treasury, diplomat, general, and every position of authority, supreme or subordinate, that comprises the hierarchy of a fully organized state. . . .

The first steps of all the new governments are marked by the establishment of *juntas* of the people. These *juntas* speedily draft rules for the calling of congresses, which produce great changes. Venezuela erected a democratic and federal government, after declaring for the rights of man. A system of checks and balances was established, and general laws were passed granting civil liberties, such as freedom of the press and others. In short, an independent government was created. New Granada uniformly followed the political institutions and reforms introduced by Venezuela, taking as the fundamental basis of her constitution the most elaborate federal system ever to be brought into existence. Recently the powers of the chief executive have been increased, and he has been given all the powers that are properly his. I understand that Buenos Aires and Chile have followed this same line of procedure, but, as the distance is so great and documents are so few and the news reports so unreliable, I shall not attempt even briefly to sketch their progress.

Events in Mexico have been too varied, confused, swift, and unhappy to follow clearly the course of that revolution. . . .

Events in Costa Firme have proved that institutions which are wholly representative are not suited to our character, customs, and present knowledge. In Caracas party spirit arose in the societies, assemblies, and popular elections; these parties led us back into slavery. Thus, while Venezuela has been the American republic with the most advanced political institutions, she has also been the clearest example of the inefficacy of the democratic and federal system for our new-born states. In New Granada, the large number of excess powers held by the provincial governments and the lack of centralization in the general government have reduced that fair country to her present state. For this reason her foes, though weak, have been able to hold out against all odds. As long as our countrymen do not acquire the abilities and political virtues that distinguish our brothers of the north, wholly popular systems, far from working to our advantage, will, I greatly fear, bring about our downfall. Unfortunately, these traits, to the degree in which they are required, do not appear to be within our reach. On the contrary, we are dominated by the vices that one learns under the rule of a nation like Spain, which has only distinguished itself in ferocity, ambition, vindictiveness, and greed.

It is harder, Montesquieu has written, to release a nation from servitude than to enslave a free nation. This truth is proven by the annals of all times, which reveal that most free nations have been put under the yoke, but very few enslaved nations have recovered their liberty. Despite the convictions of history, South Americans have made efforts to obtain liberal, even perfect, institutions, doubtless out of that instinct to aspire to the greatest possible happiness, which, common to all men, is bound to follow in civil societies founded on the principles of justice, libery, and equality. But are we capable of maintaining in proper balance the difficult charge of a republic? Is it conceivable that a newly emancipated people can soar to the heights of liberty, and, unlike Icarus, neither have its wings melt nor fall into an abyss? Such a marvel is inconceivable and without precedent. There is no reasonable probability to bolster our hopes.

More than anyone, I desire to see America fashioned into the greatest nation in the world, greatest not so much by virtue of her area and wealth as by her freedom and glory. Although I seek perfection for the government of my country, I cannot persuade myself that the New World can, at the moment, be organized as a great republic. Since it is impossible, I dare not desire it; yet much less do I desire to have all America a monarchy because this plan is not only impracticable but also impossible. Wrongs now existing could not be righted, and our emancipation would be fruitless. The American states need the care of paternal governments to heal the sores and wounds of despotism and war. The parent country, for example, might be Mexico, the only country fitted for the position by her intrinsic strength, and without such power there can be no parent country. Let us assume it were to be the Isthmus of Panamá, the most central point of this vast continent. Would not all parts continue in their lethargy and even in their present disorder? For a single government to infuse life into the New World; to put into use all the resources for public prosperity; to improve, educate, and perfect the New World, that government would have to possess the authority of a god, much less the knowledge and virtues of mankind.

The party spirit that today keeps our states in constant agitation would assume still greater proportions were a central power established, for that power—the only force capable of checking this agitation—would be elsewhere. Furthermore, the chief figures of the capitals would not tolerate the preponderance of leaders at the metropolis, for they would regard these leaders as so many tyrants. Their resentments would attain such heights that they would compare the latter to the hated Spaniards. Any such monarchy would be a misshapen colossus that would collapse of its own weight at the slightest disturbance.

Mr. de Pradt has wisely divided America into fifteen or seventeen mutually independent states, governed by as many monarchs. I am in agreement on the first suggestion, as America can well tolerate seventeen nations; as to the second, though it could easily be achieved, it would serve no purpose. Consequently, I do not favor American monarchies. My reasons are these: The well-understood interest of a republic is limited to the matter of its preservation, prosperity, and glory. Republicans, because they do not desire powers which represent a directly contrary viewpoint, have no reason for expanding the boundaries of their nation to the detriment of their own resources, solely for the purpose of having their neighbors share a liberal constitution. They would not acquire rights or secure any advantage by conquering their neighbors, unless they were to make them colonies, conquered territory, or allies, after the example of Rome. But such thought and action are directly contrary to the principles of justice which characterize republican systems; and, what is more, they are in direct opposition to the interests of their citizens, because a state, too large of itself or together with its dependencies, ultimately falls into decay. Its free government becomes a tyranny. The principles that should preserve the government are disregarded, and finally it degenerates into despotism. The distinctive feature of small republics is permanence: that of large republics varies, but always with a tendency toward empire. Almost all small republics have had long lives. Among the larger republics, only Rome lasted for several centuries, for its capital was a republic. The rest of her dominions were governed by divers laws and institutions.

The policy of a king is very different. His constant desire is to increase his possessions, wealth, and authority; and with justification, for his power grows with every acquisition, both with respect to his neighbors and his own vassals, who fear him because his power is as formidable as his empire, which he maintains by war and conquest. For these reasons I think that the Americans, being anxious for peace, science, art, commerce, and agriculture, would prefer republics to kingdoms. And, further, it seems to me that these desires conform with the aims of Europe.

We know little about the opinions prevailing in Buenos Aires, Chile, and Perú. Judging by what seeps through and by conjecture, Buenos Aires will have a central government in which the military, as a result of its internal dissensions and external wars, will have the upper hand. Such a constitutional system will necessarily degenerate into an oligarchy or a monocracy, with a variety of restrictions the exact nature of which no one can now foresee. It would be unfortunate if this situation were to follow because the people there deserve a more glorious destiny.

The Kingdom of Chile is destined, by the nature of its location, by the simple and virtuous character of its people, and by the example of its neighbors, the proud republicans of Arauco, to enjoy the blessings that flow from the just and gentle laws of a republic. If any American republic is to have a long life, I am inclined to believe it will be Chile. There the spirit of liberty has never been extinguished; the vices of Europe and Asia arrived too late or not at all to corrupt the customs of that distant corner of the world. Its area is limited; and, as it is remote from other peoples, it will always remain free from contamination. Chile will not alter her laws, ways, and practices. She will preserve her uniform political and religious views. In a word, it is possible for Chile to be free.

Perú, on the contrary, contains two factors that clash with every just and liberal principle: gold and slaves. The former corrupts everything; the latter are themselves corrupt. The soul of a serf can seldom really appreciate true freedom. Either he loses his head in uprisings or his self-respect in chains. Although these remarks would be applicable to all America, I believe that they apply with greater justice to Lima, for the reasons I have given and because of the coöperation she has rendered her masters against her own brothers, those illustrious sons of Quito, Chile, and Buenos Aires. It is plain that he who aspires to obtain liberty will at least attempt to secure it. I imagine that in Lima the rich will not tolerate democracy, nor will the freed slaves and *pardos* accept aristocracy. The former will prefer the tyranny of a single man, to avoid the tumult of rebellion and to provide, at least, a peaceful system. If Perú intends to recover her independence, she has much to do.

From the foregoing, we can draw these conclusions: The American provinces are fighting for their freedom, and they will ultimately succeed. Some provinces as a matter of course will form federal and some central republics; the larger areas will inevitably establish monarchies, some of which will fare so badly that they will disintegrate in either present or future revolutions. To consolidate a great monarchy will be no easy task, but it will be utterly impossible to consolidate a great republic.

It is a grandiose idea to think of consolidating the New World into a single nation, united by pacts into a single bond. It is reasoned that, as these parts have a common origin, language, customs, and religion, they ought to have a single government to permit the newly formed states to unite in a confederation. But this is not possible. Actually, America is separated by climatic differences, geographic diversity, conflicting interests, and dissimilar characteristics. How beautiful would be if the Isthmus of Panamá could be for us what the Ithmus of Corinth was for the Greeks! Would to God that some day we may have the good fortune to convene there an august assembly of representatives of republics, kingdoms, and empires to deliberate upon the high interests of peace and war with the nations of the other three-quarters of the globe. This type of organization may come to pass in some happier period of our regeneration. But any other plan, such as that of Abbé St. Pierre, who in laudable delirium conceived the idea of assembling a European congress to decide the fate and interests of those nations, would be meaningless.

Among the popular and representative systems, I do not favor the federal system. It is over-perfect, and it demands political virtues and talents far superior to our own. For the same reason I reject a monarchy that is part aristocracy and part democracy, although with such a government England has achieved much fortune and splendor. Since it is not possible for us to select the most perfect and complete form of government, let us avoid falling into demagogic anarchy or monocratic tyranny. These opposite extremes would only wreck us on similar reefs of misfortune and dishonor; hence, we must seek a mean between them. I say: Do not adopt the best system of government, but the one that is most likely to succeed.

By the nature of their geographic location, wealth, population, and character, I expect that the Mexicans, at the outset, intend to establish a representative republic in which the executive will have great powers. These will be concentrated in one person, who, if he discharges his duties with wisdom and justice, should almost certainly maintain his authority for life. If through incompetence or violence he should excite a popular revolt and it should be successful, this same executive power would then, perhaps, be distributed among the members of an assembly. If the dominant party is military or aristocratic, it will probably demand a monarchy that would be limited and constitutional at the outset, and would later inevitably degenerate into an absolute monarchy; for it must be admitted that there is nothing more difficult in the political world than the maintenance of a limited monarchy. Moreover, it must also be agreed that only a people as patriotic as the English are capable of controlling the authority of a king and of sustaining the spirit of liberty under the rule of sceptre and crown.

The states of the Isthmus of Panamá, as far as Guatemala, will perhaps form a confederation. Because of their magnificent position between two mighty oceans, they may in time become the emporium of the world. Their canals will shorten distances throughout the world, strengthen commercial ties between Europe, America, and Asia, and bring to that happy area tribute from the four quarters of the globe. There some day, perhaps, the capital of the world may be located—reminiscent of the Emperor Constantine's claim that Byzantium was the capital of the ancient world.

New Granada will unite with Venezuela, if they can agree to the establishment of a central republic. Their capital may be Maracaibo or a new city to be named Las Casas (in honor of that humane hero) to be built on the borders of the two countries, in the excellent port area of Bahía-Honda. This location, though little known, is the most advantageous in all respects. It is readily accessible, and its situation is so strategic that it can be made impregnable. It has a fine, healthful climate, a soil as suitable for agriculture as for cattle raising, and a superabundance of good timber. The Indians living there can be civilized, and our territorial possessions could be increased with the acquisition of the Goajira Peninsula. This nation should be called Colombia as a just and grateful tribute to the discoverer of our hemisphere. Its government might follow the English pattern, except that in place of a king there will be an executive who will be elected, at most, for life, but his office will never be hereditary, if a republic is desired. There will be a hereditary legislative chamber or senate. This body can interpose itself between the violent demands of the people and the great powers of the government during periods of political unrest. The second representative body will be a legislature with restrictions no greater than those of the lower house in England. The Constitution will draw on all systems of government, but I do not want it to partake of all their vices. As Colombia is my country, I have an indisputable right to desire for her that form of government which, in my opinion, is best. It is very possible that New Granada may not care to recognize a central government, because she is greatly addicted to federalism; in such event, she will form a separate state which, if it endures, may prosper, because of its great and varied resources. . . .

Surely unity is what we need to complete our work of regeneration. The division among us, nevertheless, is nothing extraordinary, for it is characteristic of civil wars to form two parties, *conservatives* and *reformers*. The former are commonly the more numerous, because the weight of habit induces obedience to establish powers; the latter are always fewer in number although more vocal and learned. Thus, the physical mass of the one is counterbalanced by the moral force of the other; the contest is prolonged, and the results are uncertain. Fortunately, in our case, the mass has followed the learned.

I shall tell you with what we must provide ourselves in order to expel the Spaniards and to found a free government. It is *union*, obviously; but such union will come about through sensible planning and well-directed actions rather than by divine magic. America stands together because it is abandoned by all other nations. It is isolated in the center of the world. It has no diplomatic relations, nor does it receive any military assistance; instead, America is attacked by Spain, which has more military supplies than any we can possibly acquire through furtive means.

When success is not assured, when the state is weak, and when results are distantly seen, all men hesitate; opinion is divided, passions rage, and the enemy fans these passions in order to win an easy victory because of them. As soon as we are strong and under the guidance of a liberal nation which will lend us her protection, we will achieve accord in cultivating the virtues and talents that lead to glory. Then will we march majestically toward that great prosperity for which South America is destined. Then will those sciences and arts which, born in the East, have enlightened Europe, wing their way to a free Colombia, which will cordially bid them welcome.

Such, Sir, are the thoughts and observations that I have the honor to submit to you, so that you may accept or reject them according to their merit. I beg you to understand that I have expounded them because I do not wish to appear discourteous and not because I consider myself competent to enlighten you concerning these matters.

I am, Sir, etc., etc.

SIMÓN BOLÍVAR

3. Message to the Congress of Bolivia

SIMÓN BOLÍVAR.

The address with which Bolívar submitted his draft constitution for Bolivia in May 1826 is a relatively brief and straightforward document that explains the key features of the creation but lacks the prophetic tone of the Jamaica Letter.

From: *Selected Writings of Bolívar* compiled by Vicente Lecuna, edited by Harold A. Bierck, Jr. (New York: Bolivarian Society of Venezuela, 1951), 2, pp. 596–606. Reprinted by permission.

Evident are his search for a means to reconcile liberty and order and his desire to mold institutions to the Spanish American environment. Bolívar's defense of a life-term presidency is at first glance persuasive, but it is hard to escape the conclusion that in proposing what was truly a constitutional monarchy with republican trappings, he had lost the sense of reality that had always led him to insist that monarchy *per se* could not take root in independent Spanish America.

Lima, May 25, 1826.

Legislators:

In submitting to you my draft of a constitution for Bolivia, I am overcome with embarrassment and trepidation, for I am convinced that I am not qualified as a lawgiver. When I reflect that all the wisdom of the ages has not been sufficient for the drafting of a perfect fundamental law, and that the most enlightened legislator has been the direct promoter of human misery, in travesty, as it were, of his divine mission—what can I say of a soldier who, born among slaves and isolated in the wildest section of his country, has known only captives in chains and his comrades-in-arms, pledged to unshackle them? I, a legislator! Your deception and my embarrassment may well argue for preference in this matter. I do not know who suffers most in this terrible dilemma—you, for the evils that may result from the laws you have asked of me, or I, for the opprobrium to which you have condemned me by your confidence.

I have summoned all my powers in order to expound to you my opinions relative to the manner of governing free men, in accordance with the accepted principles of civilized peoples, although the lessons of experience point only to long periods of disaster, interrupted by the briefest intervals of success. What guideposts shall we follow amidst the gloom of such disheartening precedents?

Legislators! Your duty compels you to avoid a struggle with two monstrous enemies, who, although they are themselves ever locked in mortal combat, will attack you at once. *Tyranny* and *anarchy* constitute an immense sea of oppression encircling a tiny island of freedom that is perpetually battered by the forces of the waves and the hurricane that ceaselessly threatens to submerge it. Beware, then, of the sea that you are about to cross in a fragile bark with so inexperienced a pilot at the helm.

My draft of a constitution for Bolivia provides for four branches of government, an additional one having been devised without affecting the time-honored powers of any of the others. The electoral [legislative] branch has been accorded powers not granted it in other reputedly very liberal governments. These powers resemble, in great part, those of the federal system. I have thought it expedient and desirable, and also feasible, to accord to the most direct representatives of the people privileges that the citizens of every department, province, and canton probably desire most. Nothing is more important to a citizen than the right to elect his legislators, governors, judges, and pastors. The electoral college of each province represents its needs and interests and serves as a forum from which to denounce any infractions of the laws or abuses of the magistrates. I might, with some truth, describe this as a form of representation providing the rights enjoyed by individual governments in federal systems. In this manner, additional weight has been placed in the balance to check the executive; the government will acquire greater guarantees, a more popular character, and a greater claim to be numbered among the most democratic of governments.

Every ten citizens will elect one elector, and thus the nation will be represented by a tenth of its citizens. Ability is the only prerequisite for this post. It is not necessary to possess property to have the august right of representing popular sovereignty. The elector must, however, be able to write out his ballots, sign his name, and read the laws. He must be skilled in some trade or useful art that assures him an honest living. The only disqualifications are those of crime, idleness, and utter ignorance. Understanding and honesty, rather than wealth, are the sole requirements for exercising the public trust.

The legislative body is so composed that its parts will necessarily be in harmony. It will not find itself divided for lack of an arbiter, as is the case where there are only two chambers. Since this legislature has three parts, disagreement between two can be settled by the third. The issue is thus examined by two contending parties and decided by an impartial third party. In this way no useful law is without effect; at least it shall have been reviewed once, twice, and a third time before being discarded. In all matters between two contending parties, a third party is named to render the decision. Would it not be absurd, therefore, if, in matters of the deepest concern to the nation, this expedient, dictated by practical necessity, were scorned? The chambers will thus observe toward each other the consideration which is indispensable in preserving the unity of the Congress, which must deliberate without passion and with the calm of wisdom. Our modern congresses, I shall be told, consist of only two houses. This is because England, which has provided the model, was forced to have the nobility and the people represented in two chambers; and, while the same pattern was followed in North America where there is no nobility, it may be presumed that the habits acquired under British rule inspired this imitation. The fact is that two deliberating bodies are always found to be in conflict. It was for this reason that Sieyès insisted on only one—a classic error.

The first body [I propose] is the Chamber of Tribunes. It has the right to initiate laws pertaining to finance, peace, and war. It exercises the immediate supervision of the departments administered by the executive branch with a minimum of interference by the legislative branch.

The Senators enact the codes of law and the ecclesiastical regulations and supervise the courts and public worship. The Senate shall appoint the prefects, district judges, governors, *corregidores,* and all the lesser officials in the department of justice. It shall submit to the Chamber of Censors nominations for members of the Supreme Court, archbishops, bishops, prebendaries, and canons. Everything relating to religion and the laws comes within the province of the Senate.

The Censors exercise a political and moral power not unlike that of the Areopagus of Athens and the censors of Rome. They are the prosecuting attorneys [*fiscales*] against the government in defense of the Constitution and popular rights, to see that these are strictly observed. Under their aegis has been placed the power of national judgment, which is to decide whether or not the administration of the executive is satisfactory.

The Censors are to safeguard morality, the sciences, the arts, education, and the press. The Censors exercise the most fearful yet the most august authority. They can condemn to eternal opprobrium arch criminals and usurpers of the sovereign authority. They can bestow public honors upon citizens who have distinguished themselves by their probity and public service. The sceptre of glory has been placed in their hands, for which reason the Censors must possess integrity and a conduct above reproach. For any trespass on their part, however slight, they shall be prosecuted. To these high priests of the laws I have entrusted the preservation of our sacred tablets, as it is for them to denounce the violators of these laws.

The President of the Republic, in our Constitution, becomes the sun which, fixed in its orbit, imparts life to the universe. This supreme authority must be perpetual, for in non-hierarchical systems, more than in others, a fixèd point is needed about which leaders and citizens, men and affairs can revolve. "Give me a point where I may stand," said an ancient sage, "and I will move the earth." For Bolivia this point is the lifeterm President [*presidente vitalicio*]. Upon him rests our entire order, notwithstanding his lack of powers. Not only has he been rendered headless in order that none may fear his intentions, but his hands have been tied so that he can do no harm.

The President of Bolivia enjoys many of the powers of the [North] American chief executive but with limitations that favor the people. His term of office is that enjoyed by the President of Haiti. For Bolivia, I have borrowed the executive system of the most democratic republic in the world.

The island of Haiti, if you will permit the digression, was in a state of perpetual insurrection. Having experimented with an empire, a kingdom, and a republic, in fact every known type of government and more besides, the people were compelled to call upon the illustrious Pétion to save them. After they had put their trust in him, Haiti's destinies pursued a steady course. Pétion was made President for life, with the right to choose his successor. Thus, neither the death of that great man nor the advent of a new president imperiled that state in the slightest. Under the worthy Boyer, everything has proceeded as tranquilly as in a legitimate monarchy. There you have conclusive proof that *a life-term president, with the power to choose his successor,* is the most sublime inspiration amongst republican regimes.

The President of Bolivia will be less dangerous than the President of Haiti, as the succession is provided for in a manner that better secures the interests of the state. Moreover, the President of Bolivia is deprived of all patronage. He can appoint neither governors, nor judges, nor ecclesiastic dignitaries of any kind. This limitation of powers has never before been imposed in any constituted government. One check after another has thus been placed upon the authority of the head of the government, who will in every way find that the people are ruled directly by those who exercise the significant functions of the commonwealth. The priests will rule in matters of conscience, the judges in matters involving property, honor, and life, and the magistrates or men of state in all major public acts. As they owe their position, their distinction, and their fortune to the people alone, the President cannot hope to entangle them in his personal ambitions. If to this is added the natural growth of opposition which a democratic government experiences throughout the course of its administration, there is reason to believe that, under this form of government, usurpation of the popular sovereignty is less likely to occur than under any other.

Legislators, from this day forth liberty will be indestructible in America. Observe the savage character of our continent, which of itself bars a monarchical order, for the deserts invite independence. Here, there are no great nobles or churchmen. Our wealth has amounted to little, and it is no greater today. The Church, though not without influence, is far from seeking domination as it is satisfied to insure its own preservation. Without these supporting factors, tyrants cannot survive, and, should any ambitious soul aspire to make himself emperor, there are Dessalines, Christophe, and Iturbide to warn him of what he may expect. No power is harder to maintain than that of a newly crowned prince. This truth, which is stronger than empires, defeated Bonaparte, the conqueror of all armies. If the great Napoleon could not maintain himself against an alliance of republicans and aristocrats, who then in America will undertake to establish monarchies upon a soil fired with the bright flames of liberty, which would consume the very pillars intended to support the royalist structure? No, Legislators, fear not the pretenders to a crown which will hang over their heads like the sword of Dionysius. New-found princes who should be so bold as to erect thrones upon the ruins of liberty will instead erect tombs for their own remains, which will proclaim to future ages the fact that they *preferred vain ambition to freedom and glory.*

The constitutional limitations upon the President of Bolivia are the narrowest ever known. He can appoint only the officials of the Ministries of the Treasury, Peace, and War; and he is Commander in Chief of the army. These are his only powers.

Administration is the province of the Cabinet, which is responsible to the Censors and subject to the close vigilance of every legislator, governor, judge, and citizen. The revenue officers and soldiers, who are agents of the Cabinet alone, are hardly the persons calculated to make it the object of public affection, and therefore its influence will be next to nothing.

Of all the higher officials, the Vice President is the one with the most limited power. He must obey both the legislative and the executive branches of a republican government. From the former, he receives the laws, and from the latter his instructions, and he must proceed between these two branches, following the narrowest of paths, with precipices on either side. Despite these disadvantages, this form of government is better than an absolute government. Constitutional limitations increase political consciousness, thereby giving hope of ultimately finding a beacon light which will act as a guide through the ever-present shoals and reefs. These limitations serve as dikes against the violence of our passions, which are prompted by selfish interests.

In the government of the United States it has of late become the practice for the Secretary of State to succeed the President. Nothing could be more expedient, in any republic, than this practice. It has the advantage of placing at the head of the administration a man experienced in the management of a nation. In entering upon his duties, he is fully prepared and brings with him the advantages of popularity and practical experience. I have borrowed this practice [of succession] and embodied it in the law.

The President of the Republic will appoint the Vice President, who will administer the affairs of the state and succeed the President in office. By means of this device we shall avoid elections, which result in that great scourge of republics—anarchy, which is the hand-maiden of tyranny, the most imminent and terrible peril of popular government. Compare the tremendous crises in republics when a change of rulers takes place with the equivalent situation in legitimate monarchies.

The Vice President must be a man of the loftiest character, for, should the President not appoint an honorable citizen, he will fear him as an enemy incarnate and be ever suspicious of his secret ambitions. The Vice President will have to exert himself in order to merit, through faithful service, the high esteem necessary to discharge the highest duties and to deserve that great national honor—the supreme command. The legislative body and the people will expect both ability and integrity of this high ranking office as well as a blind obedience to the principles of freedom.

If hereditary succession perpetuates the monarchical system and is all but universal, is not the plan which I have just proposed, wherein the Vice President succeeds to the presidency, much more expedient? What if hereditary princes were chosen for merit and not by fate? What if, instead of wallowing in idleness and ignorance, they were put in charge of government administration? They would unquestionably be more enlightened monarchs, and they would contribute to the happiness of their peoples. Indeed, Legislators, monarchy, which rules the world, has won its claim for approval by means of the hereditary principle, which renders it stable, and by *unity,* which makes it strong. Hence, although a ruling prince is a spoiled child, cloistered in his palace, reared on adulation, and swayed by every passion, this other prince, whom I might venture to call the impossible man, is a ruler of men, for, by virtue of power firmly and constantly applied, he maintains order and willing subordination among the citizens. Do not forget, Gentlemen, that these great advantages are combined in a life-term presidential and vice presidential tenure and a vice presidential succession.

The judicial power that I propose enjoys an absolute independence not to be found in any other nation. The people nominate the candidates, and the legislature chooses the persons who are to serve in the courts. Unless the judicial powers emanate from this source, the judiciary cannot possibly be faithful to its obligation to safeguard individual rights. These rights, Legislators, are those that insure freedom, equality, and security—all guarantees of the social order. The real foundation of liberty resides in the civil and criminal codes, and the worst kind of tyranny is that which is exercised by the courts through that powerful instrument, law. As a rule, the executive is the custodian of public affairs, but the courts are the arbiters of private affairs—of the concerns of individuals. The judicial power determines the happiness or the unhappiness of the citizens. Whatever liberty and justice the Republic enjoys is dispensed by this power. At times, the political structure is of minor importance if the civil organization is perfect, that is, if the laws are rigorously enforced and held to be as inexorable as fate.

It was to be expected that, in keeping with the ideas of our time, we should prohibit the use of torture and confessions, and that we should shorten the procedures by which law suits are made lengthy by the intricate maze of appeals.

The territory of the Republic will be governed by prefects, governors, *corregidores,* justices of the peace, and *alcaldes.* I have been unable to elaborate upon the internal organization and the exact authority of each of these positions. It is my duty, nevertheless, to commend to the Congress rules and regulations governing the administration of departments and provinces. Bear in mind, Legislators, that nations are composed of cities and towns, and that the happiness of a nation stems from their well-being. You can never give too much attention to the proper administration of the provinces. This is the crux of the legislative art, yet it is neglected only too often.

I have divided the armed forces into four parts: regular army, fleet, national militia, and internal revenue patrol. The duty of the army is to protect the border. God grant that it will never have to turn its weapons upon our citizens! The national militia will suffice to preserve order at home. Bolivia has no extensive coastline and therefore has no need of a navy, although the day may come when we will have both.[1] The internal revenue patrol is in every way preferable to a civilian guard, which is not merely superfluous but evil. Accordingly, the Republic must garrison her borders with regular troops, using the revenue patrol to combat fraud at home.

I have felt that the Constitution of Bolivia may have to be amended at intervals, in accordance with the demands of changing world conditions. The amendment procedure has been provided for in terms that I consider best adapted to the subject.

The responsibility of government officials is set forth in the Bolivian Constitution in the most explicit terms. Without responsibility and restraint, the nation becomes a chaos. I should like most forcefully to urge upon you, the legislators, the enactment of strict and well-defined laws on this important matter. Everyone speaks of responsibility, but it receives lip service only. When there is no responsibility, Legislators, the judges and all the other officials, high and low, abuse their powers, as there is no rigid check on government servants. The citizens, consequently, are the victims of this abuse. I recommend a law that will provide for an annual check on every government employee.

The most perfect guarantees have been provided for the individual. *Civil liberty* is the one true freedom; the others are nominal, or they affect the citizens slightly. The inviolability of the individual—the true purpose of society and the source of all other safeguards—is guaranteed. *Property rights* will be covered by a civil code, which you should wisely draft in due time for the good of your fellow-citizens. I have left intact that law of laws—*equality*. Neglect it, and all rights and safeguards will vanish. We must make every sacrifice for it and, at its feet, cast the dishonored and infamous relics of slavery.

Legislators, slavery is the negation of all law, and any law which should perpetuate it would be a sacrilege. What justification can there be for its

---

[1] Bolivia, until the 1870's, possessed a coastal strip between Chile and Perú (ed.).

perpetuation? Examine this crime from every aspect and tell me if there is a single Bolivian so depraved as to wish to sanctify by law this shameless violation of human dignity. One man owned by another! A man reduced to a chattel! An image of God coupled to the yoke like a beast! Where are the legal claims of the enslavers of men? Guinea did not authorize them, for Africa, devastated by fratricidal struggles, spawned nothing but crime. . . .

Legislators, I shall mention on item which my conscience has compelled me to omit. A political constitution should not prescribe any particular religion, for, according to the best doctrines, fundamental laws guarantee political and civil rights, and, since religion has no bearing upon these rights, it is by nature indefinable in the social organization, because it lies in the moral and intellectual sphere. Religion governs man in his home, within his own walls, within himself. Religion alone is entitled to examine a man's innermost conscience. Laws, on the contrary, deal with surface things; they are applicable outside the home of a citizen. If we apply these criteria, how can a state rule the conscience of its subjects, enforce the observance of religious laws, and mete out rewards and punishments, when the tribunals are in Heaven and God is the judge? Only the Inquisition could presume to do their work on earth. Would you bring back the Inquisition with its burnings at the stake?

Religion is the law of conscience. Any law that imposes it negates it, because to apply compulsion to conscience is to destroy the value of faith, which is the very essence of religion. The sacred precepts and doctrines are useful, enlightening, and spiritually nourishing. We should all avow them, but the obligation is moral rather than political.

On the other hand, what are the religious rights of man on earth? These rights reside in Heaven where there is a tribunal that rewards merit and dispenses justice according to the code laid down by the great Lawgiver. As all this is within divine jurisdiction, it would seem to me, at first sight, to be sacrilegious and profane for us to interfere with the Commandments of the Lord by enactments of our own. Prescribing religion is therefore not the task of the legislator, who, for any infractions, must provide penalties, not mere exhortations. Where there are no temporal punishments or judges to apply them, the law ceases to be law.

The moral development of man is the legislator's first concern. Once such a growth has been attained, man bases his morality upon the truths so revealed and acknowledges religion *de facto* and all the more effectively for having come to it by personal experience. Moreover, heads of families cannot neglect their religious obligations to their children. The spiritual pastors are obliged to teach the Gospel of Heaven. The example of all the true disciples of Christ is the most eloquent teacher of his divine doctrine. But doctrine cannot be commanded, nor is one who commands a teacher, for force can play no part in the giving of spiritual counsel. God and his ministers are the authorities on religion, and religion exerts its influence solely through spiritual means and bodies, never through instruments of the nation's body politic, which serves only to direct public energies toward purely temporal ends.

Legislators, as you now proclaim the new Bolivian nation, what noble, generous, and elevated thoughts must inspire you! The admission of a new state into the community of nations is just cause for man's rejoicing, for it augments the great family of nations. What a joy it is then to its founders, and to me, to see myself likened to the most renowned of the ancients—the father of the Eternal City. This honor rightly belongs to the creators of nations, who, as their very first benefactors, truly deserve the rewards of immortality. Similarly the honor done me is immortal, and it has the added factor of being gratuitous because it is undeserved. Where is the Republic, where is the city that I have founded? Your magnanimity in giving my name to a nation has far outdone any services I may have rendered, for it is infinitely superior to the service of any one man.

My embarrassment increases as I contemplate the magnitude of your reward, for even if I had contributed the talents and virtues, indeed the genius, of the greatest heroes, I should still be unworthy to give the name you have desired to take—my own! Shall I express gratitude, when gratitude alone can never express, however feebly, the emotion stirred within me by your kindness, which, like that of God himself, is infinite! Yes! God alone had sovereign power to call this land Bolivia. And what does Bolivia signify? A boundless love of liberty, and, after you had received it, you, in your enthusiasm, could conceive of nothing equal to it in value. When, carried away by the immensity of your joy, you could find no adequate way to express the sweep of your emotions, you put your own name aside and adopted mine for all time to come. This act, which is without parallel in all history, is especially so in view of the sublime disinterestedness which inspired it. Your deed shall demonstrate to the ages that as yet exist only in the infinite years of the future how strongly you cherished your right—the right to exercise political virtue, to acquire sublime talents, and to know the satisfaction of being men. Your deed, I repeat, shall prove that you were indeed fit to receive that great heavenly benediction—*the Sovereignty of the People*—the sole legitimate authority of any nation.

Legislators, happy are you who preside over the destinies of a republic that at birth was crowned with the laurels of Ayacucho, a republic destined to enduring life under benign laws which, in the calm that has followed the fearful tempest of war, shall be dictated by your wisdom.

BOLÍVAR

4. *Disillusion, Rejection and Death*

J. B. TREND

Bolívar was in Lima in late 1826 when news of factional disputes in Bogotá and Caracas persuaded him to return north. Arriving in Bogotá he learned that the Venezuelan leader, José Antonio Páez, was plotting to withdraw from the union with Gran Colombia while suggesting that Bolívar be crowned as king. Bolívar went to Caracas in January 1827 and convinced Páez to remain loyal. When he returned to Bogotá near the end of that year, he had to deal with Vice-President Francisco Paula de Santander, who was often at odds with the mercurial Liberator. Bolívar placed his hopes in a constitutional reform convention that met at Ocaña in April 1828. When it disolved with nothing accomplished, he established a frank military dictatorship that hardened after the attempt made on his life on September 24, 1828. Professor Trend provides a moving account of the assassination attempt, and of the heroism of Manuela Sáenz in enabling Bolívar to escape. He also outlines the series of events that drove Bolívar to resign the presidency in despair and to prepare to go into exile.

Bolívar had never had any great illusions on the possibility of applying democratic principles whole-heartedly in South America; and some of his biographers have considered that, once in supreme command, he took little trouble to conceal his impatience with doubting liberals. The first thing was to restore order; and he did not hesitate to sacrifice personal liberties in order to do so. To stamp out anarchy, he employed all the forces of reaction; and the chief forces which could serve his purpose, in a country where all political tradition had been lost in the wars of independence, were just those forces which were most damaging to his political ideals: the army and the church. The army was represented by ambitious generals who were hoping to carve provinces for themselves out of the remains of the Colombian Union; there was not one of sufficient stature to dream of succeeding Bolívar. Sucre might have done so, but he was murdered not long before Bolívar's own death. There remained the clergy, supported by the religiosity of the rich and the fanaticism of the poor; and these, Bolívar resolved to exploit. His decrees show him bent on suppressing liberalism, which all dictators have invariably regarded as the fountainhead of anarchy; and he increased the army to something like four times its original size. With the church on his side, and the army—and his own personal influence, which was still considerable—Bolívar thought that the Colombian Union might still be saved.

Bolívar's dictatorship was at once acknowledged by Páez. The astute

From: J. B. Trend, *Bolívar and the Independence of Spanish America* (New York: Harper & Row, 1968), pp. 250–68. Reprinted by permission.

llanero saw that the independence of Venezuela was now assured; it was already a state within a state, and he meant to keep a free hand in the country which he already ruled. Bolívar realized this; yet he was always conciliatory, and his letters to Páez are witten in the friendliest terms.

In Colombia, Bolívar's enemies took to conspiracy, though Páez would not let them cross the border and conspire on Venezuelan soil. "Behead Bolívar," one of their wits remarked, "cut off his feet, and you are left with *oliva,* the symbol of peace and tranquility." Their aim, as one of the survivors described it, 25 years afterwards, was to capture Bolívar and his ministers and put Santander at the head of the government. Santander was certainly privy to the plot. There was talk of assassination; but an attempt on Bolívar, when riding with two friends near Bogotá, was frustrated by Santander himself. That was on the 21st September; the next attempt was fixed for the 28th. But on the 25th one of the conspirators was arrested, and the others determined to act that same night before he could give anything away under cross-examination.

Bolívar had been warned, but he thought that the usual guard at the Presidential Palace—the old Palacio de San Carlos—was enough. O'Leary was away; all the other aides, except one, were on sick leave. The Liberator, too, was feeling ill and depressed. The faithful who saw eye to eye with him were few. His presence still aroused enthusiasm and devotion, but he could not himself be everywhere at once. Even his presence was not so effective as it used to be. Formerly he had only to appear in person, and the waverers became loyal again; a few days or weeks of office-work and personal rounds of inspection had always put things to rights. Now, however, there were intrigues against him personally. That, perhaps, was natural with a dictator; and in Peru, too, they had insisted on his assuming dictatorial powers. The stigma of dictatorship never left him, and his personal intervention in any question was branded by his enemies as dictatorial. The plot in Bogotá was against his dictatorial power. Though the organizers were middle-aged intriguers and wire-pullers, the actual executants were mainly young men, with the fanatical faith of storm-troopers, relying on methods of terrorism. "We could not flatter ourselves with the thought of success, except by the impression of terror which the news of Bolívar's death would produce on our opponents." One of the assassins is speaking. Vice-President Santander, without being directly implicated himself, seems to have known that a new attempt was to be made; yet he gave Bolívar no warning, and did nothing to check the movement. He too had been intriguing against the Liberator, as intercepted letters showed. Bolívar had good reason to be discouraged.

On the night of the attempt the conspirators hid in the cathedral till midnight. It had been raining—the climate of Bogotá has been compared to a cold spring in Paris—but there was bright moonlight. One brigade of artillery had been won over by the conspirators; each knew exactly what he had to do, and they felt confident of success. The clock struck 12. They came out of the cathedral and got to work.

In his depression, and the rain, and the chilly afternoon, Bolívar had sent for Manuela Sáenz. She grumbled at having to go out just then, but duly came to the Palace. Bolívar was having a hot bath. She read to him while he lay in it, and then put him to bed. He seemed to have a feverish cold, and she stayed with him.

Manuela described what happened next:

"It was about 12 when the Liberator's dogs began to bark; and there was a peculiar noise which must have been the fight with the sentries, but no shooting. I woke the Liberator, and the first thing he did was to pick up a sword and a pistol and try to open the door. I stopped him and made him dress, which he did quite calmly but quickly. He said: 'Bravo! Well, here I am dressed; what do we do now? Barricade ourselves in?' He tried to open the door again, but I prevented him. Then I remembered something I had once heard the General say. 'Didn't you tell Pepe Paris,' I said, 'that that window would do for an occasion like this?' 'You're right,' he answered and went over to the window. I prevented him getting out at first, because there were people passing; but he managed it when they had gone, just as the door was being broken open [in the next room]. I went to meet them, to give him time to get away; but I didn't have time to see him jump, or to shut the window. As soon as they saw me, they seized me and said: 'Where's Bolívar?' I told them he was at a meeting, which was the first thing that occurred to me. They searched the outer room carefully and went on to the second, and when they saw the window open, they exclaimed: 'He's got away! He's escaped.' I said: 'No, *señores,* he has not got away: he's at a meeting' . . . I said I knew there was a meeting, and that the Liberator went to it every night, but I didn't know where it was. At this they grew very angry, and dragged me away with them until we found Ibarra [an *Aide de camp*] lying wounded on the floor. 'So they've killed the Liberator?' he asked. 'No, Ibarra,' I said, 'the Liberator's alive.' I know it was stupid of us to talk, and I began to bandage him with a handkerchief. They asked me more questions; but as they couldn't get anything more they took me back to the room where they found me, and I brought the wounded man along too.

"Suddenly I heard the sound of heavy boots. I looked out of the window and saw Colonel Ferguson, running along from the house where he had been in bed with a sore throat. He saw me in the moonlight, which was bright just then. He asked for the Liberator, but I said I didn't know; and I couldn't tell him because of the guards they had left there, but I warned him not to come in because they would kill him. He answered that he would die doing his duty. In a moment I heard a shot . . . and then the blow on the head with a sabre which left him dead. . . .

"The Liberator had taken a pistol, and a sword which someone or other had given him in Europe. When he jumped into the street, his cook happened to be passing and went along with him. The General stood in the river [under a bridge] for some time; and then sent the man to see what was happening at the barracks. . . . I went as far as the cathedral, and there I saw the Liberator on a horse, talking to Santander and Padilla, with a crowd of soldiers cheering."

The rising was over in a few hours. By 4 a.m. Bolívar was back in the Presidential Palace. The conspiracy was crushed, but he had caught a chill from which he never recovered. It went to his lungs, and the effects of this attack of pleurisy never left him. The conspirators were rounded up, except for two or three who lived to conspire another day: one to write an impenitent account of the affair many years afterwards in Europe, and another to return and even become President of the Republic. Bolívar's first thought was to pardon them all; but the decision did not rest with him, and the faithful General Urdaneta had them dealt with summarily. Fourteen were shot. Santander was condemned to death, as accessory; but the sentence was commuted to one of banishment and loss of military rank, though he, too, eventually returned to be President of the Republic.

Bolívar was overwhelmed mentally and physically. He never recovered from the shock, and the tuberculosis made rapid strides. His letters, more voluble than ever, are sometimes incoherent, and his postscripts illegible.

"I am so worried," he wrote on November 15th, 1828, "that I shall go away to the country for several months, to a place where there are nothing but Indians. . . . I can't put up any longer with such ingratitude. I'm not a saint, I've no wish to suffer martyrdom. Only the luck of having a few good friends keeps me going in this torture."

The dictatorship continued, either under Bolívar personally, or exercised by others in his name. Reaction was energetically pursued, centralism accentuated. "The Liberator," a Venezuelan historian has remarked, "in spite of his understanding of the French Revolution, and his knowledge of British constitutional practice, had become a doctrinaire administrator of the Latin type. He thought in 1828 as if he were living in ancient Rome—the ancient Rome of the eighteenth-century *philosophes*. He still believed in political 'virtue' and held that dictatorship was a sovereign remedy in times of emergency; but in this way he fell into what seem to us now the greatest errors of his public life." He did not pretend that dictatorship could be a permanent system of government; "his good intentions are as evident as the error in his calculations." His reliance on the army and the church, and his persecution of liberalism, have already been referred to. Like most dictators since his time, he found himself obliged to interfere with the text-books read in schools and colleges. The books to which his attention was specially drawn were written by an Englishman—Bentham—who had personally sent Bolívar some of his writings, translated into Spanish by a liberal Catalan exile in London. They were removed from the list of works prescribed for study, although afterwards they were reinstated, and held their place for nearly a hundred years.

Other repressive measures against liberalism followed, and by 1829 very few of the liberal principles remained which had inspired the declaration of Venezuelan independence—indeed, throughout the length and breadth of Great Colombia the only revolutionary idea which was still intact was the firm resolve never to return to the domination of Spain.

At the end of 1829 Bolívar suspended all the municipal councils. In Venezuela, many people approved, forgetting that the municipal councils had been, on the whole, the only organized bodies of resistance to arbitrary government, and the only effective centres of independence. They were not, of course, democratic; they represented oligarchy and the old Creole families, as we have seen. It was on them that Páez had founded his military authority. Yet in obedience to Bolívar he dissolved them forthwith, and handed over local government to *corregidores,* regional commissioners sent down from the capital.

The Colombian Union continued to exist in a precarious state: Venezuela practically independent under Páez, Quito in a state of perpetual anarchy; and now Peru, which had once begged for a Colombian army to deliver it from the Spaniards, made war on the country which had set it free. "Neither in Colombia nor in Peru can one get anything done," Bolívar exclaimed. "Not even my own name counts for anything now. Everything has gone, for good. . . . Instinct alone makes one go on living, but [life is] almost without an object."

There was a rising in the south of Colombia, at Popayán, and almost at the same time Quito was invaded by troops from Peru. Something of the Liberator's old activity returned. With the help of the Quito general, Flores, and the Colombian General Córdoba, he succeeded in rapidly suppressing the insurgents at Popayán; while Sucre, after a campaign "rendered particularly arduous by the extraordinary and unexpected strategical mistakes of the Peruvian commander," gained at Tarqui a crushing victory over a force twice the size of his own. Bolívar's troubles were not yet over, for his own General

Córdoba rebelled in the autumn, against "the tyranny of Bolívar," and had to be routed at El Santuario by a force commanded by the faithful O'Leary.

Meanwhile the question of finding a successor to Bolívar was becoming urgent. In 1829 efforts were made to discover another man capable of holding the office of president-for-life. To the mind of the Liberator there was considerable difference between a president-for-life and a king or an emperor; but less subtle minds were unable to see this, and the idea had grown up that the life-presidency could be preserved by bringing in an English prince. The plan of a *monarquía inglesa,* a limited monarchy in the English style, has been attributed to Bolívar himself; it reappeared in 1829 and did considerable harm to his popularity. That Bolívar ever really wanted a crowned king or emperor in South America is extremely doubtful; those who attributed the idea to him were probably misled by wishful thinking, and the idea that he ever wanted a crown for himself is absurd to anyone acquainted with his character or political thought. The tragical history of the Emperor Itúrbide in Mexico showed what was likely to happen to successful Latin American generals when they aspired to the Imperial purple; and if a king were to be thought of for Great Colombia, it was essential that he should belong to one of the old royal families of Europe. The chief difficulty was that every department of Great Colombia was full of ambitious generals, or *caudillos,* ready to rise in their own immediate districts. It was plain that the Colombian Union could not continue to exist under republican institutions which demanded a presidential election every four years; and for that reason, and also because a life-presidency seemed too much like a dictatorship, opinion veered round to constitutional monarchy, for the order and stability which were believed to be inseparable from it. The Council of State in Bogotá tried to hold out to England and France the prospect of a monarchy after the Liberator's death; but Bolívar was thinking rather of some kind of mediation, influence, alliance or protectorate, by one of the great powers. He made declarations which were ambiguous and contradictory. He wrote from Quito in 1829, asking the Foreign Minister to sound the diplomatic representatives of Britain and the United States, adding that it would be impossible to prevent the outbreak of anarchy in Colombia, if some powerful state did not intervene. The choice seemed to be either anarchy or a return to something like colonial status.

"There has been a Panamá congress of American nations, but it has been despised by the nations most interested. A federation has been proposed, between the three Sovereign States of Venezuela, Colombia and Quito; but there has been such misrepresentation and such an outcry, that it could have been heard in heaven. Britain has offered to mediate between Brazil and the River Plate; it has intervened by force of arms between Turkey and Greece. Could not something also be done about Colombia?"

Nothing was done; and the monarchial project was given up.

In 1830 the Colombian Union fell to pieces. First Venezuela assumed its independence, and then Quito; Bolívar's great dream was shattered.

From May 1830 until his death in December, Bolívar's life was a continual torment. He could not even do the last thing he had set his heart on doing: get away from Colombia altogether. His friends kept insisting that he should wait and see whether, at the last minute, something could not be done to preserve the Colombian Union; though by this time the Liberator knew that all further effort was vain and useless. The increasing hold which his illness had gained upon him condemned him to inaction; and nothing that even the most elementary medical science could do could help a man who refused to submit to almost any medical treatment whatever.

Above all, he was short of money, and could not think of beginning a long voyage until funds reached him from Caracas. This was exasperating to a man who had never had to think about money-matters and was of an extremely nervous temperament. He had once been a rich man; but his plantations had been fought over and destroyed, his houses were mostly in ruins, and his fortune had been reduced to his royalties on the copper mines at Aroa— royalties which for a long time had not been paid and were at that moment the subject of litigation. His lawyers did what they could to find him ready money; but they were unable to overcome the scarcely veiled hostility of Páez, now head of the independent Venezuelan Government, or the personal spite of a Dr. Yañes, the most influential lawyer in the country. Bolívar felt the indignity of it, and more, the base ingratitude. On his resignation from the presidency of the Colombian Union, Congress had confirmed a decree of 1823 granting him an annual pension of 30,000 pesos (say £6,000); but he had never received it, nor had he accepted the pension voted him by the Congress of Peru. It was impossible for a man like the Liberator to resign himself to economies, accustomed as he was to give away all the money he had by him, in charity or presents to old friends or old soldiers. One or two old friends, of the few he still had in Venezuela, tried to help him. His musical uncle, Estéban Palacios, who long ago had played string quartets in the garden at Chacao, offered him 5,000 pesos down, and 5,000 more which were invested in Europe. Bolívar felt he could not take them and declined.

At the end of September 1830, he moved along the coast to Soledad and Barranquilla. On 1st December he reached Santa Marta, a place where the hot wind blew sand in at every door and window—quite unsuitable for a man dying of consumption. "He came ashore in a carrying chair," his French doctor reported. "He was unable to walk. He was thin and emaciated in body and restless in mind. His voice was hoarse, he coughed perpetually, and the first diagnosis was that there were extensive pulmonary lesions." Next day the French doctor saw him in consultation with an American surgeon; they diagnosed pulmonary tuberculosis. On 6th December he was moved out into the country, to the Quinta de San Pedro Alejandrino, an estate belonging to a Spaniard, Joaquín de Mier. Spain was the country above all others which had cause to hate Bolívar; without him, and his twenty years' struggle, first for freedom and then for their existence as free states, Venezuela, Colombia, Ecuador, Peru and Bolivia would still have been parts of the Spanish Empire. Yet now, when Venezuela and Colombia had turned their backs on him, Peru had forgotten him and Bolivia had set aside the constitution he had given it, it was a Spaniard who took him in, and housed him during his last illness. That action was a very Spanish thing.

In his last weeks Bolívar turned to Spanish books, particularly to *Don Quixote,* finding there, perhaps, his own image, as it was afterwards found by Unamuno.

"The three greatest *idiots* in history," he said in his bitterness, "have been Jesus Christ, Don Quixote and . . . myself!" The saying would have pleased Dostoievsky.

He had visits from a few old friends and comrades in arms; conversations with the doctor.

"Doctor, what did you come to this country to find?"

"Liberty."

"Have you found it?"

"Yes, General."

"Then you are more fortunate than I am. . . . Go back to your fair France where the tricolour is still flying. Here, in this country, no one can live. Too many crooks; *canallas.*"

At night he was delirious. He thought he was back among his own men. The watchers heard him say: "Come on now! Come on! *Vámonos!* . . . These people don't love us in this country . . . Come on, boys! This way . . ." And then: "They may take my kit aboard now."

The Bishop of Santa Marta came, and told him it was time to do his duty as a Christian. Bolívar protested; he was tired, but not so ill as all that. Then he resigned himself to it, groaning: "Oh, how shall I get out of this labyrinth!" He confessed to the parish priest of an Indian village. It is doubtful whether he could be called a Catholic; a deist rather. He belonged to the Age of Reason; yet he had lived on into times when all that was, was unreason. Romantic. He himself would one day be considered one of the living spirits of the Romantic Movement. "All a jest, all dust, all nothing." All had not been a jest, certainly; but all was dust—it was blowing into the room through every crack and cranny—and all would soon be nothing. Rather than a

Catholic or a deist, he was a *philosophe,* steeped in the thought of the French eighteenth century. Contrary to Catholic truth, he had always defended liberty of conscience and freedom for all forms of worship—except in that last exasperated period of dictatorship. Religion should be the law of the individual conscience; in the ideal constitutions which he had framed, no one religion was recognized as the established religion of the State. Yet as a public man, head of the government, he had felt bound to respect the forms and outward manifestations of Catholicism, which was the religion of the great majority of his fellow-countrymen and treat the Catholic Church as an important factor in political and social life, as it was among all people of Spanish origin.

On 10th December he made his will. He declared that he had no other property beyond the estate and mines of Aroa, and a few jewels in a safe at Cartagena. He left a gold medal to the Bolivian Congress, which had conferred it; and to the University Library at Caracas the copies of the *Contrat Social* of Rousseau and a book on military tactics which had once belonged to Napoleon, and had been given him by the father of his English A.D.C., Belford Wilson. His manservant was to receive 8,000 pesos, for long and faithful service; his residuary legatees were his sisters and his nephews. His executors were to convey a message of thanks to General Sir Robert Wilson, for the fine behaviour of his son, Colonel Belford Wilson. (Manuela Saenz was up at Bogotá, holding the position for the Liberator to the last.) After the will had been signed and witnessed, Bolívar dictated his last proclamation, "Colombians," he ended, "my latest wish is for the happiness of our country. If my death can help to put an end to party strife and consolidate the Union, I shall go down to the grave in peace."

He died a week later, on 17th December 1830. O'Leary was there, Belford Wilson, and Andrés Ibarra who had lost an arm on the night of the mutiny at Bogotá. According to the Liberator's last instructions, such papers as he had by him were burnt; but the doctor declared that he had seen among them a petition to Bolívar to allow himself to be crowned. In the margin was scribbled in pencil:

> "To accept a crown would stain my reputation. I prefer the glorious title of First Citizen of Colombia."

Bolívar's life ended in defeat and disappointment. Had he lived in vain? His last proclamation went unheeded; he himself had been driven to repudiate his own political faith; his legacy was buried with him. But a hundred years afterwards, strange things began to happen on that continent where everything is strange and few things impossible. States began to settle their differences by arbitration, instead of war. Contrary to all expectation a stable republicanism was developed. In some countries (particularly Colombia and

Uruguay) real liberalism was achieved; while between most of them a genuine, good-neighbourly feeling began to make its appearance.

Bolívar's work ended in ruins: but his ideal is still there, and the achievement of the Spanish and Portuguese Americas is one of the great facts of modern history. They are among the few peoples in the world to-day whose belief in the future has not been shaken, and whose ideals—however Utopian they may have appeared in the time of the Liberator—are now plans which can and may be put into practice, even though they may not take the form of the close political union intended by Bolívar himself.

Juan Manuel de Rosas during his first term as governor (1829–1831).

The Age of Caudillos—
Juan Manuel De Rosas

HOW TO EXPLAIN DICTATORS?

The rise and fall of *caudillos* has long been a basic theme in Latin American history. Columbus was probably the first caudillo, and there is no doubt that the institution still flourishes south of the Rio Grande. What permits them to rise to power, how they manage to stay in power, why they usually fall, and what they accomplish are highly controversial questions. It is not surprising that no *magnum opus* has yet been written on this complicated and debatable subject. One general volume with a valuable collection of representative selections is available. Its editor, in analyzing this puzzling and persistent phenomenon in Latin America, on which hundreds, if not thousands, of articles and books have been written, emphasizes "the rich variety of dictatorial types and the mulltitude of factors that condition their existence."[1]

ATTACKS ON ROSAS BY SARMIENTO

Dictators sprang up in most countries immediately following the end of European dominance. One of the most powerful and long-ruling was Juan Manuel de Rosas, who ran Argentina with an iron hand from 1829 to 1852. He has been violently attacked and stoutly defended from the time he first established his power until today. In his era, articulate exiles in neighboring Chile and Uruguay kept up a steady barrage against him in newspapers, pamphlets, and books. One of the most famous of these was Domingo Faustino Sarmiento, who in 1845 wrote a classic account entitled *Facundo, O Civilizacion I Barbarie*. This is ostensibly merely a biography

---

[1] Hugh M. Hamill, Jr., ed. *Dictatorship in Spanish America* (New York: Knopf, 1965), p. 5.

47

of Juan Facundo Quiroga, the provincial dictator, but in fact presents a profound study of the causes of dictatorship. For Sarmiento, one fundamental explanation is the nature of the *gauchos,* the rough-riding, untutored cowboys of the immense Argentine plains (Reading 1).

Rosas began to smart under the public attacks abroad of such writers as Sarmiento and Juan Bautista Alberdi. He mounted an efficient propaganda machine, directed by Pedro de Angelis, which aimed at improving the dictator's image in Europe and elsewhere with publications in English, French, and Spanish. Since Rosas, most dictators have followed his example and maintained a public relations apparatus to help keep them in power.

Inside Argentina, various methods were perfected to keep alive the pro-Rosas spirit; his wife, Encarnación, with other women aiding her, was a skillful manipulator in this field. One foreign visitor reported that puppet shows, theater performances, and the opera were opened with a display of public patriotic enthusiasm. The principal performers would assemble on the stage and cry out: "Long live the Confederación Argentina!" to which the chorus would reply: "Viva!" Then the principal characters would shout again: "Death to the savage Unitarians!" (as Rosas's opponents were called), with an answering "Mueran!" (May they perish!) from the chorus, after which the performance began.

DIVERSE ATTITUDES TOWARD ROSAS

Foreigners visiting Argentina during the Age of Rosas reacted in diverse ways. Charles Darwin, then on a scientific voyage, was favorably impressed, at least at first, whereas Anthony King denounced Rosas as an "evil genius." Historian William Spence Robertson has brought together the opinions of the French (Reading 2). Another prominent refugee from Rosas was Esteban Echeverría, who wrote a strong polemic against the dictator (Reading 3).

After Rosas fell from power in 1852, he lived quietly in England as a country gentleman until his death in 1877, but Argentines continued to deplore his "tyranny" and his personalization of power. Only toward the end of the nineteenth century did historians such as Ernesto Quesada portray Rosas as a product of his times and not as a unique monster in the annals of the Argentine nation. Following this line, José Luis Romero points out that Rosas merely continued the authoritarian tradition of colonial times (Reading 4).

ROSAS REVISIONISM

After World War I, a new Rosas revisionism developed, directed by a group of bitter, anti-foreign, anti-democratic writers who attracted a wide reading public. Some of them advocated military rule and social discipline. From 1930 on, Julio Irazusta and others began to present Rosas as a hero. Biographies, novels, and political studies were published with this theme, and in 1938 a historical institute and scholarly review were established devoted to Rosas and his regime. Irazusta and the other writers of this group denounced the Liberals' interpretation of Argentine history. They "were part of a large sector of feeling in the country which played a part in paving the way for the military rulers of Argentina from 1943 on."[2]

The pro-Rosas spirit still lives today, in the hearts of some Argentines, as demonstrated by the decree promulgated in 1964 (Reading 5). Twenty-five years later, on October 1, 1989, the Argentine government repatriated Rosas' remains from a graveyard in Southampton, England. They were interred in the Recoleta Cemetery of Buenos Aires with the honors accorded a former chief-of-state, even though Rosas never officially held that position. As President Carlos Saúl Menem explained, it was time for Argentines to forgive and forget old hostilities, and he was willing to pay any political cost to help them leave resentment behind.[3]

[2]Clifton B. Kroeber, "Rosas and the Revision of Argentine History, 1880–1955," *Inter-American Review of Bibliography*, 10 (1960), pp. 3–25.

[3]*The New York Times*, October 2, 1989.

1. The Human Background of Dictatorship, the Gaucho

DOMINGO FAUSTINO SARMIENTO

The life and work of Domingo Faustino Sarmiento became well known in the United States through his service here as Argentine minister (1865–1868) and through his friendship with Horace Mann, the Massachusetts educator whose wife translated his attack on dictatorship as *Life in the Argentine Republic in the Days of the Tyrants; or Civilization and Barbarism* (1868). The University of Michigan recognized his contributions to education in 1868 by awarding him the first honorary degree to be granted by an American university to a Latin American scholar.

Sarmiento's volume is a classic that is well worth reading in its entirety because it combines a vivid description of the geography and people of Argentina during a decisive period of its history with an informed analysis and poetic understanding of the basic forces at work and in conflict in his country. The *Revue des Deux Mondes* characterized the work when it was first published as

> full of attraction and novelty, instructive as history, interesting as a romance, brilliant with imagery and coloring. "Civilization and Barbarism" is not only one of those rare testimonials which come to us of the intellectual life of South America, but it is an invaluable document. . . . This can only be done by the philosopher, the traveller, the poet, the historian, the painter of manners and customs, the publicist. Señor Sarmiento has succeeded in realizing this object in his work, which he has published in Chili, and which proves that if civilization has enemies in those regions it also has eloquent champions. [1]

The selection here shows how clearly Sarmiento perceived the disparity between Buenos Aires and the provinces — which still exists — and the deep-rooted influence of the gauchos in the life of Argentina.

---

[1] As quoted by Mrs. Horace Mann, in *Life in the Argentine Republic in the Days of the Tyrants* (New York, 1868), pp. x–xi.

51

. . . Buenos Ayres is destined to be some day the most gigantic city of either America. Under a benignant climate, mistress of the navigation of a hundred rivers flowing past her feet, covering a vast area, and surrounded by inland provinces which know no other outlet for their products, she would ere now have become the Babylon of America, if the spirit of the Pampa had not breathed upon her, and left undeveloped the rich offerings which the rivers and provinces should unceasingly bring. She is the only city in the vast Argentine territory which is in communication with European nations; she alone can avail herself of the advantages of foreign commerce; she alone has power and revenue. Vainly have the provinces asked to receive through her, civilization, industry, and European population; a senseless colonial policy made her deaf to these cries. But the provinces had their revenge when they sent to her in Rosas the climax of their own barbarism.

The cities of Buenos Ayres and Cordova have succeeded better than the others in establishing about them subordinate towns to serve as new foci of civilization and municipal interests; a fact which deserves notice. The inhabitants of the city wear the European dress, live in a civilized manner, and possess laws, ideas of progress, means of instruction, some municipal organization, regular forms of government, etc. Beyond the precincts of the city everything assumes a new aspect; the country people wear a different dress, which I will call South American, as it is common to all districts; their habits of life are different, their wants peculiar and limited. The people composing these two distinct forms of society, do not seem to belong to the same nation. Moreover, the countryman, far from attempting to imitate the customs of the city, rejects with disdain its luxury and refinement; and it is unsafe for the costume of the city people, their coats, their cloaks, their saddles, or anything European, to show themselves in the country. Everything civilized which the city contains is blockaded there, proscribed beyond its limits; and any one who should dare to appear in the rural districts in a frock-coat, for example, or mounted on an English saddle, would bring ridicule and brutal assaults upon himself.

The whole remaining population inhabit the open country, which, whether wooded or destitute of the larger plants, is generally level, and almost everywhere occupied by pastures, in some places of such abundance and excellence, that the grass of an artificial meadow would not surpass them. . . .

Nomad tribes do not exist in the Argentine plains; the stock-raiser is a proprietor, living upon his own land; but this condition renders association impossible, and tends to scatter separate families over an immense extent of surface. Imagine an expanse of two thousand square leagues, inhabited

From *Life in the Argentine Republic in the Days of the Tyrants; or Civilization and Barbarism, from the Spanish of Domingo F. Sarmiento,* trans., with a biographic sketch, by Mrs. Horace Mann (New York, 1868), pp. 5–55, passim.

throughout, but where the dwellings are usually four or even eight leagues apart, and two leagues, at least, separate the nearest neighbors. The production of movable property is not impossible, the enjoyments of luxury are not wholly incompatible with this isolation; wealth can raise a superb edifice in the desert. But the incentive is wanting; no example is near; the inducements for making a great display which exist in a city, are not known in that isolation and solitude. Inevitable privations justify natural indolence; a dearth of all the amenities of life induces all the externals of barbarism. Society has altogether disappeared. There is but the isolated self-concentrated feudal family. Since there is no collected society, no government is possible; there is neither municipal nor executive power, and civil justice has no means of reaching criminals. I doubt if the modern world presents any other form of association so monstrous as this. . . .

Moral progress, and the cultivation of the intellect, are here not only neglected, as in the Arab or Tartar tribe, but impossible. Where can a school be placed for the instruction of children living ten leagues apart in all directions? Thus, consequently, civilization can in no way be brought about. Barbarism is the normal condition, and it is fortunate if domestic customs preserve a small germ of morality. Religion feels the consequences of this want of social organization. The offices of the pastor are nominal, the pulpit has no audience, the priest flees from the deserted chapel, or allows his character to deteriorate in inactivity and solitude. Vice, simony, and the prevalent barbarism penetrate his cell, and change his moral superiority into the means of gratifying his avarice or ambition, and he ends by becoming a party leader. . . .

In the absence of all the means of civilization and progress, which can only be developed among men collected into societies of many individuals, the education of the country people is as follows: The women look after the house, get the meals ready, shear the sheep, milk the cows, make the cheese, and weave the coarse cloth used for garments. All domestic occupations are performed by women; on them rests the burden of all the labor, and it is an exceptional favor when some of the men undertake the cultivation of a little maize, bread not being in use as an ordinary article of diet. The boys exercise their strength and amuse themselves by gaining skill in the use of the lasso and the bolas, with which they constantly harass and pursue the calves and goats. When they can ride, which is as soon as they have learned to walk, they perform some small services on horseback. When they become stronger, they race over the country, falling off their horses and getting up again, tumbling on purpose into rabbit burrows, scrambling over precipices, and practicing feats of horsemanship. On reaching puberty, they take to breaking wild colts, and death is the least penalty that awaits them if their strength or courage fails them for a moment. With early manhood comes complete independence and idleness.

Now begins the public life of the gaucho, as I may say, since his education is by this time at an end. These men, Spaniards only in their language and in the confused religious notions preserved among them, must be seen, before a right estimate can be made of the indomitable and haughty character which grows out of this struggle of isolated man with untamed nature, of the rational being with the brute. It is necessary to see their visages bristling with beards, their countenances as grave and serious as those of the Arabs of Asia, to appreciate the pitying scorn with which they look upon the sedentary denizen of the city, who may have read many books, but who cannot overthrow and slay a fierce bull, who could not provide himself with a horse from the pampas, who never met a tiger alone, and received him with a dagger in one hand and a poncho rolled up in the other, to be thrust into the animal's mouth, while he transfixes his heart with his dagger.

This habit of triumphing over resistance, of constantly showing a superiority to Nature, of defying and subduing her, prodigiously develops the consciousness of individual consequence and superior prowess. The Argentine people of every class, civilized and ignorant alike, have a high opinion of their national importance. All the other people of South America throw this vanity of theirs in their teeth, and take offense at their presumption and arrogance. I believe the charge not to be wholly unfounded, but I do not object to the trait. Alas, for the nation without faith in itself! Great things were not made for such a people. To what extent may not the independence of that part of America be due to the arrogance of these Argentine gauchos, who have never seen anything beneath the sun superior to themselves in wisdom or in power? The European is in their eyes the most contemptible of all men, for a horse gets the better of him in a couple of plunges. . . .

Country life, then, has developed all the physical but none of the intellectual powers of the gaucho. His moral character is of the quality to be expected from his habit of triumphing over the obstacles and the forces of nature; it is strong, haughty, and energetic. Without instruction, and indeed without need of any, without means of support as without wants, he is happy in the midst of his poverty and privations, which are not such to one who never knew nor wished for greater pleasures than are his already. Thus if the disorganization of society among the gauchos deeply implants barbarism in their natures, through the impossibility and uselessness of moral and intellectual education, it has, too, its attractive side to him. The gaucho does not labor; he finds his food and raiment ready to his hand. If he is a proprietor, his own flocks yield him both; if he possesses nothing himself, he finds them in the house of a patron or a relation. The necessary care of the herds is reduced to excursions and pleasure parties; the branding, which is like the harvesting of farmers, is a festival, the arrival of which is received with transports of joy, being the occasion of the assembling of all the men for twenty leagues around, and the opportunity for displaying incredible skill with the lasso. . . .

The horse is an integral part of the Argentine rustic; it is for him what the cravat is to an inhabitant of the city. In 1841, El Chacho, a chieftain of the Llanos, emigrated to Chili. "How are you getting on, friend?" somebody asked him. "How should I be getting on?" returned he, in tones of distress and melancholy. "Bound to Chili, and on foot!" Only an Argentine gaucho can appreciate all the misfortune and distress which these two phrases express.

Here again we have the life of the Arab or Tartar. The following words of Victor Hugo might have been written in the pampas:

> He cannot fight on foot; he and his horse are but one person. He lives on horseback; he trades, buys, and sells on horseback; drinks, eats, sleeps, and dreams on horseback. — *Le Rhin.*

The men then set forth without exactly knowing where they are going. A turn around the herds, a visit to a breeding-pen or to the haunt of a favorite horse, takes up a small part of the day; the rest is consumed in a rendezvous at a tavern or grocery store. There assemble inhabitants of the neighboring parishes; there are given and received bits of information about animals that have gone astray; the traces of the cattle are described upon the ground; intelligence of the hunting ground of the tiger or of the place where the tiger's tracks have been seen, is communicated. There, in short, is the Cantor; there the men fraternize while the glass goes round at the expense of those who have the means as well as the disposition to pay for it.

In a life so void of emotion, gambling exercises the enervated mind, and liquor arouses the dormant imagination. This accidental reunion becomes by its daily repetition a society more contracted than that from which each of its individual members came; yet in this assembly, without public aim, without social interest, are first formed the elements of those characters which are to appear later on the political stage. We shall see how. The gaucho esteems skill in horsemanship and physical strength, and especially courage, above all other things, as we have said before. This meeting, this daily club, is a real Olympic circus where each man's merit is tested and assayed.

The gaucho is always armed with the knife inherited from the Spaniard. More fully even than in Spain is here realized that peninsular peculiarity, that cry, characteristic of Saragossa — *war to the knife.* The knife, besides being a weapon, is a tool used for all purposes; without it, life cannot go on. It is like the elephant's trunk, arm, hand, finger, and all. The gaucho boasts of his valor like a trooper, and every little while his knife glitters through the air in circles, upon the least provocation, or with none at all, for the simple purpose of comparing a stranger's prowess with his own; he plays at stabbing as he would play at dice. So deeply and intimately have these pugnacious habits entered the life of the Argentine gaucho that custom has created a code of honor and a fencing system which protect life. The rowdy of other lands takes to his knife for the purpose of killing, and he kills; the Argentine gaucho unsheathes his to fight, and he only wounds. To attempt the life of his adversary he must be very drunk, or his instincts must be really wicked, or his rancor very deep. His aim is only to *mark* his opponent, to give him a slash in the face, to leave an indelible token upon him. The numerous scars to be seen upon these gauchos, accordingly, are seldom deep. A fight is begun, then, for the sake of shining, for the glory of victory, for the love of fame. A close ring is made around the combatants, and excited and eager eyes follow the glitter of the knives which do not cease to move. When blood flows in torrents the spectators feel obliged to stop the fight. If a *misfortune* has resulted, the sympathies are with the survivor; the best horse is available for his escape to a distant place where he is received with respect or pity. If the law overtakes him he often shows fight, and if he rushes through soldiers and escapes, he has from that time a wide-spread renown. Time passes, the judge in place has been succeeded by another, and he may again show himself in the township without further molestation: he has a full discharge.

Homicide is but a misfortune, unless the deed has been so often repeated that the perpetrator has gained the reputation of an assassin. The landed proprietor, Don Juan Manuel Rosas, before being a public man, had made his residence a sort of asylum for homicides without ever extending his protection to robbers; a preference which would easily be explained by his character of gaucho proprietor, if his subsequent conduct had not disclosed affinities with evil which have filled the world with terror. . . .

Before 1810, two distinct, rival, and incompatible forms of society, two differing kinds of civilization existed in the Argentine Republic: one being Spanish, European, and cultivated, the other barbarous, American, and almost wholly of native growth. The revolution which occurred in the cities acted only as the cause, the impulse, which set these two distinct forms of national existence face to face, and gave occasion for a contest between them, to be ended, after lasting many years, by the absorption of one into the other.

I have pointed out the normal form of association, or want of association, of the country people, a form worse, a thousand times, than that of the nomad tribe. I have described the artificial associations formed in idleness, and the sources of fame among the gauchos — bravery, daring, violence, and opposition to regular law, to the civil law, that is, of the city. These phenomena of social organization existed in 1810, and still exist, modified in many points, slowly changing in others, and yet untouched in several more. These foci, about which were gathered the brave, ignorant, free, and unemployed peasantry, were found by thousands through the country. The revolution of 1810 carried everywhere commotion and the sound of arms. Public life, previously wanting in this Arabico-Roman society, made its appearance in all the taverns, and the revolutionary movement finally brought about provincial, warlike associations, called *montoneras,* legitimate offspring of the tavern and the field, hostile to the city and to the army of revolutionary patriots. As events succeed each other, we shall see the provincial montoneras headed by their chiefs; the final triumph, in Facundo Quiroga, of the country over the cities throughout the land; and by their subjugation in spirit, government, and civilization, the final formation of the central consolidated despotic government of the landed proprietor, Don Juan Manuel Rosas, who applied the knife of the gaucho to the culture of Buenos Ayres, and destroyed the work of centuries — of civilization, law, and liberty.

2. *What the French Thought of Rosas*

WILLIAM SPENCE ROBERTSON

The late Professor William Spence Robertson was a pioneer in developing the field of Latin American history in the United States. His scholarly publications focused on the revolutionary period, and his 1929 biography of the Venezuelan revolutionary Francisco de Miranda is the standard work. His *Rise of the Spanish-American Republics as Told in the Lives of Their Liberators* (1918) may still be consulted with profit.

Among the enigmatical personages of the "Age of Dictators" in South America none played a more spectacular role than the Argentine dictator, Juan Manuel de Rosas, whose gigantic and ominous figure bestrode the Plata River for more than twenty years. So despotic was his power that Argentine writers have themselves styled this age of their history as "The Tyranny of Rosas." A political enemy named Rivera Indarte, who attacked the dictator from an asylum in Montevideo, alleged in his "tables of blood" that Rosas had assassinated 722 persons, shot 1,393, and beheaded 3,765. Indeed, until the close of the nineteenth century the name of Rosas was often anathema in his native land. A dispassionate survey of the dramatic career of this bizarre figure was indeed not made until 1898. In that year Ernesto Quesada, a lawyer, his-

From "Foreign Estimates of the Argentine Dictator, Juan Manuel de Rosas" by William Spence Robertson, *Hispanic American Historical Review,* 10 (1930), pp. 125–137, passim. Reprinted by permission.

torian, and sociologist of Buenos Aires published a monograph entitled "The Epoch of Rosas" in which he developed the thesis that this dictator was typical of his age, and furthermore that he laid broad and deep the foundations upon which the Argentine nation was successfully erected.

Still, even today among the intelligentsia of Argentina there are doubters who are loath to yield this tardy tribute to the great dictator. To paraphrase an historical sociologist: if you ask an historian who was Juan Manuel de Rosas, he will say, a tyrant; if you ask a physician, he will respond, a neurotic; ask a descendant of one of Rosas's partisans and he will retort, a great man; a publicist will dub him a clever politician; philosophers will declare that he was a son of his age; while poets will denounce him as infamous. . . .

At least this is a case in which interesting sidelights may be obtained from the other shores of the Atlantic. In the *Revue des Deux Mondes* for 1835, M. Pavie contributed an article entitled "The Indians of the Pampas," in which he expressed the opinion that, because of the civil dissensions in which they had engaged, the generals who had won the independence of Argentina had made peace more dangerous than open warfare. Pavie proceeded to give his impressions of the dictator of the Argentine Confederation, whom he had observed during a recent carnival in Buenos Aires. "In fact," said the Frenchman,

> no one can tame a colt, or break a savage horse, or hunt a cougar better than Rosas. He made a show of compelling his fine Chilean steed to gallop through the worst paved streets of the capital; then he would suddenly wheel about, retrace his steps, and pirouette over the slippery stones, dodging not only the buckets of water but also the eggs which on that day, according to custom, the women showered upon the passersby.

This clever sketch, as well as the allusions made by Pavie to the generals who had fought for Argentine independence, much provoked the government of Rosas. In a despatch to Paris, the Marquis de Peysac, the French consul at Buenos Aires, reported that both the dictator and Señor Arana, his minister of foreign relations, were full of resentment. In consequence, conferences were held between Arana and Peysac in which the latter felt called upon to inform the Argentinian that liberty of the press existed in France. But to allay the wrath of the Argentinians the marquis soon transmitted to his government an article refuting "the vile lies, and calumnious imputations concerning the political condition" of La Plata that had been published in the *Gaceta Mercantil* of Buenos Aires. This portrayal of the Argentine dictator by a partisan will perhaps serve as a foil for other characterizations.

> The dexterity, agility, and hardihood of General Rosas in horsemanship and in exercises of strength are perhaps unequalled in the Republic,

as well as his ability, experience, and knowledge with respect to all sorts of rural labors and customs. But I should add that to these estimable gifts he unites other eminent qualities; his talents, his vast knowledge, his political skill and judgment, and his valor in military campaigns have often saved the republic from ruin and desolation. Class and luminous proofs of this truth are furnished by his public life from the memorable year 1820 until the present time. He is the only man among us who has known how to unite the administrative talents of a most consummate statesman with the intrepidity, agility, and bravery of a warrior, and with the traits of a most clever gaucho. Then we must add to this happy union of singular and necessary qualities, an unshakeable patriotism, a severe virtue, and a noble disinterestedness — a combination of qualities that makes him the most perfect exemplar of the politician, the hero, the warrior, and the great citizen.

Shortly after the Marquis of Peysac had reported an interview with Rosas concerning Pavie's skit, the Duc de Broglie, who had recently become minister of foreign affairs in his own cabinet, formulated his concept of the dictator in these words:

This general is not an ordinary man. The oddities of his manner or character do not prevent me from considering him as one of the most eminent chieftains brought forth by the revolutions in South America. It is to be hoped that the value which he seems to place upon the opinions of Europe will tend to restrain him from that misuse of power which men of the New World elevated to such a position are too often inclined to permit. I have gladly acceded to the wish that he expressed to you of having published in our journals a refutation of the article he has taken so much to heart which appeared in the *Revue des Deux Mondes*. You can read this counterblast in the *Moniteur* in a version that has been rendered less bitter and more veiled.

A more interesting estimate of Rosas was furnished in 1840 by an officer of the French fleet that had blockaded the coast of Argentina largely because of the dictator's policy of requiring military service from French subjects who were domiciled in that country. This officer avowed that Rosas still enjoyed the barbarous amusements that he had loved while he lived in the country with the gauchos.

In the secrecy of his home, where he had retired with companions of these farces, Rosas gave himself up to a thousand foolish notions which are repugnant to our ideas of elegance, but which charmed those men who had grown up on the pampas in the midst of horse races and of manners and customs altogether different from those of Europe. This man, who founded his power upon the affection of the people, did not feel that he was degrading himself when he engaged in diversions which they loved. But when he found himself in the presence of a distinguished foreigner, whose esteem he desired to gain, the rude gaucho disappeared: his language became refined, his sonorous voice pleased the ear, his eye caressed, and his attentive and intelligent glance captivated. Though he had never distinguished himself by any remarkable feat of arms, yet no one ever denied that he had courage. The deep regret that seized him upon the death of his wife, as well as the extreme solicitude which he displayed toward his daughter, seemed to indicate that tender feelings had not been altogether banished from his heart. He made this cherished daughter the depositary of his most intimate thoughts and the heiress of his fortune. And because he had laid up great riches for her, he was accused of wishing to seat her upon a throne. . . .

After describing the terrible murders that had been committed by a secret society in Buenos Aires at the behest of Rosas, a French traveler who had resided some months in La Plata deemed it only fair to depict another side of the dictator's personality. This Frenchman did not maintain that by his truly great qualities Rosas had offset his disdain for life and liberty, because these were defects for which no compensation could be made. But we do recognize, he continued, that Rosas really has great qualities, and that he would have been able to render his country splendid service, if only Heaven had given him more light and a more humane heart.

His great qualities were all related to the nature of his domination. Rosas knew how to command: he possessed the secret of commanding obedience. By virtue of this quality he might have become the benefactor and saviour of his country. He indeed saw that the evil was in the anarchy which devoured the land, in the confusion of all governmental power, in the weakening of all the springs of authority, and in the insubordinate habits of soldiers and generals. Unfortunately he overemphasized the opposite tendency and gave to the power that had become irresistible in his hands an effect that was odious, destructive, and degrading. He substituted his personality for the existing institutions; he induced the entire population to adore his own portrait; he had incense burned before that portrait in the churches; he had himself drawn in a carriage by women, and by the most distinguished persons in the capital city; and he desired that discourses should be addressed to himself in public ceremonies. At least, if he did not direct this to be done, he encouraged these servile demonstrations which in their manifold forms have reduced the citizens of the capital to the moral condition of Asiatic people.

The French minister, Baron Deffaudis, who had been sent on an extraordinary mission to La Plata to settle the interminable dispute between his government and Rosas, furnishes a view from a different angle. On June 7, 1845, after an interview with the dictator, this envoy sent a dispatch to Paris conveying his impressions of that curious personage.

> Despite the care which he takes to veil them, intelligence, artifice, and determination are deeply engraven upon his face. If one were not aware that he held the lives of his adversaries very cheap, one would perhaps never divine this at all; but when one knows this, one is not in the least astonished at his physiognomy. On the other side, age begins to leave its mark upon him. His postures are awkward and somewhat weak. His body is ten years older than his face. One does not notice in him the agility, skill, and vigor that placed him, as he once said, at the forefront of the gauchos. He has the air of a townsman endowed with a strong constitution, who has become corpulent and enervated by a sedentary life. In fact, he scarcely leaves his apartments, particularly when he is in the city, and only takes the air on the terrace of his house. Then, too, he has been attacked by a cruel malady, the gravel, which leaves him only certain intervals of repose. I further believe that those Europeans who represent him as rather disposed to spring into a saddle to resume the vagrant life of the pampas than to yield to the more just and moderate demands of foreign diplomacy are interpreting him by traits that are out of date. . . .
>
> Each successive day General Rosas is becoming more and more a man of the cabinet: in this role he is now more redoubtable than as a gaucho. In the cabinet, in fact, he is a man full of will and perseverance as well as of astuteness and suppleness. He is absolutely indifferent about the nature of the means by which to gain success and clever to find the means which are suitable to his ends. He believes that men are full of vices and weaknesses, and boasts of his ability to discern by the first glance of his eye the species of seduction or corruption to which any particular man is susceptible. An indefatigable worker, he spends his days in supervising the smallest details of ministerial affairs, in corresponding directly with the civil and military authorities of the provinces in matters touching his personal policy, and finally in dictating and even correcting with his own hand an infinite number of articles destined for journals not only in his own country but also in foreign lands. The object of these articles is above all to depict his administration in the most attractive colors, to repel the attacks which are made upon it from every quarter, and also to make the most bitter criticism of every act of those governments with which he finds himself in disagreement.

Another French diplomat, Count Walewski, who was later sent on an identical errand to La Plata, thus conveyed the impressions that General Rosas made upon him during an interview that lasted five or six hours.

> General Rosas is ordinarily prolix and diffuse. His periods are long; and he departs with great facility from the main topic in order to engage in digressions that immeasurably lengthen the conversation. From time to time he tries the effects of eloquence or of gestures, and his intonations are cleverly calculated to impress the hearer.

The count affirmed that it was very difficult to pursue an argument with Rosas. "Warned in advance of this digressive tendency," said Walewski,

> while listening religiously, I was forced constantly to lead him back to the question at issue, and it was only because of these persistent efforts on my part that we were able to consider the principal points in the negotiation. Otherwise twenty-four hours would not have been sufficient. Aside from this, the course of his argument was admirably arranged, and if his premises were well founded, there was nothing that could have been said against him.

These personages terminated their interview by an exchange of diplomatic courtesies. Rosas declared that he had always desired that his political conduct would meet with "the approval of France," and particularly with "the approbation of her king," for whose person he professed in lofty terms a high admiration. The dictator mellifluously avowed that he considered Louis Philippe as

> the most enlightened of those sovereigns who today occupy the thrones of the world, and as the greatest statesman of the century.

An attache of the mission named Brossard, who was present at this interview, was more successful than his master in discerning the salient traits of Rosas. A few years later, on a broad canvas and with a variety of pigments, this diplomat painted what was perhaps the best portrait ever made of the crafty despot. Here it is:

> General Rosas is a man of medium height, quite stout, and apparently endowed with great physical vigor. His features are regular; he has a light complexion and blonde hair, and does not at all resemble a Spaniard. One might well exclaim upon beholding him, "Here is a Norman gentleman." His physiognomy is a remarkable mixture of craft and force. He is generally tranquil, and even mild; but upon occasion, the contraction of his lips gives him a singular expression of deliberate severity. He expresses himself with much facility, and as one who is a

perfect master of his thoughts and his words. His style in conversation varies: now he uses well-chosen and even elegant phrases; and again he indulges in trivial expressions. There is perhaps a little affectation in the way in which he expresses himself. His remarks are never categorical; they are diffuse and complicated by digressions and incidental phrases. This prolixity is evidently premeditated and intended to embarrass the interlocutor. In truth it is quite difficult to follow General Rosas in the detours of his conversation. . . .

The dictator showed himself by turns to be a consummate states-man, an affable individual, an indefatigable dialectician, a vehement and passionate orator; as the emergency arose, he displayed with rare perfection, anger, frankness, and bonhomie. One realizes that, when en-countered face to face, he could intimidate, or deceive, or seduce.

Walewski's aide also contributed so discerning a political analysis of Rosas that in quoting it one scarcely knows where to stop:

Endowed with a reflective and persistent will, Juan Manuel is essen-tially an absolute ruler. Although force — that is to say, the principle of persons who have no principles — is the basis of his government, and although he constantly consults in his policies the necessities of his per-sonal position, yet he is much pleased to be considered as a man of well-founded convictions. He professes a great horror for secret societies, *lojias* as they are designated, even though the *Mazorca* which he founded was nothing else than a secret society, which became publicly known be-cause of its excesses. He becomes indignant when one supposes that he has the least affinity with revolutionists who are enemies of the social order; and as a statesman he assumes in his maxims a great austerity that does not exist in his private morals. "I know," he avowed in his interviews, "that a good example should be highly esteemed by all peo-ple."

Up to a certain point he has justified his pretensions and his words by reestablishing material order throughout the country and in the ad-ministration, by causing the civil laws to be obeyed, and by enveloping his dictatorship with the constitutional forms that were observed before his advent. He busies himself with all the details of administration and carefully supervises them; he labors assiduously from fifteen to sixteen hours every day in the transaction of public business, and does not allow anything to pass without a minute inspection. Thus, as he has said, the entire burden of governmental responsibility falls upon himself. . . .

Raised to supreme power by astuteness, General Rosas has seen his domination violently attacked, and he has not known how to maintain himself except by force. Vindictive and imperious by education and by temperament, he was precipitated into despotism, and has cheapened in the interior of the country that liberty of which he has spoken so much. He resembles those men portrayed by Tacitus who placed liberty to the fore in order thereby to overthrow the existing order, and, who, when they became masters of the empire, turned upon their mistress. Because of this tendency he has committed those sanguinary acts that have surrounded him with an aureola of terror. Because of this tendency he has been obliged to concede extravagant favors to abandoned men, who are bound irrevocably to his chariot by their vices and crimes as well as by his favors and whose prosperity is an insult to morale and to public misery. From this tendency there has arisen the system of legal oppression by which he persecutes all his enemies, who, it must be said, compose the most polished and intellectual part of the nation.

A man from the country, Rosas has in fact been the leader of the reaction of the men of the campo against the predominant influence of the capital city. Imbued with the prejudice of Castilian pride, he detests *en masse* those foreigners whose labor and capital could enrich his country, and accords them only a niggardly hospitality. An agriculturist by birth, by education, and by taste, he does not appreciate industry. . . . Nourished in the monopolistic maxims of Spanish colonial law, he neither understands nor permits trade except when it is hemmed in by prohibitive tariffs and rigorous regulations.

On the other side, General Rosas is much occupied with the means by which a government may influence the morale of a people. Thus it is that he attaches great importance to matters concerned with public education; for he considers both education and religion as means of political influence. This same motive causes him to intervene actively in the periodical press. He subsidizes periodicals in France, in England, in Portugal, in Brazil, in the United States, and directs his journals of Buenos Aires, namely, the *Gaceta Mercantil,* the *Archivo Americano,* and the *British Packet.*

In the belief that persons of the so-called Latin race have an insight into each other's character that is often denied to Anglo-Saxons, I have purposely used estimates of Rosas that emanated from French contemporaries. They present the concepts of foreigners whose viewpoint though prejudiced was much more detached than that of Argentine observers. My study convinces me that the treasure trove of unexploited material in the French archives will cast a glow of interpretative light upon both the domestic and the foreign policies of the Hispanic-American nations. So far as Rosas is concerned, these unedited papers demonstrate that he was a consummate poseur. They convey hints that his iron constitution was corroding. These papers further reveal that the dictator maintained an insidious diplomatic as well as journalistic propaganda both at home and abroad. At many points they confirm the view of other contemporaries with regard to the personal methods, the genuine ability, the strength, the resourcefulness, the astuteness, and the unscrupulousness of the gaucho tyrant — traits which he possessed in a more marked degree than many other Hispanic-American tyrants. In truth he was compared by one contemporary with the gloomy Paraguayan dictator Francia, while another contemporary likened him unto the French nationalistic monarch Louis XI. The iteration and reiteration of the cruelty and ruthlessness of Rosas in these accounts indeed provoke the query whether in the rehabilitation of the tyrant the historic pendulum may not have been swung from the extreme of denunciation too far in the direction of justification, and whether as fresh and discriminating sources are utilized the historian of the future may not bring the pendulum back to a median position. In any event this brief study brings up the perennial problem of the good and the evil in dictatorial rule in Hispanic America.

3. *An Argentine Writer Condemns Rosas* in The Slaughter House

ESTEBAN ECHEVERRÍA

Latin American writers have been preoccupied with the tyranny of dictatorship from the early revolutionary years until today. A large anthology of antidictatorial works could be easily compiled, for every dictator has aroused passionate opposition by some of the most creative literary figures of their times.

Against Rosas were ranged Sarmiento and the writers who introduced romanticism to Argentina — Esteban Echeverría (1805–1851) and José Marmol (1817–1871). The latter produced a two-volume novel, *Amalia,* which was one of the most widely read denunciations of the tyrant and won him the title of "the poetic hangman of Rosas." As is often the case with intellectuals in Latin America, he was once imprisoned and twice had to flee abroad for his life. After Rosas fell in 1852, he returned to Argentina and became director of the National Library.

Echeverría had visited France, a custom still followed by Latin Americans, and there became an ardent follower of the romantic movement. On his return to Buenos Aires, he founded a secret revolutionary society and wrote his famous novel *The Slaughter House,* denouncing tyranny. As Arturo Torres-Ríoseco, the Chilean literary historian, describes it:

> Even nowadays, when blood-curdling realism is commonplace, it is hard to find the equal of this sketch, scrawled off at top speed by an author under peril of his life.

The action of *The Slaughter House,* as the name implies, takes place in an actual *matadero* where fifty head of cattle are being butchered. The savage scene is minutely described: the red banners of the Rosas faction, the slaughtering and the distribution of meat, the escape of one of the bulls who gores a child to death, leaving the headless trunk to spout blood! For this is more than an ordinary slaughterhouse; it is the rendezvous of the *mashorca* (the "gallows-plus") or band of assassins who keep the despot in power. And just at the height of the bloody spectacle, a passing Unitarian is sighted by the butchers, a youth of twenty-five with his beard cut in the shape of a U. The leader of the hangmen, "Killer of Seven," falls upon him, pulling him from his horse; the youth is bound hand and foot and his beard clipped into the Federalist pattern. The thugs then prepare to beat him — but at this moment, the young Unitarian, struggling to free himself, breaks bleeding from his bonds and dies before the eyes of his astonished executioners. The whole story is a sombre and terrible vignette, against a background of howling curs, bedraggled Negresses, circling vultures — a slaughterhouse that represents the real *matadero* tyranny of Rosas.[1]

The Convalescencia, or Alto Slaughter House, is located in the southern part of Buenos Aires, on a huge lot, rectangular in shape, at the intersection of two streets, one of which ends there while the other continues eastward. The lot slants to the south and is bisected by a ditch made by the rains, its shoulders pitted with ratholes, its bed collecting all the blood from the Slaughter House. At the junction of the right angle, facing the west, stands what is commonly called the *casilla,* a low building containing three small rooms with a porch in the front facing the street and hitching posts for tying the horses. In the rear are several pens of ñandubay picket fence with heavy doors for guarding the steers.

In winter these pens become veritable mires in which the animals remain bogged down, immobile, up to the shoulder blades. In the casilla the pen taxes and fines for violation of the rules are collected, and in it sits the judge of the Slaughter House, an important figure, the chieftain of the butchers, who exercises the highest power, delegated to him by the Restorer, in that small republic. It is not difficult to imagine the kind of man required for the discharge of such an office.

The casilla is so dilapidated and so tiny a building that no one would notice it were it not that its name is inseparably linked with that of the terrible judge and that its white front is pasted over with posters. "Long live the Federalists! Long live the Restorer and the Heroine Doña Encarnación Escurra! Death to

---

[1] Arturo Torres-Ríoseco, *The Epic of Latin American Literature* (Berkeley and Los Angeles: University of California Press, 1961), pp. 66–67.
From *El Matadero* [The Slaughter House] by Esteban Echeverría, trans. and ed. Angel Flores (New York: Las Americas Publishing Company, 1959), pp. 15–35, passim. Reprinted by permission.

the savage Unitarians!" Telling posters, indeed, symbolizing the political and religious faith of the Slaughter House folk! But some readers may not know that the above mentioned Heroine is the deceased wife of the Restorer, the beloved patroness of the butchers, who even after her death is venerated by them as if she were still alive, because of her Christian virtues and her Federalist heroism during the revolution against Balcarce. The story is that during an anniversary of that memorable deed of the *mazorca,* the terrorist society of Rosas' henchmen, the butchers feted the Heroine with a magnificent banquet in the casilla. She attended, with her daughter and other Federalist ladies, and there, in the presence of a great crowd, she offered the butchers, in a solemn toast, her Federalist patronage, and for that reason they enthusiastically proclaimed her patroness of the Slaughter House, stamping her name upon the walls of the casilla, where it will remain until blotted out by the hand of time.

From a distance the view of the Slaughter House was now grotesque, full of animation. Forty-nine steers were stretched out upon their skins and about two hundred people walked about the muddy, blood-drenched floor. Hovering around each steer stood a group of people of different skin colors. Most prominent among them was the butcher, a knife in his hand, his arms bare, his chest exposed, long hair dishevelled, shirt and sash and face besmeared with blood. At his back, following his every movement, romped a gang of children, Negro and mulatto women, offal collectors whose ugliness matched that of the harpies, and huge mastiffs which sniffed, snarled, and snapped at one another as they darted after booty. Forty or more carts covered with awnings of blackened hides were lined up along the court, and some horsemen with their capes thrown over their shoulders and their lassos hanging from their saddles rode back and forth through the crowds or lay on their horses' necks, casting indolent glances upon this or that lively group. In mid-air a flock of blue-white gulls, attracted by the smell of blood, fluttered about, drowning with strident cries all the other noises and voices of the Slaughter House, and casting clear-cut shadows over that confused field of horrible butchery. All this could be observed at the very beginning of the slaughter.

But as the activities progressed, the picture kept changing. While some groups dissolved as if some stray bullet had fallen nearby or an enraged dog had charged them, new groups constantly formed: here where a steer was being cut open, there where a butcher was already hanging the quarters on the hook in the carts, or yonder where a steer was being skinned or the fat taken off. From the mob eyeing and waiting for the offal there issued ever and anon a filthy hand ready to slice off meat or fat. Shouts and explosions of anger came from the butchers, from the incessantly milling crowds, and from the gamboling street urchins. . . .

The slaughtering had been completed by noon, and the small crowd which had remained to the end was leaving, some on foot, others on horseback, others pulling along the carts loaded with meat.

Suddenly the raucous voice of a butcher was heard announcing: "Here comes a Unitarian!" On hearing that word, the mob stood still as if thunderstruck.

"Can't you see his U-shaped side whiskers? Can't you see he carries no insignia on his coat and no mourning sash on his hat?"

"The Unitarian cur!"

"The son of a bitch!"

"He has the same kind of saddle as the gringo!"

"To the gibbet with him!"

"Give him the scissors!"

"Give him a good beating!"

"He has a pistol case attached to his saddle just to show off!"

"All these cocky Unitarians are as showy as the devil himself!"

"I bet you wouldn't dare touch him, Matasiete."

"He wouldn't, you say?"

"I bet you he would!"

Matasiete was a man of few words and quick action. When it came to violence, dexterity, skill in the handling of an ox, a knife, or a horse he did not talk much, but he acted. They had piqued him; spurring his horse, he trotted away, bridle loose, to meet the Unitarian.

The Unitarian was a young man, about twenty-five years old, elegant, debonair of carriage, who, as the above-mentioned exclamations were spouting from these impudent mouths, was trotting towards Barracas, quite fearless of any danger ahead of him. Noticing, however, the significant glances of that gang of Slaughter House curs, his right hand reached automatically for the pistolcase of his English saddle. Then a side push from Matasiete's horse threw him from his saddle, stretching him out. Supine and motionless he remained on the ground.

"Long live Matasiete!" shouted the mob, swarming upon the victim.

Confounded, the young man cast furious glances on those ferocious men and hoping to find in his pistol compensation and vindication, moved towards his horse, which stood quietly nearby. Matasiete rushed to stop him. He grabbed him by his tie, pulled him down again on the ground, and whipping out his dagger from his belt, put it against his throat.

Loud guffaws and stentorian vivas cheered him.

What nobility of soul! What bravery, that of the Federalists! Always ganging together and falling like vultures upon the helpless victim!

"Cut open his throat, Matasiete! Didn't he try to shoot you? Rip him open . . . !"

"What scoundrels these Unitarians! Thrash him good and hard!"

"He has a good neck for the 'violin' — you know, the gibbet!"

"Better use the Slippery-One on him!"

"Let's try it," said Matasiete, and, smiling, began to pass the sharp edge of his dagger around the throat of the fallen man as he pressed in his chest with his left knee and held him by the hair with his left hand.

"Don't behead him, don't!" shouted in the distance the Slaughter House Judge as he approached on horseback.

"Bring him into the casilla. Get the gibbet and the scissors ready. Death to the savage Unitarians! Long live the Restorer of the laws!"

"Long live Matasiete!"

The spectators repeated in unison "Long live Matasiete! Death to the Unitarians!" They tied his elbows together as blows rained upon his nose, and they shoved him around. Amid shouts and insults they finally dragged the unfortunate young man to the bench of tortures just as if they had been the executioners of the Lord themselves.

The main room of the casilla had in its center a big, hefty table, which was devoid of liquor glasses and playing cards only in times of executions and tortures administered by the Federalist executioners of the Slaughter House. In a corner stood a smaller table with writing materials and a notebook and some chairs, one of which, an armchair, was reserved for the Judge. A man who looked like a soldier was seated in one of them, playing on his guitar the "Resbalosa," an immensely popular song among the Federalists, when the mob rushing tumultuously into the corridor of the casilla brutally shoved in the young Unitarian.

"The Slippery-One for him!" shouted one of the fellows.

"Commend your soul to the devil!"

"He's furious as a wild bull!"

"The whip will tame him."

"Give him a good pummeling!"

"First the cowhide and scissors."

"Otherwise to the bonfire with him!"

"The gibbet would be even better for him!"

"Shut up and sit down," shouted the Judge as he sank into his armchair. All of them obeyed, while the young man standing in front of the Judge exclaimed with a voice pregnant with indignation:

"Infamous executioners, what do you want to do with me?"

"Quiet!" ordered the Judge, smiling. "There's no reason for getting angry. You'll see."

The young man was beside himself. His entire body shook with rage: his mottled face, his voice, his tremulous lips, evinced the throbbing of his heart and the agitation of his nerves. His fiery eyes bulged in their sockets, his long black hair bristled. His bare neck and the front of his shirt showed his bulging arteries and his anxious breathing.

"Are you trembling?" asked the Judge.

"Trembling with anger because I cannot choke you."

"Have you that much strength and courage?"

"I have will and pluck enough for that, scoundrel."

"Get out the scissors I use to cut my horse's mane and clip his hair in the Federalist style."

Two men got hold of him. One took his arms and another his head and in a minute clipped off his side whiskers. The spectators laughed merrily.

"Get him a glass of water to cool him off," ordered the Judge.

"I'll have you drink gall, you wretch!"

A Negro appeared with a glass of water in his hand. The young man kicked his arm and the glass smashed to bits on the ceiling, the fragments sprinkling the astonished faces of the spectators.

"This fellow is incorrigible!"

"Don't worry, we'll tame him yet!"

"Quiet!" said the Judge. "Now you are shaven in the Federalist style — all you need is a mustache, don't forget to grow one!"

"Now, let's see: why don't you wear any insignia?"

"Because I don't care to."

"Don't you know that the Restorer orders it?"

"Insignia become you, slaves, but not free men!"

"Free men will have to wear them, by force."

"Indeed, by force and brutal violence. These are your arms, infamous wretches! Wolves, tigers, and panthers are also strong like you and like them you should walk on all fours."

"Are you not afraid of being torn to pieces by the tiger?"

"I prefer that to have you pluck out my entrails, as the ravens do, one by one."

"Why don't you wear a mourning sash on your hat in memory of the Heroine?"

"Because I wear it in my heart in memory of my country which you, infamous wretches, have murdered."

"Don't you know that the Restorer has ordered mourning in memory of the Heroine?"

"You, slaves, were the ones to order it so as to flatter your master and pay infamous homage to him."

"Insolent fellow! You are beside yourself. I'll have your tongue cut off if you utter one more word. Take the pants off this arrogant fool, and beat him on his naked ass. Tie him down on the table first!"

Hardly had the Judge uttered his commands when four bruisers bespattered with blood lifted the young man and stretched him out upon the table.

"Rather behead me than undress me, infamous rabble!"

They muzzled him with a handkerchief and began to pull off his clothes. The young man wriggled, kicked, and gnashed his teeth. His muscles assumed now the flexibility of rushes, now the hardness of iron, and he squirmed like a snake in his enemy's grasp. Drops of sweat, large as pearls, streamed down his cheeks, his pupils flamed, his mouth foamed, and the veins on his neck and forehead jutted out black from his pale skin as if congested with blood.

"Tie him up," ordered the Judge.

"He's roaring with anger," said one of the cutthroats.

In a short while they had tied his feet to the legs of the table and turned his body upside down. In trying to tie his hands, the men had to unfasten them from behind his back. Feeling free, the young man, with a brusque movement which seemed to drain him of all his strength and vitality, raised himself up, first upon his arms, then upon his knees, and collapsed immediately, murmuring: "Rather behead me than undress me, infamous rabble!"

His strength was exhausted, and having tied him down crosswise, they began undressing him. Then a torrent of blood spouted, bubbling from the young man's mouth and nose, and flowed freely down the table. The cutthroats remained immobile and the spectators, astonished.

"The savage Unitarian has burst with rage," said one of them.

"He had a river of blood in his veins," put in another.

"Poor devil, we wanted only to amuse ourselves with him, but he took things too seriously," exclaimed the Judge, scowling tiger-like.

"We must draw up a report. Untie him and let's go!"

They carried out the orders, locked the doors, and in a short while the rabble went out after the horse of the downcast, taciturn Judge.

The Federalists had brought to an end one of their innumerable feats of valor.

Those were the days when the butchers of the Slaughter House were apostles who propagated by dint of whip and poignard Rosas' Federation, and it is not difficult to imagine what sort of Federation issued from their heads and knives. They were wont to dub as savage Unitarians (in accordance with the jargon invented by the Restorer, patron of the brotherhood) any man who was neither a cutthroat nor a crook; any man who was kindhearted and decent; any patriot or noble friend of enlightenment and freedom; and from the foregoing episode it can be clearly seen that the headquarters of the Federation were located in the Slaughter House.

4. Rosas Continued the Authoritarian Colonial Tradition

JOSÉ LUIS ROMERO

José Luis Romero has played an active part in the troubled history of the University of Buenos Aires during the last generation. His study of political ideas and political events in Argentina from the colonial period onward gives him an excellent perspective from which to judge Rosas.

Juan Manuel de Rosas was a powerful *hacendado* in the province of Buenos Aires, whose political prestige grew unchecked after 1820. As an *estanciero,* he was able to count on great resources to gain control of the countryside; as the chief of a military force organized at his own expense — the "Colorados del Monte," or "Red Rangers" — he was able to influence decisively the events in the capital during the crisis brought on by Lavalle's seizure of power and the later execution of Dorrego. Rosas saw clearly that this was his chance to impose his authority, and he declared himself in favor of federalism. Henceforth his importance in the capital was unequalled, his power grew to near omnipotence, and at the end of 1829 he was made governor of the province.

His first government lasted until the end of 1832. In that period [General José María] Paz, who might have been his worthy rival, fell prisoner, and the League of the Interior, which Paz had organized, collapsed. At about the same time, the League of the Littoral was organized. With the disappearance of Paz, other provinces joined the new League, and they, like the original signatories of the pact, delegated to Rosas the conduct of the foreign relations of the country. Thus Rosas, on leaving power, had contributed to the establishment of a loose national regime — the Confederation — which merited the cooperation of the *caudillos* and permitted Buenos Aires to exercise a certain hegemony that did not weigh greatly on the economy of the other provinces.

Reprinted from *A History of Argentine Political Thought* by José Luis Romero, introduction and translation by Thomas F. McGann, (Stanford: Stanford University Press. 1963). Reprinted by permission.

From 1832 to 1834, the provincial government of Buenos Aires was in the hands of men on whom Rosas could rely, yet who were zealously watched by his followers. His authority was by now unchallengeable, and it increased — as did his wealth — thanks to the campaign he led against the Indians of the desert. The popular masses and the most reactionary anti-Rivadavian groups supported him, especially the estancieros, whose interests Rosas rigidly defended, since they were also his interests. This coalition of forces propelled him to power for a second time, despite his tactics of pretended reticence by which he succeeded in obtaining the grant of "Extraordinary Powers," which was contrary to all republican tradition.

Events favored him, but he had the cunning to create favorable conditions for his own plans. Although he sought only to exercise exceptional powers as governor of Buenos Aires, he counted on obtaining de facto authority over the entire country. To that end, he conceived the plan to leave control of the provinces in the hands of caudillos who were all-powerful in local affairs, and later to bring those leaders under his own influence. The only obstacle to this plan of action was the presence of two caudillos who exercised notorious control over vast regions: Estanislao López and Juan Facundo Quiroga. But Rosas knew how to dominate them, and with a lucid mind, marked sagacity, and, above all, long patience and invincible tenacity, he accomplished his plans.

His views on the problems of the political organization of the country were expressed in two notable documents in 1834, shortly before his second ascent to power. As a result of a conflict between the governors of Salta and Tucumán, Quiroga was given the responsibility of mediating between the two men, and from the governor of Buenos Aires he received instructions that doubtlessly had been inspired by Rosas:

> Señor Quiroga should take advantage of every opportunity to make all the people whom he will meet during his trip understand that a congress ought to be convened as soon as possible, but that at present it is useless to demand a congress and a federal constitution, since each state has not arranged its internal affairs and does not give, within a stable, permanent order, practical and positive proofs of its ability to organize a federation with the other provinces. For in this system, the general government is not united, but rather is sustained by union, and the State represents the people who comprise the republic in their relations with other nations; neither does the State resolve the disputes between the people of one province and those of another, but rather limits their activities in compliance with the general pacts of the federation — to watch over the defenses of the entire republic, and to direct their negotiations and general interests in relation to those of other States,

since in cases of discord between two provinces, the constitution usually has an agreed way of deciding them, when the contenders do not arbitrate the dispute.

So expressed, this statement shows a sound and justifiable grasp of the situation. But these ideas have real significance only if one takes into account the fact that at last some of the caudillos — even Quiroga himself — were beginning to recognize the need to establish a national government, although under a federal system. Rosas' plan, therefore, was both the result of his interpretation of existing conditions and the disclosure of a scheme. His plan had been sketched out in the instructions that the mediator officially carried with him. But Rosas assumed that Quiroga was not convinced of the advantages of the plan, and tried to reinforce his arguments at a meeting; afterward he summarized his ideas in a letter he wrote to Quiroga in December 1834, at the Hacienda de Figueroa, before the two leaders separated:

> After all that experience and evidence have taught and counseled, is there anyone who believes that the remedy is to hasten the constitutional organization of the State? Permit me to make some observations in this regard, since, although we have always been in agreement on such important matters, I wish to entrust to you with bold anticipation, and for whatever service it may be to you, a small part of the many thoughts that occur to me, and about which I must speak.
>
> No one is more persuaded than you and I of the necessity to organize a general government as being the only means of giving responsible existence to our republic.
>
> But who can doubt that this ought to be the happy result of employing all the means suited to its accomplishment? Who may hope to reach an objective by marching in the opposite direction? Who, in order to form an organized, compact entity, does not first seek out and arrange, by thorough, permanent reforms, the elements that ought to compose it? Who organizes a disciplined army from groups of men without leaders, without officers, without obedience, without rank — an army in which not a moment passes without internal spying and fighting, and thus involves others in its disorders? How may a living, robust being be created out of members that are dead, torn, and diseased by corrupting gangrene, since the life and strength of this new, complex being can be no greater than what it receives from the elements of which it must be composed? Please observe how costly and painful experience has made us see in a practical way that the federal system is absolutely necessary for us because, among other powerful reasons, we totally lack the elements required for a unified government. Furthermore, because our

country was dominated by a party that was deaf to this need, the means and resources available to sustain the State were destroyed and annulled. That party incited the people, perverted their beliefs, set private interests against each other, propagated immorality and intrigue, and split society into so many factions that they have not left even the remnants of its common bonds. They extended their fury to the point of breaking the most sacred of those bonds, the only one that could serve to re-establish the others — religion. With the country in this pitiful condition, it is necessary to create everything anew, first laboring on a small scale and piecemeal, and thereby prepare a general system that may embrace everything. You will observe that a federal republic is the most chimerical and disastrous that can be imagined in all cases when it is not composed of internally well-organized States. Since each part preserves its sovereignty and independence, the central government's authority over the interior of the republic is almost nonexistent; its principal, almost its only role, is purely representative — to be the voice of the people of the confederated states in their relations with foreign governments. Consequently, if within each individual state there are no elements of power capable of maintaining order, the creation of a general, representative government serves only to agitate the entire republic over each small disorder that may occur and to see to it that an outbreak in one state spreads to all the others. It is for this reason that the Republic of North America has not admitted to its new confederation the new people and provinces that have been formed since independence, but rather has admitted them when they have put themselves in a condition for self-rule; meanwhile, they have been left without representation as States, and have been considered as adjuncts of the Republic.

Considering the disturbed condition of our people, contaminated as they all are by Unitarians, lawmakers, seekers after political power, the secret agents of other nations, and the great secret Lodges that spread their nets over all of Europe, what hope can we have of tranquility and calm for making a federal compact, the first step a congress of federation must take? And in the impoverished state to which political agitation has driven our people, with what funds can they pay for a permanent congress and a general administration?

Steadfast in his ideas, Rosas set out to maintain the status quo of the country, and he put off every attempt to organize the State. But if that was his intent in its legal aspect, his practical plans were quite different. What he sought was that the de facto power of the caudillos be brought under his own de facto power, on which there were no legal restrictions and for which there were no predetermined forms. Quiroga's death, which occurred on his return from his mission to the North, eliminated Rosas' most important rival, one whose goal seems to have been the prompt constitutional organization of the country. A few years later, in 1838, Estanislao López also died, in Santa Fe; henceforth, there was no one in the interior who could rival the governor of Buenos Aires, who exercised his authority over the whole country and progressively brought the caudillos under his control with threats, promises, or gifts. As Domingo F. Sarmiento wrote in 1845, in *Facundo:*

> At last we have our centralized republic — and all of it bent under the arbitrary rule of Rosas. The old issues debated by the political parties of Buenos Aires have been stripped of all significance; the meaning of words has been changed; the laws of the cattle ranch have been introduced into the government of the republic, which was once the most war-like and the most enthusiastic for liberty, and sacrificed most to achieve it. The death of López delivered Santa Fe to Rosas; the death of the Reinafé brothers gave him Córdoba; Facundo's death gave him the eight provinces on the slopes of the Andes. To take possession of all these, a few personal gifts, some friendly letters, and some hand-outs from the treasury sufficed.

On this basis a national State with unusual characteristics took form, founded on a system of alliances and on the authority of an all-powerful chief — principally the latter, because, since Rosas' State lacked legal form, it was merely an extension of his personal power.

An analysis of the characteristics of this situation, and of the idea of power it involved, is highly suggestive. Intelligent — more than that, supremely astute and profoundly knowledgeable in the psychology of the creoles — Rosas had succeeded in creating among the people the deep-rooted conviction of his natural right to exercise authority. Only he appeared to be capable of restoring the traditional way of life and of putting an end to civil strife; this belief, which was held by his most devoted adherents, was corroborated by the plebiscite that he had demanded be taken before he accepted the grant of total authority. In effect, this belief was generally held, and his prestige quickly turned it into idolatry, and not without magical overtones pointing to the mysterious origin of his power:

> He, with his talent and his science
> keeps the country secure,
> and that is why he gets his help
> from Divine Providence.

So the people sang, and Rosas himself tried to make them believe it, allowing his image to appear in the churches, where it received popular homage. The vague awareness of the force behind his authority facilitated the shift to autocracy, and no person or thing altered his will or succeeded in decisively influencing his resolution. "During the time I presided over the government of Buenos Aires, charged with the foreign relations of the Argentine Confederation and holding total authority, as granted to me by law" — he wrote in 1870 — "I governed according to my conscience. I am solely responsible for all my acts, good or bad, and for my errors as well as for my successes." Rosas became so powerful that years later, his nephew, Lucio V. Mansilla, could say: "There was no discussion during the time of Rosas; no criticism; no opinion." His was a personal power, independent of that granted to him by law, and he was so sure that his authority sprang from himself alone that he once hinted at the possibility of transmitting his power to his daughter, Manuelita.

Despite the broad popular basis of his support, Rosas had many influential enemies. From the outset, he was opposed by the followers of Rivadavia, against whom he had fought as a federalist; later, he had enemies among all the groups that had any sense of honor, which was an obstacle to the submission that he demanded. Rosas was implacable with all his opponents: many fled to foreign lands, and many suffered violent persecution. As Paz said: "The historian who undertakes the job of narrating these events will be hard put not to give the appearance of exaggerating what happened, and posterity will have to work as hard to persuade itself that the events we have witnessed were possible." Thanks to the use of violence, thanks to the skill with which he managed the instincts and inclinations of the creole masses, Rosas obtained apparently unanimous support. He who was not unconditionally with Rosas was his enemy — "a savage, filthy Unitarian." The fact is that Rosas succeeded in planting in the minds of the people the conviction that all their enemies — among whom were doctrinaire Federalists and many old Unitarians who had later become convinced of the advantages of federation — made up a single group, characterized by unswerving centralist beliefs and by alien, anti-creole attitudes. And these qualities were precisely the most hateful ones to the masses.

Rosas' ideology stemmed directly from a colonial inheritance that is noticeable as early as the May Revolution. As Sarmiento wrote: "Where, then, did this man learn about the innovations that he introduced into his government, in contempt of common sense, tradition, and the conscience and immemorial practices of civilized peoples? God forgive me if I am wrong, but this idea has long possessed me: he learned them from the cattle ranch, where he has spent his whole life, and from the Inquisition, in whose tradition he has been educated." The author of *Facundo* was correct: not only was Rosas the culmination of the secessionist movement that had appeared after 1810 and that was, in a strict sense, more than mere federalism; also he was the distillation of the antiliberal movement that was part of the authoritarian tradition of the colony and that retained its vigor among the rural masses.

These trends may be clearly seen if one analyzes the symbols he employed with such marked success. Defense of the Catholic faith had been the order of the day of Quiroga, whose motto was "Religion or Death," and it was seemingly one of the basic objectives of the Rosas dictatorship. The ultramontane party, represented by men like Francisco Tagle and Father Gregorio Castañeda, had struggled hard to enthrone Rosas; their faithful followers were known as the "Apostolic Party," and when the people wanted to describe their enemies, they said that they were

> mocking religion; the result:
> heretics who had blasphemed
> what is most holy, what most sacred
> of our divine cult.

Ultramontane reaction was but one aspect of the antiliberalism that followed the revolution of 1830 in France. Anything that recalled the ideas of the men of the Enlightenment, of whom the followers of Rivadavia were the direct heirs, was violently condemned by the partisans of Rosas, as is conclusively shown by General Mansilla's comment to his son, Lucio, on the day he found him reading Rousseau: "My friend, when one is the nephew of Rosas, he does not read the *Social Contract* if he intends to remain in the country, or he gets out of the country if he wishes to read the book with profit." This antiliberalism, seen clearly in the political and economic views that Rosas put into effect during his long period of rule, was intermingled with creole reaction. If he was called the "Restorer of the Laws," it was not so much because the people regarded him particularly as the defender of legal norms, but because they felt he was the guardian of the traditions of the common folk and the zealous defender of a way of life that seemed to be condemned to extinction. This explains his political xenophobia, which was, nonetheless, compatible with his alliances with the governments of countries that traded with the estancieros and with the producers of hides and salted meats. It explains the devoted support given him by the masses, who were proud of their "Americanism," and who were by tradition and by inertia opposed to progress, and infatuated with the superiority of their virtues as a pastoral people — courage and manual dexterity.

Along these lines Rosas built the indisputable popular basis for his policies, and this support allowed the all-powerful governor of Buenos Aires and proprietor of its port to impose his authority on the Confederation, which was the elementary form in which he conceived the national State. No doubt he unified the country, as Sarmiento said, but he exhausted the Confederation's possibilities during his long rule, and gradually he awakened the desire to attain unity through a solidly founded constitutional system. It cannot be denied that he fulfilled a mission, despite the overtones of barbarism that darkened his labors as governor, although it is certain that he would have been able to achieve this result by other means if such violent prejudices and rancor had not been at work within him.

5. *Rosas Still Lives in the Hearts of Some Argentines!*

This effusive tribute to Rosas demonstrates that there is still some popular support for him in Argentina, where citizens are notoriously historically-minded and patriotic. This decree was formally issued in 1964 by a municipality in the Chaco on the occasion of the naming of one of its avenues in honor of "Brigadier General Juan Manuel de Rosas."

Whereas: The naming of streets has always had as its purpose the commemoration of the attitudes, deeds, or conduct of personalities who have distinguished themselves in ways the remembrance of which should not be neglected; and

Considering: That it is therefore proper to honor the name of one of the forgers of our nationality and that this resolve is all the more fitting because the province to which this city belongs has been one of the last to be integrated as a Federal State within the vast Argentine Fatherland;

That the heroes of our National Organization effected the triumph of the Argentine Confederation already perfected and founded by Brigadier General Juan Manuel de Rosas by means of the Organic Pact of 1831;

That the said Confederation was sustained by its founder for more than two decades while he struggled against internal conspiracies and foreign coalitions under conditions that would have discouraged any other ruler or military leader;

That as governor of the province of Buenos Aires, Juan Manuel de Rosas created, by means of novel systems for the production, distribution, and commercialization of goods, useful sources of employment for the rural and pro-

From Clifton B. Kroeber, *Rosas y la revisión de la historia Argentina*, trans. J. L. Muñoz Azpiri (Buenos Aires: Fondo Editor Argentino, 1965), pp. 87–90. Reprinted by permission.

letarian workers, thereby materially improving the general welfare to which the constitution of 1853 refers;

That the rancher, businessman, and exporter Juan Manuel de Rosas founded . . . the so-called "mother industry of the country" — cattle-raising — the products of which he exported in ships flying the Argentine flag and belonging to the first Argentine National Merchant Marine, whose tonnage was surpassed only in 1943;

That he dignified the worker by assuming with national pride the name of "gaucho," which was used at that time to refer disdainfully to humble Argentines;

That he caused this name to be respected by the powers of the earth through the exercise of intelligence and arms;

That he initiated the first ordinance of national economic independence in the famous Customs Law of 1831, which provided financial controls and protection for our industries and crafts;

That he professed to be permanently honored "with the friendship of the poor" and to hold himself aloof from the privileges of the so-called oligarchy of Buenos Aires;

That he recovered thousands of leagues from the wilderness and founded the centers of civilization called Bahía Blanca, Junín, and 25 de Mayo;

That during twelve years of international conflict he defended Argentine sovereignty with immortal dignity, preserving it "as whole and unblemished as when it left the hands of the Almighty," and he fulfilled and for the first time brought about the true fulfillment of the oath of July 9, 1816;

That he declared the ninth of July a national holiday;

That he enjoyed the admiration of the world's leading statesmen and publicists, who considered him the champion of the rights of South American sovereignty;

That he brought dignity to the name of Argentina because of his irreproachable conduct in his personal and private life and his scrupulous management of public funds;

That he strengthened the privileges of the Church and revoked measures of persecution against Catholicism which had been dictated by previous doctrinaire governments, thereby fortifying Argentina's civil unity, one of the sources of which is the strength and solidarity of the Christian faith;

That he made the Argentine Army a specialized and technical body, providing it with industries and laboratories and establishing the bases of military manufacturing in the model barracks and workshops of Santos Lugares;

That he converted our fledgling diplomatic service into a corps of professionals and specialists in international politics and in the art of negotiation, among them Arana, Guido, Manuel Moreno, and Mariano Balcarce;

That he was the first to honor the Father of the Country by decreeing that a plaza in Buenos Aires bear the name of the Liberator during his lifetime;

That the name of Juan Manuel de Rosas survives in the bosom of this region, the latest to be recovered from the wilderness of the Argentine Chaco, as the symbol and epitome of the purest national essence;

That his heroic name, pronounced by the humble and patriotic hearts of Argentina's generous soil, will always prevent humiliations or slights to our Fatherland;

That he deserved the highest posthumous honors that any Argentine citizen has hitherto received upon setting forth on his voyage to the tomb, accompanied by the sword of San Martín and the flag of Arenales;

That the present resolution fulfills one of the desires of the Father of the Country, General José de San Martín, who in a letter to General Rosas dated on May 6, 1850, in Boulogne sur Mer expressed the hope "that upon ending his public life he would be overwhelmed by the just gratitude of every Argentine."

For all these reasons:

The Municipal Council of Roque Saenz Peña directs that:

Article 1. The name Brigadier General Juan Manuel de Rosas be given to the present Avenue of Labor along its entire length.

Article 2. The Subsecretariat of Public Works take action to put up the appropriate street signs.

Baron and Viscount Mauá at the Age of Forty-three

Nineteenth-Century Economic Affairs

INFLUENCE OF THE WORLD ECONOMY ON LATIN AMERICA

The late Professor Sanford A. Mosk of the University of California, Berkeley, stated a quarter of a century ago that "the economic history of Latin America has been a neglected field," and this is still true despite some recent advances. His essay on the way in which the world economy influenced the development of Latin America in the period 1850–1914 explains better than any other article the fundamental aspects of the subject (Reading 1). He was convinced that we will be handicapped in our understanding of the contemporary economic problems and trends in Latin America until we have "a better balanced and more accurate picture of Latin American history."

One way to attempt to meet the need will be by setting forth case studies of entrepreneurship in individual countries as illustrations of the broad, general lines of economic influences that Professor Mosk has analyzed in his wide-ranging exposition.

ENTREPRENEURSHIP IN BRAZIL

To begin with, let us consider Brazil where a conservative Emperor Pedro II made life difficult for an adventurous capitalist such as the Baron Mauá (Reading 2). Mauá and the other economic innovators of the years 1840–1880 at times yielded to the dangerous temptation to overextend themselves by engaging in too many enterprises simultaneously and had difficulty matching capital resources with technical competence and administrative ability. They were all influenced by Britain and British values, particularly the willingness to risk money for the sake of possible profits, which was the essence of the Victorian age. The spirit stood in direct opposition to the static agrarian life of Brazil, dominated as it was by the landed gentry who considered profits akin to usury. Mauá particularly was deeply influenced by the vision of an industrialized, modern society which he derived from an early visit to England.

AMERICAN ENTREPRENEURS

Latin Americans for many years have had to suffer superactive Yankees eager to sell nutmegs or assist in one way or another the "development" of their countries, usually with some profit to themselves. A classic example was Edward A. Hopkins who felt called to bring various benefits to Paraguay (Reading 3). Another such promoter was Henry Meiggs, a genial figure who knew how to ingratiate himself with Peruvians and whose remarkable exploits in building railroads in the difficult Andean terrain won for him the title of "Yankee Pizarro" (Reading 4).

Railroads built by Meiggs helped to develop the country economically, but the price paid in human suffering was very high, particularly by the thousands of Chinese coolies who were practically enslaved to the dirty work. And the basic economic and social problem—the debased condition of the mass of peasants who constituted the majority of the population—was not affected either by railroads or by the exploitation of guano (bird droppings) that created a boom in the middle of the nineteenth century, benefiting a few Peruvians and foreign entrepreneurs.

In Reading 5 the American novelist John Dos Passos paints an ironic picture of Meiggs' nephew, Minor Cooper Keith, who built railroads in Central America and made a fortune in the nascent banana industry.

1.   Latin America and the World Economy, 1850–1914

SANFORD A. MOSK

Some studies are so imaginatively conceived and soundly presented that
they have a perennial value, despite the appearance of much new information on the subject. Such an article is this work by the late Professor Mosk,
to whom we are indebted for his convincing guidelines for understanding
the economic history of Latin America in modern times.

The fact that the Spanish colonies broke up into a large number of independent governments makes it harder to deal with the national period than
with the colonial, when centralized authority gave a large degree of unity to
affairs throughout the whole area. In the colonial period, too, geographic unity
was matched by continuity through time. In the republican period, on the other
hand, turbulence and kaleidoscopic political changes make it difficult to find
a continuity in development and to appraise the long-run significance of individual events. The historian of the colonial period also enjoys an advantage
in source materials. The documentary sources for colonial history are not only
voluminous but they have been readily available in a few centralized archives.
Materials on the national period are by no means lacking, but on the whole
they been less satisfactory for the historian, for reasons which are inherent in the political and social structure of Latin America. A sense of
loyalty to political and family connections has unquestionably made its influence felt in the selection of records to be preserved and to be made available to scholars. . . .

   Our understanding of the national period, therefore, in all its phases can
hardly be called satisfactory. What needs to be studied in particular is the
way in which institutions have been modified and, reshaped since independence. It is probable that some Latin American institutions which are ordinarily viewed as a product of the colonial system will turn out on a closer

From "Latin America and the World Economy, 1850–1914" by Sanford A. Mosk, Inter-
American Economic Affairs, 2 (1948), no. 3, pp. 53–82, passim. Reprinted by permission.

inspection to bear only a superficial resemblance to institutions of colonial times and to be something very different in content. I would certainly expect such a revaluation to occur with respect to Latin American economic institutions. The commercialization of economic life in the nineteenth and twentieth centuries has not gone nearly as far in Latin America as in other parts of the world such as Western Europe and the United States. Nevertheless, it has played its part. To cite but one example, in penetrating economic life in Latin America since the middle of the nineteenth century, commercialization has brought about important changes in the heritage of colonial times with respect to land ownership and the relations between landowners and peasants.

These observations are in no sense intended to deny the importance of knowledge about the colonial period. Such knowledge — and also an understanding of pre-Columbian cultures — is basic to an understanding of Latin America. The perspective of the historian, however, has given too little weight to what has taken place since independence. Probably this deficiency has been greater in the treatment of Latin America's economic development than in any other phase of Latin American history. Certainly it has been acute in the economic field. In most of the textbooks and other general works on Latin American history there is an implicit, if not an explicit, underemphasis upon the economic development of the national period. The treatment of this subject tends to be fragmentary, sketchy, and lacking in generalizations. In all these respects, and usually too in amount of space, it falls far short of the treatment accorded the economy of colonial times.

This weakness obviously needs to be overcome if we are to have a better balanced and more accurate picture of Latin American history. Until it is overcome, too, we are handicapped in our understanding of the contemporary economic problems and trends of Latin America. Right now a number of countries in Latin America are trying to bring about significant changes in their economic structure. In doing so, it may truly be said that they are writing off the economic heritage of the colonial period. But it may be said with equal truth that they are also writing off the economic heritage of the late nineteenth and early twentieth centuries.

My purpose in writing this essay is to call attention to certain propositions about economic development since the middle of the nineteenth century which help to give meaning to the economic history of Latin America, and which thereby contribute to the understanding and analysis of today's economic problems in Latin America. It is not my intention to give a rounded sketch of Latin American economic history in this period, but rather to stress certain things which I believe have been inadequately appreciated by the historians. . . .

The opening of new areas took a variety of forms. One of the most striking and significant cases was the settlement and economic development of the interior of the United States, which made the virgin grasslands of the Mississippi Valley a principal source of cheap food for European consumption. Other grasslands, such as those of Argentina, Australia, and Canada were also newly colonized and developed as suppliers of agricultural products for Europe in the late years of the nineteenth century and early years of the twentieth. In still other cases, areas long before settled, such as southern Russia and India, expanded their production of grain for export as the cheap and regular transportation provided by the railroad and the steamship made it possible for them to reach distant markets with ease. Even without new colonization these regions helped to bring about an expanding economic horizon.

In large part, the territorial expansion of the period 1850–1914 consisted of the opening of continental interiors outside of Europe. This process did not always involve new settlement, as we have noted above. And even where new settlement occurred, it did not always involve large numbers of persons or even permanent occupation. The exploitation of new mineral resources was often achieved by a handful of men in a mining camp or similar outpost, located in an otherwise uninhabited region and connected with markets and supply sources by a single thread of transport running to the nearest seaport. Large settlement was unnecessary. Furthermore, mining camps were often abandoned because resources played out. Such lack of permanence in settlement has been even more common in the exploitation of timber resources than in minerals.

The true significance of the territorial expansion we have been dealing with is not found in the factor of settlement, but rather in the exploitation of new and highly productive natural resources — soils, minerals, and forests. The economic resources of the world were greatly expanded. Moreover, the new additions were important because of their quality as well as their quantity. Thus, like technical improvements, they contributed to a reduction in real costs of production of basic articles of consumption — of staple items of diet, of fuel, of fabricated goods, etc.

Still another broad force making for economic advance after the middle of the nineteenth century was a great increase in population. It is estimated that in 1850 the world contained 1.2 billion inhabitants. The increase thereafter brought the total to an estimated 1.6 billion in 1900, and by 1940 it is calculated that a figure of 2.2 billion was attained. Roughly, it appears that the world's population has doubled in the last hundred years. This multiplication of consumers and of human productive power contributed to the great expansion in world output of goods and services after the middle of the nineteenth century. More people had to be fed and clothed and housed, while on the other side, more people meant more labor for productive effort. . . .

To show how the world setting of the years 1850–1914 influenced economic development in Latin America, we may refer to the economic experience of Argentina. In the middle of the nineteenth century the pulse of economic life in Argentina was faint indeed. The great pampa region was given over mainly to the hunting of wild cattle, as it had been in earlier times, an activity that cannot properly be called stockraising. No effort was made to improve the breeds of stock. Cattle were hunted and slaughtered mostly for their hides, the principal product which could be shipped to export markets. Some tallow was also exported, and a certain amount of salt beef was shipped to the West Indies and Brazil. Economically and technically the sheepraising industry was more advanced than cattle production, and wool exports were on the increase. Corn and wheat were raised, but for domestic consumption rather than for export. Actually Argentina found it necessary to import wheat and flour regularly to meet her requirements. The economy of Argentina around the middle of the nineteenth century was picturesque, but it was hardly productive.

About 1880, however, the pace of economic life began to quicken, and thereafter Argentina underwent a rapid economic transition. Within a generation the economy of Argentina was completely transformed. Possibly the most striking feature of this change was an expansion in grain production and the emergence of Argentina as a major supplier of grain for world markets. In 1870 the total cultivated acreage in Argentina amounted to only about one million acres. By 1895 over 12 million acres were under cultivation, and by 1914 an additional fivefold increase had brought the total to approximately 63 million. Lands formerly idle or used as pasturage were converted to the tillage of wheat, corn, alfalfa, and flax.

Argentina's exports reflected these new trends in crop acreage and production. In the 1880's wheat exports averaged less than 100,000 tons per year, but in the following decade the annual average was in the neighborhood of 1,000,000 tons. When the First World War broke out, Argentina was exporting approximately 2,500,000 tons of wheat each year. In the exportation of corn even greater gains were made in the years just prior to the war. The increased production of flax led to an expansion in linseed exports which rivaled that of corn in percentage terms. Alfalfa, of course, was exported in the form of livestock products.

In the same period Argentina's livestock industry assumed an entirely new character. Successful experiments with refrigerated shipping in the last quarter of the nineteenth century led to the establishment of freezing plants (*frigoríficos*) in Argentina to prepare meat for shipment to expanding overseas markets. A demand was thus created for better grades of meat than could be provided by the wild and semi-wild cattle of the pampas. Improved breeds were imported, such as Shorthorns and Herefords from Great Britain, and mixed with the native stock. A true stockraising industry was developed. To maintain the new improved breeds called for care and vigilance, and thus it became common to fence in ranches rather than to graze cattle on the open range. Further enclosures were made necessary by an intermingling of crop lands and grazing lands, such as arose in connection with the raising of alfalfa on the cattle ranches (*estancias*). Much of the cultivation of crop lands on the ranch was carried out by tenants. Tenancy had been known earlier in Argentina, but it was unimportant until the high tide of immigration began to run in the late years of the nineteenth century. Immigrants and their descendants became the nucleus of a permanent class of tenant farmers, and new types of sharecropping and other rental arrangements were worked out. In scope and nature, tenancy in Argentina in 1914 was a very different institution from the tenancy of 60 years earlier.

Perhaps all these changes in cattle-raising can be summed up by saying that a new industry was created, new types of land use appeared, and new kinds of landowner-tenant relations were fashioned.

We have already observed that a new meat-processing industry was also created in Argentina with the advent of the frigoríficos. This industry expanded rapidly after 1900. Exports of frozen beef rose from about 25,000 tons in 1900 to over 365,000 tons (frozen and chilled beef combined) in 1914. Although the number of frigoríficos was not increased greatly, the plants were expanded in size and capacity, and production was rationalized and standardized. In the year just prior to 1914, also, the frigoríficos were diversifying their output by expanding the production and exportation of canned meat.

Of strategic importance in the expansion of crop and livestock production, and in the development of the meat-processing industry, was the building of railways. In 1860 Argentina had only about 25 miles of railroads. Annual increases occurred thereafter, but it was not until about 1885 that construction was undertaken actively. Between 1885 and 1914 Argentina increased its railway mileage from 2,800 to 21,000. By 1914 most of the trunk lines across the pampa had been completed and a true network of feeder and branch lines had been created. In reaching into the interior, the railroads were typically built when settlement was still sparse, and thus they were a vital force in stimulating internal colonization. Obviously, too, the expanded production of wheat, corn, and meat for overseas markets would have been impossible without the development of a railroad network to haul these products to Rosario, Buenos Aires, and other seaports.

The preceding paragraphs have brought out the main lines of development in Argentina in the generation prior to the First World War. Figures could be cited to show advances in other branches of the economy, such as internal trade, banking operations, and public finance, but we need not pause to do so here. For our purpose it is sufficient to point out that levels of performance all through the economy were raised as Argentina became a vital factor in the world's trade in food products.

What needs to be stressed is that the true historical perspective for Argentina's economic transformation is the pattern of world economic development after the middle of the nineteenth century. It is no exaggeration to say that the new Argentine economy was a product of (1) technical advances in manufacture and in transportation which originated in the industrialized countries, and (2) a workable international economy characterized by relatively great freedom for trade, extensive migrations of people, and a large volume of international investment.

On the technical side, one of the most decisive developments for Argentina was the invention of barbed wire in the United States in the early 1870's. Imported into the pampa country, barbed wire provided an effective fencing material for enclosing improved breeds of livestock. It was important, therefore, in grading up the quality of Argentine beef. Also, the barbed wire fence made it possible to combine crop-raising with grazing in the pampa region, and thus it played its part in the expansion of output of wheat, corn, and alfalfa. In the meat-processing industry, the critically important methods of refrigeration were introduced from abroad, and other technical improvements of substantial influence came in with the American companies that started to operate in 1908. In transportation, the railroad, the steamship, and refrigerated shipping were technical developments of strategic importance for revolutionizing the Argentine economy.

These technical developments, and others which might be mentioned, could not have exerted the influence they did had it not been for the existence of an international economy. The great agricultural production of Argentina — wheat, corn, linseed, and meat — was destined for export markets in the United Kingdom and other industrialized countries of western Europe. Only a small fraction of the output of meat was consumed in Argentina itself. In 1914, for example, about one-eighth of the meat slaughtered was used for domestic consumption. For linseed, the Argentine market was negligible, and almost the whole output was shipped abroad. For wheat and corn the home market was relatively larger, but it hardly took over a third of the annual production in the years prior to 1914. Clearly the bulk of Argentina's productive effort, especially if one takes account of transport and other services connected with exportation, was directed toward foreign markets. Thus the Argentine economy was part of the larger framework of international trade.

The Argentine economy also benefited from immigration. Apart from the United States, which was in a class by itself, Argentina was one of the principal absorbers of European emigrants before the First World War. Immigration began to reach significant proportions in the 1880's, building up to a peak of 260,000 in the year 1889. This was followed by a sharp drop, but by 1896 immigration had recovered to the average levels of the 80's. The upward trend continued, and by 1906 the peak of 1889 had been surpassed. In 1912 almost 380,000 immigrants were recorded.

It is true that not all of these immigrants settled permanently in Argentina. On the basis of emigration figures compiled by the Argentine government it is estimated that roughly 45 per cent of the immigrants returned to their native lands. But even the temporary immigrants made their contribution to Argentina's economic expansion. Indeed, many of the Italians, who together with Spaniards comprised the majority of the immigrants, were seasonal workers who came each year to Argentina to do harvesting. They met a peak requirement without putting a strain on the Argentine economy during the remainder of the year. The movements of these immigrants, who were known as *golondrinas* (swallows), are a striking illustration of the interconnections and flexibility of the international economic order of pre-1914 times.

The annual cycle of migration began in October and November, when the seasonal laborers left their homes in Italy. Cheap steerage transportation brought them to Argentina where most of them first found employment in harvesting flax and wheat in the northern part of the pampa country. Thereafter they followed the course of harvesting to the south, moving much of the time on foot. By February they had begun to work in the harvesting of corn. When this task was finished in April the golondrinas returned to Italy in time to participate in the spring planting. It is, of course, impossible to know how much expansion of crop acreage in Argentina was made possible by these migratory workers. Nevertheless, those who have studied Argentine agricultural development are unanimous in saying that the expansion of acreage and output would have been much less rapid than it was prior to the First World War if the golondrinas had not been available.

Foreign capital also played a prominent part in the economic development of pre-1914 Argentina. Most of the railroads were built by British capital and operated by British companies. In 1914 over 70 per cent of the railway mileage in Argentina was owned and operated by British concerns. Other public utilities, such as streetcar systems and gas plants, were also largely British-owned, although appreciable amounts of German, French, and Italian capital were invested in such enterprises. The Argentine government, and provincial and municipal governments as well, were large borrowers of foreign funds. Here, again, Great Britain was the principal source. Not all of this borrowing, of course, was used for purposes directly relating to Argentina's economic development, but some of it went into the construction of public works which contributed to an expansion in production.

Foreign capital was also a major factor in the development of Argentina's meat-processing industry. The first frigoríficos were established by British capital with a certain amount of Argentine participation. British investment was dominant in this industry until 1908, when one of the larger American packing houses entered the Argentine industry. Three other American packers soon followed suit, and by 1914 American investment was an important feature in the meat-processing industry. This was the only sphere in which American capital was significant in Argentina before the First World War.

Precise estimates of international investment for the period before World War I are hard to come by. All such estimates, however, must be considered subject to a wide margin of error. Nevertheless, some idea of the order of magnitude involved can be gained from the following figures reported by American consular representatives in Buenos Aires. By 1913, British investments in Argentina were valued at $1,551 million; French, $771 million; German, $298 million; Belgian, $180 million; Spanish, $80 million; American, $20 million. These foreign investments in Argentina at the time, aggregated $2.9 billion. Without the inflow of this foreign capital during the preceding 25 to 30 years, Argentina could not possibly have attained the economy it had at the time of the First World War.

The influence of the pre-1914 world economy in shaping economic development in Latin America is probably shown more clearly in Argentina than in any of the other republics. The influence, however, was pervasive, and in most countries it was strongly felt. The pattern of economic specialization in Latin America in 1914 (and, therefore, today) was very different from that of 1850. Some of the differences were clear-cut differences in kind. Others represented changes in degree, but of such large degree that they also amounted to changes in kind.

To illustrate this last proposition we may refer to copper production. Numerous copper deposits in Latin America were worked in the colonial period, and even in pre-Columbian times. Some expansion took place after 1800, but it was not until the latter part of the nineteenth century that the output of copper reached substantial amounts. The decisive factor was the growth of the electrical industry. Prior to the development of this industry, copper was used principally for ornamentation, kitchen utensils, and ships' bottoms. The widespread use of electricity created new, large demands for copper in power transmission, telegraph and telephone lines, electric motors, etc. All over the world new levels of production were attained after the middle of the nineteenth century. The world as a whole produced five times more copper in the last 25 years of the century than it had in the first 50. In South America, Chile and the other copper-producing countries produced about ten times as much copper in the last half of the century as they had in the first half.

It should also be observed that the exploitation of Latin American copper resources since the middle of the nineteenth century has been carried out mostly by foreign capital. Most of the copper mines of Latin America have been operated by American companies. Much American capital, too, has gone into silver-mining in Latin America during the same period. Thus, although silver-mining was an important industry in earlier times, it has assumed new characteristics in the last 100 years. Moreover, the amount of silver production has been carried to entirely new levels. Mexico, the world's leader in silver production, is estimated to have produced about 2 billion ounces from the beginning of the colonial period to 1850, a span of more than 300 years. In the 65 years from 1851 to 1915 Mexico produced 2.2 billion ounces of silver.

In agricultural production, as in mining, new kinds of specialization emerged in Latin America in the late nineteenth and early twentieth centuries. The commercial production of bananas in Middle America did not begin to assume importance until about 1870. Shortly after 1900 the introduction of refrigerated shipping into the banana trade provided a great stimulus to the industry. The principal market for bananas was the United States, and the capital which developed the production and traffic in bananas was almost exclusively American.

The cultivation of coffee in the Caribbean region began as early as the first part of the eighteenth century, but it was not until the late years of the nineteenth that it assumed importance. After 1875, too, a shift occurred in the center of coffee production within the region. Leadership passed from the islands to the north coast of South America and the Pacific Coast of Central America, the two areas where it has remained to the present day.

The world's greatest coffee-producing country is Brazil. Here, again, we find a development mainly of the period after 1875. Not that coffee production was unknown in Brazil before that time. Actually, production and exports were increasing steadily before 1875, and Brazil had come to account for about one-half of world coffee production in that year, whereas 50 years before she had produced less than one-fifth of the world's supply. But it was in the last quarter of the nineteenth century that the industry mushroomed. By 1900 Brazil's exports of coffee were about three times as large as they had been in 1875, and they continued to mount in the early years of this century. Brazil also improved her relative position in world coffee production after 1875. In the years 1895–1899 Brazil produced two-thirds of the world's coffee supply, and in the following five-year period she accounted for as much as three-fourths of the world total.

The great expansion in Brazilian coffee acreage and production took place in the province of Sao Paulo. To this province came large numbers of immigrants, especially from Italy. By 1875 Negro slavery was dying out in Brazil, and it was finally abolished in 1888. Italian immigrants became a principal source of labor for the coffee growers, who, through their own associations and through the provincial government, did much to encourage immigration. Advertising campaigns were conducted in Italy, and free transportation was provided from Italy to Sao Paulo. In 1875 there were very few Italians in Sao Paulo. From 1875 to 1886 about 21,000 arrived, and in the years which followed the flow of Italian immigrants became even larger. From 1887 to 1906 more than 800,000 entered the province of Sao Paulo. Although these Italian immigrants were not the sole source of labor for coffee-raising, they were in a majority and it is extremely unlikely that Brazil could have achieved its great expansion in coffee production without their work.

The foregoing observations on certain Latin American mineral and agricultural products have been offered as illustrations of the importance of the changes which took place after the middle of the nineteenth century — changes which originated mainly in the world economy of the period. Although pertinent data are not always easy to come by, similar patterns of development can be traced for commodities other than those which have been cited. The development of petroleum production in Latin America, as elsewhere, has been essentially confined to the present century. The commercial production of sugar and cotton in Peru, two important items in Peruvian exports nowadays, goes back only to the end of the nineteenth century. The same dating applies to tin-mining in Bolivia. Nitrate production in South America has a somewhat longer commercial history, but it, too, must be regarded as a development of the period since 1880. . . .

This essay has dealt with the world economy of the period 1850–1914 and with its effects on the economic development of Latin America. These effects were in many ways salutary. Certainly the world economy provided the main stimulus for commercial production. However, it should not be inferred that the economic picture in Latin America was a wholly benign one in that period. . . .

Furthermore, the exports of the colonial economies represented by far the major part of their commercial production. In some countries production of food for local consumption may have been larger than production for export, but always a large percentage of the food raised was for subsistence purposes. It did not enter commercial channels. As a general rule, the colonial economies were but small consumers of their own commercial output. Their own consumption tended to be a negligible fraction of their total production. Thus their export markets — viz., the advanced industrial nations — were of the utmost importance to the colonial economies.

Before 1914 this dependence upon export markets did not give rise to acute problems. The consumption of primary materials by the manufacturing countries was an expanding one, and it was little affected by cyclical disturbances in business conditions. Also, the international economic factor functioned smoothly in that period, as we have seen, thus helping to maximize the advantages of international trade for all participating countries.

Nevertheless, it must be recognized that the colonial economies did not share equally with the industrialized nations the fruits of world economic development. The great improvements in technology and the opening up of new, highly productive resources brought about a decrease in real costs of production. Looked at from the standpoint of the consumer, this meant that a given amount of money could buy a larger amount of goods and services. On the average, therefore, people were able to consume more, to live better. In other words, average standards of living were raised.

The gains in standards of living, however, were largely confined to the industrialized countries. . . .

The lag of the colonial economies in standards of living was due to complex causes. In some cases, a deficiency in natural resources, or some other physical condition such as a difficult climate in which to work, played an important part by restricting the total productivity of the whole economy. As a general rule, however, the lag was inherent in the social and political structures of the non-industrialized regions. These conditions were not the same everywhere, but they were similar in fostering a high degree of inequality in income distribution. A large fraction of the national income in the colonial economies went to a handful of persons, while the average income for the bulk of the people was very low. The average person in such areas, therefore, was prevented from increasing his consumption of goods and services by internal social and political conditions.

The economic specialization of the colonial economies, which was a part of the international economic order of pre-1914 days, also bore a share of the responsibility, although probably a small one, for the lower living standards prevailing in such areas. Economic specialization in the form of raw-material production for export fitted in with and strengthened the existing social order in the colonial economies. Economic diversification, on the other hand, tends to weaken such a social order by creating opposing forces — as, for example, in the historical case of the rise of a middle class. The existence of a workable world economy, by creating conditions favorable to the maintenance of one-sided economies in the non-industrialized areas, tended to fortify those very qualities of social and political organization which prevented a wide distribution of national income and thus prevented the enjoyment of higher standards of living by the mass of the people in those areas.

The main causes of the relatively lower standards of living in the colonial economies were internal. But the international economy also operated in the same direction. It is true that in other ways the international economy worked in the direction of spreading higher average standards of living in the colonial economies, but this effect was clearly insufficient to offset the results of internal social and political conditions.

The most expansive, flexible, and workable international economy the world has ever known, therefore, could not insure reasonably high standards of living in Latin America and the other colonial economies. Moreover, in gearing themselves to export markets and to external sources of capital, the Latin American countries became extremely dependent upon the smooth functioning of the world economy. The First World War dealt a blow to the international economy from which it never recovered. Attempts to reconstruct it during the 1920's were only partly successful, and what was reconstructed began to break down again toward the end of that decade. In the depression of the 1930's the remainder of the international economy collapsed completely. It is beyond the scope of this essay to deal with the period subsequent to World War I, but I do want to stress, in concluding, that the economic history of Latin America in the last 30 years is in large part a reflection of the breakdown and collapse of the world economy of the preceding generation.

2. Emperor Pedro II Gave the Banker Baron Mauá a Hard Time

ANYDA MARCHANT

Miss Marchant is a member of the bar of Virginia and of the Supreme Court who has an abiding interest in the history of Brazil. In 1965 she published the standard work *Viscount Mauá and the Empire of Brazil: A Biography of Irenêo Evangelista de Souza (1813–1889).* The present selection comes from an earlier statement.

Brazilian historians have never paid much attention to the economic history of Brazil, and, indeed, have generally maintained a deprecatory attitude toward the businessman and his effect on the country. Involved in this neglect is the figure of Irenêo Evangelista de Souza, Baron and Viscount Mauá (1813–1889), still an almost unknown and little-studied man, even though he was Brazil's pioneer railroad builder and industrialist, an imaginative entrepreneur, and a daring innovator in investment banking.

From "A New Portrait of Mauá the Banker: A Man of Business in Nineteenth-Century Brazil" by Anyda Marchant, *Hispanic American Historical Review,* 30 (1950), pp. 411–431, passim. Reprinted by permission.

Mauá's business life began when he was an orphan at the age of nine, in the shop of a Portuguese merchant in Rio de Janeiro in 1822. By the time he was sixteen, he had become the confidential clerk of Richard Carruthers, an English merchant and importer of English manufactured goods. Carruthers taught him the English language and English business methods, and introduced him to the variety of industry and the concepts of credit that were commonplace then in England but unknown in Brazil. When Carruthers retired to England in the late 1830's, he left his favorite clerk as managing partner of his business in Rio. By 1840, Irenêo was an important member of the business community of Rio — "Senhor Iréneo," as his English acquaintances seem characteristically to have mispronounced his name. By 1850, he was an industrialist as well as a merchant and ready to embark on investment banking in a large way.

One of the things that the boy Irenêo had learned in Carruther's firm was the idea of financial credit as a basis for industrial expansion. The most important practical result of his first trip to England in 1840 had undoubtedly been the founding, in Manchester, of the firm of Carruthers, De Castro and Company, because Carruthers' name was invaluable when his protegé needed to raise capital in England to float many of his early enterprises. Mauá's banking career was based on Carruthers' international connections, for Carruthers had his own web of international credit: his firm in London, a branch of the Manchester house; Carruthers, Souza and Company in Buenos Aires; Carruthers, Dixon and Company in New York. As the old man withdrew more and more from an active part in these businesses, Joseph Reynell de Castro, who was linked to Irenêo by boyhood friendship as well as by business partnership, took over the direction of these English affairs.

Mauá's financial network in Brazil grew so quickly that when he had decided by 1850 to have his own banking house in Rio he easily connected it intimately with the Manchester firm. In July, 1851, he founded the Banco Mauá e Companhia with a capital of ten thousand *contos*. It did not have the power to issue notes, but in heated debates over its charter in the Chamber of Deputies it had won the right to issue drafts and bills of exchange. These drafts and bills were for a term of five days with a value of not less than two hundred *milreis* (about $100 or £25) and their total at any time could not be more than one third of the bank's actual funds.

Mauá had not hesitated after he had the head office going and the business sprang at once into busy life. In 1853, he established branches in São Paulo and in Rio Grande do Sul. In 1851, the bank's deposits had been valued at 214 contos, and by March, 1854, had grown to 950 contos. In 1851, it had held discounted bills for over one thousand contos; in 1854, for over nine thousand. Only the Banco Commercial, with a total sum of over ten thousand contos in discounted bills in 1853 could equal it in volume of business.

Indeed, this very prosperity precipitated Mauá's first conflict with the Emperor and those who advised him on the financial policy of the Empire. . . .

In the period between 1851 and 1856, Brazil was enjoying exceptional prosperity. There was plenty of gold in the country. But the businessmen complained of only one unfavorable element: there was not enough paper money to keep pace with the demands of business. Caught up in the rapidly developing modern methods of business, they were fast leaving behind the idea that the only real money was specie or cash in hand.

The Minister of the Treasury in 1853, however, was more conservative. The political life of Joaquim José Rodrigues Torres, Viscount Itaboraí, dated from the days of the Regency, and he was therefore a man who carried considerable weight with the Emperor, whose favorite financial adviser he was until his death in 1872. He believed that paper money was a snare and a delusion and that real money was specie. It took much persuasion to make him concede that a bank with the right to issue paper money was a boon to the country, and he certainly did not believe that such a bank should be a private concern.

The result of the constant pressure from businessmen was the reluctant giving of his approval to the creation of the third Bank of Brazil as a bank of issue, to be formed from the forced merger of the Banco Commercial with Mauá's bank. Eighty thousand shares were distributed to the shareholders of the two banks. Thirty thousand were offered for public sale in Rio itself, and when more than three thousand eager buyers presented themselves for this lot, offering 10 per cent above the nominal price, the Treasury made a profit of six hundred contos. The new bank finally began operations on August 10, 1854, under the direction of Viscount Paraná.

The fifty thousand shares that Mauá and his shareholders received for their share in the merger did not reconcile Mauá to the high-handed destruction of his house. At first he could not believe that the government really intended to drive his bank out of business, or, rather, absorb it, but Itaboraí soon made it plain that such was the case. . . .

In the late 1850's and early 1860's, as a man in his forties, Mauá was in his prime. He was a man of average height, with brown hair, a fair skin, penetrating dark eyes under straight eyebrows, a long nose and a firmly closed mouth. His very attitude in standing for his portrait distinguished him from the typical Brazilian public man of his day, the inheritor and perpetuator of traditional gestures. He stood straight, energy apparent in every line of his figure, as if he had only paused for a moment to interrupt his all-absorbing affairs, with a trace of preoccupation still in his expressive yet reserved glance.

In private life, he was a family man of very simple tastes, a devoted husband and father. He never went on his frequent long journeys without taking his wife and some of the older children with him. When he was in Rio and came home in the evening preoccupied with financial affairs, he would walk up and down in his wife's sitting room, thinking aloud in English, for one result of his early training was that English had become his personal language, the language in which he thought, preferred to write his letters and, on provocation, swore.

His working day ended late, in the office he kept next to his bedroom, where he sat and wrote letters for half the night. He began a new day sharp at nine o'clock, reaching his downtown office before the clerks, and often in the press of business he forgot to eat. Especially on the days when the steam packets left for Europe, when he had long letters, full of detailed instructions and advice, to prepare for his partners, MacGregor in London and De Castro in Manchester, he stayed at his desk and the porter brought him food from the nearest hotel.

His memory was prodigious, for he could carry in his head the balance sheets and business details of all his enterprises, which at one time numbered twenty or more. He paid good wages and was liberal with bonuses. The old business habits he had learned with Carruthers remained with him, with the concept that a well-paid employee was worth the money in the loyalty and willingness thus obtained. His manner with his employees was a part of his art of managing his affairs. He never shouted at them, even when work was badly done, but instead questioned and advised, and, if he gave orders, gave them in a low voice. If he was dealing with a man expert in some technical field, like metallurgy or shipbuilding, in which he had only his own practical genius to guide him, he never presumed to give orders. In a subject in which he was really a master, like accountancy, he always had a reasonable explanation and the patience to present it in persuading those who worked under him to do as he said. But in spite of these soft manners, there was never any doubt when he had made up his mind.

A delicate, cheerful courtesy was a part of his nature, and he made no distinction between high and low concerning whom should receive such treatment from him. Intrigue, bad faith, personal attack could make him angry and even violent and abusive, but mistakes and a lack of understanding in those under his orders never awoke in him anything but a tolerant patience. His confidence in himself gave him a steadiness and optimism in dealing with other people that overcame all but his most implacable enemies. Unlike the typical public man of his day, raised in the enervating climate of slavery and a society of manners and privilege, he was not touchy, arrogant, autocratic. He was vain of only one thing: his own abilities to solve financial and economic problems.

. . . His views were based on a simple idea: one does not develop a vast, wild country, full of natural resources but needing an immense amount of initial outlay, with gold that one carries about in one's pocket. . . .

But if the fortunes of the house remained bright, the general economic scene became darker. Three great international firms with important Brazilian holdings — Baring Brothers, Peabody and Company, and Brown, Shipley and Company — were badly affected by the approaching Civil War in the United States. The Brazilian government also felt the repercussions of bad news nearer at hand. To the south, across the border in the old Banda Oriental, trouble was brewing that was to culminate in 1865 in the Paraguayan War. But, despite every sign of approaching danger, most people in Brazil who had put their money in banks were caught without warning by the sudden financial collapse of 1864 — the "September crisis." It was the most extraordinary monetary crisis, said William Scully, the editor of the *Anglo-Brazilian Times,* that had occurred since the days of Law and the South Sea Bubble. The great firm of Souto and Company closed its doors on September 10, 1864. Its bankruptcy was a signal for runs on all the banking houses. The streets were full of people trying to withdraw their money. The police was called out to control the mobs. So great was the effect of the panic that the Bank of Brazil lost its right to issue paper money, which henceforth became a function exclusively of the Treasury.

Mauá, MacGregor and Company was not spared from the run on the banks, yet, with other houses crashing all around, it weathered the storm. In fact, the firm flourished. Perhaps Mauá saw a grim retribution in the panic, for, as he wrote to Ribeiro, unhappily there "did not exist a public spirit sufficiently energetic, on the part of the governed, to require the governors to march in accordance with public opinion." The governors could therefore go on with their own ideas until the results, which were sometimes catastrophic, as in the case of the September Crisis, convinced them of their mistakes.

Ribeiro was in a position to know how Mauá regarded the inflexible and anachronistic financial policy of "the governors," because as early as 1860 Mauá had thus written to him:

> In place of the ranch-owner, the husbandman, the landowner, the lawyer, and all others keeping what they own unproductively in money in their houses, we must induce them to bring these sums, great and little, and deposit them in the Mauá firm and its branches. When the masses understand the immense advantage of drawing credit from their money, what great sums may accumulate in our branches, to be newly employed with advantage, aiding labor and industry, producing conditions of prosperity in different localities, and what benefits will result from this impetus, and how much faster will march the creation of

wealth in our country! In the United States there is a branch bank or agency in all localities where more than fifty houses are built. In England, despite the small size of the country and because of the denser population, there are three thousand seven hundred banks, banking houses and their agencies! which occupy themselves exclusively in concentrating the money capital for useful employment, and from this fact arises the amazing creation of wealth that thus operates to transform these countries day by day. . . .

Optimist as he often appeared to be, he never deceived himself about his Brazil or his place in it. His financial successes in the 1850's and 1860's left him little to desire, but he knew that money alone and the power it gave him were not enough to make for him a comfortable place in the Empire. In Dom Pedro II's Brazil, there was really no place for the combination of gifts and disadvantages that he possessed. To the Emperor himself, Mauá was always a suspect person, a dangerous man because he was powerful and not thoroughly subordinate to the dictates of the Emperor's court. Dom Pedro did not care for moneyed men whose wealth was not tied up in *fazendas* and slaves and who had sources of influence and strength outside the Emperor's sphere of control. Mauá could at times be irritated at the Emperor's coldness and indirectly expressed distrust, but to him the main complaint was the time and energy he had to spend in managing public men, from the Emperor down, whose grasp of finance and whose theories of economic development he thought both rudimentary and out of key with the times and the needs of the country. . . .

With such an attitude, it is not surprising that his greatest successes in creating a banking system based on the deposits of middle-class people were achieved outside Brazil. In Brazil, such a success was necessarily limited, for the middle class was still negligible. In the River Plate countries, however, free of the incubus of slavery, there was more opportunity, and the House of Mauá had never neglected opportunity.

Though doing business in Brazil in spite of the Emperor was a problem large enough to try the patience and exercise the ingenuity of the cleverest banker. Mauá never lacked boldness in looking for money from people who wished speculative profits from what he considered first-rate securities. He wanted capital for investment and he raised it in banking transactions. The loans for his railroads were particularly involved and difficult to manage. The money had to be raised in London for such enterprises; there was not nearly enough capital to be found in Brazil, or at least it was unwilling to come forward. But English investors, putting money into South American railways, were speculating. They did not consider such uses for their money as sound long-term investment and they naturally expected speculative profits. Seen from the other side of the Atlantic, Brazil was a place to make a fortune quickly. Mauá, on the other hand, his head full of the immense economic possibilities of the New World, insisted that such investment could be first-rate and comparable to the best to be found anywhere else in the world. He was aware of the problems presented by slavery, governmental inertia, and a sparse, thinly spread population, but he was also aware of the dangers to sound credit that arose from too much of the get-rich-quick mentality among many of his shareholders.

The wish that he had expressed to Carruthers for leisure for recreation and European travel could not be fulfilled for several years. His manifold interests in the River Plate and, indeed, all his financial affairs were now gradually being drawn into the involvement of the Empire and the whole River Plate region in the preliminaries of the Paraguayan War. In 1864, he apparently saw no fruitful continuation of the existing situation, and, no longer postponing action every few months as each new crisis arose, broke off his affairs abruptly. He had a new scheme in mind — the merger of his house with the London and Brazilian Bank.

Much to the surprise of the international money market, he arranged the merger in London to create a new company to be known as the London, Brazilian and Mauá Bank. It was to be an international house, with branches in Portugal, Argentina, and Uruguay. For Mauá, the merger with one of the most solid banking houses of the period would have consolidated all his banking operations in Argentina, Uruguay, and Brazil. Each of the countries except Brazil approved the charter within a few days, but for effectiveness in Brazil approval by the Emperor's government was also needed.

Perhaps it was the very fact of the merger's concentrating tremendous power in the River Plate countries in Mauá's hands that frightened the Emperor's government. And that government was easily alarmed at this period as it found itself with fewer and fewer ways of escape from the events that were leading it into its first foreign war. The Emperor's Council of State thought about the matter for two months. In the end, the Council, ignoring the considerable strength that the new company would have given the Empire at a time when it needed aid in international affairs, rejected the charter.

It was the final triumph of the men of conservative beliefs in regard to banking who were in the Emperor's government. The subsequent history of Mauá's banking schemes, especially in the River Plate, merely emphasized this rejection by the Brazilian government of his theories of banking practice. Yet his banking house, in spite of consistent official disfavor and because of the vigor and ingenuity that he brought to its management, only collapsed, in 1875, after a long struggle and as a result of the disastrous effects on the Empire itself of the Paraguayan War and the disintegration of the slave-based economy. When that collapse came, there was then left, not merely the debris of Mauá's financial structure but of an epoch in the history of Brazil.

3. Edward A. Hopkins: A Pioneer Promoter in Paraguay

HAROLD F. PETERSON

Professor Emeritus Harold F. Peterson of the State University of New York at Buffalo specialized in the history of the Río de la Plata area and published the standard volume, *Argentina and the United States, 1810–1960* (1964). Here he gives a lively and informative picture of a well-known type in Latin America — the eager-beaver American bent on modernizing what he considers a "backward" society.

It is likely that no American schoolboy ever heard the name of Edward Augustus Hopkins. On the other hand, few Paraguayan students have not learned of Hopkins. Throughout a decade in the middle of the last century Hopkins was a stormy petrel in the politics of the Plata region. Recurrently, for nearly a century, this turbulent son of Vermont has been the dependable whipping-boy of Paraguayan law students, publicists, and public men.

Edward Hopkins gave all fifty of his adult years to opening up and exploiting interior South America. No *El Dorado* lured a *conquistador* more unremittingly than the Plata Valley seduced Hopkins. He became a kind of composite of Cabeza de Vaca, Commodore Perry, James G. Blaine, Henry Meiggs, and Edward Tomlinson. Like Cabeza de Vaca he tramped through the bush and bramble of Southern Brazil to reach Asunción — not once, but three times. Like Commodore Perry, he was an instrument in opening to the world a long-secluded nation — the hermit people of Dr. José Gaspar Rodríguez Francia. A generation before Blaine, Hopkins envisaged a congress of the American nations — with all the confidence, though without the success, of that seasoned politician. With the audacity of Henry Meiggs, he contrived transportation and industrial projects for the South American tropics. No less energetically than Edward Tomlinson did he describe the "new roads to riches in the other Americas."

Before he reached the age of thirty-two, Hopkins had served five years in

From "A Pioneer Promoter in Paraguay" by Harold F. Peterson, *Hispanic American Historical Review,* 22 (1942), pp. 245–261, passim. Reprinted by permission.

the United States Navy, had been twice appointed and recalled as special agent and consul to Paraguay, and had made six trips to South America. He had offered the fruits of his lively imagination to the public officials and business-men of seven nations. He had won, first the hearing, then the enduring venom of two of Latin America's most assertive dictators. He had promoted an American corporation for the exploitation of the reputed riches of the Para-guayan treasure-house. To a decade of such animated activity, the remaining forty years of his career could be but a lively postlude.

The manifold activities of this son of an Episcopalian bishop deepened his distinctive traits. His energy, enthusiasm, and endurance were unbounded. In one period of six years he made three round trips from New York to Asun-ción. On one occasion he rode a thousand miles in nine days; on another he went fifty-six hours with no sustenance but tobacco. His industry and perse-verance minimized obstacles, and cut through political red tape and diplomatic convention that defied his contemporaries. His sharp intelligence and his fund of miscellaneous information inspired faith in his schemes. But Hopkins' activities were never restricted by "excessive modesty," and his advances sometimes approached arrogance. . . . Edward Hopkins was the Yankee entrepreneur at his best and, sometimes, at his worst.

When he was but seventeen, Hopkins had forsaken his too sedate positions as church organist and tutor to enlist as a midshipman in the United States Navy. During the next five years he twice sailed to South America, cruising for extended periods with the Brazil Squadron. Neither the small decks of American warships nor the exotic cities of South America were adequate to contain his repressed vitality. Three times he was brought to the bar of court-martial, for charges ranging from "disobedience of orders" to "scandalous conduct tending to destruction of good morals.". . . Hopkins' unbecoming conduct in the Navy was no bar to the greater plans he had conceived. From his frequent stops at ports of call in the South Atlantic, he had contracted a consuming ambition to visit the recently weaned "children" of Dr. Francia and to explore the upper reaches of the rivers Paraná and Paraguay. Even before his resignation from the Navy he was considered by the Department of State for an appointment as special agent to Asunción. Up to this moment his experiences had consisted of six years as church organist, school teacher, and rebellious midshipman; he was now twenty-two. This was the equipment he offered to the Polk administration. His personal resignation from the Navy was dated June 9th; President Polk made him special agent to Paraguay on June 10th. Surely this was amateur diplomacy at its zenith!

Still, Buchanan apparently knew the man he was sending as the nation's first representative to Asunción. He complimented Hopkins upon his "industry and zeal," then fatherly-like, bade him control his temper and act with utmost prudence. But these admonitions were only the sequel to instructions that imposed a responsibility of considerable weight. Hopkins was to determine the readiness of Paraguay for recognition, always "abstaining from the least intimation that you are a government agent, unless when this shall be clearly necessary to accomplish the objects of your mission."

Such a charge was all Hopkins needed to inject his vigor into the complicated politics of Anglo-French intervention in the Río de la Plata. The mud from his exacting thousand-mile hike from Rio Grande, Brazil, to Asunción was hardly dry on his boots when he violated every counsel Buchanan had given him. In his first conference with President López — on the third day after his arrival — Hopkins assured the dictator "that the next Congress of the United States would recognize the independence of Paraguay." Moreover, he said that he "was authorized to offer the mediation of the United States, between the Governments of Paraguay and Buenos Ayres." During his two months stay in Asunción Hopkins sent only one despatch to Washington, but that was a comprehensive report of some seven thousand words, in which he revealed that he had assumed full diplomatic powers. From Rio de Janeiro, two months later, he assured Buchanan that Paraguay was, "next to our own country, *the most united, the richest, and the strongest nation of the new world.*"

Even these extraordinary indiscretions did not constitute the extent of Hopkins' rashness. Completely ignoring Buchanan's admonitions of prudence, the agent secured the invitation of President López to bear propositions to General Rosas. But Hopkins' impressive scheme to unite the Americas against the Anglo-French interference was destined to collapse on the twin rocks of his own arrogance and Rosas' refusal to accept his overtures. . . .

First in Buenos Aires, then in Montevideo, ambitious designs for a far grander drama were whirling in his brain. He would revive Bolívar's plan for a congress of American states. Such a congress would arrange the definitive boundaries of the South American countries, would "regulate by definite & conclusive laws the rights of all to the navigation of the rivers," and would crush forever the peril of European interference in the New World. "Throughout America," he wrote, "ideas of fraternity & community in interests" would soon abound. The congress would assemble in New Orleans, and Hopkins would procure American warships to convey the delegates. He had already submitted his proposals — or so he claimed — to General Rosas, to the diplomats of Uruguay, Paraguay, Brazil, and Peru, and, through them, to officials of Chile and Colombia. But this grand vision — honest and zealous though its dreamer probably was — faded with Hopkins' early recall to Washington.

Hopkins' career now suddenly changed from that of an amateur diplomat to that of a propagandist. Half of the next five years he spent in Paraguay and adjoining provinces. Twice more he fought his way from Rio Grande to Asunción, swimming rivers, riding hundreds of half-wild horses, sometimes sleeping in the saddle. In Paraguay he came to know the leading citizens, and familiarized himself with all sections of the country. He explored every important tributary of the rivers Paraguay and Alto Paraná, enduring toils and privations, pushing his canoe to the Brazilian frontier. He came to know Paraguay better, perhaps, than any Paraguayan; certainly he was the best-informed American on its politics and resources.

Back in his homeland between South American journeys, Hopkins sought to focus the interest of commercial groups in the vast new regions which awaited their enterprise. Of all the new nations in the valley of the Río de la Plata, he contended, Paraguay was most deserving of American attention. . . .

But Hopkins' glowing reports were much more than empty bleatings. He was the harbinger of several fundamental policies the Department of State was to pursue during the next generation. As early as 1846 he urged the United States to become the champion of the principle of free navigation of international rivers, a policy not officially adopted until seven years later. With reference to the Monroe Doctrine, he complained because President Polk failed "to carry it out as it was originally intended." He pleaded for the appointment of diplomatic representatives to Latin America on some more rational basis than "the reward of sycophancy, relationship, and oftentimes unscrupulous party services, without one single reference to competency for the office." He advocated the despatch of a governmental hydrographic survey long before Lieutenant Thomas J. Page entered the Paraná with the celebrated *Water-Witch*.

Moreover, during these years of travel and writing, Hopkins was laying the groundwork for his own promotional ventures. His frequent contacts with Paraguayan leaders gave him the inside track. He proposed a steamship company which would operate boats on Paraguayan rivers. If he were assured exclusive rights for fifteen years, he said, he could form a company with capital of $300,000. If he were guaranteed a monopoly on the machines and inventions he should introduce, he could organize a manufacturing company. He proposed to found an agricultural school for Paraguayan boys, and was assured free land and exemption from taxation. No one of these early projects materialized.

Meanwhile, Hopkins sought reappointment to the post from which he had once been summarily dismissed. With suppliant letters of application he and his father bombarded President Fillmore, Secretaries Clayton, Webster, and Everett, and members of Congress. The sin of his petulant letter to Rosas, however, continued to militate against him until 1852, when he was finally rewarded with the appointment.

Now, at last, Hopkins was ready for his greatest adventure. Armed with his commission as United States Consul, he would have official position from which to direct his commercial undertakings. Home from his third trip to Paraguay, he set about the organization of a company to underwrite his enterprises. He induced a group of Rhode Island capitalists to charter a corporation, with an initial capitalization of $100,000. The chief purpose of The United States and Paraguay Navigation Company was to build and navigate vessels on the seas and rivers of South America, although it was also authorized to transact any "other lawful business." A prime mover in the corporation was Samuel G. Arnold, lieutenant-governor of Rhode Island, who, in wide travels, had visited Chile and Argentina, where he had formed friendships with Bartolomé Mitre and Domingo F. Sarmiento. Hopkins was made agent for the area south of the equator. He was to receive a salary of $2,000 and five per cent of the profits until his share should amount to $30,000, when he would be paid $10,000 in cash and $20,000 in the stock of the company. Paraguay, of course, was selected as the area of operations.

The first expedition was soon sent out. It was a river steamer, loaded with all manner of the latest American machinery — steam engines, road scrapers, paper-cutting machines, agricultural and blacksmithing supplies, cigar-making equipment, a steam sawmill, a sugar-mill, and a brick-making machine — together with knocked-down ships, stoves, safes, and seventeen varieties of clocks. Several scores of American and Cuban workmen — machinists, cigar-makers, common laborers — accompanied the expedition.

Upon the arrival of the men and equipment in Paraguay, the company immediately acquired land and buildings at Asunción and at San Antonio, ten miles below the capital, where water power could be developed. The company was aided by the promises of López and by public decrees which granted patent rights to foreigners who first introduced implements or manufacturing processes. Various enterprises were soon under way, and by the early months of 1854 business seemed to be thriving. The company put into operation the first steam sawmill in Paraguay, the profits from which were expected to approach $32,725 a year, and the brick-making machine, which it was hoped would turn out ten thousand bricks a day. Land was soon brought under cultivation with the new American implements, and the manufacture of cigars was begun. Hopkins, at last, seemed about to realize his cherished dream. Now he could bring the fruits of civilization to a country, "more worthy of her rights in the family of nations, than any other republic on this Continent save our own," as he had once described Paraguay.

Nevertheless, Hopkins' great hopes for Paraguay — and for himself and his company — were never to be realized. The domain of López, which the Consul had so zealously advertised for ten years, was no longer the hospitable paradise he had envisaged. The Paraguayan people, who had received him with "a joy and a cordiality," now seemed to him "the retrograde slaves of the Jesuits, an infernal mixture of all the original types of the human race."

President López, who had appeared "a man possessing a high degree of talent, much determination of character, good information, some tenacity, and a large share of sensitiveness lest he should be thought ignorant," was now an insolent, raging, old tyrant. The prospective paradise became a sea of troubles, and in less than a year Hopkins had lost his *exequatur* as consul, and all his enterprises had been closed.

The responsibility for this sudden turn in Hopkins' fortunes lay on both sides. By the introduction of improvements from industrial nations President López had planned a new day for his country. But, undoubtedly, he hoped, too, for personal enrichment. Like Gómez in Venezuela, he sought monopolistic control of prospering business enterprises. Moreover, he may have feared that the Americans were bringing his people ideas of liberty and natural rights as well as the skills they so much needed. Therefore, he speedily took steps to break up the company by hedging it about with unreasonable restrictions and by confiscating some of its properties.

On the other hand, because of Hopkins' character and reputation, it seems extremely doubtful that he was entirely guiltless in any quarrel with a jealous dictator. By the testimony of his own employees "he had a swaggering, bullying way with him," and "his deportment was always tyrannical and overbearing." Moreover, the arrogance and enthusiasm which had so often perplexed his associates undoubtedly helped to produce the annoyances that drove his company from Paraguay. At any rate, Hopkins' promotional career in Paraguay was finished.

The sequel to this curious episode was equally grotesque. The United States and Paraguay Navigation Company immediately filed claims with the Department of State, not only for the losses it incurred, but also for the profits it might have made. Other grievances against López accumulated — his attack upon the *Water-Witch* and his failure to ratify a commercial treaty — and by 1858 President Buchanan resolved to liquidate them. He dispatched to the Río de la Plata 19 vessels and 2500 men — the largest naval force sent from American shores up to that time. A special commissioner, James B. Bowlin, accompanied the fleet, only part of which was sent up the river to Asunción. Bowlin negotiated two treaties with Paraguay, one of friendship and commerce, another providing settlement or arbitration of accumulated disputes. Buchanan reported the "happy effect" of the expedition, although the claims of the company were never satisfied. Hopkins had no share in these negotiations.

In the meantime, the frustrated promoter repaired to Argentina, where a more progressive people, recently rid of Rosas, was preparing to grapple with its frontiers. Hopkins, still only thirty-two, quickly plunged into the second phase of his South American promotions. All of his remaining thirty-seven years he devoted to the development of growing Argentina. First he inaugu-

rated steam navigation on the Paraná, sendin
river ports where steamboats had never been
construct and operate wharves and dock f
Corrientes. The Argentine government g
thousand dollars and freed his boats fr
Buenos Aires he was commissioned to cons.
out through the suburbs of Palermo, Belgrano, an
Argentina's need for manpower, in 1857 he presente
memorial to the legislature, incorporating a model law for u.
of immigration. In Argentina Hopkins was restricted by none
which had cut down his enterprises in Paraguay.

During the sixties, in spite of the war with Paraguay, Hopkins continued
receive support for new ventures. The Argentine Congress legalized his
schemes for deepening the channel of the river Capitán and for building a telegraph line to Rosario, Mendoza, and Santiago de Chile. With Hinton R.
Helper, he induced Argentina to authorize an annual subvention of $20,000
to any company which would establish direct steamship communication between New York and Buenos Aires. To support this much-needed project
Hopkins prepared for the American House of Representatives two petitions,
one of which was signed by many prominent South Americans, including
seven supreme court justices of Argentina and Uruguay. The close of the long
Paraguayan War brought forth the most pretentious of all Hopkins' abortive
proposals. He would build a railroad and telegraph line to connect the river
Pilcomayo in the Chaco with Lake Titicaca. Such a road, he argued, would be
far more practical than that to Santiago, which had been proposed, and would
bring into the sphere of Argentine economy several millions of new consumers. But, like so many of Hopkins' schemes, this bubble, too, was destined to
collapse.

During the thirty-seven years of his Argentine residence, Hopkins made at
least five trips to the United States. On each of these he used every opportunity to tell the nation of the importance of improved trade facilities with
South America. He addressed such groups as the New York Chamber of
Commerce; he presented memorials to Congress. Even on his last trip in 1891
he came as secretary of the Argentine delegation to an international railway
conference.

Though he often toiled in vain, Hopkins gave a lifetime to pioneer promotions in the valley of the Río de la Plata. His energy and overzealousness often
brought embarrassment and annoyance to himself, to his associates, and to
his country. As United States Consul, he revealed amateur diplomacy at its
worst. As a propagandist, he shared in one of his country's rediscoveries of
Latin America. As a pioneer promoter, his failures outweighed his achievements. . . .

4. *Henry Meiggs, Yankee Railroad Builder*

J. FRED RIPPY

Americans were in the forefront of railroad building in Latin America, and Henry Meiggs was one of the most colorful and successful, despite the difficult Peruvian terrain in which he worked. Professor Emeritus J. Fred Rippy, one of the *veteranos* in the field, here tells how Meiggs was able to do the job in Peru.

Henry Meiggs was perhaps the most remarkable railroad builder who ever appeared on the Latin-American scene. Landing in Chile early in 1855, a stranger and "like a thief in the night," he obtained his first railway contract three years later, and by the end of 1867 had managed the construction of nearly 200 miles, a good part of it across the Chilean coastal range. In 1868 he went to Peru, where the railway era was at its dawn, with less than 60 miles in operation. At his death in Lima on September 30, 1877, Peru had approximately 1,200 miles of track, more than 700 miles of which had been built under Meiggs's direction. . . .

As early as 1862 the Peruvian minister in Chile had urged that Meiggs should be induced to come to Peru and build its railroads. Five years later Meiggs sent his first proposals to the Peruvian government; but his first railway contract in Peru was not awarded until April 30, 1868, three months after his arrival in Lima. A few weeks afterward he set his engineers and labor crews to work on the Arequipa line.

Already his fame was so great that no further evidence of his capacity was required. Three additional contracts were almost thrust upon him before the Arequipa road was finished. By the end of 1871 the total of his contracts mounted to seven, which required the construction of some 990 miles of railway. The aggregate contract price, in cash and in bonds taken by Meiggs at considerably below par, was more than 130,000,000 Peruvian *soles;* and at

From *Latin America and the Industrial Age* by J. Fred Rippy. (New York: G. P. Putnam & Sons, 1944). Reprinted by permission.

that time a Peruvian sol was almost the equivalent of a United States gold dollar.

Not only did nearly all the Meiggs railways in Peru run up steep canyons into the giant Andes or along lofty plateaus higher than the highest passes of the North American Sierras and Rockies; floods or scarcity of water accentuated these baffling topographical barriers. The seven railroads, their length, and the dates of the contracts signed with Meiggs are as follows:

1. Mollendo to Arequipa, 107 miles, April 30, 1868.
2. Callao to Oroya, 136 miles, December 18, 1869.
3. Arequipa to Puno, 218 miles, December 18, 1869.
4. Pacasmayo to Magdalena, 91 miles, December 13 and 24, 1870.
5. Ilo to Moquegua, 63 miles, January 12, 1871.
6. Chimbote to Huaraz, 166 miles, October 31, 1871.
7. Juliaca to Cuzco, 210 miles, December 2, 1871.

On February 3, 1877, Meiggs was awarded his eighth and last railway contract. It provided for the construction of a railroad from Oroya to the Cerro de Pasco silver and copper mines, a distance of some 85 miles.

Meiggs did not live to complete these railways. Only the Arequipa, the Puno, and the Ilo-Moquegua lines were finished at his death. He had managed, however, to build the major part of the others, except the Juliaca to Cuzco and the Oroya to Cerro de Pasco roads. No doubt he would have built them all if the national finances had not failed. He made a tremendous attack on the formidable Andes; and often he dreamed of laying rails down their rugged eastern slopes to the mighty Amazon.

The most difficult of the Meiggs railroads to build were the lines from Mollendo to Arequipa and from Callao to Oroya. The longest was the line from Arequipa to Puno, with hardly a mile of its 218 lower than 7,500 feet above the sea and with two passes at an altitude of more than 14,500 feet — higher than Pikes Peak or Mount Evans. But the terrain, in this case, was comparatively smooth and the climate fairly healthful.

Most of the Mollendo-Arequipa line had to be pushed through desert and mountains. The cost of providing a water supply for the railway after it was finished was nearly two million soles, to say nothing of the expense of transporting it during the period of construction. The mountains and canyons required, of course, many fills, excavations, curves, bridges, and culverts. On one stretch tons of drifting sand were confronted and mastered. Disease and accidents took a heavy toll of the laborers — 2,000, it is said — and bloody fights sometimes occurred between the Chilean and Peruvian workers.

The Oroya Railway arouses the admiration of all who see it. After a journey over the road in the 1930's Christopher Morley declared that Meiggs "was one of the world's great poets," for he "built a rhyme loftier than

Lycidas." A Peruvian journalist, many years before, had called the enterprise a great hymn with notes running all the tones from "the dull blow of the pickaxe . . . to the shrillest whistle of the locomotive." Some have called it the "railway to the moon." It is, to say the least, a marvelous railroad. The first thirty miles or so run over a gradually rising coastal plain; but the railway then enters the narrow, deep gorge of the River Rímac, as formidable as any on earth. There are 61 bridges, 65 tunnels, and 26 switchbacks; the passenger hardly knows whether he is coming or going. The towering, artistic Verrugas bridge, destroyed years later by an avalanche, was the pride of Peru. The Galera Tunnel runs under Mount Meiggs at an elevation of 15,645 feet. The construction of the road is said to have cost ten thousand lives. Fatal accidents were numerous; mortal fever swept repeatedly through the ranks of the workmen. Only 87 miles were in operation at Meiggs's death.

The gauge of all the Meiggs roads except the Chimbote line was standard: four feet, eight and one half inches. Yet he sent the locomotives higher than they had ever gone before.

Meiggs was the last man to claim exclusive credit for what he did. He was not a trained engineer; he was merely a great executive and a dynamic personality. He imported his experts from all the skillful nations of the world, but mostly from the United States. Some of the managers and technicians were his kinsmen, his brother John G. Meiggs and his nephew Henry Meiggs Keith among them. Prominent among his construction engineers were John L. Thorndike and William H. Cilley. He also employed a few Peruvian technicians who had learned how to build railways. Among his physicians were George A. Ward, Juan Martínez Rosas (a Peruvian), Henry Kinney, Isaac T. Coates, and Edwin R. Heath, who was later to make himself famous by his explorations in the Amazonian jungle. The hard labor was done mostly by Peruvians, Chileans, Bolivians, and Chinese coolies — all employed on a scale seldom witnessed in Latin America. As many as twenty or twenty-five thousand were working for Meiggs at the height of his construction enterprises in 1872.

Meiggs paid his laborers well and was seldom indifferent about their welfare. They were exposed, of course, to the hazards of precipices, landslides, rolling boulders, falling stones, and work trains, as well as to those of climate and disease; but their food was better than they had been accustomed to, and while the medical service was often clearly inadequate it was superior to any they had known before. Of the Chilean *rotos* whom he employed both in their home country and in Peru, Meiggs once said: "I have treated them like men and not like dogs, as is the custom, for they are good if one knows how to direct them." Sometimes his peons were roughly handled by labor bosses or Peruvian soldiers; but that was almost unavoidable in view of the Latin-American attitude toward the lower classes at the time. Criticized in some quarters because of the high death rate among the men working on the Oroya, Meiggs once remarked that people were accustomed to die in Peru as elsewhere. The remark did not signify, however, that he was not grieved. He was careful regarding the food of even the Chinese.

Meiggs had to import nearly everything he used in building his railroads. Peru furnished only the powder for blasting, the rights-of-way, rock for ballast, and a part of the food, medicines, and clothing for the workers. Purchasing agents were located both in England and the United States; but all of the rolling stock and most of the tools, machinery, and materials for construction came from the United States. The bulk of the ties and lumber was shipped in from Washington, Oregon, and California.

Meiggs knew how to win Latin-American sympathies. He was a great dramatist and a great orator. His banquets, celebrations, and charities were long remembered both in Chile and Peru. A Chilean declared that he was a true philanthropist. He distributed thousands of pesos and soles among the poor and the victims of earthquakes. He spent tens of thousands on ceremonies and entertainments, chiefly in connection with his railways.

Work was begun on the Valparaíso-Santiago Railway with a gorgeous fiesta; interrupted to dedicate a monument created by Meiggs himself to the memory of a Chilean Revolutionary hero; concluded with magnificent ceremonies that extended from one end of the line to the other. Trains received the blessings of the higher clergy; Chileans drank toasts to Don Enrique Meiggs the Great Builder; Meiggs compared the Chilean officials of the day with the intrepid founders of the nation, paid glowing tribute to his railway experts, and praised the Chilean *roto* to the skies. For five years thereafter he was a social lion in Chile.

One of the banquets Meiggs gave in Lima during the celebration that marked the beginning of work on the Oroya Railway was attended by 800 of the double cream of society. On that occasion he promised eternal fame to the top-flight officials who were soon to collaborate in unlocking the treasure vaults of the nation and expanding its role in history:

> This happy event proclaims . . . a great social revolution whose triumph and whose benefits are entrusted to the locomotive, that irresistible battering ram of modern civilization. At its pressure will fall those granite masses which physical nature until today has opposed to the . . . aggrandizement of the Peruvian nation. Its whistle will awaken the native race from . . . [its] lethargy. . . .
>
> Peru, ever noble and generous, will . . . inscribe in the book of its glorious history, at the head of its lofty benefactors, the names of all the illustrious citizens to whose indefatigable exertions and patriotism is due the establishment of this iron road.

The Peruvians called Meiggs the "Messiah of the Railway." After the elaborate ceremonies ended he published an apology in the newspapers to those whom "unintentionally" he had failed to invite to the feast. . . .

Two weeks of celebration marked the opening of the Arequipa Railway to public traffic late in 1870. Four steamers were required to transport Meiggs's guests to Mollendo and five trains were employed to haul them up to Arequipa. The president and all the members of the cabinet and Congress were in the party. The locomotives received a sprinkling of holy water from the bishop. Many speeches were made at both ends of the line.

At Mollendo, Meiggs spoke with deep emotion of the cost of his technological triumph. "I do not refer to money," he said. "I speak of the blood and the lives poured out by hundreds of Chileans, Peruvians, Bolivians, Frenchmen, Irishmen, and even Anglo-Americans who have died on this work. Let us drink here in silence to the memory of those who died. . . ." The Bolivian minister called Meiggs a "colossus of fortune and credit," a "contractor without fear," a wizard who had come to Latin America to erase the word "impossible" from all the dictionaries, a miracle-man who had joined Valparaíso and Santiago and brought Arequipa down to the sea, and who would on the morrow place Puno, Cuzco, Oroya, perhaps even distant Potosí and "dear" Sucre "close to the breakers of the Pacific." After the banquet was over the guests began to dance. They spent the night in Mollendo, their temporary abode the railway buildings; they were provided by Meiggs with food, drinks, good mattresses, pillows, sheets, and — for the ladies — even mosquito nets.

In Arequipa, which recently had been gravely damaged by an earthquake, the railway was described as a "present from heaven to compensate for the sufferings of the past." Almighty God, President José Balta, and Henry Meiggs were praised and thanked. Handing Balta the hammer and the last spike, Meiggs declared:

> Be certain, most excellent sir, that as you place the last rail . . . the civilized nations will look upon you as the collaborator of Newton, Fulton, and Humboldt in science, and that the history of the fatherland will open to you its pages alongside those which Bolívar and San Martín occupy, because the steam and the iron with which you are endowing your country affirm also the liberty and independence of nations.

Always less fluent than most Latins, Balta was almost speechless with elation. He gazed about for a moment in silence, then spoke a few words and drove home the golden spike that completed the first of Meiggs's Peruvian railroads. After more feasting, oratory, poetry, and dancing the party returned to Lima, where they left with Meiggs many souvenirs of their profound appreciation.

Such pageantry was never surpassed even in the glittering days of the colonial viceroys. Much of the Latin temperament seems to have entered Meiggs's soul. He was welcomed into the best social circles of Peru.

The closing scene of the Meiggs drama was most impressive. He died poor. The debts he left behind probably exceeded the value of his mortgaged property. He could build no more railways and there was no more money for charity. But twenty or thirty thousand people, the majority of them Peruvian peons, came to witness the last rites. The ceremony took place in La Merced, a Catholic church in Lima, and the body was buried in a private cemetery on the Meiggs estate. As the corpse was being transferred from the church to the flower-covered hearse drawn by four white horses a great crowd of humble people surged forward. They demanded the privilege of bearing the metal casket to the open grave, two or three miles away, and took the heavy burden on their tired shoulders. "Harry" Meiggs must have enjoyed his funeral.

Meiggs's spectacular career is not free from the stain of dishonesty and corruption. Having overspeculated in California real estate, he sold forged warrants and issued unauthorized stock in an effort to save himself and his friends. When his crime was about to be discovered he fled to Chile to avoid prosecution — perhaps even execution — by irate citizens determined to take "justice" into their hands. Although his record in Chile is untainted and it is said that he later made amends for his financial sins in California, he has been accused of resorting to large-scale bribery in Peru. He is also charged with major responsibility for bankrupting the nation.

The millions spent on his railways and others of the period did bring Peru at least to the very brink of bankruptcy; and the unsuccessful war with Chile that followed in 1879–1883 sent the country over the precipice. In 1890 the Peruvian Corporation, an English enterprise organized to bail out European bondholders and salvage the wreck of Peruvian finances, took over most of the railways of the nation. And the Peruvian railways are still dominated by this English corporation. In the midst of their calamities it was natural for the Peruvians to search for a scapegoat, and some of them found one in Henry Meiggs.

Meiggs probably bribed several politicians. Bribery seems to have been the custom in those days, not only in Peru but in a number of other countries. It is likely that Meiggs had to buy some of the Peruvians in order to obtain permission to build the railways. And the drive for bribes, along with the Meiggs pageantry, no doubt contributed to the railway boom. But other factors were involved. The earning capacity of railroads and their power to stimulate economic development were vastly overestimated — perhaps honestly so by many — and enthusiasm for the new means of transportation was already tremendous among the members of the ruling class before Meiggs reached Lima. It is doubtful whether he originated a single railway project upon which he actually began construction. Certainly most of the lines he finished or started had been discussed for years before he arrived in Peru.

The conclusion seems clear. Peruvian leaders must share much of the blame for the nation's calamities. At times Henry Meiggs was a scoundrel; but he had his good traits and he built some remarkable railways. Few have ever accused him of shoddy workmanship or the use of any but the best of materials. His iron roads may not last as long as the Inca palaces; but they are sure to endure for many years.

5. *Emperor of the Caribbean*

JOHN DOS PASSOS

When Minor C Keith died all the newspapers carried his picture, a bright-eyed man with a hawknose and a respectable bay window, and an uneasy look under the eyes.

Minor C. Keith was a rich man's son, born in a family that liked the smell of money, they could smell money half way round the globe in that family.

His Uncle was Henry Meiggs, the Don Enrique of the West Coast. His father had a big lumber business and handled real-estate in Brooklyn;

young Keith was a chip off the old block

(Back in 49 Don Enrique had been drawn to San Francisco by the gold rush. He didn't go prospecting in the hills, he didn't die of thirst sifting alkalidust in Death Valley. He sold outfits to the other guys. He stayed in San Francisco and played politics and high finance until he got in too deep and had to get aboard ship in a hurry.

The vessel took him to Chile. He could smell money in Chile.

He was the capilista yanqui. He'd build the railroad from Santiago to Valparaiso. There were guano deposits on the Chincha Islands. Meiggs could smell money in guano. He dug himself a fortune out of guano, became a power on the West Coast, juggled figures, railroads, armies, the politics of the local caciques and politicos; they were all chips in a huge pokergame. Behind a big hand he heaped up the dollars.

He financed the unbelievable Andean railroads.)

When Tomas Guardia got to be dictator of Costa Rica he wrote to Don Enrique to build him a railroad;

Meiggs was busy in the Andes, a $75,000 dollar contract was hardly worth his while,

so he sent for his nephew Minor Keith.

From: *The 42nd Parallel* by John Dos Passos (New York: Harper & Brothers, 1930), pp. 249–252. Reprinted by permission.

They didn't let grass grow under their feet in that family:
at sixteen Minor Keith had been on his own, selling collars and ties in a clothingstore.
After that he was a lumber surveyor and ran a lumber business.
When his father bought Padre Island off Corpus Christi Texas he sent Minor down to make money out of it.
Minor Keith started raising cattle on Padre Island and seining for fish,
but cattle and fish didn't turn over money fast enough
so he bought hogs and chopped up the steers and boiled the meat and fed it to the hogs and chopped up the fish and fed it to the hogs,
but hogs didn't turn over money fast enough,
so he was glad to be off to Limon.

Limon was one of the worst pestholes on the Caribbean, even the Indians died there of malaria, yellow jack, dysentery.
Keith went back up to New Orleans on the steamer John G. Meiggs to hire workers to build the railroad. He offered a dollar a day and grub and hired seven hundred men. Some of them had been down before in the filibustering days of William Walker.
Of that bunch about twentyfive came out alive.
The rest left their whiskyscalded carcases to rot in the swamps.
On another load he shipped down fifteen hundred; they all died to prove that only Jamaica negros could live in Limon.

Minor Keith didn't die.

In 1882 there were twenty miles of railroad built and Keith was a million dollars in the hole;
the railroad had nothing to haul.
Keith made them plant bananas so that the railroad might have something to haul, to market the bananas he had to go into the shipping business;
this was the beginning of the Caribbean fruittrade.
All the while the workers died of whiskey, malaria, yellow jack, dysentary.
Minor Keith's three brothers died.
Minor Keith didn't die.
He built railroads, opened retail stores up and down the coast in Bluefields, Belize, Limon, bought and sold rubber, vanilla, tortoiseshell, sarsparilla, anything he could buy cheap he bought, anything he could sell dear he sold.
In 1898 in cooperation with the Boston Fruit Company he formed the United Fruit Company that has since become one of the most powerful industrial units in the world.

In 1912 he incorporated the International Railroads of Central America;
all of it built out of bananas;
in Europe and the United States people had started to eat bananas,
so they cut down the jungles through Central America to plant bananas,
and built railroads to haul the bananas,
and every year more steamboats of the Great White Fleet
steamed north loaded with bananas,
and that is the history of the American empire in the Caribbean,
and the Panama canal and the future Nicaragua canal and the marines and
the battleships and the bayonets.

Why that uneasy look under the eyes, in the picture of Minor C. Keith the
pioneer of the fruit trade, the railroad builder, in all the pictures the newspapers carried of him when he died?

Punishment of Slaves in Brazil. Historians have devoted much attention in recent years to the question of whether slaves were better treated in Brazil than in the United States or elsewhere. Though no simple or general answer may be given, since punishment often depended on the individual master and other circumstances, it is clear that slaves were punished in Brazil, as available sources show, including this scene from the Illustrated London News *of 1845.*

SECTION IV

African Slavery in Brazil

Slavery hangs like a dark cloud over the history of Brazil from the sixteenth century until today. Historians contemplating this system of forced labor have concluded that its establishment in America was one of the great ironies: "By the sixteenth and seventeenth centuries Europeans had arrived at the greatest dualism of them all—the momentous division between an increasing devotion to liberty in Europe and an expanding mercantile system based on Negro labor in America."[1]

The fundamental importance of African slavery in the history of Brazil did not diminish with the passage of time. Many of the most important movements and events of the nineteenth century—immigration, the growth of republicanism, the onset of modernization, the War of the Triple Alliance, the fall of the monarchy—were directly or indirectly related to the fate of the "peculiar institution."

Today more attention than ever is devoted to assessments of the true nature of slavery and its continuing influence on the life of Latin America's largest and most populous nation. A sophisticated school of social anthropologists and historians in Brazil is producing a large and interesting literature on many diverse aspects of slavery, and so much attention is being paid to the comparison of African slavery in Brazil with the institution in other parts of the Americas that the field has become a flourishing growth industry.

The intense desire to learn about slavery and Brazilian society began in the early years of the nineteenth century. The many travelers from Europe and the United States who visited this huge country almost always discoursed upon African slavery, in much the same way that visitors to our antebellum South did. No Latin American country has a richer travel literature in the nineteenth century than Brazil. A representative collection of writings has been selected to illustrate the varying attitudes manifested toward slavery (Readings 1–4). The few samples given here will surely whet the reader's appetite for more.

---

[1] David Brion Davis, *The Problem of Slavery in Western Culture* (Ithaca, N.Y.: 1970), p. 108.

121

Travelers see only a part of the reality they attempt to describe, and they are often affected in their judgements by their personal convictions. It remains for the historian to sift all essential sources to present a more comprehensive and evaluative view of the past. One of the first to consider the role of slavery was Gilberto Freyre, the gifted Pernambucan writer who almost singlehandedly revolutionized the writing of Brazilian history in the years since 1930. His major book, *The Masters and the Slaves,* was first published in English in 1946, and slightly abridged in a paperback edition in 1964. Freyre's thesis that slavery was relatively mild in Brazil when compared with slavery in the United States and elsewhere in the Americas is reflected in his essay "Social Life in Brazil in the Middle of the Nineteenth Century," which was based on his Master's thesis written at Columbia University (Reading 5).

More recently historians such as Robert Conrad have argued that Freyre's conclusions about the nature of slavery in Brazil are not supported by the facts.[2] The University of São Paulo has produced a vigorous school of sociologists and historians whose researches have laid the basis for a new approach to the complicated study of African slavery. One of these scholars, Emilia Viotti da Costa, has concluded that the real emancipation of blacks from their slave status is "a process still under way," a view that is shared by many other Brazilian scholars (Reading 6). The debate will doubtless grow in intensity, and may well lead to a reevaluation of the history of the Western Hemisphere.

[2] For more detailed information on this and other aspects of this complicated subject, see his monograph, *The Destruction of Brazilian Slavery 1850–1888* (Berkeley: University of California Press, 1973). See also Robert Brent Toplin, *The Abolition of Slavery in Brazil* (New York: Atheneum, 1972).

1. Slaves in Brazil Have More Tolerable Lives than Those in Other Countries

HENRY KOSTER

Henry Koster was an English merchant who traveled about Brazil during the period 1808–1818, principally in the northeast. His view that Brazilian slaves were less abused than those in the British West Indies served as an important source for Frank Tannenbaum and others who supported this interpretation. However, Koster also attested to the brutality of the slave trade and noted the large number of suicides among Brazilian slaves.

The general equity of the laws regarding free persons of colour in the Portuguese South American possessions, has been, to a certain degree, extended to that portion of the population which is in a state of slavery: and the lives of the slaves of Brazil have been rendered less hard and less intolerable than those of the degraded beings who drag on their cheerless existence under the dominion of other nations. The Brazilian slave is taught the religion of his master: and hopes are held out of manumission from his own exertions: but still he is a slave, and must be guided by another man's will; and this feeling alone takes away much of the pleasure which would be felt from the faithful discharge of his duty, if it was voluntarily performed. . . .

Slaves, however, in Brazil, have many advantages over their brethren in the British colonies. The numerous holidays of which the Catholic religion enjoins the observance, give to the slave many days of rest or time to work for his own profit: thirty-five of these, and the Sundays besides, allow him to employ much of his time as he pleases. Few masters are inclined to restrain the right of their slaves to dispose of these days as they think fit: or, at any rate, few dare, whatever their inclinations may be, to brave public opinion in depriving them of the intervals from work which the law has set apart as their own, that their lives may be rendered less irksome. The time which is thus afforded,

From *Travels in Brazil in the Years from 1809–1815* by Henry Koster (Philadelphia: M. Carey and Son, 1817), 2, pp. 189–217, passim.

enables the slave, who is so inclined, to accumulate a sum of money: however this is by law his master's property, from the incapability under which a slave labours of possessing any thing which he can by right call his own. But I believe there is no instance on record in which a master attempted to deprive his slave of these hard-earned gains. The slave can oblige his master to manumit him, on tendering to him the sum for which he was first purchased, or the price for which he might be sold, if that price is higher than what the slave was worth at the time he was first bought. This regulation, like every one that is framed in favour of slaves, is liable to be evaded, and the master sometimes does refuse to manumit a valuable slave: and no appeal is made by the sufferer, owing to the state of law in that country, which renders it almost impossible for the slave to gain a hearing; and likewise this acquiescence in the injustice of the master proceeds from the dread, that if he was not to succeed, he would be punished, and that his life might be rendered more miserable than it was before. Consequently a great deal depends upon the inclinations of the master, who will, however, be very careful in refusing to manumit, owing to the well-known opinion of every priest in favour of this regulation, to the feelings of the individuals of his own class in society, and to those of the lower orders of people: and likewise he will be afraid of losing his slave. He may escape with his money: and the master will then run much risk of never seeing him again, particularly if the individual is a creole slave. In general, therefore, no doubts are urged, when application is made for manumission by a slave to his master; who is indeed oftentimes prepared for it by the habits of industry and regularity of his slave, and by common report among the other slaves and free persons upon the estate, that the individual in question is scraping together a sum of money for this purpose. The master might indeed deprive the slave of the fruits of his labour: but this is never thought of; because the slave preserves his money in a secret place, or has entrusted it to some person upon whom he can depend, and would suffer any punishment rather than disclose the spot in which his wealth lies concealed. A still more forcible reason than any other, for the forbearance of the master, is to be found in the dread of acting against public opinion: in the shame which would follow the commission of such an act; and perhaps the natural goodness which exists in almost every human being, would make him shun such gross injustice, would make him avoid such a deed of baseness.

A slave is often permitted by his owner to seek a master more to his liking; for this purpose a note is given, declaring that the bearer has leave to enter into the service of any one, upon the price which the master demands being paid by the purchaser. With this the slave applies to any individual of property whom he may wish to serve; owing to having heard a good report of his character towards his slaves, or from any other cause. This is a frequent practice; and at least admits the possibility of escape from a severe state of bondage to one that is less irksome.

A considerable number of slaves are manumitted at the death of their masters: and indeed some persons of large property fail not to set at liberty a few of them during their own life-time. A deed of manumission, however simply it may be drawn out, cannot be set aside. A register of these papers is preserved at the office of every notary-public, by which any distress that might be occasioned by the loss of the originals is provided against; for the copy, of course, holds good in law. A slave who has brought into the world, and has reared ten children, ought to be free, for so the law ordains. But this regulation is generally evaded: and besides, the number of children is too great for many women to be benefited by it. The price of a new-born child is 5*l.* (20,000 *mil-reis*), and the master is obliged to manumit the infant at the baptismal font, on the sum being presented. In this manner, a considerable number of persons are set at liberty; for the smallness of the price enables many freemen who have had connections with female slaves to manumit their offspring; and instances occur of the sponsors performing this most laudable act. Not unfrequently female slaves apply to persons of consideration to become sponsors to their children, in the hopes that the pride of these will be too great to allow of their god-children remaining in slavery. Thus by their own exertions, by the favour of their masters, and by other means, the individuals who gain their freedom annually, are very numerous. . . .

All slaves in Brazil follow the religion of their masters; and notwithstanding the impure state in which the Christian church exists in that country, still such are the beneficent effects of the Christian religion, that these, its adopted children, are improved by it to an infinite degree; and the slave who attends to the strict observance of religious ceremonies, invariably proves to be a good servant. The Africans, who are imported from Angola, are baptized in lots before they leave their own shores: and on their arrival in Brazil they are to learn the doctrines of the church, and the duties of the religion into which they have entered. These bear the mark of the royal crown upon their breasts, which denotes that they have undergone the ceremony of baptism, and likewise that the king's duty has been paid upon them. The slaves which are imported from other parts of the coast of Africa, arrive in Brazil unbaptized, and before the ceremony of making them Christians can be performed upon them, they must be taught certain prayers, for the acquirement of which one year is allowed to the master, before he is obliged to present the slave at the parish church. The law is not always strictly adhered to as to the time, but it is never evaded altogether. The religion of the master teaches him that it would be extremely sinful to allow his slave to remain a heathen: and indeed the Portuguese and Brazilians have too much religious feeling to let them neglect any of the ordinances of their church. The slave himself likewise wishes to be made a Christian; for his fellow-bondmen will, otherwise, in every squabble or trifling disagreement with him, close their string of opprobrious epithets with the name of *pagam* (pagan). The unbaptized negro feels that he is considered as an inferior being: and although he may not be aware of the value which the whites place upon baptism, still he knows that the stigma for which he is upbraided, will be removed by it; and therefore he is desirous of being made equal to his companions. The Africans who have been long imported, imbibe a Catholic feeling; and appear to forget that they were once in the same situation themselves. The slaves are not asked whether they will be baptized or not. Their entrance into the Catholic church is treated as a thing of course: and indeed they are not considered as members of society, but rather as brute animals, until they can lawfully go to mass, confess their sins, and receive the Sacrament.

The slaves have their religious brotherhoods as well as the free persons: and the ambition of the slave very generally aims at being admitted into one of these, and at being made one of the officers and directors of the concerns of the brotherhood. Even some of the money which the industrious slave is collecting for the purpose of purchasing his freedom, will oftentimes be brought out of its concealment for the decoration of a saint, that the donor may become of importance in the society to which he belongs. The negroes have one invocation of the Virgin (or I might almost say one virgin), which is peculiarly their own. Our Lady of the Rosary is even sometimes painted with a black face and hands. It is in this manner that the slaves are led to place their attention upon an object in which they soon take an interest, but from which no injury can proceed towards themselves, nor can any through its means be by them inflicted upon their masters. Their ideas are removed from any thought of the customs of their own country; and are guided into a channel of a totally different nature, and completely unconnected with what is practised there. . . .

The Portuguese language is spoken by all the slaves: and their own dialects are allowed to lie dormant until they are by many of them quite forgotten. No compulsion is resorted to, to make them embrace the habits of their masters: but their ideas are insensibly led to imitate and adopt them. The masters at the same time imbibe some of the customs of their slaves: and thus the superior and his dependent are brought nearer to each other. I doubt not that the system of baptizing the newly imported negroes, proceeded rather from the bigotry of the Portuguese in former times than from any political plan: but it has had the most beneficial effects. The slaves are rendered more tractable. Besides being better men and women, they become more obedient servants. They are brought under the control of the priesthood: and even if this was the only additional hold which was gained by their entrance into the church, it is a great engine of power which is thus brought into action. . . .

The slaves of Brazil are regularly married according to the forms of the Catholic church. The banns are published in the same manner as those of free persons: and I have seen many happy couples (as happy at least as slaves can be) with large families of children rising around them. The masters encourage marriages among their slaves; for it is from these lawful connections that they can expect to increase the number of their creoles. A slave cannot marry without the consent of his master; for the vicar will not publish the banns of marriage without this sanction. It is likewise permitted that slaves should marry free persons. If the woman is in bondage, the children remain in the same state: but if the man is a slave, and she is free, their offspring is also free. A slave cannot be married until the requisite prayers have been learnt, the nature of confession be understood, and the Sacrament can be received. Upon the estates the master or manager is soon made acquainted with the predilections of the slaves for each other: and these being discovered, marriage is forthwith determined upon, and the irregular proceedings are made lawful. In towns there is more licentiousness among the negroes, as there is among all other classes of men. . . .

The great proportion of men upon many of the estates, produces, of necessity, most mischievous consequences. A supply is requisite to keep up the number of labourers. The women are more liable to misconduct, and the men imbibe unsettled habits. But if an adequate number of females are placed upon the estate, and the slaves are trained and taught in the manner which is practised upon well-regulated plantations, the negroes will be as correct in their behaviour, as any other body of men: and perhaps their conduct may be less faulty than that of other descriptions of persons, who have less to occupy their time, though their education may be infinitely superior. That many men and many women will be licentious, has been and is still the lot of human nature, and not the peculiar fault of the much injured race of which I speak.

I shall now state the manner in which the Africans are transported from their own country to Brazil, and the disposal of them on their arrival in South America; the characters of the several African nations with which the ships are loaded; the condition of those who are employed in Recife — upon the sugar-plantations — in the Mata or cotton estates — and in the Sertam or cattle districts.

As the voyage from the coast of Africa to the opposite shores of South America is usually short, for the winds are subject to little variation, and the weather is usually fine, the vessels which are employed in this traffic are generally speaking small, and are not of the best construction. The situation of captain or master of a slave ship is considered of secondary rank in the Portuguese merchant-service: and the persons who are usually so occupied, are vastly inferior to the generality of the individuals who command the large and regular trading vessels between Europe and Brazil. The slave ships were formerly crowded to a most shocking degree; nor was there any means of preventing this. But a law has been passed for the purpose of restricting the number of persons for each vessel. However, I more than suspect, that no attention is paid to this regulation — that means are made use of to evade the law. On the arrival at Recife of a cargo of slaves, the rules of the port direct that they shall be disembarked, and taken to St. Amaro, which is an airy spot, and sufficiently distant from the town to prevent the admittance of any infectious disorder, if any such should exist among the newly imported negroes; and yet the place is at a convenient distance for the purchasers, St. Amaro being situated immediately opposite to Recife, upon the inland bank of the expanse of waters which is formed by the tide, on the land side of the town. However, like many others, this excellent arrangement is not attended to: and even if the slaves are removed for a few days to St. Amaro, they are soon conveyed back to the town. Here they are placed in the streets before the doors of the owners, regardless of decency, of humanity, and of due attention to the general health of the town. The small pox, the yaws, and other complaints have thus frequent opportunities of spreading. It is probable, that if the climate was not so very excellent as it is, this practice would be discontinued; but if it was not put a stop to, and the country was subject to pestilential complaints, the town would not be habitable.

In the day-time, some of the streets of Recife are in part lined with miserable beings, who are lying or sitting promiscuously upon the foot-path, sometimes to the number of two or three hundred. The males wear a small piece of blue cloth round their waists, which is drawn between the legs and fastened behind. The females are allowed a larger piece of cloth, which is worn as a petticoat: and sometimes a second portion is given to them, for the purpose of covering the upper parts of the body. The stench which is created by these assemblages is almost intolerable to one who is unaccustomed to their vicinity; and the sight of them, good God! is horrid beyond any thing. These people, do not, however, seem to feel their situation, any farther than that it is uncomfortable. Their food consists of salt meat, the flour of the mandioc, beans, and plantains occasionally. The victuals for each day are cooked in the middle of the street in an enormous caldron. At night, they are driven into one or more warehouses: and a driver stands to count them as they pass. They are locked in: and the door is again opened at day-break on the following morning. The wish of these wretched creatures to escape from this state of inaction and discomfort is manifested upon the appearance of a purchaser. They start up willingly, to be placed in the row for the purpose of being viewed and handled like cattle: and on being chosen they give signs of much pleasure. I have had many opportunities of seeing slaves bought; for my particular friends at Recife lived opposite to slave-dealers. I never saw any demonstrations of grief at parting from each other: but I attributed this to the dread of punishment, if there had been any flow of feeling, and to a resigned or rather despairing sensation, which checks any shew of grief, and which has prepared them for the worst, by making them indifferent to whatever may occur: besides, it is not often that a family is brought over together: the separation of relatives and friends has taken place in Africa. It is among the younger part of the assemblage of persons who are exposed for sale, that pleasure is particularly visible at the change of situation, in being removed from the streets of the town; the negroes of more advanced age do whatever the driver desires, usually with an unchanged countenance. I am afraid that very little care is taken to prevent the separation of relations who may chance to come over in the same ship: and any consideration on this point lies entirely with the owner of the cargo. A species of relationship exists between the individuals who have been imported in the same ship. They call each other *malungos:* and this term is much regarded among them. The purchaser gives to each of his newly bought slaves a large piece of baize and a straw hat; and as soon as possible marches them off to his estate. I have often in travelling met with many parties going up to their new homes, and have observed that they were usually cheerful — any thing is better than to sit at the door of the slave merchant in Recife. The new master, too, does everything in his power to keep them in good humour at first, whatever his conduct may afterwards be towards them. . . .

The slaves who are employed in Recife, may be divided into two classes; household slaves, and those which pay a weekly stipend to their owners, proceeding from the earnings of some employment which does not oblige them to be under the immediate eye of the master. The first class have little chance of gaining their freedom by their own exertions; and are subject to the caprice and whims of their superiors. But some few are manumitted by the kindness of those whom they have served: and the clothing and food which is afforded to them is generally better than that which the other class obtains. This second class consists of joiners, shoemakers, canoemen, porters, &c. and these men may acquire a sufficient sum of money to purchase their own freedom, if they have the requisite prudence and steadiness to allow their earnings to accumulate. But too often, the inducements to expend them foolishly are sufficiently powerful, to make these people swerve from their purpose. They generally earn more each day than the master exacts, and have besides the Sundays and holidays as their own; and if the slave feeds and clothes himself, to these are added the Sundays of every week. I think that allowing largely for him to supply every thing requisite for his support and decent appearance, and yet something for what may to a person in such a rank in life be accounted luxury, a slave so circumstanced may in ten years purchase his freedom. If his value is great, it is because his trade is lucrative; so that these things keep pace with each other. The women have likewise some employments by which they may be enabled to gain their liberty. They make sweetmeats and cakes, and are sent out as cooks, nurses, house-keepers, &c.

Creole negroes and mulattos are generally accounted quicker in learning any trade than the Africans. This superior aptitude to profit by instruction is doubtless produced by their acquaintance from infancy with the manners, customs, and language of their masters. From the little experience, however, which I have had, and from the general remarks which I have gathered from others, who might be judged better acquainted than myself with slaves, I think that an African who has become cheerful, and seems to have forgotten his former state, is a more valuable slave than a creole negro or mulatto. He will be generally more fit to be trusted. Far from the latter submitting quietly to the situation in which they have been born, they bear the yoke of slavery with impatience. The daily sight of so many individuals of their own casts, who are in a state of freedom, makes them wish to be raised to an equality with them: and they feel at every moment their unfortunate doom. The consideration with which the free person of mixed casts are treated, tends to increase the discontent of their brothers who are in slavery. The Africans do not feel this; for they are considered by their creole brethren in colour, as being so completely inferior, that the line which, by public opinion, has been drawn between them, makes the imported slave feel towards the creoles as if they had not been originally of the same stock.

Miserable objects are at times seen in Recife, asking alms in various quarters of the town, aged and diseased. Some of these persons have been slaves: and when, from infirmity they have been rendered useless, their masters have manumitted them; and thus being turned away to starve in their old age, or in a crippled state, their only resource is to beg in the public streets. These instances of gross injustice and depravity in masters, are not many: but that they should occur, is sufficient to cause the aid of law to be called in, that the *existence* of them should be prevented.

2. *"A Horrid Traffic": Life on a Slave Ship*

ROBERT WALSH

Despite the efforts of the British who, for a variety of humanitarian and commercial reasons, applied external pressure on Portugal to abolish the slave trade, the trade between Africa and Brazil lingered on until 1850—albeit with a series of restrictions. In 1810 England forced Portugal to limit the trade to her colonies in Africa. In 1815 all trade was restricted to the colonies south of the equator. In 1817 the British navy received permission to stop and search Portuguese vessels believed to be violating the conditions imposed on the trade.

Robert Walsh, an English clergyman, who lived in Brazil during 1828 and 1829, here recounts an incident in which a British ship halted and inspected a Portuguese slave ship on the high seas. Only a year before, the Brazilians had agreed to terminate all trade by 1829. They did not honor this agreement for another twenty years.

After about an hour standing towards us she [a suspected slaver] tacked, as if not liking our appearance, and alarmed at our approach, and stood away directly before the wind. We crowded all sail in chase. The breeze freshened, and at four bells we had neared so much that we had a distinct view of her hull, and we were now certain she was a slaver, and also perhaps a pirate, and that she had at least five or six hundred slaves on board. This opinion was formed on that sagacity that a long experience on the coast of Africa, and a familiar acquaintance with such vessels had imparted. We were, therefore, all on the alert, exulting in the prospect of liberating so many fellow-creatures, and bartering and bargaining for our share of the ransom-money, for it seemed almost certain that she could not escape us. She resembled, however, a fox doubling in all directions, and every moment seeming to change her course to avoid us.

The captain now ordered a gun to be fired to leeward, and the English union flag to be hoisted; we had the wind right aft, and were running right down upon her, distant about four miles. She took no notice of our gun and flag, and another was fired with as little effect. Orders were then given that one of the long guns at the bows should be shotted and sent after her. We all crowded to the forecastle to witness the effect. The ball went ricochetting along the waves, and fell short of her stern; in a little time afterwards she hoisted a flag, which we perceived was Brazilian. Two shot more were sent after her with as little effect, and the wind began dying away, our coming up with her before dark seemed very doubtful. To increase the way of the ship, the long guns of the bows were brought midships, but without effect; we were evidently dropping astern. We kept a sharp look-out with intense interest, leaning over the netting, and silently handing the glass to one another, as if a word spoken would impede our way. At length the shades of evening closed on us, and we applied night-glasses. For some time we kept her in view on the horizon, but about eight o'clock she totally disappeared.

All night we were pointing our glasses in the direction in which she lay, and caught occasional glimpses of her, and when morning dawned, we saw her like a speck on the horizon, standing due north. We followed in the same track, the breeze soon increased our way to eight knots, and we had the pleasure to find we were every moment gaining on her. We again sent long shot after her, but she only crowded the more sail to escape; and we observed her slinging her yards, that is, hanging them with additional cords, that they might be supported if the proper lifts were shot away.

We could now discern her whole equipment; her gun streak was distinctly

From *Notices of Brazil in 1828 and 1829* by Robert Walsh (London: Richardson, Lord & Holdbrook, 1831) pp. 476–494, passim.

seen along the water, with eight ports of a side; and it was the general opinion that she was a French pirate and slaver, notorious for her depredations. At twelve o'clock, we were entirely within gunshot, and one of our long bow-guns was again fired at her. It struck the water alongside, and then, for the first time, she showed a disposition to stop. While we were preparing a second, she hove-to, and in a short time we were alongside her, after a most interesting chase of thirty hours, during which we ran 300 miles.

The first object that struck us, was an enormous gun, turning on a swivel, on deck, the constant appendage of a pirate; and the next, were large kettles for cooking, on the bows, the usual apparatus of a slaver. Our boat was now hoisted out, and I went on board with the officers. When we mounted her decks, we found her full of slaves. She was called the *Veloz,* commanded by Captain José Barbosa, bound to Bahia. She was a very broad-decked ship, with a mainmast, schooner-rigged, and behind her foremast was that large formidable gun, which turned on a broad circle of iron, on deck, and which enabled her to act as a pirate, if her slaving speculation had failed. She had taken in, on the coast of Africa, 336 males, and 226 females, making in all 562, and had been out seventeen days, during which she had thrown over-board fifty-five. The slaves were all enclosed under grated hatchways, between decks. The space was so low, that they sat between each other's legs, and stowed so close together, that there was no possibility of their lying down, or at all changing their position, by night or day. As they belonged to, and were shipped on account of different individuals, they were all branded, like sheep, with the owners' marks of different forms,

These were impressed under their breasts, or on their arms, and, as the mate informed me, with perfect indifference, "queimados pelo ferro quento — burnt with the red-hot iron." Over the hatchway stood a ferocious looking fellow, with a scourge of many twisted thongs in his hand, who was the slave-driver of the ship, and whenever he heard the slightest noise below, he shook it over them, and seemed eager to exercise it. I was quite pleased to take this hateful badge out of his hand, and I have kept it ever since, as a horrid memorial of reality, should I ever be disposed to forget the scene I witnessed.

As soon as the poor creatures saw us looking down at them, their dark and melancholy visages brightened up. They perceived something of sympathy and kindness in our looks, which they had not been accustomed to, and feeling instinctively that we were friends, they immediately began to shout and clap their hands. One or two had picked up a few Portuguese words and cried out "Viva! viva!" The women were particularly excited. They all held up their arms, and when we bent down and shook hands with them, they could not contain their delight; they endeavoured to scramble upon their knees, stretching up to kiss our hands, and we understood that they knew we were come to liberate them. Some, however, hung down their heads in apparently hopeless dejection; some were greatly emaciated, and some, particularly children, seemed dying.

But the circumstance which struck us most forcibly, was, how it was possible for such a number of human beings to exist, packed up and wedged together as tight as they could cram, in low cells, three feet high, the greater part of which, except that immediately under the grated hatchways, was shut out from light or air, and this when the thermometer, exposed to the open sky, was standing in the shade, on our deck, at 89°. The space between decks was divided into two compartments, 3 feet 3 inches high; the size of one was 16 feet by 18, and of the other 40 by 21; into the first were crammed the women and girls; into the second, the men and boys: 226 fellow-creatures were thus thrust into one space 288 feet square; and 336 into another space 800 feet square, giving to the whole an average of 23 inches, and to each of the women not more than 13 inches, though many of them were pregnant. We also found manacles and fetters of different kinds, but it appears that they had all been taken off before we boarded.

The heat of these horrid places was so great, and the odour so offensive, that it was quite impossible to enter them, even had there been room. They were measured as above when the slaves had left them. The officers insisted that the poor suffering creatures should be admitted on deck to get air and water. This was opposed by the mate of the slaver, who, from a feeling that they deserved it, declared they would murder them all. The officers, however, persisted, and the poor beings were all turned up together. It is impossible to conceive the effect of this eruption — 507 fellow-creatures of all ages and sexes, some children, some adults, some old men and women, all in a state of total nudity, scrambling out together to taste the luxury of a little fresh air and water. They came swarming up, like bees from the aperture of a hive, till the whole deck was crowded to suffocation, from stem to stern; so that it was impossible to imagine where they could all have come from, or how they could have been stowed away. On looking into the places where they had been crammed, there were found some children next the sides of the ship, in the places most remote from light and air; they were lying nearly in a torpid state, after the rest had turned out. The little creatures seemed indifferent as to life or death, and when they were carried on deck, many of them could not stand.

After enjoying for a short time the unusual luxury of air, some water was brought; it was then that the extent of their sufferings was exposed in a fearful manner. The all rushed like maniacs towards it. No entreaties, or threats, or blows, could restrain them; they shrieked, and struggled, and fought with one another, for a drop of this precious liquid, as if they grew rabid at the sight of it. There is nothing which slaves, in the mid-passage, suffer from so much as want of water. It is sometimes usual to take out casks filled with sea water, as ballast, and when the slaves are received on board, to start the casks, and refill them with fresh. On one occasion, a ship from Bahia neglected to change the contents of the casks, and on the mid-passage found, to their horror, that they were filled with nothing but salt water. All the slaves on board perished! We could judge the extent of their sufferings from the afflicting sight we now saw. When the poor creatures were ordered down again, several of them came, and pressed their heads against our knees, with looks of the greatest anguish, at the prospect of returning to the horrid place of suffering below.

It was not surprising that they should have endured much sickness and loss of life, in their short passage. They had sailed from the coast of Africa on the 7th of May, and had been out but seventeen days, and they had thrown overboard no less than fifty-five, who had died of dysentery and other complaints, in that space of time, though they had left the coast in good health. Indeed, many of the survivors were seen lying about the decks in the last stage of emaciation, and in a state of filth and misery not to be looked at. Evenhanded justice had visited the effects of this unholy traffic, on the crew who were engaged in it. Eight or nine had died, and at that moment six were in hammocks on board, in different stages of fever. This mortality did not arise from want of medicine. There was a large stock ostentatiously displayed in the cabin, with a manuscript book, containing directions as to the quantities; but the only medical man on board to prescribe it was a black, who was as ignorant as his patients.

While expressing my horror at what I saw, and exclaiming against the state of this vessel for conveying human beings, I was informed by my friends, who had passed so long a time on the coast of Africa, and visited so many ships, that this was one of the best they had seen. The height, sometimes, between decks, was only eighteen inches; so that the unfortunate beings could not turn round, or even on their sides, the elevation being less than the breadth of their shoulders; and here they are usually chained to the decks, by the neck and legs. In such a place, the sense of misery and suffocation is so great, that the negroes, like the English in the black-hole at Calcutta, are driven to frenzy. They had, on one occasion, taken a slave vessel in the river Bonny: the slaves were stowed in the narrow space between decks, and chained together. They heard a horrid din and tumult among them, and could not imagine from what cause it proceeded. They opened the hatches, and turned them up on deck. They were manacled together, in twos and threes. Their horror may well be conceived, when they found a number of them in different stages of suffocation; many of them were foaming at the mouth, and in the last agonies — many were dead. A living man was sometimes dragged up, and his companion was a dead body; sometimes, of the three attached to the same chain, one was dying, and another dead. The tumult they had heard, was the frenzy of those suffocating wretches in the last stage of fury and desperation, struggling to extricate themselves. When they were all dragged up, nineteen were irrecoverably dead. Many destroyed one another, in the hopes of procuring room to breathe; men strangled those next to them, and women drove nails into each other's brains. Many unfortunate creatures, on other occasions, took the first opportunity of leaping overboard, and getting rid, in this way, of an intolerable life.

They often found the poor negroes impressed with the strongest terror at their deliverers. The slave dealers persuaded them that the English were cannibals, who only took them to eat them. When undeceived, their joy and gratitude were proportionately great. Sometimes, a mortal malady had struck them before they were captured, from which they could never recover. They used to lie down in the water of the lee scuppers, and notwithstanding every care, pined away to skin and bone, wasted with fever and dysentery; and, when at length they were consigned to the deep, they were mere skeletons. Unlike other impressions, habit had not rendered these things familiar, or hardened the hearts of my companions. On the contrary, the scenes they had witnessed made them only more susceptible of pity on the present occasion; and the sympathy and kindness they now showed these poor slaves, did credit to the goodness of their hearts.

When I returned on board the frigate, I found the captain of the slaver pacing the deck in great agitation; sometimes clasping his hands, and occasionally requesting a drink of water; and when asked whether he would have any other refreshment, he replied, turning his head and twisting his mouth, with an expression of intense annoyance, "nada, nada — nothing, nothing." Meantime, his papers were rigidly examined, to ascertain if they bore out his story. He said that he was a Brazilian, from Bahia, and that his traffic was strictly confined to the south of the line, where, by treaty, it was yet lawful; that he made Bengo bay, on the coast of Angola, nine degrees south of the line, traded along that coast, and took in all his slaves at Cabinda, and was returning directly home; that his ship had only received on board the number allowed by law, which directs that five slaves may be taken in for every two tons; and that his complement was under that allowance. All this, his chart and log corresponded with. As the tale, however could be easily fabricated, and papers were written to correspond, a strict scrutiny was made into other circumstances. Some of the poor slaves said they came from Badagry, a place in six degrees north latitude. Two of the crew, whose persons were recognized by some of our people, confessed they were left at Whida, by another ship, where they had been seen; and above all, the slave captain had endeavoured to escape by every means in his power, as conscious of his guilt; and it was not till after a persevering chase of 300 miles that he was at length taken, and that too, sailing in a northerly direction, when his course to Bahia would have been south-west. He said, in reply, that the slaves might have been originally from Badagry, and sent, as is usual, to Cabinda, where he bought them; that the two men entered at Cabinda, to which they had been brought in a Spanish ship from Whida; and finally, that he did not bring-to when required, because he imagined the *North Star* to be one of the large pirates which infest these seas, whom he endeavored to escape from by every means in his power; and in fact in his log, our ship was designated "hum briganda." All this was plausible, and might be true.

The instructions sent to king's ships as to the manner of executing the treaty of Brazil, are very ambiguous. They state in one place that "no slave ship is to be stopped to the south of the line, on any pretext whatever." Yet in another, a certain latitude is allowed, if there is reason to suspect that the slaves on board "were taken in, to the north." By the first, the ship could not be detained at all, and it was doubtful if there was just reason for the second. Even if there were the strongest grounds for capturing and sending her to Sierra Leone for adjudication, where the nearest mixed commission sat, a circumstance of very serious difficulty occurred. It would take three weeks, perhaps a month or more, to beat up to windward to this place, and the slaves had not water for more than half that time, and we could not supply her. A number had already died, and we saw the state of frenzy to which the survivors were almost driven, from the want of this element. On a former occasion, a prize of the *North Star,* sent to Sierra Leone, had lost more than 100, out of a very small complement, while beating up the coast, notwithstanding every care; and it seemed highly probable that in this case but few could survive. Under these doubtful circumstances, then, it appeared more legal and even more humane to suffer them to proceed on their course to Bahia, where it is probable, after all, the remnant left alive would be finally sent, after an investigation by the commissioners, as having been taken in, within the limits of legal traffic. It was with infinite regret, therefore, we were obliged to restore his papers to the captain, and permit him to proceed, after nine hours' detention and close investigation. It was dark when we separated, and the last parting sounds we heard from the unhallowed ship, were the cries and shrieks of the slaves, suffering under some bodily affliction.

It should appear, then, that notwithstanding the benevolent and persevering exertions of England, this horrid traffic in human flesh is nearly as extensively carried on as ever, and under circumstances, perhaps, of a more revolting character. The very shifts at evasion, the necessity for concealment, and the desperate hazard, cause inconvenience and sufferings to the poor creatures in a very aggravated degree. The restriction of slaving to the south of the line was in fact nugatory, and evaded on all occasions. . . .

Two difficulties, however, remain, which ought to be removed for the final and effectual prevention of this traffic. By treaties with Spain, Portugal, the Netherlands, and Brazil, mutual right of search is allowed to the cruisers of each nation, and mixed commissions for adjudication reside at Sierra Leone, Havannah, Rio de Janeiro, and Surinam; but no right of mutual search exists with France or North America, and slaves are continually transported with impunity under their flags. Surely, if nations are sincere in this great cause of God and man, they will no longer suffer the little etiquettes of national vanity to oppose it.

It also happens that the right of capture is cunningly evaded by the slavers, as vessels are only liable to seizure when they have actually slaves on board. Ships frequently enter the mouths of rivers, or other parts of the coast, having every apparatus on board for the reception of slaves, which are collected in the vicinity, and ready to embark on the first opportunity. This is known to our ships, who often watch them for a considerable time, while the slaver remains quietly and securely at anchor. When from any cause the attention of the cruiser is called away, the slaves are all embarked in one night; and when the cruiser resumes his station, the slaver has disappeared with her full cargo. The cruiser has little chance of overtaking the slaver, even though she should be in the immediate neighbourhood. The superior class of vessels employed by the Spaniards, is so well calculated for escape in this way, that our ships of war have no chance of overtaking them at sea. To defeat this, an additional article in the treaty with the Netherlands provides, that all vessels are to be considered as slavers, and treated as such, when they have an apparatus evidently intended for the reception of slaves, even though none be found on board.

If therefore, when the whole coast of Africa is protected from this commerce, and no vessel of any nation is permitted to traffic on any part of it, the right of mutual search is acknowledged, and acted on by all civilized nations, and every ship found with the damning proofs on board be confiscated, and the crews treated as pirates, then, and not till then, can we hope to see this horrid traffic finally abolished.

3. *Slavery Is Doomed in Brazil*

D. P. KIDDER AND J. C. FLETCHER

The American Protestant missionaries Kidder and Fletcher wrote probably the most popular book on Brazil ever published in the United States. They attempted to give a balanced picture of Negro slavery, particularly as it existed in Rio de Janeiro in the years immediately following the cutting off of international traffic in 1850. Slavery was doomed in Brazil, they felt, and they were convinced that Brazilian Negroes had greater opportunities for advancement than those in the United States.

The subject of slavery in Brazil is one of great interest and hopefulness. The Brazilian Constitution recognises, neither directly nor indirectly, color as a basis of civil rights; hence, once free, the black man or the mulatto, if he possesses energy and talent, can rise to a social position from which his race in North America is debarred. Until 1850, when the slave-trade was effectually put down, it was considered cheaper, on the country-plantations, to use up a slave in five or seven years and purchase another, than to take care of him. This I had, in the interior, from intelligent native Brazilians, and my own observation has confirmed it. But, since the inhuman traffic with Africa has ceased, the price of slaves has been enhanced, and the selfish motives for taking greater care of them have been increased. Those in the city are treated better than those on the plantations: they seem more cheerful, more full of fun, and have greater opportunities for freeing themselves. But still there must be great cruelty in some cases, for suicides among slaves — which are almost unknown in our Southern States — are of very frequent occurrence in the cities of Brazil. Can this, however, be attributed to cruelty? The negro of the United States is the descendant of those who have, in various ways, acquired a knowledge of the hopes and fears, the rewards and punishments, which the Scriptures hold out to the good and threaten to the evil: to avoid the crime of suicide is so strongly inculcated as to avoid that of

From *Brazil and the Brazilians* by D. P. Kidder and J. C. Fletcher (Philadelphia: Childs & Peterson, 1857), pp. 132–139.

murder. The North American negro has, by this very circumstance, a higher moral intelligence than his brother fresh from the wild freedom and heathenism of Africa; hence the latter, goaded by cruelty, or his high spirit refusing to bow to the white man, takes that fearful leap which lands him in the invisible world.

In Brazil every thing is in favor of freedom; and such are the facilities for the slave to emancipate himself, and when emancipated, if he possess the proper qualifications, to ascend to higher eminences than those of a mere free black, that *fuit* will be written against slavery in this Empire before another half-century rolls around. Some of the most intelligent men that I met with in Brazil — men educated at Paris and Coimbra — were of African descent, whose ancestors were slaves. Thus, if a man have freedom, money, and merit, no matter how black may be his skin, no place in society is refused him. It is surprising also to observe the ambition and the advancement of some of these men with negro blood in their veins. The National Library furnishes not only quiet rooms, large tables, and plenty of books to the seekers after knowledge, but pens and paper are supplied to such as desire these aids to their studies. Some of the closest students thus occupied are mulattoes. The largest and most successful printing-establishment in Rio — that of Sr. F. Paulo Brito — is owned and directed by a mulatto. In the colleges, the medical, law, and theological schools, there is no distinction of color. It must, however, be admitted that there is a certain — though by no means strong — prejudice existing all over the land in favor of men of pure white descent.

By the Brazilian laws, a slave can go before a magistrate, have his price fixed, and can purchase himself; and I was informed that a man of mental endowments, even if he had been a slave, would be debarred from no official station, however high, unless it might be that of Imperial Senator.

The appearance of Brazilian slaves is very different from that of their class in our own country. Of course, the house-servants in the large cities are decently clad, as a general rule; but even these are almost always barefooted. This is a sort of badge of slavery. On the tables of fares for ferry-boats, you find one price for persons wearing shoes (*calçadas*), and a lower one for those *descalças,* or without shoes. In the houses of many of the wealthy Fluminenses you make your way through a crowd of little wooly heads, mostly guiltless of clothing, who are allowed the run of the house and the amusement of seeing visitors. In families that have some tincture of European manners, these unsightly little bipeds are kept in the background. A friend of mine used frequently to dine in the house of a good old general of high rank, around whose table gambolled two little jetty blacks, who hung about their *"pai"* (as they called him) until they received their portions from his hands, and that, too, before he commenced his own dinner. Whenever the lady of the house drove out, these pets were put into the carriage, and were as much offended at being neglected as any spoiled only son. They were the children of the lady's nurse, to whom she had given freedom. Indeed, a faithful nurse is generally rewarded by manumission.

The appearance of the black male population who live in the open air is any thing but appetizing. Their apology for dress is of the coarsest and dirtiest description. Hundreds of them loiter about the streets with large round wicker-baskets ready to carry any parcel that you desire conveyed. So cheaply and readily is this help obtained, that a white servant seldom thinks of carrying home a package, however small, and would feel quite insulted if you refused him a *preto de ganho* to relieve him of a roll of calico or a watermelon. These blacks are sent out by their masters, and are required to bring home a certain sum daily. They are allowed a portion of their gains to buy their food, and at night sleep on a mat or board in the lower purlieus of the house. You frequently see horrible cases of elephantiasis and other diseases, which are doubtless engendered or increased by the little care bestowed upon them.

The coffee-carriers are the finest race of blacks in Brazil. They are almost all of the Mina tribe, from the coast of Benin, and are athletic and intelligent. They work half clad, and their sinewy forms and jetty skins show to advantage as they hasten at a quick trot, seemingly unmindful of their heavy loads. This work pays well, but soon breaks them down. They have a system among themselves of buying the freedom of any one of their number who is the most respected. After having paid their master the sum required by him daily, they club together their surplus to liberate the chosen favorite. There is now a Mina black in Rio remarkable for his height, who is called "The Prince," being, in fact, of the *blood-royal* of his native country. He was a prisoner of war, and sold to Brazil. It is said that his *subjects* in Rio once freed him by their toil: he returned, engaged in war, and was a second time made prisoner and brought back. Whether he will again regain his throne I know not; but the loss of it does not seem to weigh heavily on his mind. He is an excellent carrier; and, when a friend of mine embarked, the "Prince" and his troop were engaged to transport the baggage to the ship. He carried the largest case on his head the distance of two miles and a half. This same case was pronounced unmanageable in Philadelphia by the united efforts of four American negroes, and it had to be relieved of half its contents before they would venture to lift it up-stairs.

From time to time the traveller will meet with negroes from those portions of Africa of which we know very little except by the reports of explorers like the intrepid Livingstone and Barth. I have often thought that the slaves of the United States are descended not from the noblest African stock, or that more than a century of bondage has had upon them a most degenerating effect. We find in Brazil very inferior spiritless Africans, and others of an almost untamable disposition. The Mina negro seldom makes a good house-servant, for he is not contented except in breathing the fresh air. The men become coffee-carriers, and the women *quitandeiras,* or street pedlars.

These Minas abound at Bahia, and in 1838 plunged that city into a bloody revolt — the last which that flourishing municipality has experienced. It was rendered the more dreadful on account of the secret combinations of these Minas, who are Mohammedans, and use a language not understood by other Africans or by the Portuguese.

When the delegation from the English Society of Friends visited Rio de Janeiro in 1852, they were waited upon by a deputation of eight or ten Mina negroes. They had earned money by hard labor and had purchased their freedom, and were now desirous of returning to their native land. They had funds for paying their passage back to Africa, but wished to know if the coast were really free from the slavers. Sixty of their companions had left Rio de Janeiro for Badagry (coast of Benin) the year before, and had landed in safety. The good Quakers could scarcely credit this last information, thinking it almost impossible that any who had once been in servitude "should have been able and bold enough to make so perilous an experiment"; but the statement of the Minas was confirmed by a Rio ship-broker, who put into the hands of the Friends a copy of the charter under which the sixty Minas sailed, and which showed that they had paid four thousand dollars passage-money. A few days after this interview, Messrs. Candler & Burgess received from these fine-looking specimens of humanity "a paper beautifully written in Arabic by one of their chiefs, who is a Mohammedan."

In Rio the blacks belong to many tribes, some being hostile to each other, having different usages and languages. The Mina negroes still remain Mohammedans, but the others are nominal Roman Catholics.

Many of them, however, continue their heathen practices. In 1839, Dr. Kidder witnessed in Engenho Velho a funeral, which was of the same kind as those curious burial-customs which the African traveller beholds on the Gaboon River. You can scarcely look into a basket in which the *quitandeiras* carry fruit without seeing a *fetisch.* The most common is a piece of charcoal, with which, the abashed darkey will inform you, the "evil eye" is driven away. There is a singular secret society among the negroes, in which the highest rank is assigned to the man who has taken the most lives. They are not so numerous as formerly, but from time to time harm the unoffending. These blacks style themselves *capoeiros,* and during a festa they will rush out at night and rip up any other black they chance to meet. They rarely attack the whites, knowing, perhaps, that it would cost them too dearly.

The Brazilians are not the only proprietors of slaves in the Empire. There are many Englishmen who have long held Africans in bondage — some for a series of years, and others have purchased slaves since 1843, when what is called Lord Brougham Act was passed. By this act it is made unlawful for

Englishmen to buy or sell a slave in any land, and by holding property in man they are made liable, were they in England, to prosecution in criminal courts. The English mining-company, whose stockholders are in Great Britain, but whose field of operations is S. João del Rey in Brazil, own about eight hundred slaves, and hire one thousand more.

Frenchmen and Germans also purchase slaves, although they have not given up allegiance to their respective countries.

If it be asked, "Who will be the laborers in Brazil when slavery is no more?" the reply (given more at length in the account of a visit to the colony of Senator Vergueiro) is that the supply will come from Germany, Portugal, and Azores and Madeira, and other countries.

It is a striking fact that emigrants did not begin to arrive from Europe by thousands until 1852. In 1850 and '51 the African slave-trade was annihilated, and in the succeeding year commenced the present comparatively vigorous colonization. Each year the number of colonists is increasing, and the statesmen of the Empire are now devoting much attention to discover the best means for thus promoting the advancement of the country.

Almost every step in Brazilian progress has been prepared by a previous gradual advance: she did not leap at once into self-government. She was raised from a colonial state by the residence of the Court from Lisbon, and enjoyed for years the position of a constituent portion of the Kingdom of Portugal. The present peaceful state of the Empire under D. Pedro II was preceded by the decade in which the capabilities of the people for self-government were developed under the Regency. The effectual breaking up of the African slave-trade is but the precursor of a more important step.

Slavery is doomed in Brazil. As has already been exhibited, when freedom is once obtained, it may be said in general that no social hinderances, as in the United States, can keep down a man of merit. Such hinderances do exist in our country. From the warm regions of Texas to the coldest corner of New England the free black man, no matter how gifted, experiences obstacles to his elevation which are insurmountable. Across that imaginary line which separates the Union from the possessions of Great Britain, the condition of the African, socially considered, is not much superior. The Anglo-Saxon race, on this point, differs essentially from the Latin nations. The former may be moved to generous pity for the negro, but will not yield socially. The latter, both in Europe and the two Americas, have always placed merit before color. . . .

Thus far reason and Christianity have proved impotent in rooting out this prejudice, or in doing away with these social hinderances, which, more than slavery, will ever render the black man "a hewer of wood and a drawer of water" to the Anglo-American, and which, unjust as they are, I fear can never be eradicated. These insurmountable obstacles, it seems to me, like plain providences, point to Liberia as the nearest land where the North-American-born negro may enjoy the full freedom and the social equality enjoyed by the African descendants in the most enlightened Government of South America.

4. Slavery Is a Curse for Both Negroes and Whites

HERBERT H. SMITH

Herbert H. Smith, the American naturalist who saw all the major regions of Brazil during 1874–1868, was one of the many scientists who have been attracted to Brazil by the tremendous variety of flora and fauna. He also observed slavery, and he emphasized the harm it did to the masters by influencing them toward "indolence and pride and sensuality and selfishness."

I came to Brazil, with an honest desire to study this question of slavery in a spirit of fairness, without running to emotional extremes. Now, after four years, I am convinced that all other evils with which the country is cursed, taken together, will not compare with this one; I could almost say that all other evils have arisen from it, or been strengthened by it. And yet, I cannot unduly blame men who have inherited the curse, and had no part in the making of it. I can honor masters who treat their slaves kindly, albeit they are owners of stolen property.

In mere animal matters, of food and clothing, no doubt many of the negroes are better off than they were in Africa; no doubt, also, they have learned some lessons of peace and civility; even a groping outline of Christianity. But it would be hard to prove that the plantation slave, dependent, like a child, on his master, and utterly unused to thinking for himself, is better, mentally, than the savage who has his faculties sharpened by continual battling with the savage nature around him. Slavery is weakening to the brain; the slave is worse material for civilization than the savage is, and worse still with every generation of slavery.

That is not the main evil, however. The harm that slavery has done to the black race is as nothing to the evils it has heaped upon the white one, the masters. If every slave and free negro could be carried away to Africa, if every

From *Brazil: The Amazons and the Coast* by Herbert H. Smith (New York: Charles Scribner's Sons, 1879), pp. 466–470.

drop of cursed mixed blood could be divided, the evils would be there yet, and go down to the children's children with a blight upon humanity.

Indolence and pride and sensuality and selfishness, these are the outgrowths of slavery that have enslaved the slavemakers and their children. Do you imagine that they are all rich men's sons, these daintily clad, delicate young men on the Ouvidor? The most of them are poor, but they will lead their vegetable lives, God knows how, parasites on their friends, or on the government, or on the tailor and grocer, because they will not soil their hands with tools. "Laborers!" cries Brazil. "We must have labor!" and where will she get honest workmen, if honest work is a degradation? Slavery has made it so. For generations the upper classes had no work to do, and they came to look upon it as the part of an inferior race. So they have kept their hands folded, and the muscle has gone from their bones, and indolence has become a part of their nature. Still, they will be sham lords, if they cannot be real ones; so their money — what they have of it — goes for broadcloth coats and silk hats, and sensuality; a grade below that, they are yet shabby-genteel figures, with an eye to friendly invitations to dinner; and below that, they sink out of sight altogether, from mere inanition.

The rich men's sons are not parasites; sharp enough, many of them are, to keep the money they have, and double it. But from their cradle, the curse of slavery is on them. The black nurse is an inferior, and the child knows it, and tyrannizes over her as only a child can. The mother is an inferior, by her social station, and she does not often venture to thwart the child. The father, with whom authority rests, shirks it back on the irresponsible ones, who may not venture to lay sacrilegious hands on the heir of power. The amount of it is, that a child's training here consists in letting it have its own way as much as possible; and the small naughtinesses and prides develop into consuming vanity and haughtiness. It is characteristic of the Brazilians, this vanity; it may come out in snobbism, or over-confidence, or merely a fiery sensitiveness; but there it is plainly; in the best of them. Slavery is to blame for it; black slavery, and woman slavery that gives the mother no authority.

Of the sensuality that comes from slavery, the mixed races that overrun Brazil are a sufficient witness, as they are in our Southern States. But in Brazil, the proportion of these mixed races is vastly greater; I am safe in saying that not a third of the population is pure-blooded; social distinctions of color are never very finely drawn, though they are by no means abolished, as some writers would have us believe.

People who talk of "amalgamation," as a blessing to be hoped for, should study its effects here, where it is almost an accomplished fact. The mixed races are invariably bad; they seem to combine all the worst characteristics of the two parent stocks, with none of the good ones; and the evil is most apparent where the "amalgamation" is most complete. A light mulatto, or an almost black one, may be a very decent kind of a fellow; but the brown half-and-half is nearly always lazy and stupid and vain. So with the whites and Indians, or the Indians and blacks; the *mamelucos* are treacherous, and passionate, and indolent; the *mestiços* are worse yet; but a dash of mixed blood may not spoil the man that has it.

The treatment of slaves in Brazil depends, of course, on the master; largely, too, on the district. In the provinces north of the São Francisco, I am bound to say that they are treated with great kindness; on the Amazons, they would be, from necessity, if not from choice, for every ill-used slave would run off to the woods, as many have done, out of mere laziness; freedom, considered abstractly, is not likely to have much influence on the negro mind. But around Rio and Bahia, where the vast majority of the slaves are now owned, there are masters who treat their servants with a severity that is nothing short of barbarism. We shall see something of this, when we come to study the coffee-plantations.

Yet Brazil should have a certain credit above other slave-holding countries, present and past; for she alone has voluntarily set herself to getting rid of her shame. Other nations have done it by revolutions, or because they were forced to by a stronger power, or because the system died out of itself. But Brazil, among all, has had nerve to cut away the sore flesh with her own hand; to cut it away while it was yet strong, while it seemed her best vitality. Would to God that she could cut away the scar as well! But the scar will be there, long after emancipation has done its work.

By the present law, slavery will cease to exist in 1892; essentially, I think, the northern provinces will free their slaves before that time. At Pernambuco, especially, the emancipation-spirit is very strong; it has come out in the form of an abolition society, which embraces nearly every prominent man in the place; many slaves have been freed by subscription, at the meetings of this society; there, and elsewhere, the masters frequently celebrate days of public rejoicing, by releasing some old servant. Sometimes a rich man frees his entire household, by testament.

The slaves have been drained into the southern provinces for years. It is common to find three or four hundred of them on the Rio coffee-plantations; rarely, there will be as many score on the sugar-estates of Pernambuco or Pará. Now mark the result. At Rio there is a constant cry for workmen; the slaves are not sufficient, yet free laborers cannot compete with the forced ones; the planters work their negroes as they would never work their mules, yet complain that they reap no profits. In the northern provinces, there is free labor, enough and to spare; poor men have a chance in the world; rich ones are content with the fair returns that their money brings them; society is far more evenly balanced, and the level of private character is far higher than in the south. Of course, there are humane masters at Rio also; the city, in this instance, is better than the country around. Many of the negro porters are slaves; great, brawny fellows, who run in gangs through the streets, each one with a hundred and thirty pounds of coffee on his head. Sometimes we see five or six of them, trotting together, with a piano; the weight evenly distributed on the woolly craniums; the men erect, moving in time to the leader's rattle, and to a plaintive chant. The porters pay their masters a certain sum per day; what they earn over this, is their own. The best of them sometimes buy their freedom from their savings.

5. The Majority of the Brazilians in the 1850s Were Living in the Middle Ages

GILBERTO FREYRE

Gilberto Freyre became interested in social history while a graduate student at Columbia University. There he fell under the spell of Franz Boas, the grand old man of American anthropology, and other teachers in the social sciences who were stimulating interest in cultural history. His thesis for the Master's degree, "Social Life in Brazil in the Middle of the Nineteenth Century," was such a well-written study and so firmly based on an impressive variety of primary sources that it was promptly published in the *Hispanic American Historical Review*.

On his return to Brazil he quickly developed an individual style and personal approach to the study of the history of his country. His stimulating generalizations on the peaceful intermingling of races in Brazil have not been wholly accepted by everyone, but few writers on the history of Brazil during the last forty years have been uninfluenced by his ideas.

In their material environment and, to a certain extent, in their social life, the majority of Brazilians of the fifties were in the Middle Ages: the élite only was living in the eighteenth century. Only a few men, such as the emperor himself, and a few women, such as Nisia Floresta, were conscious of the Europe of John Stuart Mill, hoop-skirts, Sir Charles Lyell, George Sand, four-wheeled English carriages, and Pius IX. Politically the English type of government was

From "Social Life in Brazil in the Middle of the Nineteenth Century" by Gilberto Freyre, *Hispanic American Historical Review*, 5 (1922), pp. 599–627, passim. Reprinted by permission.

the model after which a sensible, and even sophisticated, oligarchy, in whose power the stern emperor often intruded like a big moral policeman, governed the country. Among some of those oligarchs such subtleties and nuances of political theory as "what is the nature and what are the limits of the moderating power in a parliamentary monarchy?" were often discussed. But more practical subjects occupied their attention: the better administration of civil justice, the building of railways, the relations with the boisterous republics to the south, the slave trade. They were studious and took their responsibilities seriously. The imperial senate was, during the fifties and early sixties, an assembly of brilliant minds. Machado de Assis has left us a graphic description of the senate he knew in 1860 — the senate of the old Marquis of Itanhaem, of Rio Branco, Nabuco de Araujo, Zacarias de Goes — a place where public affairs were discussed in an able, entertaining, sometimes caustic, but always dignified, way. . . .

In an examination of the economic structure of Brazilian society in the middle of the nineteenth century we find on one side a class of landowners and slaveholders; on the other, the mass of slaves, and between the two a few "petits bourgeois" and small farmers, not counting the bureaucracy and leaving out the mercantile interests — the bulk of which was foreign. A sort of medieval landlordism prevailed. Land was owned by coffee planters in the south, cattle-proprietors in the inland provinces and Rio Grande do Sul, by *senhores de engenho* (sugar planters) in the Northeast, especially in Pernambuco. Along the coast and in scattered points of the interior were extensive monastic estates. The class of small farmers were the *"roceiros,"* not a few of whom were colored freedmen. Most of the *petit bourgeoisie* was composed of *marinheiros,* or newly arrived Portuguese. Some of these were able to rise, by their perseverance, from being keepers of kiosks or small grocershops, and *mascates,* or peddlers, to the comfortable merchant class — the fathers of future statesmen, diplomats, and judges. The liberalism of the empire, so eager to recognize individual merit, was favorable to newcomers.

By the middle of the nineteenth century the population of Brazil was, roughly speaking, seven millions. . . . Of these he [F. Nunes de Souza] classed 2,120,000 as whites: 1,100,000 as free colored, 3,120,000 as negro slaves, 180,000 as free native African, and 800,000 as Indians. Miscegenation was going on freely. As early as 1818 or 1819 the French naturalist Auguste de Saint-Hilaire found such a mixture of races in São Paulo that he described it as an "étrange bigarrure d'où resultent des complications également embarrassantes pour l'administration et dangereuses pour la morale publique." Alfred R. Wallace found in Para "a most varied and interesting mixture of races."

"There is" he writes, "the fresh-colored Englishman, who seems to thrive as well here as in the cooler climates of his country, the sallow American, the swarthy Portuguese, the more corpulent Brazilian, the merry Negro and the apathetic but finely formed Indian; and between these a hundred shades and mixtures which it requires an experienced eye to detect." The American, C. S. Stewart, U.S.N., who visited Brazil in the early fifties, was surprised at "the fearfully mongrel aspect of the population.". . .

It was in the fifties that the first railways were built in Brazil but only in the seventies did they become a serious factor in the economic and social life of the country. . . . Steam navigation made notable progress in Brazil during the fifties. It was followed by improvements in the towns it touched. Para, for instance, gained much from the line of regular steamers on the Amazon, inaugurated in 1854. Such luxuries as camphene lights and macadam generally followed steam-navigation. Hence the progress noted by foreign observers in coast and riverside towns. The others were hardly affected by any touch of progress until railways penetrated the country. They remained truly medieval — no public lighting, no street cleaning, no macadam. And medieval they were in their customs and in their relations to the great landowners around whose estates the towns and villages were scattered.

The power of the great planters was indeed feudalistic, their patriarchalism being hardly restricted by civil laws. Fletcher, who traveled through the interior of Brazil, wrote: "The proprietor of a sugar or cattle estate is, practically, an absolute lord." And he adds: "The community that lives in the shadow of so great a man is his feudal retinue: and, by the conspiracy of a few such men, who are thus able to bring scores of lieges and partisans into the field, the quiet of the province was formerly more than disturbed by revolts which gave the government much trouble." Oliveira Lima says that those communities living in the shadow of the great planters were very heterogeneous: he compares them to the army of lieges that the Portuguese nobles of the eighteenth century kept in their states: *bravi* or rascals, bull fighters, friars, guitarrists, etc. The large Brazilian estate was a self-sustaining unit — economically and socially — depending little on the world outside its large wood gates. It had its cane-fields or its coffee-plantations, and plantations of mandioc, black beans, and other produce, for its own consumption. Its population included, besides the owner and his family, *feitores,* or overseers, *vaqueiros,* or shepherds, sometimes a chaplain and a tutor, carpenters, smiths, masons, and a multitude of slaves. Fletcher visited a coffee estate in Minas Geraes which contained an area of sixty-four square miles. Besides the rows of coffee trees he noticed large tracts of mandioc, cotton and sugar, an abundance of cattle, and one hundred and fifty hives with bees. . . .

The work people of the plantations were well-fed, and attended to by their master and mistress as a "large family of children." They had three meals a day and a little rum (*caxaca*) in the morning. Their breakfast consisted of farina or *pirão,* with fruits and rum; at midday they were given a very substantial meal of meat or fish; in the evening, black beans, rice, and vegetables. On holidays it was customary on certain estates to have an ox killed for the slaves and a quantity of rum was given to make them merry. Then they would dance the sensuous measures of the *batuque* or other African dances or sing or play the *marimba*.

As a rule the slaves were not overworked in the households either in the plantations or in the city. It is true that much was being said in the fifties, of cruel treatment of slaves in Brazil, by the British anti-slavery propaganda. Later on the British dark account of conditions was to be repeated in Brazil by Brazilian anti-slavery orators such as the young Nabuco and Sr. Ruy Barbosa — men inflamed by the bourgeois idealism of Wilberforce as well as by a very human desire for personal glory — and they did it in so emphatic a language that the average Brazilian believes today that slavery was really cruel in his country. The powerful fancy won over reality. For, as a matter of fact, slavery in Brazil was anything but cruel. The Brazilian slave lived the life of a cherub if we contrast his lot with that of the English and other European factory-workers in the middle of the last century. Alfred R. Wallace — an abolitionist — found the slaves in a sugar plantation he visited in North Brazil "as happy as children.". . . But it is an English clergyman — the Reverend Hamlet Clark, M.A., who strikes the most radical note: "Nay indeed, we need not go far to find in free England the absolute counterpart of slavery: Manighew's London Labour, and London Poor, Dicken's Oliver Twist, Hood's Song of the Shirt and many other revelations tell of a grinding, flinty-hearted despotism that Brazilian slaveowners never can approach." As Professor Hayes points out, in England, "audiences wept at hearing how cruel masters licked their cowering slaves in Jamaica: but in their own England little Englishmen and Englishwomen ten years old were being whipped to their work," sometimes "in the factories of some of the anti-slavery orators."

At sunset the whistle of the sugar-mill closed the day's work on the Brazilian plantation. The workpeople came then for their last meal, after which they went to bed. But first they came to ask their master's and mistress' blessing: "Bençáo, nhonho!" Bençáo Nhanha!" holding out their right hand. Then the master and the mistress would say: "Deus te abençoe" (God bless you), making at the same time the sign of the cross.

In a typical Brazilian city-home of the higher class — say, the home of a custom-house officer — slaves numbered on the average fifteen or twenty. Since slaves were plentiful, certain necessities, and even luxuries, were produced at home, under the careful oversight of the mistress; cloth was cut and made into dresses, towels and undergarments; wine was distilled; lace and crivo (a sort of embroidery) were manufactured. Besides this the housewife superintended the cooking, the preserving, the baking of cakes, the care of the sick; taught her children and their black playmates the Lord's Prayer, the Apostles' Creed, and the Ave Maria. . . .

Slaves were plentiful. The staff of a large city-house included cooks, those trained to serve in the dining room, wet-nurses, water carriers, footmen, chambermaids — the latter sleeping in their mistresses' rooms and assisting them in the minutest details of their toilette, such as picking lice, for instance. Sometimes there were too many slaves. A lady told Doctor Fletcher that she "had nine lazy servants at home for whom there was not employment" and another one that she could not find enough work to keep her slaves out of idleness and mischief. It is easy to imagine how some housewives became pampered idlers, spending their days languidly in gossiping, or at the balcony, or reading some new novel of Macedo or Alencar. . . .

It is true that the Brazilian lady of the fifties did not go out for her shopping. She was a house prisoner. Moorish prejudices kept her from those pretty shops of fancy goods, bonnets, jewelry, *bijouterie,* which travelers admired so much in Rio de Janeiro, the Italian naval officer Eugenio Rodriguez describing them as "elegantissimi magazini." But at home she did not stay in her hammock. In a typical home works of all kinds went on during the day. Linen, silk, millinery, fancy goods, were bought from samples and pattern-books, after much running of negro boys from shop to the house: or, in many cases, from the peddler who came once or twice a week, making a noise with his yardstick. It was not necessary to go to the market to buy vegetables, fruit, or eggs since venders of these rural products, as well as of milk, meat, and fish, came to the home. There were itinerant coppersmiths who announced themselves by hitting some old stewpan with a hammer. Even novels were sold at the door. Paulo Barreto tells that Alencar and Macedo — "the best sellers" of the period — had negroes go from house to house, selling their novels in baskets. Therefore, the fact that the Brazilian woman did not go to the shops does not mean that she was too lazy to do her own shopping. She did it. And after the shopping was done in the morning it was she who superintended the various kinds of work going on in the household. . . . Fletcher who, though a Protestant clergyman, enjoyed the intimacy of many a home in Brazil, thought that the Brazilian housewife answered to the description of the "good woman" in the last chapter of Proverbs: "she looketh well to the ways of her household and eateth not the bread of idleness." Carlos de Laet — the last brilliant mind of a departed order — tells us that "to accuse a lady of not knowing how to manage her household was then the most unpleasant offence to her." Oliveira Lima characterizes the Brazilian housewife of this period as possessing "ability to manage" (*capacidade administrativa*), without which it was impossible to keep such large households going. Others might be quoted to show that in this matter the weighing of evidences reveals an active, rather than an idle woman, as the typical Brazilian housewife in slavery days.

The double standard of morality prevailed in the fifties: the lily-like woman was idolized while incontinence in the man was slightly regarded. It is true that the Emperor Dom Pedro II. made the standards of sexual morality stricter for those who were around him or who aspired to political eminence. He was a sort of Queen Victoria in breeches — only more powerful — and watched the statesmen like a moral detective. It is commonplace that he refused to appoint men to eminent positions on account of irregularities in their private life — a tradition which the Republican leaders found too foolish to maintain. But the emperor's influence was only felt in the high spheres of officialdom. In the large country estates irregularities went on freely, the colored girls constituting a disguised harem where either the master or his sons satisfied their exotic sexual tastes. . . .

In his attitude towards his wife the Brazilian of the fifties was a true patriarch of the Roman type. She was given authority in the household, but not outside. Outside she was to be, legally and socially, the shadow of her husband. "A promenade below, with the chance of a flirtation, is denied her," the American C. S. Stewart remarks in his book. Pointing out the virtues of the Brazilian matron in the *ancien régime,* of which he is the most eminent survivor, the Count Carlos de Laet says that "she knew how to obey her husband." Monsieur Expilly, a French feminist who visited Brazil in the fifties, was indignant at what he calls "le despotisme paternel" and "la politique conjugale.". . .

While the woman spent most of her time indoors, the man — the city man — spent most of his, out — in the street, in the plaza, at the door of some French hotel or in his office or warehouse. The condition was much like that in ancient Greece where people thought, with the wise old Xenophon, that "it is not so good for a woman to be out-of-doors as in, and it is more dishonourable for a man to stay in than to attend to his affairs outside." Brazilian men, like the Greeks, enjoyed the easy fellowship of the street and the plaza — and in the street and the plaza they discussed politics, Donizetti, the Aberdeen Bill, and transacted business. We are told by Sampaio Ferraz, in his excellent work "O Molhe de Olinda," that in Pernambuco, during the last half of the nineteenth century, the most important business was transacted outdoors, under the trees of Lingoeta. Lithogravures of the period, which I examined in Oliveira Lima's collection, show the streets — Rua Direita and Largo da Alfandega in Rio, Lingoeta in Pernambuco, and so on — full of groups of men, talking, smoking, taking snuff, while coffee or sugar carriers run with their cargoes, their half-naked bodies shining with oily sweat. The sentiment of home was not strong among the Brazilian men when the patriarchal family was in its full vigor. Nor did they have mundane clubs — unless if we accept as such the Masonic lodges. The street was their club.

This may serve as an explanation of the fact that the city Brazilians of the fifties did not seem to have attractive homes. Twenty years before a French traveler, Louis De Freycinet, had observed that the Brazilians spent most of their time sleeping, or outdoors, or, sometimes, receiving their friends: therefore they only needed — the Frenchman thought — a reception room and the bedrooms. . . .

At eight or nine the girl was sent to a religious boarding school and kept there until she was thirteen or fourteen. There her training, begun at home, was continued. She was trained in that fine art — the art of being a woman. Music, dancing, embroidery, prayers, French, and sometimes English, a thin layer of literature — such were the elements of a girl's education in the boarding school. She came back a very romantic, and sometimes bewitching, little creature, reading Sue, Dumas, and George Sand, besides the gossiping *pacotilhas* such as *A Marmota* and Alencar's saccharine, but often erotic, *folhetins*. And how she could pray! And how she could dance! The dances of the period were the quadrille, the lanciers, and the polka; to dance them well, to be light as a feather and tiny as a piece of lace, was the highest ideal of a girl — I was told by a lady who took dancing lessons from the same teacher as Princess Isabel.

Ladies bloomed early. The years of giddy childhood were short. At fourteen or fifteen the girl dressed like a lady. Docility, and even timidity, was considered a grace. The girl was trained to be timid or, at least, to look timid before people — as timid as a little boy before the circus elephant. The Brazilian girl of the fifties was everything that the so called "very modern" girl is not. "Perhaps they were too timid" — Carlos de Laet writes of the girls of that period — "but they were adorable in the timidity." Those very timid girls were playful and talkative when given a chance. Max Radiguet tells of the custom of the Brazilian society girls going to the imperial chapel in Rio de Janeiro, where an excellent orchestra assisted by a choir of Italian soprani played every Friday evening. There "pendant toute la durée de ce concert religieux les femmes accroupées sur leur caire de tapisserie prenaient sans scruple des sorbets et des glaces avec les jeunes gens qui venaient converser avec elles dans le lieu saint." When such merry rendezvous, in the shadow of the church, were not possible — and the custom was discontinued just as dances in the churches were discontinued — love-making had to be even more platonic. There was, for instance, love-making by means of a fan — that is, girls could make their fans speak a particular language of love which all lovers were supposed to understand. "It all depended on how the fan was held," an old lady explained to me while her tapering, white fingers handled a delicate fan in a thousand and one ways.

But as a rule marriage did not result from romantic lovemaking. The man whom the girl married in her early teens was seldom her own choice. He was her parents', or her father's, choice. An English traveler describes how betrothals were made: "Some day the father walks into the drawing room, accompanied by a strange gentleman, elderly or otherwise. 'Minha Filha,' he remarks, 'this is your future husband.' " Sometimes the "future husband" was a pleasant surprise — a pale youth of twenty-three or twenty-five, a ruby or an emerald sparkling from his forefinger, his moustaches perfumed, his hair smooth, oily . . . a hero who had escaped from some bright German oleogravure or from the pages of a novel. And romantic love developed between the contracting parties. But other times the "future husband" was some fat, solid, newly-rich Portuguese, middle-aged, his neck short and his hands coarse. Perhaps a very fine person — inside; but what a death-blow for a sentimental girl of the fifties. And yet she often accepted him — the potbellied one — such a marriage being nothing more than a business partnership. Unfortunate marriages of the latter type became a favorite theme with Brazilian writers of fiction in the sixties and seventies, Guimaraes' *Historia de Uma Moça Rica* being typical of that literature. But one should be discriminating in the matter: some marriages arranged by the girl's parents were as happy as marriages ordinarily are.

Early marriages meant early procreation. At fifteen a girl was generally a mother. Sometimes she was a mother at fourteen and even thirteen. The Reverend Walter Colton wrote in his diary: "A Brazilian lady was pointed out to me to-day who is but twelve years of age, and who has two children, who were frolicking around her steps. . . ." And he adds ". . . ladies here marry extremely young. They have hardly done with their fictitious babies, when they have the smiles and tears of real ones." As a consequence, girls faded early, having tasted in a hurry the joy of careless youth.

The boy, too, was born middle-aged. Dom Pedro's prematurity may be taken as typical. He was made an emperor at fifteen, and he was then very thoughtful and serious; at twenty he was an old man. Youth flew from him in a gallop. Brazilian education favored then, more than in a later day, the prematurity of the boy. Very early he was sent to the *collegio,* where he lived and boarded. Though his home might be a street or two off, very seldom — usually once a month — was he allowed to go there. He often got from home boxes of cakes and bon-bons, but no such things as toys. Toys were for little boys; he was nine or ten, nearly a man. As a rule he studied hard his Latin grammar, his rhetoric, his French classics, his sacred history, his geography. When that big occasion — the final examinations — came, he shone, answering well all that Padre So-and-So asked about Horace, Noah, Rebecca, rules of punctuation, the verb *amare;* and all that some other teacher asked about Racine, Vesuvius, and what not.

At fifteen or sixteen the boy finished his studies in the *collegio.* It was time to go to the professional school. Here, as in the girls' betrothal, it was the father's or family's choice that generally prevailed. The tendency was to scatter the boys in different schools, so that the family would be represented in different professions. One was picked to go to Pernambuco or São Paulo to study law or diplomacy; another to enter the medical school; a third to be a cadet in the military school; a fourth to go to the seminary. Among the most pious families it was considered a social, as well as a moral, failure not to have a son studying for the priesthood. Sometimes the youngest son, though of no churchly turn of mind, was the scapegoat. The family simply had to have a *padre*. As to the stupid son, who could not make good anywhere, the sensible parents sent him to business, which was looked down upon by gentlemen.

The flower of the family was picked for the law school — the law school being the training-ground, not for magistracy only, but for the parliament and the cabinet also, and for diplomacy. There were two law schools — that of Olinda, in Pernambuco, and that of São Paulo. Writing from São Paulo in 1855 Doctor Kidder said of its law school: "It is here and at the Pernambuco Law School (which contains three hundred students in the regular course) that the statesmen of Brazil receive that education which so much better fits them for the Imperial Parliament and the various legislative assemblies of their land than any preparatories that exist in the Spanish-American countries."

The "regular course," to which Doctor Kidder refers, came after a sort of pre-law course which included Latin, geometry, rational and moral philosophy, and other subjects. The "regular course" extended over a period of five years, the following subjects being studied: philosophy of law, public law, analysis of the imperial constitution, Roman law, diplomacy, ecclesiastical law, civil law, mercantile and maritime law, political economy, and theory and practice of general law. . . .

But this churchly atmosphere in the day time did not prevent most of the students from being merry, boisterous, and even wicked, after sunset. They did not care a rap for rowing or any ball game — not even for cockfighting, which some of their elders enjoyed. Making love to actresses was their favorite sport. There were generally two rival actresses, like Candiani and Delmatro, in São Paulo, and Eugenia Camara and Adelaide do Amaral, in Pernambuco, and surrounding each, a fervent group of admirers — some platonic, some not. Each group had a "poet" instead of a "cheer leader," and oratorical duels were fought in the theaters. . . . It was in the shadow of the theater that the young men enjoyed themselves, writing verses to actresses, fighting for actresses, spending money on merry suppers with actresses. . . .

It is amazing how the Brazilians of the fifties managed to live in such miserable conditions of dirt and bad smell as they did. There was practically no public hygiene to speak of. It is in a semi-official outline of the history of public health services in Brazil that the following description appears, of Rio de Janeiro in the middle of the nineteenth century: "A filthy city, in which, it may be said, there was no air, no light, no sewers, no street cleaning; a city built upon bogs where mosquitoes freely multiplied." Mme. Ida Pfeiffer saw, as she walked through the streets of Rio, carcasses of dogs, cats, and even a mule, rotting. She also refers to "le manque complet d'égouts" — the complete lack of sewers. This condition was common to the other cities of the empire — even to Pernambuco, where the Dutch had left a touch of their cleanliness. Charles Darwin, who was there in the thirties, writes of its filthy streets and offensive smells, comparing it to oriental towns. In all the towns of the empire the removal of garbage, ashes, decaying matter, and vegetables, and human excrements was made in the crudest and also the most picturesque way. Those wastes were put in pipes or barrels, nicknamed *tigres,* and carried on the heads of slaves who dumped them into rivers, the seashore, and alleys. Sometimes as a witness referred to a later-day Brazilian hygienist, "the bottom of the barrel would cast off, the contents soiling both the carrier and the streets." The decaying material was left near the bridges or on the seashores, flocks of carrion crows being depended upon to do the work of scavengers. The removal of the garbage and human waste was generally made after the church bells rang "ten o'clock." In Pernambuco the *tigres* were emptied from the bridges into the rivers Capibaribe and Beberibe: in Rio they were taken on the heads of slaves to be emptied "into certain parts of the bay every night, so that walking in the streets after 10 o'clock is neither safe nor pleasant." This quotation is from Ewbanks who adds: "In this matter Rio is what Lisbon is and what Edinburg used to be."

As there were no sewers to carry off the drainage there was no plumbing in the houses. The system of water supply was that of the *chafariz,* or public fountain. There was a constant dashing to and fro of big negro water carriers, taking water for the houses, sometimes to the third or fourth floor, where the kitchen was located. Those water carriers worked harder, perhaps, than any other class of slaves; for Brazilians made free use of water, thus making up in personal cleanliness what was lacking so painfully in public hygiene. Next to his hot coffee and his snuff, a Brazilian loved a hot bath best of all. Everywhere — in cities and in the great as well as the humble houses of the interior — water, soap, and a large clean towel welcomed a guest. On examining statistics of the period, I found that more than one third of the seventy-two factories then existing in the empire were soap factories.

Though there was no plumbing in the houses and bathtubs were unknown, rich and poor took a sheer joy in bathing. Poor people bathed in rivers, under the public eye. Landing in Para, the American, John Esaias Warren, was attracted to the freedom with which people bathed and swam in the river. "The first spectacle which arrested our attention," he writes, "was that of a number of persons of both sexes and all ages, bathing indiscriminately together in the waters of the river, in a state of entire nudity." And his comment is: "The natives of Para are very cleanly and indulge in daily ablutions; nor do they confine their baths to the dusky hours of the evening but may be seen swimming about the public wharfs at all hours of the day." While the well-to-do in the cities used·"gamellas" or large wooden bowls for their ablutions those in the country states — gentlemen and ladies alike — went to the nearest stream where they could also enjoy a good swim. The suburban *chacaras* in Pernambuco, along the Capibaribe river, had crude bathhouses made of coconut palms. There the ladies undressed and then dipt into the water in free, white, nakedness, like happy mermaids.

It was customary to wash one's hands before and after a meal, the slaves bringing bowls with beautifully embroidered towels. Doctor Fletcher noticed this in Rio as well as in the interior of Minas, where he traveled in an oxcart. Not many years before Saint-Hilaire had been delighted at the apostolic simplicity with which the small farmers in Minas Geraes came themselves with a basin and a towel to wash their guest's feet before he went to bed. Children had their feet washed by their mothers or negro nurses before going to bed. On this occasion their feet were also examined, so that *bichos de pe* might be extracted with a pin, if found. . . .

6. *Brazilian Paternalism was a Myth*

EMILIA VIOTTI DA COSTA

In the 1950s and 1960s, a new generation of Brazilian sociologists and historians, mostly hailing from Sao Paulo, began to scrutinize Freyre's views. Writing from a Marxist perspective, they presented Brazilian slavery as a far less benign institution than had been previously thought, and questioned whether the slave systems of the United States and Brazil were all that dissimilar. While Emilia Viotti da Costa has given considerable attention to slave life and conditions, her principal concern is not so much the slaves themselves, as the impact of slavery on the economic development of Brazil. Here she challenges the myth that Brazilian slaveowners were paternalistic.

Too much has been said recently about the paternalism of the slaveowners. Historians have argued that paternalism was more than just a myth—an

From *The Brazilian Empire: Myth and Histories* by Emilia Viotti da Costa (Chicago: University of Chicago Press, 1985), pp. 137–145. Reprinted by permission.

actual practice regulating the relations between master and slaves—a means of social control. This opinion, however, seems questionable when contrasted with the overwhelming evidence suggesting the violence of the system. Masters may have resorted to rewards as well as to punishment; they may have tried to impose order and discipline by presenting themselves as father figures. But all this should not blind us to the ultimate violence of a system which made slaves the property of their masters—a property that could be bought and sold and whose fate depended on the master's whim.

The forms of ritual kinship *(compadrío)* and the paternalistic relationships that slaveholding society developed as mechanisms of accommodation and social control could not eliminate the barriers that separated the two opposing and irreconcilable worlds of the slave and the master. Racial prejudice always separated the owner from the owned. Most whites, even those who considered slavery an economic and political aberration, believed in the moral inferiority and political and social incapacity of the African race. Racial prejudice served to maintain and legitimize the distance between a world of privileges and rights and one of deprivation and duties.

Even if the slaveholders often rewarded good behavior by granting manumission or conferring to their most loyal slaves a position of prestige within the slave community, more often they resorted to threats or punishments to keep up the rhythms of work, prevent escapes or revolts, and keep slaves obedient and submissive. Physical punishment was universally accepted as a method of coercion, although society disapproved of both the masters who were excessive in their punishments and the ones who were overly benevolent. Leniency and cruelty were considered equally dangerous.

Religion was another means of social control. Since the colonial period, the Church had undertaken to reconcile the masters' financial interests with the dictates of religion and philanthropy. Discipline on the *fazendas,* according to one traveler in the mid-nineteenth century (who did not include paternalism as one of the means of social control), had two forms: the whip and the confessional. Patience, resignation, and obedience were the cathechism the priests taught the slaves. Some went so far as to say that blacks were "cursed" and constituted a condemned race whose salvation depended on their serving whites patiently and with devotion. Others played the role of mediators between masters and slaves, preaching moderation and benevolence to the masters and obedience to the slaves. But whatever the priests' role was, most people believed that religion and the confessional were the best antidotes to insurrections.

When rewards, admonition, and advice did not produce the desired result, slaveholders resorted to punishment. The most common methods were the *palmatória,* the stocks, and various kinds of whips and lashes. Rare, but not absent, were neck shackles, manacles, iron rings for squeezing fingers, brass masks, and imprisonment. Whipping and the *palmatória* were common disciplinary punishments, recognized and authorized by law. Slaves were not alone: soldiers and sailors were also whipped when they committed certain offenses, and children were subjected to the *palmatória* in school. Sometimes lower-class free men were also beaten when they displeased a slaveholder or failed to treat him with "proper" respect. In the nineteenth century, social relations were based on dominance and oppression; on the power of father over son, of husband over wife, of master over slave, of the rich over the poor. Physical violence was an integral part of most people's lives.

The harshest punishments were applied to slaves who committed murder, led other slaves to run away, or instigated rebellions. A murderer was condemned to death if the crime was carried out against the planter or his family and to chain gangs or prison otherwise. Runaways received three hundred lashes, administered over several days. For a long time it was the custom to brand slaves with a hot iron. Even on the eve of abolition, the newspapers carried advertisements of runaway slaves who could be identified by those brands. All these devices for torture and punishment were in frequent use until the middle of the nineteenth century. Such practices declined thereafter, but the history of Brazilian slavery is replete with cases of death or permanent injury from excessive punishment, enough to make us doubt the paternalistic pretensions of the masters.

Various travelers in nineteenth-century Brazil praised the excellence of the legislation that sought to protect the slave. They forgot, however, that the effectiveness of a law always depends on compliance and enforcement. And it is difficult to believe that these laws were implemented when, as we have seen before, slaveowners often interfered with the action of the courts. Before the abolitionist campaign, the slave was always seen as guilty by the jury, while the master always seemed to be in the right. Thus, most of the time the law was ineffective in the defense of the slaves but quite effective on behalf of the slaveholders.

In spite of all the mechanisms conceived to keep the slave population submissive, the planters lived in perpetual fear of slave insurrection. At the least rumor, severe measures were taken to prevent an uprising. The news spread swiftly: troops were mobilized, slaveholders warned, suspects arrested and interrogated, and the guilty severely punished. Laws were enacted to strengthen security measures. Both municipal and provincial legislatures reinforced the legal provisions that limited the slaves' movements. In the towns, every slave found on the street after curfew without his master's authorization was arrested. Slaves were prohibited from congregating in shops or public places, and they were forbidden to enter gambling houses or taverns. The sale of arms or poison to slaves was severely punished, as was the renting of rooms or houses to them. It was illegal to buy any merchandise from slaves, unless they showed authorization from their masters. This was intended to reduce thefts, but neither vigilance nor repressive measures worked. Masters constantly complained that roadside stores traded in goods stolen by the slaves.

Despite the rumors of insurrections that periodically alarmed the slaveholding class, large-scale revolts were rare in nineteenth-century Brazil. Some of those that did occur, however, were quite impressive. The most famous slave revolts of this period had a religious character and were provoked by Muslim blacks. They occurred in the cities, where communication among the insurgents was easier than in the country and the concentration of slaves from the same part of Africa was greater. Those revolts took place principally in the Northeast, where many Muslim blacks were to be found. The Malè revolts in Alagoas (1815) and Bahía (1835) were of this type. In Minas Gerais a famous uprising occurred shortly before independence. Some 15,000 slaves assembled in Ouro Preto and another 6,000 in Sao João do Morro. They spoke of a constitution and freedom and spread the rumor that in Portugal a constitution had already been approved in which blacks had been made equal to whites. Revolts of such size, however, were rare in the coffee areas and only occasionally took on the frightening aspects of the one that broke out in Vassouras in 1838, when about three hundred slaves, mostly Haussás, rose in revolt and troops had to be summoned from Rio de Janeiro to suppress them.

The repressive mechanisms that slave society had developed against uprisings were usually quite effective, and when a revolt did break out, it was quickly put down by the police or the army. But even careful vigilance could not prevent slaves from escaping to the forests and raiding plantations and villages. Communities of runaway slaves, known as *quilombos,* had been widespread since the colonial period, and in the nineteenth century some became famous, such as Jabaquara in São Paulo and Gávea in Rio de Janeiro. *Quilombos* grew in importance during the final years of slavery because slaves could count on the help of abolitionists and on the goodwill of the urban population.

Insurrections, crimes, work badly done, orders not fulfilled, lies, negligence were the many ways slaves fought oppression. But most of all, they ran away. The newspapers of the period are filled with advertisements dealing with escaped slaves and promising rewards to anyone who captured them. In 1855, up to 30$000 was offered. Twenty years later, when slave prices had risen to two and a half *contos* (2:500$000) or even more, some owners would offer up to 400$000 for the capture of a runaway slave.

The profession of *capitão do mato* (hunter of runaway slaves) had existed since the colonial period. In the nineteenth century, *capitães do mato* did not hesitate to put advertisements in the newspapers offering their services. But with the spread of abolitionist ideas they gradually became targets of popular satire and sometimes even of physical attacks.

The slaves' potential for rebellion was contained not only by repression, but also by the rivalries and enmities that divided the slave community. In rural areas, the household servants often considered themselves better than slaves who worked in the fields. Maids, cooks, seamstresses, coachmen, pages, washerwomen, and nursemaids received special treatment and had greater opportunities to gain their freedom through manumission than did fieldhands. The household servants often lived more or less separated from their fellow slaves. Their apparent superior status tended to separate them from their natural group and imposed on them a code of etiquette full of prohibitions. They did not belong to the slave quarter, but they were not accepted in the world of the masters. Their position was not without ambiguities, and ambiguous was their behavior. Some were bound by ties of affection to the master's family; others hated their masters to such an extent that they did not hesitate to eliminate them. The accounts of crimes committed by household slaves kept the master class apprehensive and watchful as long as slavery lasted.

Many other forms of rivalry further divided the slave population. In the cities blacks often organized themselves by "nations" (their places of origin). And sometimes they kept old hierarchies. Some African princes are said to have maintained the respect of their subjects in slavery. To the traditional African hierarchical positions, new distinctions were added based on occupation. As one traveler noted at midcentury, "A well-dressed and well-turned out high-class female slave feels no compassion or sympathy for her ragged and dirty fellow." The master's position also reflected on the slave, and one who belonged to a plantation owner felt himself superior to another who worked for a modest official—even though he might be subject to a more rigorous discipline. In spite of these divisions, feelings of solidarity also developed among slaves. And in the second half of the nineteenth century the activities of the abolitionists were important not only in spurring the slaves to join together in winning their freedom but in providing them with the means to do so.

African traditions had an important role to play in keeping the slave community united. Cultural traditions were apparently more easily retained in the cities than in the countryside. In urban areas, blacks from the same parts of Africa had at least the possibility of seeing one another and forming groups. On the plantations, where masters tried to prevent the formation of homogeneous groups, such contacts were more difficult. People of different cultural traditions were mixed together. The family or kin that had constituted the basis of the social structure in Africa fell apart. The traditional collective symbolic systems took on new meanings. Cults and rituals brought from Africa underwent a process of interpretation based on new circumstances imposed by slavery.

Music, religion, and magic were intimately related and played an immense part in the life of the slaves. Some masters permitted their slaves to dance and sing on Saturdays, Sundays, or holidays. In the cities and towns, African songs and dances were usually prohibited, out of a fear that any gathering of slaves could degenerate into a subversive movement. The only authorized celebrations were those of a Christian character, such as that of Nossa Senhora do Rosário, patron saint of blacks, and a few dances, such as the *congadas.*

For the most part, however, Christianity was little more than a veneer over African traditions and practices. Few masters made much effort at Christianizing their slaves. Although most plantations had chapels, mass was rarely celebrated. Priests were in short supply, and the few who appeared from time to time had no opportunity to initiate the slaves in the real practices of Christianity. Household rites and family prayers prevailed. The master would lead prayers, aided by the slaves, who repeated them mechanically often without understanding their meaning. In practice, African and Christian traditions became thoroughly mixed, and African deities survived under Christian guise. The inclusion of African cultural elements in Catholicism made possible their preservation under a Christian exterior. But in this process, many African deities acquired a sinister character and often the warlike ones came to be preferred. The Muslim slaves, who were heavily concentrated in the Northeast, were the most resistant to Christianity, and some even managed to maintain their own places of worship. Nevertheless, slavery often made it impossible to observe religious requirements strictly, and it was mainly among free blacks that African traditions survived, however modified.

The fate of the slave actually depended as much on the prosperity of the master as on his benevolence and humanity. And it varied from region to region, from one plantation to another. It was said that Rio was better than Maranhão and that the worst masters were to be found in Campinas. "I will sell you to Campinas," said masters in western São Paulo to rebellious or lazy slaves. In Bahía, unruly blacks were threatened with being sent to the south. In Pernambuco the threat was to sell them to Maranhão. There was considerable mystification in this insinuation, but slave treatment did vary with the productivity of the various regions. In areas suffering from soil exhaustion—but still productive—such as the Paraiba Valley after 1870, the planter demanded longer hours and the care of a larger number of trees from his slaves to compensate for the decline in productivity of the coffee trees. In totally decadent areas, poverty sometimes brought slave and master closer together, and when slaves were not sold, master and slave relations became somewhat more civilized as they both struggled for survival. In the most prosperous areas, where productivity was higher and labor abundant, living conditions for the slaves were usually better.

On the whole, living conditions seem to have improved after the abolition of the slave trade in 1850, when the price of slaves increased and slaveowners became more concerned with keeping their slaves in good health. In the twenty years from 1855 to 1875, slave prices almost trebled, going from one *conto* to two and a half and even three. While slave prices in Rio and São Paulo (in the coffee areas) maintained an upward trend from mid-century to about 1880, rising abruptly in the 1850s and then more gradually during the next decades, in the sugar areas prices began to decrease from the late 1850s on, reaching their lowest point in the 1870s. The fall of slave prices was related to changes in commodity prices; while sugar prices tended to decline, coffee prices reached their highest levels during the 1870s. The difference between slave prices in the Northeast and in the South and the higher demand for slaves in the South led to a dislocation of the slave population from the Northeast to the South. The majority of bondsmen sold in the southern provinces, however, seem to have come not from plantations but from urban areas or small farms less dependent on slave labor.

During the first years after the interruption of the slave trade, there was a movement of slaves from the less productive regions to the more productive, from the cities to the countryside. Intra- and interprovincial trade replaced the external trade. Slave traders scoured the Northeast, offering high prices for slaves whom they then sold to the coffee planters of the South. Concerned about this loss of labor, the governments of the northeastern provinces tried to limit departures by imposing high taxes on them. A report by the president of the province of Maranhão in 1853 noted that the tax on the export of slaves had brought in more than in prior years because of the high slave prices prevailing in the Rio de Janeiro market. In Pernambuco the tax on slaves leaving the province, which was 5$000 in 1842, reached 200$000 in 1859. In 1866 the provincial president reported that from 1855 to 1864, 4,023 slaves had been transferred to other provinces. In Bahía in1860, over 200:000$000 was collected in taxes on slaves leaving the province. The situation was similar in Alagoas, where the largest source of revenue in 1862 was the tax on the export of slaves. Wanderley, representing the planters of Bahía, tried unsuccessfully in 1854 to secure approval in the House of Representatives for a bill prohibiting the interprovincial slave trade. The interests of large-scale agriculture in the South were stronger. The northeastern provinces, suffering from chronic crisis, thus lost much of their slave population.

SECTION V

Porfirio Díaz: Dictator of Mexico

No nineteenth-century caudillo has been so much written about as Porfirio Díaz, who first became provisional president of Mexico in 1876 by revolting with the cry "No re-election" and then by 1884 had the country so thoroughly dominated that he was able to get himself "elected" term after term until the Mexican Revolution overthrew him in 1911. The *Porfiriato,* as this long period is called, produced peace and some economic progress, but these were achieved only at a great price.

The intellectuals did not go into exile as they had when Juan Manuel de Rosas held sway over Argentina, and in fact General Díaz received strong support from the positivists. As one Mexican historian explains:

> His figure came to symbolize the order and peace for which the men trained in positivism had clamored. Materialism and dehumanization were converted into models of life for the generation which developed during his regime: industry, money, railroads, and always more money. Progress definitely seemed to triumph. The social evolution seemed to be moving forward with gigantic steps, but . . . freedom was forgotten, the very thing for which it was said that order had been established.[1]

The fault was by no means his alone, but in his long years of power the people as a whole did not advance and remained illiterate. While the celebrants of the centenary of Mexican independence and of the dictator's eightieth birthday drank twenty carloads of champagne and consumed many delicacies, the masses verged on starvation, for they had suffered a steady reduction in their incredibly low living standards during the long Porfiriato.

[1] Leopoldo Zea, *The Latin-American Mind,* trans. James H. Abbott and Lowell Dunham (Norman: University of Oklahoma Press, 1963), p. 284.

Yet in many ways Díaz was a great man; one of his severest United States critics concludes:

> He accomplished what none of his countrymen had been able to do before him — to maintain a generation of peace. . . . But the overshadowing fact — to remember — is that the Mexico he left in 1911 had all its problems, the problems of four centuries, still to solve.[2]

During the Porfiriato, Americans began to go to Mexico in ever-increasing numbers — to invest money, to build railroads, to buy ranches, to write books, to report for newspapers, or just to pay a tourist visit. It was during this period that the moving picture camera began to record the living scenes of Mexican history. Salvador Toscano produced enough film on a French machine that a remarkable documentary could be made, the "Memorias de un Mexicano," which is now being seen by many students at American universities thanks to the initiative of the Committee on Mexican History of the Conference on Latin American History. Newspaper photographers also began to arrive in the last years of the Porfiriato and the early years of the Revolution, so that the documentation is both varied and rich.

The accounts written by visitors from the United States are particularly revealing. One reporter, James Creelman, made the long journey from New York to Mexico City for the sole purpose of interviewing the aged dictator, who unexpectedly remarked that he would be retiring in a couple of years and hence welcomed an opposition (Reading 37). This was the beginning of the end for Díaz. But two years later he was still in the saddle, and another American, John Kenneth Turner, attacked his harsh and high-handed rule that resulted in his complete control of Mexico (Reading 2).

Another visitor was a young Harvard student from Minneapolis, Charles Flandrau, who went to Mexico to visit a brother for some months and whose delightful record of experiences there, entitled *Viva Mexico!*, constitutes an amusing and interesting view of Mexican life but also includes some sharp criticism of the Church there which helps to explain the anticlerical spirit of the Revolution when it broke out a few years later. Flandrau learned "of a powerful bishop whose 'wife' and large family of sons and daughters are complacently taken for granted by the entire diocese," and was "warned by a devout Catholic never under any circumstances to allow one's American maid servants to converse with a priest or to enter his home on any pretext whatever."[3] Flandrau himself experienced clerical commercialism when he described a village confirmation ceremony in 1908, when the bishop

[2] Ernest Gruening, *Mexico and Its Heritage* (New York: Century, 1928), p. 65.
[3] Ibid., p. 270.

arrived in Mizantla because many children were unconfirmed since his last visit there "five or eight" years ago:

> The bishop, with three priests behind him was standing at the top of the altar steps. He was wearing his mitre, and the tips of his fingers lightly touched one another, as a bishop's fingers should, on the apex of his stomach. It was a thrilling moment.
>
> Then combining, in a quite wonderful fashion, extreme rapidity with an air of ecclesiastical calm, he made his confirmatory way down one side of the nave, across the end, and up the other, preceded by one priest and followed by two. The first gathered up the certificates (no laying on of hands unless one has paid one's twenty-five centavos) and read the name of the child next in line to the bishop, who murmured the appropriate formula, made a tiny sign of the cross on a tiny forehead with the end of a dirty thumb and moved on. The second, with a bit of absorbent cotton, dipped in oil, swabbed the spot on which the cross had been signed, while the third, taking advantage of the general rapture, gently relieved everyone of his blessed candle (it had never been lighted) and carried it away to be sold again. But by the time the first priest reached my family party he had grown tired and careless. Instead of collecting the certificates singly, he began to take them in twos and threes with the result that they became mixed, and Gerónimo was confirmed, not as Gerónimo, but as "Saturnina," which happened to be the name of the little snub-nosed Totonac girl standing next to him. When I realized this had happened, I protested. Whereupon his grace and I proceeded to have "words." With exceeding bitterness he then reperformed the rite, and if the eyes of the first priest could have killed, I should have withered on my slender stalk. The priest with the cotton sought to annihilate me with an undertoned remark to the effect that my conduct was a *barbaridad,* but the third was not only *simpático* — he was farther away from the bishop: As, with much tenderness, he disengaged Gerónimo's reluctant fingers from the candle, he severely looked at me and winked.[4]

Flandrau also noted the widespread intoxication of the villagers and marveled "not, like the tourist of a week, that they are dirty, but that under the circumstances they are as clean as they are; not that so many of them are continually sick, but that any of them are ever well; not that they love to get drunk, but that they can bear to remain sober." [5]

4 Ibid., pp. 258–259.
5 Ibid., p. 540.

Porfirio Díaz

Knowledge of Mexican history has greatly increased in recent years under the impetus supplied by Daniel Cosío Villegas and his colleagues at the Colegio de México, and by historians at the University of Mexico (Reading 4). The Porfiriato is inextricably linked to the Revolution, and any fair appraisal must include the ten years of chaos that followed his fall.

The Porfiriato had its defenders and two apologists for the regime, Toribio Esquivel Obregón and Emilio Rabasa, who argued that the Revolution was unjustified because Mexico did not have a land problem: the rural, largely

Indian population owned more than enough land to support itself. Professor William B. Taylor, whose recent researches have demonstrated that in fact the Oaxaca land distribution was radically different from the large hacienda type holdings in northern Mexico, points out that these apologists for the Porfiriato used examples from Oaxaca to support their argument.[6] Here again we have an example of the dangers of generalizing on Latin America!

1. *President Díaz: Hero of the Americas*

JAMES CREELMAN

James Creelman represented that breed of American journalists who go abroad on their restless search for a "newsworthy" story. When his interview with President Díaz appeared in the March 1908 issue of *Pearson's Magazine,* it created a commotion in Mexico, for Díaz announced the end of his rule. As Ernest Gruening stated, in his solid volume of enduring value on Mexico: "An earthquake would have caused far less commotion. Mexico was accustomed to earthquakes. But such sentiments from the lips of Don Porfirio were startling, unprecedented, incredible. Many Mexicans refused to believe them. But no denial was forthcoming and the political ferment began."[1]

Did Díaz seriously intend to retire, or was this interview a clever ruse to test the loyalty of his henchmen? Gruening believed that "in the light of subsequent events the interview appears as a typical piece of Díaz duplicity, designed to test out his entourage. It was wholly in keeping with Porfirian policy that matters of such transcendent importance were revealed to an American journalist, while Mexican newspapermen were denied even a further interview on the same subject."[2]

The obsequious praise lavished on the dictator in the Creelman article was typical of the times: "Apart from the subsidized press and countless books, and the paeans of the beneficiaries, much of this enthusiasm was genuine."[3] Nor was Creelman unusual. Here is one dedication of a book by an American writer: "To Señor General Don Porfirio Díaz, The Illustrious President Of Mexico, Whose Intrepid Moral Character, Distinguished Statesmanship, And Devoted Patriotism Make Him The Pride And Glory Of His Country, Is Dedicated This Volume, Describing A Beautiful And Prosperous Land, Whose Free Flag Never Waved Over A Slave, And Whose Importance As A Nation Is Due To The Patriot Under Whose Administration Mexico Now Flourishes And Holds Its Proud Position Among The Republics Of The World."[4]

[6] William B. Taylor, *Landlord and Peasant in Colonial Oaxaca* (Stanford: Stanford University Press, 1972), p. 199.

[1] Gruening, *Mexico and Its Heritage* (New York: Century, 1928), p. 91.

[2] Ibid., p. 92.

[3] Ibid., p. 62.

[4] Marie Robinson Wright, *Picturesque Mexico* (Philadelphia: Lippincott, 1897).

From the heights of Chapultepec Castle President Diaz looked down upon the venerable capital of his country, spread out on a vast plain, with a ring of mountains flung up grandly about it, and I, who had come nearly four thousand miles from New York to see the master and hero of modern Mexico — the inscrutable leader in whose veins is blended the blood of the primitive Mixtecs with that of the invading Spaniards — watched the slender, erect form, the strong, soldierly head and commanding, but sensitive, countenance with an interest beyond words to express.

A high, wide forehead that slopes up to crisp white hair and overhangs deep-set, dark brown eyes that search your soul, soften into inexpressible kindliness and then dart quick side looks — terrible eyes, threatening eyes, loving, confiding, humorous eyes — a straight, powerful, broad and somewhat fleshy nose, whose curved nostrils lift and dilate with every emotion; huge, virile jaws that sweep from large, flat, fine ears, set close to the head, to the tremendous, square, fighting chin; a wide, firm mouth shaded by a white mustache; a full, short, muscular neck; wide shoulders, deep chest; a curiously tense and rigid carriage that gives great distinction to a personality suggestive of singular power and dignity — that is Porfirio Diaz in his seventy-eighth year, as I saw him a few weeks ago on the spot where, forty years before, he stood — with his besieging army surrounding the City of Mexico, and the young Emperor Maximilian being shot to death in Querétaro, beyond those blue mountains to the north — waiting grimly for the thrilling end of the last interference of European monarchy with the republics of America.

It is the intense, magnetic something in the wide-open, fearless, dark eyes and the sense of nervous challenge in the sensitive, spread nostrils, that seem to connect the man with the immensity of the landscape, as some elemental force.

There is not a more romantic or heroic figure in all the world, nor one more intensely watched by both the friends and foes of democracy, than the soldier-statesman, whose adventurous youth pales the pages of Dumas, and whose iron rule has converted the warring, ignorant, superstitious and impoverished masses of Mexico, oppressed by centuries of Spanish cruelty and greed, into a strong, steady, peaceful, debt-paying and progressive nation.

For twenty-seven years he has governed the Mexican Republic with such power that national elections have become mere formalities. He might easily have set a crown upon his head.

From "President Diaz: Hero of the Americas" by James Creelman, *Pearson's Magazine*, 19, March 1908, pp. 231–277. A facsimile reproduction of the interview, together with a Spanish translation, appears in *Entrevista Díaz-Creelman*, Cuadernos del Instituto de Historia, Serie Documental, no. 2 (Mexico: Universidad Nacional Autónoma de México, 1963).

Yet to-day, in the supremacy of his career, this astonishing man — foremost figure of the American hemisphere and unreadable mystery to students of human government — announces that he will insist on retiring from the Presidency at the end of his present term, so that he may see his successor peacefully established and that, with his assistance, the people of the Mexican Republic may show the world that they have entered serenely and preparedly upon the last complete phase of their liberties, that the nation is emerging from ignorance and revolutionary passion, and that it can choose and change presidents without weakness or war.

It is something to come from the money-mad gambling congeries of Wall Street and in the same week to stand on the rock of Chapultepec, in surroundings of almost unreal grandeur and loveliness, beside one who is said to have transformed a republic into an autocracy by the absolute compulsion of courage and character, and to hear him speak of democracy as the hope of mankind.

This, too, at a time when the American soul shudders at the mere thought of a third term for any President.

The President surveyed the majestic, sunlit scene below the ancient castle and turned away with a smile, brushing a curtain of scarlet trumpet-flowers and vine-like pink geraniums as he moved along the terrace toward the inner garden, where a fountain set among palms and flowers sparkled with water from the spring at which Montezuma used to drink, under the mighty cypresses that still rear their branches about the rock on which we stood.

"It is a mistake to suppose that the future of democracy in Mexico has been endangered by the long continuance in office of one President," he said quietly. "I can say sincerely that office has not corrupted my political ideals and that I believe democracy to be the one true, just principle of government, although in practice it is possible only to highly developed peoples."

For a moment the straight figure paused and the brown eyes looked over the great valley to where snow-covered Popocatapetl lifted its volcanic peak nearly eighteen thousand feet among the clouds beside the snowy craters of Ixtaccihuatl — a land of dead volcanoes, human and otherwise.

"I can lay down the Presidency of Mexico without a pang of regret, but I cannot cease to serve this country while I live," he added.

The sun shown full in the President's face but his eyes did not shrink from the ordeal. The green landscape, the smoking city, the blue tumult of mountains, the thin, exhilarating, scented air, seemed to stir him, and the color came to his cheeks as he clasped his hands behind him and threw his head backward. His nostrils opened wide.

"You know that in the United States we are troubled about the question of electing a President for three terms?"

He smiled and then looked grave, nodding his head gently and pursing his lips. It is hard to describe the look of concentrated interest that suddenly came into his strong, intelligent countenance.

"Yes, yes, I know," he replied. "It is a natural sentiment of democratic peoples that their officials should be often changed. I agree with that sentiment."

It seemed hard to realize that I was listening to a soldier who had ruled a republic continuously for more than a quarter of a century with a personal authority unknown to most kings. Yet he spoke with a simple and convincing manner, as one whose place was great and secure beyond the need of hypocrisy.

"It is quite true that when a man has occupied a powerful office for a very long time he is likely to begin to look upon it as his personal property, and it is well that a free people should guard themselves against the tendencies of individual ambition.

"Yet the abstract theories of democracy and the practical, effective application of them are often necessarily different — that is when you are seeking for the substance rather than the mere form.

"I can see no good reason why President Roosevelt should not be elected again if a majority of the American people desire to have him continue in office. I believe that he has thought more of his country than of himself. He has done and is doing a great work for the United States, a work that will cause him, whether he serves again or not, to be remembered in history as one of the great Presidents. I look upon the trusts as a great and real power in the United States, and President Roosevelt has had the patriotism and courage to defy them. Mankind understands the meaning of his attitude and its bearing upon the future. He stands before the world as a statesman whose victories have been moral victories. . . .

"Here in Mexico we have had different conditions. I received this Government from the hands of a victorious army at a time when the people were divided and unprepared for the exercise of the extreme principles of democratic government. To have thrown upon the masses the whole responsibility of government at once would have produced conditions that might have discredited the cause of free government.

"Yet, although I got power at first from the army, an election was held as soon as possible and then my authority came from the people. I have tried to leave the Presidency several times, but it has been pressed upon me and I remained in office for the sake of the nation which trusted me. The fact that the price of Mexican securities dropped eleven points when I was ill at Cuernavaca indicates the kind of evidence that persuaded me to overcome my personal inclination to retire to private life.

"We preserved the republican and democratic form of government. We defended the theory and kept it intact. Yet we adopted a patriarchal policy in the actual administration of the nation's affairs, guiding and restraining popular tendencies, with full faith that an enforced peace would allow education, industry and commerce to develop elements of stability and unity in a naturally intelligent, gentle and affectionate people.

"I have waited patiently for the day when the people of the Mexican Republic would be prepared to choose and change their government at every election without danger of armed revolutions and without injury to the national credit or interference with national progress. I believe that day has come. . . .

"In the old days we had no middle class in Mexico because the minds of the people and their energies were wholly absorbed in politics and war. Spanish tyranny and misgovernment had disorganized society. The productive activities of the nation were abandoned in successive struggles. There was general confusion. Neither life nor property was safe. A middle class could not appear under such conditions."

"General Diaz," I interrupted, "you have had an unprecedented experience in the history of republics. For thirty years the destinies of this nation have been in your hands, to mold them as you will; but men die, while nations must continue to live. Do you believe that Mexico can continue to exist in peace as a republic? Are you satisfied that its future is assured under free institutions?"

It was worth while to have come from New York to Chapultepec Castle to see the hero's face at that moment. Strength, patriotism, warriorship, prophethood seemed suddenly to shine in his brown eyes.

"The future of Mexico is assured," he said in a clear voice. "The principles of democracy have not been planted very deep in our people, I fear. But the nation has grown and it loves liberty. Our difficulty has been that the people do not concern themselves enough about public matters for a democracy. The individual Mexican as a rule thinks much about his own rights and is always ready to assert them. But he does not think so much about the rights of others. He thinks of his privileges, but not of his duties. Capacity for self-restraint is the basis of democratic government, and self-restraint is possible only to those who recognize the rights of their neighbors.

"The Indians, who are more than half of our population, care little for politics. They are accustomed to look to those in authority for leadership instead of thinking for themselves. That is a tendency they inherited from the Spaniards, who taught them to refrain from meddling in public affairs and rely on the Government for guidance.

"Yet I firmly believe that the principles of democracy have grown and will grow in Mexico."

"But you have no opposition party in the Republic, Mr. President. How can free institutions flourish when there is no opposition to keep the majority, or governing party, in check?"

"It is true there is no opposition party. I have so many friends in the republic that my enemies seem unwilling to identify themselves with so small a minority. I appreciate the kindness of my friends and the confidence of my country; but such absolute confidence imposes responsibilities and duties that tire me more and more.

"No matter what my friends and supporters say, I retire when my present term of office ends, and I shall not serve again. I shall be eighty years old then.

"My country has relied on me and it has been kind to me. My friends have praised my merits and overlooked my faults. But they may not be willing to deal so generously with my successor and he may need my advice and support; therefore I desire to be alive when he assumes office so that I may help him."

He folded his arms over his deep chest and spoke with great emphasis.

"I welcome an opposition party in the Mexican Republic," he said. "If it appears, I will regard it as a blessing, not as an evil. And if it can develop power, not to exploit but to govern, I will stand by it, support it, advise it and forget myself in the successful inauguration of complete democratic government in the country.

"It is enough for me that I have seen Mexico rise among the peaceful and useful nations. I have no desire to continue in the Presidency. This nation is ready for her ultimate life of freedom. At the age of seventy-seven years I am satisfied with robust health. That is one thing which neither law nor force can create. I would not exchange it for all the millions of your American oil king."

His ruddy skin, sparkling eyes and light, elastic step went well with his words. For one who has endured the privations of war and imprisonment, and who to-day rises at six o'clock in the morning, working until late at night at the full of his powers, the physical condition of President Diaz, who is even now a notable hunter and who usually ascends the palace stairway two steps at a time, is almost unbelievable.

"The railway has played a great part in the peace of Mexico," he continued. "When I became President at first there were only two small lines, one connecting the capital with Vera Cruz, the other connecting it with Querétaro. Now we have more than nineteen thousand miles of railways. Then we had a slow and costly mail service, carried on by stage coaches, and the mail coach between the capital and Puebla would be stopped by highwaymen two or three times in a trip, the last robbers to attack it generally finding nothing left to steal. Now we have a cheap, safe and fairly rapid mail service throughout the country with more than twenty-two hundred post-offices. Telegraphing was a difficult thing in those times. To-day we have more than forty-five thousand miles of telegraph wires in operation.

"We began by making robbery punishable by death and compelling the execution of offenders within a few hours after they were caught and condemned. We ordered that wherever telegraph wires were cut and the chief officer of the district did not catch the criminal, he should himself suffer; and in case the cutting occurred on a plantation the proprietor who failed to prevent it should be hanged to the nearest telegraph pole. These were military orders, remember.

"We were harsh. Sometimes we were harsh to the point of cruelty. But it was all necessary then to the life and progress of the nation. If there was cruelty, results have justified it."

The nostrils dilated and quivered. The mouth was a straight line.

"It was better that a little blood should be shed that much blood should be saved. The blood that was shed was bad blood; the blood that was saved was good blood.

"Peace was necessary, even an enforced peace, that the nation might have time to think and work. Education and industry have carried on the task begun by the army.". . .

"And which do you regard as the greatest force for peace, the army or the schoolhouse?" I asked.

The soldier's face flushed slightly and the splendid white head was held a little higher.

"You speak of the present time?"

"Yes."

"The schoolhouse. There can be no doubt of that. I want to see education throughout the Republic carried on by the national Government. I hope to see it before I die. It is important that all citizens of a republic should receive the same training, so that their ideals and methods may be harmonized and the national unity intensified. When men read alike and think alike they are more likely to act alike."

"And you believe that the vast Indian population of Mexico is capable of high development?"

"I do. The Indians are gentle and they are grateful, all except the Yacquis and some of the Mayas. They have the traditions of an ancient civilization of their own. They are to be found among the lawyers, engineers, physicians, army officers and other professional men."

Over the city drifted the smoke of many factories.

"It is better than common smoke," I said.

"Yes," he replied, "and yet there are times when common smoke is not such a bad thing. The toiling poor of my country have risen up to support me, but I cannot forget what my comrades in arms and their children have been to me in my severest ordeals."

There were actually tears in the veteran's eyes.

"That," I said, pointing to a hideously modern bull-ring near the castle, "is the only surviving Spanish institution to be seen in this landscape."

"You have not noticed the pawnshops," he exclaimed. "Spain brought to us her pawn-shops, as well as her bull-rings.". . .

There are nineteen thousand miles of railways operated in Mexico, nearly all with American managers, engineers and conductors, and one has only to ride on the Mexican Central system or to enjoy the trains de luxe of the National Line to realize the high transportation standards of the country.

So determined is President Diaz to prevent his country from falling into the hands of the trusts that the Government is taking over and merging in one corporation, with the majority stock in the Nation's hands, the Mexican Central, National and Inter-oceanic lines — so that, with this mighty trunk system of transportation beyond the reach of private control, industry, agriculture, commerce and passenger traffic will be safe from oppression.

This merger of ten thousand miles of railways into a single company, with $113,000,000 of the stock, a clear majority, in the Government's hands, is the answer of President Diaz and his brilliant Secretary of Finances to the prediction that Mexico may some day find herself helplessly in the grip of a railway trust.

Curiously enough, the leading American railway officials representing the lines which are to be merged and controlled by the Government spoke to me with great enthusiasm of the plan as a distinct forward step, desirable alike for shippers and passengers and for private investors in the roads.

Two-thirds of the railways of Mexico are owned by Americans, who have invested about $300,000,000 in them profitably.

As it is, freight and passenger rates are fixed by the Government, and not a time table can be made or changed without official approval.

It may surprise a few Americans to know that the first-class passenger rate in Mexico is only two and two-fifths cents a mile, while the second-class rate, which covers at least one-half of the whole passenger traffic of the country, is only one cent and one-fifth a mile — these figures being in terms of gold, to afford a comparison with American rates.

I have been privately assured by the principal American officers and investors of the larger lines that railway enterprises in Mexico are encouraged, dealt with on their merits and are wholly free from blackmail, direct or indirect. . . .

More than $1,200,000,000 of foreign capital has been invested in Mexico since President Diaz put system and stability into the nation. Capital for railways, mines, factories and plantations has been pouring in at the rate of $200,000,000 a year. In six months the Government sold more than a million acres of land.

In spite of what has already been done, there is still room for the investment of billions of dollars in the mines and industries of the Republic.

Americans and other foreigners interested in mines, real estate, factories, railways and other enterprises have privately assured me, not once, but many times, that, under Diaz, conditions for investment in Mexico are fairer and quite as reliable as in the most highly developed European countries. The President declares that these conditions will continue after his death or retirement.

Since Diaz assumed power, the revenues of the Government have increased from about $15,000,000 to more than $115,000,000, and yet taxes have been steadily reduced.

When the price of silver was cut in two, President Diaz was advised that his country could never pay its national debt, which was doubled by the change in values. He was urged to repudiate a part of the debt. The President denounced the advice as foolishness as well as dishonesty, and it is a fact that some of the greatest officers of the government went for years without their salaries that Mexico might be able to meet her financial obligations dollar for dollar.

The cities shine with electric lights and are noisy with electric trolley cars; English is taught in the public schools of the great Federal District; the public treasury is full and overflowing and the national debt decreasing; there are nearly seventy thousand foreigners living contentedly and prosperously in the Republic — more Americans than Spaniards; Mexico has three times as large a population to the square mile as Canada; public affairs have developed strong men like José Yves Limantour, the great Secretary of Finances, one of the most distinguished of living financiers; Vice-president Corral, who is also Secretary of the Interior; Ignacio Mariscal, the Minister of Foreign Affairs, and Enrique Creel, the brilliant Ambassador at Washington.

And it is a land of beauty beyond compare. Its mountains and valleys, its great plateaus, its indescribably rich and varied foliage, its ever blooming and abundant flowers, its fruits, its skies, its marvelous climate, its old villages, cathedrals, churches, convents — there is nothing quite like Mexico in the world for variety and loveliness. But it is the gentle, trustful, grateful Indian, with his unbelievable hat and many-colored blanket, the eldest child of America, that wins the heart out of you. After traveling all over the world, the American who visits Mexico for the first time wonders how it happened that he never understood what a fascinating country of romance he left at his own door.

It is the hour of growth, strength and peace which convinces Porfirio Diaz that he has almost finished his task on the American continent.

Yet you see no man in a priest's attire in this Catholic country. You see no religious processions. The Church is silent save within her own walls. This is a land where I have seen the most profound religious emotion, the most solemn religious spectacles — from the blanketed peons kneeling for hours in cathedrals, the men carrying their household goods, the women suckling their babies, to that indescribable host of Indians on their knees at the shrine of the Virgin of Guadalupe.

I asked President Diaz about it while we paced the terrace of Chapultepec Castle.

He bowed his white head for a moment and then lifted it high, his dark eyes looking straight into mine.

"We allow no priest to vote, we allow no priest to hold public office, we allow no priest to wear a distinctive dress in public, we allow no religious processions in the streets," he said. "When we made those laws we were not fighting against religion, but against idolatry. We intend that the humblest Mexican shall be so far freed from the past that he can stand upright and unafraid in the presence of any human being. I have no hostility to religion; on the contrary, in spite of all past experience, I firmly believe that there can be no true national progress in any country or any time without real religion."

Such is Porfirio Díaz, the foremost man of the American hemisphere. What he has done, almost alone and in such a few years, for a people disorganized and degraded by war, lawlessness and comic-opera politics, is the great inspiration of Pan-Americanism, the hope of the Latin-American republics,

Whether you see him at Chapultepec Castle, or in his office in the National Palace, or in the exquisite drawing-room of his modest home in the city, with his young, beautiful wife and his children and grandchildren by his first wife about him, or surrounded by troops, his breast covered with decorations conferred by great nations, he is always the same — simple, direct and full of the dignity of conscious power.

In spite of the iron government he has given to Mexico, in spite of a continuance in office that has caused men to say that he has converted a republic into an autocracy, it is impossible to look into his face when he speaks of the principle of popular sovereignty without believing that even now he would take up arms and shed his blood in defense of it.

Only a few weeks ago Secretary of State Root summed up President Diaz when he said:

> It has seemed to me that all of the men now living, General Porfirio Diaz, of Mexico, was best worth seeing. Whether one considers the adventurous, daring, chivalric incidents of his early career; whether one considers the vast work of government which his wisdom and courage and commanding character accomplished; whether one considers his singularly attractive personality, no one lives to-day that I would rather see than President Diaz. If I were a poet I would write poetic eulogies. If I were a musician I would compose triumphal marches. If I were a Mexican I should feel that the steadfast loyalty of a lifetime could not

be too much in return for the blessings that he had brought to my country. As I am neither poet, musician nor Mexican, but only an American who loves justice and liberty and hopes to see their reign among mankind progress and strengthen and become perpetual, I look to Porfirio Diaz, the President of Mexico, as one of the great men to be held up for the hero-worship of mankind.

2. The Díaz System

JOHN KENNETH TURNER

John Kenneth Turner had an entirely different approach from that of Creelman, for he had seen with his own eyes the conditions suffered by the Indians in Yucatán and the Valle Nacional.

The slavery and peonage of Mexico, the poverty and illiteracy, the general prostration of the people, are due, in my humble judgment, to the financial and political organization that at present rules that country — in a word, to what I shall call the "system" of General Porfirio Diaz.

That these conditions can be traced in a measure to the history of Mexico during past generations, is true. I do not wish to be unfair to General Diaz in the least degree. The Spanish Dons made slaves and peons of the Mexican people. Yet never did they grind the people as they are ground today. In Spanish times the peon at least had his own little patch of ground, his own humble shelter; today he has nothing. Moreover, the Declaration of Independence, proclaimed just one hundred years ago, in 1810, proclaimed also the abolition of chattel slavery. Slavery was abolished, though not entirely. Succeeding Mexican governments of class and of church and of the individual held the people in bondage little less severe. But finally came a democratic movement which broke the back of the church, which overthrew the rule of caste, which adopted a form of government as modern as our own, which freed the slave in fact as well as in name, which gave the lands of the people back to the people, which wiped the slate clean of the blood of the past. . . .

It was under Porfirio Diaz that slavery and peonage were re-established in Mexico, and on a more merciless basis than they had existed even under the

From *Barbarous Mexico* by John Kenneth Turner (Chicago: Charles H. Kerr & Company, 1910), pp. 120–137, passim.

Spanish Dons. Therefore, I can see no injustice in charging at least a preponderance of the blame for these conditions upon the system of Diaz.

I say the "system of Diaz" rather than Diaz personally because, though he
is the keystone of the arch, though he is the government of Mexico more
completely than is any other individual the government of any large country
on the planet, yet no one man can stand alone in his iniquity. Diaz is the central prop of the slavery, but there are other props without which the system
could not continue upright for a single day. For example, there is the collection of commercial interests which profit by the Diaz system of slavery and
autocracy, and which puts no insignificant part of its tremendous powers to
holding the central prop upright in exchange for the special privileges that it
receives. Not the least among these commercial interests are American,
which, I blush to say, are quite as aggressive defenders of the Diaz citadel as
any. Indeed . . . these American interests undoubtedly form the determining
force of the continuation of Mexican slavery. Thus does Mexican slavery
come home to us in the full sense of the term. . . .

In order that the reader may understand the Diaz system and its responsibility in the degradation of the Mexican people, it will be well to go back and
trace briefly the beginnings of that system. Mexico is spoken of throughout
the world as a Republic. That is because it was once a Republic and still pre-
tends to be one. Mexico has a constitution which has never been repealed, a
constitution said to be modeled after our own, and one which is, indeed, like
ours in the main. Like ours, it provides for a national congress, state legislatures and municipal aldermen to make the laws, federal, state, and local judges
to interpret them, and a president, governors and local executives to administer them. Like ours, it provides for manhood suffrage, freedom of the press
and of speech, equality before the law, and the other guarantees of life, liberty
and the pursuit of happiness which we ourselves enjoy, in a degree, as a
matter of course.

Such was Mexico forty years ago. Forty years ago Mexico was at peace
with the world. She had just overthrown, after a heroic war, the foreign
prince, Maximilian, who had been seated as emperor by the armies of Napoleon Third of France. Her president, Benito Juarez, is today recognized in
Mexico and out of Mexico as one of the most able as well as unselfish patriots of Mexican history. Never since Cortez fired his ships there on the gulf
coast had Mexico enjoyed such prospects of political freedom, industrial
prosperity and general advancement.

But in spite of these facts, and the additional fact that he was deeply
indebted to Juarez, all his military promotions having been received at the
hands of the latter, General Porfirio Diaz stirred up a series of rebellions for
the purpose of securing for himself the supreme power of the land. Diaz not
only led one armed rebellion against a peaceable, constitutional and popularly

approved government, but he led three of them. For nine years he plotted as a common rebel. The support that he received came chiefly from bandits, criminals and professional soldiers who were disgruntled at the antimilitarist policy which Juarez had inaugurated and which, if he could have carried it out a little farther, would have been effective in preventing military revolutions in the future — and from the Catholic church. . . .

In defiance of the will of the majority of the people of Mexico, General Diaz, thirty-four years ago, came to the head of government. In defiance of the will of the majority of the people he has remained there ever since — except for four years, from 1880 to 1884, when he turned the palace over to an intimate friend, Manuel Gonzalez, on the distinct understanding that at the end of the four years Gonzalez would turn it back to him again.

Since no man can rule an unwilling people without taking away the liberties of that people, it can be very easily understood what sort of regime General Diaz found it necessary to establish in order to make his power secure. By the use of the army and the police powers generally, he controlled elections, the press and public speech and made of popular government a farce. By distributing the public offices among his generals and granting them free rein to plunder at will, he assured himself of the continued use of the army. By making political combinations with men high in the esteem of the Catholic church and permitting it to be whispered about that the church was to regain some of its former powers, he gained the silent support of the priests and the Pope. By promising full payment of all foreign debts and launching at once upon a policy of distributing favors among citizens of other countries, he made his peace with the world at large. . . .

Take, for example, Diaz's method of rewarding his military chiefs, the men who helped him overthrow the government of Lerdo. As quickly as possible after assuming the power, he installed his generals as governors of the various states and organized them and other influential figures in the nation into a national plunderbund. Thus he assured himself of the continued loyalty of the generals, on the one hand, and put them where he could most effectively use them for keeping down the people, on the other. One variety of rich plum which he handed out in those early days to his governors came in the form of charters giving his governors the right, as individuals, to organize companies and build railroads, each charter carrying with it a huge sum as a railroad subsidy.

The national government paid for the road and then the governor and his most influential friends owned it. Usually the railroads were ridiculous affairs, were of narrow-gauge and of the very cheapest materials, but the subsidy was very large, sufficient to build the road and probably equip it besides. During his first term of four years in office Diaz passed sixty-one railroad acts containing appropriations aggregating $40,000,000, and all but two or three of these acts were in favor of governors of states. In a number of cases not a mile of railroad was actually built, but the subsidies are supposed to have been paid, anyhow. In nearly every case the subsidy was the same, $12,880 per mile in Mexican silver, and in those days Mexican silver was nearly on a par with gold.

This huge sum was taken out of the national treasury and was supposedly paid to the governors, although Mexican politicians of the old times have assured me that it was divided, a part going out as actual subsidies and a part going directly into the hands of Diaz to be used in building up his machine in other quarters.

Certainly something more than mere loyalty, however invaluable it was, was required of the governors in exchange for such rich financial plums. It is a well authenticated fact that governors were required to pay a fixed sum annually for the privilege of exploiting to the limit the graft possibilities of their offices. For a long time Manuel Romero Rubio, father-in-law of Diaz, was the collector of these perquisites, the offices bringing in anywhere from $10,000 to $50,000 per year.

The largest single perquisite whereby Diaz enriched himself, the members of his immediate family, his friends, his governors, his financial ring and his foreign favorites, was found for a long time in the confiscation of the lands of the common people — a confiscation, in fact, which is going on to this day. Note that this land robbery was the first direct step in the path of the Mexican people back to their bondage as slaves and peons.

. . . The lands of the Yaquis of Sonora were taken from them and given to political favorites of the ruler. The lands of the Mayas of Yucatan, now enslaved by the *henequen* planters, were taken from them in almost the same manner. The final act in this confiscation was accomplished in the year 1904, when the national government set aside the last of their lands into a territory called Quintana Roo. This territory contains 43,000 square kilometers or 27,000 square miles. It is larger than the present state of Yucatan by 8,000 square kilometers, and moreover is the most promising land of the entire peninsula. Separated from the island of Cuba by a narrow strait, its soil and climate are strikingly similar to those of Cuba and experts have declared that there is no reason why Quintana Roo should not one day become as great a tobacco-growing country as Cuba. Further than that, its hillsides are thickly covered with the most valuable cabinet and dyewoods in the world. It is this magnificent country which, as the last chapter in the life of the Mayas as a nation, the Diaz government took and handed over to eight Mexican politicians.

In like manner have the Mayos of Sonora, the Papagos, the Tomosachics — in fact, practically all the native peoples of Mexico — been reduced to peonage, if not to slavery. Small holders of every tribe and nation have gradually been expropriated until today their number as property holders is almost down to zero. Their lands are in the hands of members of the governmental machine, or persons to whom the members of the machine have sold for profit — or in the hands of foreigners.

This is why the typical Mexican farm is the million-acre farm, why it has been so easy for such Americans as William Randolph Hearst, Harrison Gray Otis, E. H. Harriman, the Rockefellers, the Guggenheims and numerous others each to have obtained possession of millions of Mexican acres. This is why Secretary of Fomento Molina holds more than 15,000,000 acres of the soil of Mexico, why ex-Governor Terrazas, of Chihuahua, owns 15,000,000 acres of the soil of that state, why Finance Minister Limantour, Mrs. Porfirio Diaz, Vice-President Corral, Governor Pimentel of Chiapas, Governor Landa y Escandon of the Federal District, Governor Pablo Escandon of Morelos, Governor Ahumada of Jalisco, Governor Cosio of Queretaro, Governor Mercado of Michoacan, Governor Canedo of Sinaloa, Governor Cahuantzi of Tlaxcala, and many other members of the Diaz machine are not only millionaires, but they are millionaires in Mexican real estate.

Chief among the methods used in getting the lands away from the people in general was through a land registration law which Diaz fathered. This law permitted any person to go out and claim any lands to which the possessor could not prove a recorded title. Since up to the time the law was enacted it was not the custom to record titles, this meant all the lands of Mexico. When a man possessed a home which his father had possessed before him, and which his grandfather had possessed, which his great-grandfather had possessed, and which had been in the family as far back as history knew; then he considered that he owned that home, all of his neighbors considered that he owned it, and all governments up to that of Diaz recognized his right to that home.

Supposing that a strict registration law became necessary in the course of evolution, had this law been enacted for the purpose of protecting the land owners instead of plundering them the government would, naturally, have sent agents through the country to apprise the people of the new law and to help them register their property and keep their homes. But this was not done and the conclusion is inevitable that the law was passed for the purpose of plundering.

At all events, the result of the law was a plundering. No sooner had it been passed than the aforesaid members of the governmental machine, headed by the father-in-law of Diaz, and Diaz himself, formed land companies and sent out agents, not to help the people keep their lands, but to select the most desirable lands in the country, register them, and evict the owners. This they did on a most tremendous scale. Thus hundreds of thousands of small farmers lost their property. Thus small farmers are still losing their property. . . .

Another favorite means of confiscating the homes of small owners is found in the juggling of state taxes. State taxes in Mexico are fearfully and wonderfully made. Especially in the less populous districts owners are taxed inversely as they stand in favor with the personality who represents the government in their particular district. No court, board or other responsible body sits to review unjust assessments. The *jefe politico* may charge one farmer five times as much per acre as he charges the farmer across the fence, and yet Farmer No. 1 has no redress unless he is rich and powerful. He must pay, and if he cannot, the farm is a little later listed among the properties of the jefe politico, or one of the members of his family, or among the properties of the governor of the state or one of the members of his family. But if he is rich and powerful he is often not taxed at all. American promoters in Mexico escape taxation so nearly invariably that the impression has got abroad in this country that land pays no taxes in Mexico. Even Frederick Palmer made a statement to this effect in his recent writings about that country.

Of course such bandit methods as were employed and are still employed were certain to meet with resistance, and so we find numerous instances of regiments of soldiers being called out to enforce collection of taxes or the eviction of time-honored landholders. . . .

. . . Hardly a month passes today without there being one or more reports in Mexican papers of disturbances, the result of confiscation of homes, either through the denunciation method or the excuse of nonpayment of taxes. . . .

Graft is an established institution in the public offices of Mexico. It is a right vested in the office itself, is recognized as such, and is respectable. There are two main functions attached to each public office, one a privilege, the other a duty. The privilege is that of using the special powers of the office for the amassing of a personal fortune; the duty is that of preventing the people from entering into any activities that may endanger the stability of the existing regime. Theoretically, the fulfillment of the duty is judged as balancing the harvest of the privilege, but with all offices and all places this is not so, and so we find offices of particularly rosy possibilities selling for a fixed price. Examples are those of the jefes politicos in districts where the slave trade is peculiarly remunerative, as at Pachuca, Oaxaca, Veracruz, Orizaba, Cordoba and Rio Blanco; of the districts in which the drafting of soldiers for the army is especially let to the jefes politicos; of the towns in which the gambling privileges are let as a monopoly to the mayors thereof; of the states in which there exist opportunities extraordinary for governors to graft off the army supply contracts.

Monopolies called "concessions," which are nothing more nor less than trusts created by governmental decree, are dealt in openly by the Mexican government. Some of these concessions are sold for cash, but the rule is to give them away gratis or for a nominal price, the real price being collected in political support. The public domain is sold in huge tracts for a nominal price or for nothing at all, the money price, when paid at all, averaging about fifty Mexican *centavos* an acre. But never does the government sell to any individual or company not of its own special choice; that is, the public domain is by no means open to all comers on equal terms. Public concessions worth millions of dollars — to use the water of a river for irrigation purposes, or for power, to engage in this or that monopoly, have been given away, but not indiscriminately. These things are the coin with which political support is bought and as such are grafts, pure and simple.

Public action of any sort is never taken for the sake of improving the condition of the common people. It is taken with a view to making the government more secure in its position. Mexico is a land of special privileges extraordinary, though frequently special privileges are provided for in the name of the common people. An instance is that of the "Agricultural Bank," which was created in 1908. To read the press reports concerning the purpose of this bank one would imagine that the government had launched into a gigantic and benevolent scheme to re-establish its expropriated people in agriculture. The purpose, it was said, was to loan money to needy farmers. But nothing coud be farther from the truth, for the purpose is to help out the rich farmer, and only the richest in the land. The bank has now been loaning money for two years, but so far not a single case has been recorded in which aid was given to help a farm that comprised less than thousands of acres. Millions have been loaned on private irrigation projects, but never in lumps of less than several tens of thousands. In the United States the farmer class is an humble class indeed; in Mexico the typical farmer is the king of millionaires, a little potentate. In Mexico, because of the special privileges given by the government, medievalism still prevails outside the cities. The barons are richer and more powerful than were the landed aristocrats before the French Revolution, and the canaille poorer, more miserable.

And the special financial privileges centering in the cities are no less remarkable than the special privileges given to the exploiters of the *hacienda* slave. There is a financial ring consisting of members of the Diaz machine and their close associates, who pluck all the financial plums of the "republic," who get the contracts, the franchises and the concessions, and whom the large aggregations of foreign capital which secure a footing in the country find it necessary to take as coupon-clipping partners. The "Banco Nacional," an institution having some fifty-four branches and which has been compared flatteringly to the Bank of England, is the special financial vehicle of the government camarilla. It monopolizes the major portion of the banking business of the country and is a convenient cloak for the larger grafts, such as the railway merger, the true significance of which I shall present in a future chapter.

Diaz encourages foreign capital, for foreign capital means the support of foreign governments. American capital has a smoother time with Diaz than it has even with its own government, which is very fine from the point of view of American capital, but not so good from the point of view of the Mexican people. Diaz has even entered into direct partnership with certain aggregations of foreign capital, granting these aggregations special privileges in some lines which he has refused to his own millionaires. These foreign partnerships which Diaz has formed has made his government international insofar as the props which support his system are concerned. The certainty of foreign intervention in his favor has been one of the powerful forces which have prevented the Mexican people from using arms to remove a ruler who imposed himself upon them by the use of arms.

When I come to deal with the American partners of Diaz I mention those of no other nationality in the same breath, but it will be well to bear in mind that England, especially, is nearly as heavily as interested in Mexico as is the United States. While this country has $900,000,000 (these are the figures given by Consul General Shanklin about the first of the year 1910) invested in Mexico, England (according to the South American Journal) has $750,000,000. However, these figures by no means represent the ratio between the degree of political influence exerted by the two countries. There the United States bests all the other countries combined. . . .

3. The Díaz Regime Was Unconcerned with the Needs of the Masses and Ignorant of Their Potential Power

CHARLES C. CUMBERLAND

The late Professor Charles C. Cumberland of Michigan State University was one of the many students who developed their capacity for understanding Mexican history under Professor Charles W. Hackett at the University of Texas. Professor Cumberland's competent analysis of the beginnings of the Revolution demonstrates how closely connected were the years of the dictatorship and the violent period of the Revolution.

When in September, 1910, Mexico played host to the embassies of the world at the magnificent spectacle celebrating a century of Mexican independence, the special delegates vied with one another in extolling the virtues and strength of the Díaz regime. General Porfirio Díaz was completing his seventh term as constitutional president of Mexico, having been the dictator of his country for

From *Mexican Revolution: Genesis under Madero* by Charles C. Cumberland (Austin: University of Texas Press, 1952), pp. 3–28, passim. Reprinted by permission.

thirty-four years, and was then about to embark upon his eighth term. His nation was honored and respected; as a head of state Díaz had been phenomenally successful in stabilizing Mexico and bringing her material prosperity. The power and prestige of the aged dictator, who appeared to be hale and vigorous in spite of his eighty years, had never been greater; his government was believed to be impervious to attack, his power unassailable, his country assured of a peaceful future. And yet, within the space of eight months the Díaz government crumbled, the dictator and most of his chief advisors fled into exile, and a revolution of tremendous force began.

That the Díaz government was a dictatorship no one denied. Even its strongest supporters freely admitted that the Constitution of 1857 had been perverted, that the branches of government were nonexistent inasmuch as Díaz was the final arbiter in all questions, and that "democracy" was merely a term used indiscriminately. As Francisco Bulnes expressed it, the question was not whether Díaz was a dictator, since the Mexicans in the past had possessed neither liberty nor democracy, but whether he was a good or a bad dictator. His task, on assuming control in 1876, had been to weld the Mexican people into a peaceful unit, to stabilize the government and pacify the country, and to bring material gain and prosperity to the nation. Each part of the task impinged on the other; failure in one would have meant almost inevitable failure in the other two. . . .

Within a relatively short time after coming to power, Díaz managed to obtain the active or tacit support of the great majority of the Mexican people of all classes by attempting to meet the special interests of each class. Through this practice, supplemented by a policy of harsh repression against revolutionaries and bandits, he brought peace to Mexico, the first peace the nation had known since the colonial period, and laid the foundation for an amazing material development. Railway lines, which in 1876 had been negligible, totaled more than fifteen thousand miles in 1910. During the same period, exports and imports increased nearly tenfold, with a favorable balance of trade in most years. Smelting of precious and semiprecious metals increased fourfold, petroleum production became a major industry, textile mills were built by the hundreds, sugar mills sprang up in the southern states, and numerous smaller but important industries began. The prosperity of the epoch was reflected in the favorable relationship between national debt and national income, and in the foreign-credit standing. Mexican bonds on foreign markets sold at a premium, the national debt declined until in the early 1900's it was the smallest in the country's history, revenues increased more than tenfold, and reserves accumulated annually. The domestic and foreign financial standing of the Mexican government, under the direction of the dictatorship, was very sound. . . .

It was the economic advances and their by-products . . . that served as a stimulus for most of the support of, and much of the opposition to, the dictatorship. In view of the general financial condition of Mexico and her people when Díaz came to power — the government was heavily in debt and the people had little cash reserve for new investment — it was absolutely necessary to encourage a flow of foreign capital to Mexico if there was to be material development. From the beginning of his administration, Díaz deliberately fostered foreign investment on terms highly advantageous to the investor. The policy brought money to Mexico, but the zealous regard for the interests of the foreigner created another class in Mexican society and added to the already prejudicial social and economic stratification. The foreigner, particularly the American, was now considered the most important element in society, with much of the economic legislation framed to favor his group. The concessions made to foreigners, especially in the changes in the mining code, worked to the grave disadvantage of the nation, inasmuch as the government's proportion of income from the mines was lessened and speculation in mining properties was encouraged. The preference granted to foreigners was constantly humiliating to the nationals and was one of the most irritating facets of the dictatorship. On the other hand, often the robber was robbed, for the majority of foreigners who invested in Mexico were victimized by ignorance and sharp dealing, even though many of those who came to the country did amass fortunes.

The emphasis on industrialization had other evil effects as well, for with the development of monopolies the already clearly defined difference between rich and poor became even more marked. Mexico's economy was largely controlled by a small group of businessmen and financiers who completely dominated money and credit, controlled the most lucrative concessions, and soon became the "arbiters of the prosperity of the Mexicans." For example, of the sixty-six financial, transportation, insurance, and industrial corporations listed in the 1908 report of the Banco Central Mexicano, thirty-six had common directors from a group of thirteen men; and nineteen of the corporations had more than one of the thirteen. One of the thirteen men was on the boards of nine banks, one railroad, one insurance company, and four industrial concerns. This tight control by a small group led to many of the economic and social abuses of which the Díaz government was accused, and brought into being what a Díaz opponent called "mercantilism." "It was this 'mercantilism,'" he said, "which overwhelmed the nation, increased despotism, despoiled the people, implanted degrading speculation, and sustained infamous and depraved governors." As the monopolists became more opulent, they were blinded by their own prosperity and became less able than ever to see the needs of the less fortunate. Their own prosperity, too, bolstered by the statistics of production, foreign trade, and finances, convinced them that Mexico as a nation was prosperous and that their own interests were synonymous with national interests.

In the last decade of the nineteenth century, a few men representing the new moneyed class banded together under Díaz' father-in-law, Manuel Romero Rubio, into a group which soon came to be called the Científicos. Hardly a political party at its inception, the organization was nonetheless allied closely with a political party formed in 1892 and came to exercise all the functions of a party. The group soon determined that the most effective means of guaranteeing a continuation of the economic system that had developed would be to control the government in so far as possible during Díaz' life and absolutely after his death. Until the formation of the Científicos, Díaz had maintained his early policy of meeting the demands of the mestizos; but as the Científicos grew in power, they successfully drew him away from the mestizos and convinced him of the necessity for supporting the creoles. Looked upon by many in the nineties and in the early years of the new century as the hope for a regenerated Mexico, the Científicos came to be feared and hated, even by men who had previously been their ardent supporters. . . .

There were many evidences, tenuous to be sure, of economic instability after 1904, even in [Minister of Hacienda José Ives] Limantour's own special province — banking. Adoption of the gold standard in 1905, followed by the 1907 money panic in the United States and an export price decline, brought shrinking national revenues, which necessitated foreign borrowing, and at the same time placed a heavy strain on domestic financial institutions. The banks, although outwardly prosperous, demonstrated symptoms of instability which endangered the entire Mexican financial structure. Limantour himself recognized the symptoms and called a national conference of bankers early in 1908 for the purpose of studying the situation and proposing new laws to rectify the existing weaknesses. The banks had obviously been indulging in speculation, lending enormous sums on poor security; institutions authorized to issue bank notes were particularly at fault, engaging in practices which sometimes brought large returns but which were generally unsound. As a consequence of the conference and Limantour's recommendations, a new banking law to correct some of the dangerous policies and to encourage the establishment of investment and mortgage banks was passed in the summer of 1908.

The new regulations, however, did not correct all the evils. Less than a year later the Banco Central Mexicano, the central reserve institution, was in a condition that approached the critical. The weakness of the bank was largely the responsibility of the government itself, which at various times had "suggested" to the bank that loans be made to administration friends. When the public learned that the central bank had absorbed enough worthless paper to impair its capital, confidence in all credit and financial institutions was seriously undermined. . . .

As might be expected in such a financial situation, inflation was rampant during most of the latter part of the Díaz regime. The cost of most items, particularly the staples on which the mass of the population depended, increased enormously; there was not a corresponding increase in the wages of agricultural and industrial workers. The wage earners were therefore forced into a constantly deteriorating position. What was happening to corn, a basic part of the diet of 85 per cent of the population, indicates the trend. Between 1893 and 1906 the value of corn per unit increased on the average by 50 per cent, and after 1906 the increase was more rapid. Occasionally the government would sell corn at "much lower prices than those established by the speculators," to use Díaz' words, but these sales were temporary expedients only and were usually confined to the capital itself. Somewhat the same trend was noted in other staples. Even more destructive of the well-being of the masses was the violent fluctuation in the price of staples from day to day and from place to place; a change of 400 per cent in a matter of days was not unusual. The government, in spite of the obvious need for price stabilization, did nothing permanently constructive. . . .

While basic commodity prices were on the increase, there was no ascertainable rise in salaries. In the early nineteenth century Baron Alexander von Humboldt had estimated the average daily wage to be approximately twenty-five centavos; in 1891 the prevailing wage was between twenty-five and fifty centavos, with the average nearer the lower figure; in 1908 the daily wage was almost exactly what it had been one hundred years earlier. In sum total, the static wage and the increasing cost of commodities meant a drastic decline in real wages. . . .

In the face of his rapidly deteriorating economic position, the laborer was helpless. Not only were there no labor laws to aid the worker but as Díaz became more closely allied with the creoles and their interests he became less sympathetic to the predicament of the mestizos and Indians, who composed the working class. A cheap labor supply being one of the principal assets which Mexico could offer to foreign investors and Mexican industrialists, and the general standard of work among the laborers being rather poor, the government never considered that protection of the laborer was either necessary or desirable. In vain did some intellectuals demand an improvement of conditions; in vain did Wistano Luis Orozco, scholar and humanitarian, insist that the lower classes were the brothers of the remainder of society and had a right to demand improvement, "morally and physically." The alliance between government and special privilege was too strong. Labor organizations were practically unknown before 1900; and even if the workers had been organized, they would have found it almost impossible to act in their own behalf. In most states and territories the laws forbade strikes; in the Federal District heavy fines and imprisonment could be imposed on any person attempting to use physical or moral force for the purpose of increasing salaries or wages. Even in areas where no specific law applied to striking, various means were used, often with the aid of public officials, to defeat the aims of the workers.

But these industrially idyllic conditions, in which the laborer worked for a pittance without question, could not continue indefinitely. The syndicalist and anarchist concepts, though late in penetrating into Mexico, became known after the turn of the century through the work and writing of Spaniards and Mexicans, the most important of whom was the Mexican Ricardo Flores Magón. Accordingly, the workers, "better taught than before to look out for their own interests, resented . . . oppression and resolutely aspired to improve their condition." Beginning in 1906, the laborers insisted that wages be raised and hours shortened; as a result of the industrialists' adamant refusal to meet these demands, a period of unrest developed. Although the strikes were defeated in most cases through government intercession, most industrial centers saw strife of varying intensity, and the workers were at last beginning to realize their potential strength, even though industrial labor constituted only a small proportion of the country's total labor force. . . .

The poor condition in which the industrial worker found himself had its counterpart, perhaps exaggerated to a degree, in the situation of the vast number of Indians whose primary source of livelihood was the land. The rural inhabitants, largely Indian, had been at the mercy of the Spaniard and the creole during the colonial epoch and continued in that state after independence. But many Indian villages had been allowed to retain the community holdings which were in their possession prior to the Conquest, and many more had been granted land by the Spanish crown. These areas, called *ejidos* though actually divided into five distinct classifications, served as a guarantee of partial independence for members of the community, but in the immediate postindependence period considerable difference of opinion arose among liberals over the question of the Indian and his relation to the land. Some, arguing that the Indian did not have a European concept of ownership, insisted that the village ejidos be left undisturbed; others, convinced that communal holding was evidence of backwardness and was not conducive to progress, favored a distribution of village land among the inhabitants of the village, with the individuals holding the parcels in fee simple. It was this last contention which prevailed when the triumphant liberals, after defeating Santa Anna and his conservative supporters in the Revolution of Ayutla, drafted the Constitution of 1857. The Ley Lerdo, which had been passed the previous year and which prohibited civil or religious corporations from owning real property not directly necessary for the functioning of the corporations, was written into the constitution. The village lands were therefore open to distribution among the members of the communities.

In the meantime the haciendas, enormous holdings of land often poorly and incompletely cultivated, were becoming increasingly important as an institution — economic, social, and political — in the rural areas. Many haciendas dated from the colonial period, but with the application of the Ley Lerdo and the Reform Laws effectuated a few years later, and with the confiscation, during both the War of Reform and the French Intervention, of much of the property belonging to the losing factions, the hacienda system was extended and a new hacienda class developed. . . .

It was on this foundation that the Díaz land system developed, and it was in the agrarian field that the Díaz government recorded one of its greatest failures. In a nation which depended heavily on agriculture, the Díaz government made no attempt to improve agricultural production through education or experimentation. Although much of the country was arid or semiarid and needed irrigation planning on a national scale, the government did practically nothing. It did not attempt to relieve the critical food shortage by encouraging increased production of cereals or other items consumed by the masses; although statistics indicate an annual increase in agricultural production, the increase was largely in items for export and gave little aid to the mass of the population. These were errors of omission; much more serious were the errors of commission in land legislation.

Díaz was not completely responsible for the development which robbed the villages of their land and forced the major portion of the Indian population into economic slavery; previous legal and constitutional provisions had set the pattern. The first interpretations of the constitutional provision had stipulated that the *suertes,* or *terrenos de común repartimiento* — agricultural lands attached to the villages at the time of the Conquest — were not subject to parceling, and as long as that interpretation prevailed many villages in the heart of the agricultural districts would retain their independence. By successive decrees in 1889 and 1890, however, Díaz brought all village lands within the categories to be parceled, and from that time forward the laws were more stringently applied. The new owner, unaccustomed to thinking in terms of private ownership and not given proper protection by the government, was easily victimized by unscrupulous officials and by individuals who legally or illegally gained control of the land. In the final analysis, the Indian villager too often found that as a result of the distribution he no longer had access to any land of his own and was forced to seek employment at the nearest hacienda.

Not all the Indian villages, however, lost their land through the instrumentality of the distribution law; many were victimized outright by a variety of other means. In some cases grasping government officials, charged with the responsibility of parceling the land and dispensing justice to the villagers, merely sold all village property to a company or an individual; such sales were irregular and illegal, of course, but the despoliation was effectuated nevertheless. In many cases the village was destroyed when an outsider gained control of the water supply and forced the village to sell. But the most disastrous practice, in so far as the loss of village lands was concerned, resulted from a series of surveying laws passed in 1863, 1883, 1894. Under these laws, each more advantageous than the last to the surveying companies and demanding fewer responsibilities from them, national lands were surveyed by individuals and companies and the surveyors allowed to gain control of enormous amounts of land. Under the 1894 law any parcel to which a legal title could not be produced could be declared *terrenos baldíos,* or untilled national lands, and any individual could file a claim to purchase the property at a set cash price. . . . Through the operation of the laws, and through official or quasi-official chicanery, enormous quantities of land came under the control of a small group of men or companies. One estimate indicates that over two and one-quarter million acres of good land, representing the means of livelihood of tens of thousands of Indians, passed from the Indian communities to the *hacendados;* this was in addition to the untold millions of acres of bona fide national lands which were alienated.

A combination of the above forces and practices meant disaster to the Indian village, and tremendous growth to the haciendas. The free agricultural village — one in which the majority of the residents had access to sufficient lands to make a living — was disappearing, and concentration of land ownership was intensifying. Between 1881 and 1889, 14 per cent of the arable land was concentrated in twenty-nine companies or individuals; by 1894, more than 20 per cent was controlled by fewer than fifty holders; and by 1910, less than 1 per cent of the families owned or controlled about 85 per cent of the land. . . .

Had the land acquired by the haciendas been profitably used, and had the villagers now forced to work for the haciendas been properly treated, the situation would not have been so disastrous. But the haciendas were not economically successful: they left too much arable land uncultivated, and they were not so productive, proportionally, as the smaller holdings. The rapid development of the hacienda system under Díaz constituted a burden on, and a retrogression of, the agricultural economy, rather than, as its proponents insisted, an improvement. . . .

Díaz' attitude toward rural and industrial labor is indicative of his loss of political perception. In contrast to his remarkable acumen in recognizing the paramount interest of each important group and in catering to those interests before 1900, after the turn of the century he was no longer able to see the forces or to adjust his policies accordingly. Labor was rapidly becoming a factor to consider in national politics, and yet Díaz and his advisors could think of nothing more constructive than suppression. When confronted with somewhat the same condition in 1876 with respect to bandits, Díaz had adroitly obtained the support of a sufficient number to counterbalance those who were recalcitrant. To labor he made no concession at all, and after 1900 labor constituted a greater potential force than had the bandits in 1876. . . .

Díaz was also unconcerned with the nationalism which had been developing rapidly in the latter part of the nineteenth century. The constant condescension displayed by the President and his government to everything Mexican, and the near adulation for everything foreign, were irritating to the younger generation. The foreigner was treated with the deference of an invited guest, the mining laws governing concessions and subsoil rights were reframed to conform with foreign concepts and practices, enormous areas of land were sold or practically given to foreigners, and foreigners were regularly favored in Mexican courts. Since citizens of the United States were the most numerous among the foreigners, one bitter critic summed it up by saying that the regime "destroyed national honor in the face of Yankee demands." Díaz was not alone in his preference for foreigners; most of the social elite were prejudiced in favor of foreign goods, foreign literature, and foreign ideas. Industrial concerns, whether under the control of Mexicans or aliens, regularly paid higher wages to foreign employees than to natives; the policy was probably justified by the foreigners' greater technical skill, but it did not endear the government or the industrialists to the laborers. All those who were proud to be Mexicans resented the rank favoritism which seemed to be common.

Even the upper classes were mixed in their support of the government after 1900. Díaz, consistently refusing to allow widespread political participation to the social and economic plutocracy, destroyed the public spirit of the class and weakened it as a bulwark of the regime. To be sure, the moneyed groups gave unstinting praise to Díaz' government, but they were without organization and without leadership other than that formed by the government. In his anxiety to protect himself against the political ambitions of this group, Díaz had enervated a potentially powerful support.

Without quite realizing what had happened, Díaz gradually lost the active support of most elements in Mexican society. Many mestizos were alienated by his gradual orientation toward creoles and foreigners, as well as by the treatment accorded labor and small proprietors. The proprietors, allied with the labor leaders, became a solid core of opposition before the end of the regime. The Indians, while not openly hostile except in rare instances, generally were becoming more and more restive as a result of agrarian developments which either threatened their independent existence or left them destitute. Members of the upper class not directly connected with the regime were either not allowed to render public service or were driven into partial opposition by the government's bland assumption that all able men served the government and that all who questioned the policies were either knaves or fools. Added to the insult was the economic injury which seemed to be impending; the rather precarious economic situation after 1905 forced many men who previously had been staunch Díaz supporters to question the safety of the Mexican economy under Díaz' continued administration. The group whose economic interests were in danger did not always actively oppose the administration; but when the revolution came, the plutocracy gave Díaz little help.

Díaz still had strong support, particularly among those who profited directly, or hoped to profit, from his government. More important to the future of the nation, and more widespread, than the support to Díaz himself was the belief in his philosophy of government. Many of those who turned against the Díaz administration, or who no longer supported it, did so because they detected weaknesses in his government rather than because they opposed the principles upon which he acted. These men, including many of the great hacendados and financiers, were quite willing to see Díaz removed from office, even though they looked with horror upon fundamental changes in the governmental or social structure. They were the men who made possible a successful revolution against Díaz, but at the same time their attitude would make it difficult for a reform government to function. As a class they foresaw a revolution, but they did not foresee the nature of the struggle; they believed it would take place after Díaz' death and would be nothing more than a quarrel over political power among the upper class. They did not recognize the symptoms of a social revolution developing in Morelos, for example, where "ragged plebeians, with their thin veneer of rudimentary civilization, were acting like savage gluttons of human carrion" during the 1908 gubernatorial election. They were unconcerned with the needs of the masses, and being unconcerned they were ignorant of the potential of those masses.

4. The Porfiriato: Legend and Reality

DANIEL COSÍO VILLEGAS

Licenciado Daniel Cosío Villegas is something of a phenomenon even in Mexico, where many independent and intelligent spirits flourish. Trained as an economist, he has served as a professor, ambassador, publisher, and more recently as a historian and columnist. He has been more responsible than anyone else for opening up in a decisive and stimulating way the study of the history of modern Mexico. Thanks to his investigations and to his stimulus, we now begin to see the true Porfirio Díaz; a dictator, yes, but also a patriot who defended well some of the national interests of Mexico.[1]

The Porfiriato must have been, as the legend has it, an era of consolidation. The tranquility of the period suggests that divisions or differences were neither so violent nor so irreconcilable as to lead to war. It was, moreover, an era in

[1] For a judicious evaluation of past and present interpretations of Díaz, see Martín Quirarte, *Historia Mexicana,* 15 (1965–1966), no. 2–3, pp. 416–422.
From "El porfiriato, era de consolidación" by Daniel Cosío Villegas, *Historia Mexicana,* 13 (1963), pp. 76–87, passim. Reprinted by permission.

which means of communication improved significantly, thereby increasing opportunities for Mexicans to become acquainted and have contact with one another. Finally, one suspects that consolidation was also furthered by the undeniably authoritarian character of the regime, for extraordinary power makes itself felt on everything and everyone, impressing a uniform cast on the entire society.

Such must have been the Porfiriato. To be certain, however, one would have to ask whether the process of consolidation was general or selective. According to the legend, the regime was notably successful in promoting the consolidation of two areas at least: Mexican nationality and institutions. . . .

The consolidation of the Mexican nation has been the result of a very long process. Perhaps it dates from the incipient imperialism of the Aztecs, which . . . imposed some unity on the political and cultural diversity of the numerous Indian groups of the period. The conquest and domination of the Spaniards, despite the elements of profound disparity which they introduced, gave to the native civilizations elements of community, language, religion, and government which they had hitherto lacked. The consequences did not take long to appear, for the first clear manifestations of a spiritual nationalism were evident in the eighteenth century. But it was above all during that calumniated first half of the nineteenth century that the process of national formation was accelerated, precisely because of the misfortunes that befell the newly born nation. . . . The war with the United States and the very loss of territory helped, like few other events, to consolidate our nationality, first through the sensation of danger and the feeling of hatred for the aggressor — sentiments which constitute a negative force but a tremendously effective one when a weak people is involved. Secondly, no matter how unjust and painful the loss of half of our national territory was, it is undeniable that it drastically reduced the material and spiritual task of forging the nation, as well as the time that would be needed to accomplish this task. Finally, this unhappy war also taught us that when our internal struggles passed certain limits of rancor and persistence, the danger of aggression and the irreparable loss of the nation would become real and substantial.

It does not seem that the country made use of this sad but beneficial lesson, for in a very short time, during the wars of the Reform and Intervention, the two contenders, blinded by immediate partisan interests, appealed for foreign aid. But this occurred for the last time because it became apparent that with the aid came the foreign soldier, that is, the flesh-and-blood enemy of Mexican nationhood. These two wars [were] fought so bitterly that, by way of a reaction, they created a conciliatory climate that bore fruit throughout the entire period of the Restored Republic. . . .

[By 1876], then, Mexico, as a result of so many painful and seemingly sterile struggles, was beginning to gather the positive fruits of its misfortunes;

it had gone a long way toward placing general interests before partial interests.

Does all this mean that the Porfiriato did not contribute in any way to the task of consolidating the Mexican nation? By no means. It merely means that the process was lengthy, that it was initiated a long time before 1876, and that the principal direct contributions had been made previously. The contribution of the Porfiriato, while it was very important, seems to me to have had an indirect character. With the railroads, telegraph, and telephone, with the general improvement of communications and transportation, particularly of the press, the circulation of Mexicans, as well as of their wealth, ideas, and sentiments, also improved.

It is less easy to define and very difficult to assess another factor in the consolidation of the nation which appeared in a singularly active manner during the Porfirian age. Mexico had always lived under the thumb of regional caciques; accordingly, federalism had a reality that was political, social, and economic, as well as geographic and ethnic. Only Juárez emerged in 1867 as a great national figure; but the impossibility of preserving the unity of the liberal party and Juárez' need to lead his own faction in order to defend himself and prevail over the factions of Lerdo and Díaz made him lose to a large extent the general and superior character of a national figure. Díaz, on the other hand, less scrupulous in his political practices and born of a revolutionary coup and not of lawful elections, had far more liberty of action. Finding the field already sowed and blessed with better luck, he at length succeeded in putting an end to the regional caudillos and in transforming himself into the sole caudillo, that is, into the national caudillo. To this must be added the popular aura that Díaz always had, the memory of his glorious campaigns against the foreign invader, his very age, his granite-like physical appearance, and his conscious effort to acquire and exhibit the air of a man who was superior to petty and fleeting passion; his was the air of the guardian of the permanent interests of the country, the air of a monarch who receives homage not only from his own subjects but also from the outside world, the civilized world.

But Porfirio Díaz did not become merely a decorative national symbol, like the flag or anthems which evoke and exalt patriotic sentiments upon reaching the eyes or ears, not even in the more intellectual sense of serving as a symbol of national unity, like the English monarch. He was also authority, and in many respects the sole authority; he was power, and in many respects the sole power. Family disputes were laid before him, as well as disputes involving towns, authorities, or interests. All the organs of public power depended on him: legislatures, courts, judges, governors, political and military chiefs. Not only was he seen everywhere, like God, but he also made himself felt everywhere. . . .

There can be no doubt that, as the legend claims, juridical, economic, and social institutions were consolidated to some extent. One merely has to consider the peacefulness, prosperity, and longevity of the regime to admit this; when there is peace, wealth, and time, there are opportunities and resources for the undertaking of projects that in turbulent periods are left for "better times." Unfortunately, history requires more than generalities; it requires analysis and a body of facts.

With respect to juridical institutions, the work had already begun. The first great bodies of law antedated the Porfiriato: the constitution itself, the organic law of public instruction (1867), the law governing juries in criminal cases (1869), the organic law on the recourse of *amparo* (1869), the penal code (1871), the civil code (1871), the code of civil procedure (1872), the code pertaining to aliens (1876), etc. But these were few in number and limited in influence, in part because most of them could be applied only in the Federal District and in part because the conditions of the country were not sufficiently normal for their beneficial influence to be felt. During the Porfiriato, these same codes were revised, made more consistent, and complemented with new ones . . . while important legislation, such as the law on credit institutions, was also enacted. To this body of true juridical creation, there ought to be added the regulatory and administrative achievement. These gains placed the country on the path to a normal, regular existence, which in many respects became ideally impersonal. In addition, the law in general appeared to attain a respectability, a stature, that made it impervious to human negation or threats.

All this is very well, but how can one forget that political institutions are a part of juridical institutions? Can it be sustained that political institutions were consolidated during the Porfiriato? They simply disappeared, and something that does not exist is not susceptible of consolidation or dispersion.

In this matter there is no defense or qualification. No Porfirista — not even the most passionate, nor the most timid, nor the most shameful, nor the most cynical — has ever dared to affirm that Mexico progressed politically during the Díaz regime. This is the explanation of [Rafael de] Zayas Enríquez: the people of Mexico voluntarily ceded their political rights to Porfirio Díaz so that he might return them little by little as the Mexicans learned how to be free. This is the opinion of [Francisco] Bulnes: "it passes the limits of stupidity to assail General Díaz for not having done the impossible — to be a democratic president in a nation of slaves.". . .

According to Emilio Rabasa, one of the few Mexican political writers of true talent, "the dictatorship of Díaz was characterized, *above all,* by respect for *legal forms,* which he always preserved in order to keep alive in the people the sentiment that their laws were respected even though they were not enforced, and that they remained on the books so that they might recover their ascendancy in the not-too-distant future." This is the point that truly deserves investigation, for on it depends the answer to the question of whether political institutions were consolidated during the Porfiriato.

Is it possible to respect a law that is not enforced? Can a law which is not enforced remain in force? Can a law which is not enforced someday recover its ascendancy? To me, it is as clear as daylight that a law which is not enforced provokes mockery, compassion, but never respect; a law which is not enforced is a dead law, and what is dead can never remain in force; a law which is not enforced has no power and in consequence can never recover what it never had. Finally, to describe as the "not-too-distant future" an era which, like that of Díaz, lasted for thirty-five years is to forget that in so long a time a whole generation was born and raised in the delightful atmosphere of the law that is not enforced but is respected. I would say exactly the opposite of Rabasa: that nothing degrades and demoralizes a people so much as the constant, repeated, daily spectacle of the non-enforcement of the law. . . .

It is this attitude toward the law, especially the political laws, that indicates the gulf between Porfirio Díaz and the great liberals of the Reform. The latter had a blind faith in the law as a pick-axe to strike down old and noxious institutions and in the law as a cherished mould for shaping new ones. For this reason they respected the law, and to preserve or change it, they were capable of risking their lives or their futures. . . .

Porfirio Díaz, who fought for the liberal cause from his boyhood, who once accused Juárez of conservatism, did not have that respect and veneration for the law which was the very essence of Mexican liberalism. For Díaz, the law was a dead letter and consequently lacked spirit. For him, the *fact* was the instrument of change, and the fact, of course, was power and might. Because he despised the law, he did not change it or trouble himself about it; he simply forgot it and sought power in the invincible fact of being stronger than everyone else. . . .

The conclusion of all this seems obvious to me, as well as logical. Some juridical institutions were consolidated during the Porfiriato, and some were not. Those that were consolidated were the secondary ones, while the major ones — the political institutions — simply disappeared.

SECTION VI

Conflicting Latin and Yankee Attitudes at the Turn of the Twentieth Century

One of the most difficult problems students and teachers of Latin American history in the United States face is the gulf of misunderstanding that separates north from south. When "Latin" and "Yankee" values are compared, chauvinism and ignorance often play leading roles.

For their part, Latin American intellectuals have nurtured a love-hate relationship with their neighbor to the north. Once their nations had liberated themselves from Spain and Portugal, they were faced with the enormous problem of developing their own way of life. Throughout the nineteenth century many Latin Americans observed the material progress of the United States with great interest; some hoped their own countries would emulate the Yankees; others questioned or attacked mere economic improvement as dangerous to their way of life.

By the end of the century the positivists who had enjoyed considerable influence in Brazil, Mexico, and elsewhere found less fertile ground for propagating their views about the beauty of material progress generated by the courtship of foreign investors. A new and powerful sentiment began to be widely expressed: the fear that the United States would increasingly intervene to transform the Caribbean into a North American lake dominated by dollars and marines. One of the first to articulate this fear was Cuban poet and revolutionary José Martí (Reading 1). From 1881 to 1895 Martí lived in exile in New York City and contributed, to Latin American newspapers, articles describing political, economic and cultural developments in the U.S. Martí found much to admire, but he expressed mounting concern over the rise of monopolistic and imperialist tendencies. A few days before his death, he was apparently convinced that the U.S. would try to swallow up Cuba, for he wrote, "I know the monster because I have lived in its lair, and my sling is that of David." Martí returned to Cuba to renew the struggle for independence from Spain, and died in battle on May 19, 1895.

The easy victory of the United States over Spain in 1898 bore out the apprehensions of many Latin Americans that they would be engulfed by the materialism and brute force emanating from the "Colossus of the North." In 1900 the Uruguayan José Enrique Rodó urged Latin Americans to reaffirm the essential elements of their culture against the North American threat. In ten years his beautifully written book, *Ariel*, (Reading 2) went through eight editions. The work became a kind of bible for those Latin Americans intimidated by North American power, because they felt Rodó legitimized their own potential. Eight years later Rubén Darío echoed this same theme in his famous "Ode to Roosevelt" (Reading 3). At a time when the United States was building a canal through Panama and intervening actively with its economic and military strength in Central America and the Caribbean, this poet from Nicaragua triumphantly proclaimed that the United States might be rich and powerful but that Spanish America was far superior, for it had many poets and God. But it was Rodó's message in *Ariel* that was quoted most often, particularly when Latin American intellectuals began to use the work as an important weapon in their battle against the United States and the values they felt the northern republic represented. Today, though Rubén Darío and *Ariel* may be somewhat passé, Latin Americans continue to search for their own expression, their distinctive contribution to the culture of the world.

For their part, after their surprisingly easy victory over Spain in 1898, many North Americans indulged in a jingoistic imperialism unprecedented in earlier history. Exuberant and complacent, they accepted the notion that Yankee expansion into the Caribbean was an "inexorable" stage of American development, and that the creation of empires was the inevitable "penalty of greatness" that obliged "the ascendant nation to extend law and order for the benefit of everybody." Yankee assertions of superiority with regard to Latin Americans were strongly flavoured with a deepseated bias against colored people faintly masked by condescension and paternalism. All these attitudes are openly expressed by George W. Crichfield, an American businessman, who published in 1908 a two-volume work entitled *American Supremacy* advocating the complete takeover of Latin America (Reading 4). Crichfield made his point of view quite clear when he dedicated his book as follows:

> "To the Great American Voter, the man behind the ballot, the man who makes governments and unmakes them, the man before whose dread

opinion the mighty of the earth stand in awe, the man in whose hands is confided the destiny of the Western Hemisphere, the man of multifarious and perplexing mien, but whose heart is true as steel and pure as gold, I inscribe this work, in the profound conviction that while we may neglect our opportunities and evade our responsibilities, we cannot escape the inevitable consequences of so doing." (I, v.)

Unfortunately Crichfield's attitudes about Latin America have continued to shape U.S. policy toward the region throughout the twentieth century. In a book entitled *Our Jungle Diplomacy*,[1] William Franklin Sands records the following conversation between the British Foreign Secretary Lord Grey and the U.S. ambassador to Britain Walter Hines Page during Woodrow Wilson's administration:

Grey: Suppose you have to intervene, what then?
Page: Make 'em vote and live by their decisions.
Grey: But suppose they will not so live?
Page: We'll go in again and make 'em vote again.
Grey: And keep this up for 200 years?
Page: Yes. The United States will be here for 200 years and it can continue to shoot men for that little space till they learn to vote and rule themselves.

On the eve of World War II, another American ambassador to Great Britain, Joseph P. Kennedy, appealed to his countrymen to keep the hemisphere out of war: "If any of the Latin Americans act up, kick them in the teeth."[2] Today U.S. policy in Central America is much debated, but no one can deny that racism, paternalism and condescension still play a role.

[1] William Franklin Sands, *Our Jungle Diplomacy* (Chapel Hill, 1944), p. 121.
[2] Louis M. Lyons, *Newspaper Story* (Cambridge, MA, 1971), p. 292.

José Martí

1. José Marti (1853–1895)

HAROLD E. DAVIS

Poet-journalist-revolutionist, José Martí devoted his life, most of it spent in exile, to achieving the independence of Cuba. As he said in Caracas in 1878, Cuban independence would be "the last strophe" of the incomplete "poem of 1810." But he also saw in it the beginning of a new and broader revolutionary movement, in the support of which he aspired "to arouse the world." America, he said, must go her own way, but she must march with Bolívar on one side and Herbert Spencer on the other. Later, during his fourteen year stay in the United States, he was influenced by the writings of Henry George and other North Americans sympathetic to the ideas of socialism. Some Cubans have tried to stamp him with the mark of materialist-socialist doctrine. Others have emphasized his individualism and devotion to democratic-liberal ideas. But Martí defies categorization. Even the Cuban communist, Juan Marinello, has called him "the poet [who], expressing reality in an unaccustomed manner, transforms it within himself, makes it a part of his internal tumult, of his spiritual state, of his dominating emotion." Hence, Martí is best understood as expressing the frequently contradictory emotions and anxieties of Cuba and Latin America at the end of the nineteenth century, rather than as the exponent of any particular ideology. In this sense he may be considered a precursor of the inquietude of Latin America which finds expression in its twentieth century revolutionary movements.

José Martí grew up during the Ten Years War (1868–78) for Cuban independence. Entering the Colegio de San Pablo two years before the war began, he studied under the revolutionary poet and journalist, Rafael Mendive, until the latter was imprisoned for his revolutionary activities. A visit to his imprisoned teacher left an impression on the mind of the thirteen year old boy which was never erased. Later he published his first, revolutionary, poem, "Abdala," in *La Patria Libre,* edited by Mendive and Cristobal Madán. At the age of sixteen he was condemned to six years imprisonment at hard labor because of a letter he and a fellow student had written to another student of

From *Latin American Social Thought* by Harold E. Davis, 2nd American edition (Washington, D.C.: The University Press, 1966), pp. 256–66. Reprinted by permission.

Mendive, then in the Spanish service, urging him to return to the Cuban cause. Released after two months because of ill health and a wound on his ankle from the iron grill he wore as a prisoner—a wound which required several surgical operations for its cure—he was permitted to go to the Isle of Pines and later to Spain to continue his studies.

In Spain, then undergoing a series of kaleidoscopic political changes following the overthrow of Queen Isabella in 1868, Martí was as much political agitator as student. He published a scathing denunciation of Spanish treatment of political prisoners in Cuba, and his poetic ode to the student demonstrators shot on the streets of Havana on November 27, 1871 had an electric effect on Spanish public opinion. During the historic siege in Zaragoza, he stirred the republican sympathies of the city with his fiery oratory. After the establishment of the Republic (1873) he pleaded the Cuban cause in a pamphlet, *The Spanish Republic Confronting the Cuban Revolution*.

Years of exile followed the overthrow of the Republic—first in Mexico, where he began in his writing to urge the development of an American, rather than European, education, literature, thought, and institutions, and later in Guatemala, where he lectured in the Normal School and published the *Revista Guatemalteca*. Returning to Cuba, briefly, after the Ten Years War, he was soon imprisoned and deported to Spain (1878). Escaping from prison, he made his way to Paris, New York, and finally Caracas, where he vowed to "arouse the world" to the Cuban cause. Because of differences with the dictator-president, he soon left Caracas for New York, around which the last fourteen years of his life centered. Recognized as the moral and intellectual leader of Cuban independence, he devoted his energies to arousing support for that cause, while earning his living as a journalist. It was a severe blow when United States officials stopped the departure of two vessels equipped at great expense to initiate an invasion of Cuba. But Martí and his followers, undaunted, made their way to Cuba to begin hostilities in February 1895. On May 19, at Dos Rios, he was killed in the first charge of the rebel forces.

Martí's martyrdom made him an idol of the next generation of Latin American youth, while his poetic and vigorous expression of a new revolutionary philosophy, decrying the notion of Latin American political incapacity derived from the prevalent evolutionary positivist concepts, anticipated some of the new trends in twentieth century social thought in the Hispanic countries. Absorbed in the daily tasks of the journalist and in revolutionary planning, his life cut short at forty-two, he never wrote the volumes he planned on such subjects as education and the Negro race. His thought must therefore be culled from speeches, newspaper and magazine articles, letters, and the preliminary notes for books never written.

Crawford has called him a practical mystic, utopian yet at the same time realist. While obviously influenced by Marxism, much of his writing, like that of Rodó, is an eloquent plea for a spiritual revolution, with an ethics based upon love. His great admiration for Cecilio Acosta of Venezuela embraced the latter's appreciation of the ethical basis of Anglo-American democracy, and his frequent denunciations of the materialism he found in the United States should be interpreted in that light. He spoke out clearly against racism, defending the cause of the recently emancipated Negroes of Cuba. He urged education for the Indians and Negroes of all of America, an education which would be practical rather than literary, agrarian reform which would include division of the land, and an independence for Cuba which would be not only political, but economic and cultural as well. Thus his concepts of the social revolution required in America make him a predecessor of José Mariátegui and Victor Raúl Haya de la Torre, while his appeal to the idealism of youth links him with José Rodó, José Ingenieros, and José Vasconcelos.

THE MORAL BASIS OF REVOLUTION

BY José Martí

We know and believe that human nature, evil by chance but in essence noble, once committed to the exercise of its most honorable prerogatives, only exchanges or declines them for advantages so pleasing that they may worthily compensate for the ineffable pleasure produced by rational self-control. . . . Only virtues produce in peoples a continuous and serious well being.

*   *   *

This is not merely the revolution of anger. It is the revolution of reflection. It is the prudent conversion to a useful and honorable objective of inextinguishable elements, restless and active, which if they are neglected, would certainly lead us to serious permanent unrest and to solutions achieved under threats. It is the only way in which we can attend in time to interests which are at the point of death, which constitute our sole element of economic prosperity, and which have nothing to hope for from interests absolutely opposed. At this moment in which, from one and another side of the continent, the ocean threatens to leave its bounds to carry the artistic riches of the white peoples to the yellow peoples—at this point in human history in

From an address to Cuban emigrés in Steck Hall, New York, January 24, 1880, in Felix Lizaso, José Martí, Ideario separatista La Habana: Ministerio de Educatión, 1947 pp. 42–43, 48–52.

which, by amazing exertion, it seems that the world is initiating an era of greater understanding and happiness, we Cubans stand in the gravest danger of losing forever the easiest, simplest, and most advantageous means of raising our abused *patria* to an unanticipated height of strength and wealth. Because this epoch, looked upon by some as one of transition and trying disturbances for Cuba, is rather a decisive one, never to recur, in which, if we do not effect change energetically, we shall lose, together with the sole diminishing and threatened wealth which remains to us, the natural and probable possession of one of the most abundant veins of fortune which the commerce of this age offers. And these problems through which, dulled by the sight of the gallows and the yoke, we usually pass without casting an eye upon them, as in the case of all real and pressing problems, add up to a little more than the narrow proposals, imperfect aspirations, and timid suggestions with which, as individuals and aimlessly, the corrupt and uncertain Cuban delegation fights in the Spanish Cortes. And because they are so dispirited, behold them frustrated and conquered, looked upon as strangers and not abused as the illustrious men of other times were; because with a single meritorious exception they have had neither the daring spirit, nor the vital speech, nor the sure judgment the latter had.

One must do in each moment what is necessary in each moment. Time should not be wasted in attempting what there is good reason for believing is not to be achieved. To postpone is never to decide, above all since now neither palpitating memories, nor painful resentments, nor serious impending catastrophes permit another opportunity. To foresee is a duty of those who undertake to lead. To go ahead of others requires seeing more than they do. Peoples know not how to live in the compromising uncertainty of those protected by the advantages which prudence yields, who do not feel within their cloistered homes the tempests of the countryside, nor in their torpid hearts the real cry of a country stoned and betrayed.

Despots do not know that the people, the suffering mass, is the true head of revolution; and they caress that other brilliant mass which, because it seems intelligent, appears to influence and direct [affairs]. And it does in fact direct, with a leadership necessary and useful in so far as it obeys—to the extent that it is inspired—the energetic desires of those who entrust to them their destiny with blind faith and generous confidence. But when they in their own weakness neglect the trust of the people and give up their task in fright, when those who had been considered and chosen as good by their smallness belittle everything and by their vacillation defeat it, the proud country casts off the burden of these men and goes on its way, leaving behind those who had insufficient valor to go on. The opportunistic policy, as it is now called, pretending to make a special school of what is merely the predominance of good sense in the conduct of public affairs—the opportunistic policy, which does not consist in hoping blindly despite everything but in being impatient when there is a right to hope, cannot be the mad effort to feign them [hopes] when there is no cause whatever to nourish or justify them. The price of liberty is very high, and one must either resign himself to live without it or decide to buy it at its price.

From the vibrant and varied elements which palpitate in Cuba; from the impotence for good and the incapacity for government of Spanish policy; from the habits contracted during the long campaign, not lessened by later benefits, but strengthened by new offenses; from the custom of fighting which agitates some and from the custom of being free which disquiets others; from the shame of having contributed to a general decline; from the complete absence of the hoped for resources *(caudales recelosos)* in the largest and neediest part of the island; from the unthinking and traitorous abundance of promises, which thereupon caused the deception to be felt more keenly; from the hopeless misery which afflicted all; from the patriotic ardor which burned in all, fed by such varied causes—[from all of these] the revolution had to surge, in spite of those who did not feel so keenly these deeply wounding evils *(punzantes males)*. It had to surge up disorderly and fierce, as an explosion of wrath and a tempestuous rebirth of varied and angry hopes which needed no previous agreement to throw themselves into the battle. . . . When an evil is necessary, the evil occurs. And since nothing now avails to avoid it, the wise thing is to study it and guide it so that it will not exhaust and overwhelm us with its excesses. Thus, the revolution having occurred when valor, decorum, and the sentiment of honor, primary laws of life, were lacking—and they alone had sufficient force to produce—a popular motive of convenience and a narrow logical reasoning invigorated, set the tone, and gave form to a movement which it was not now possible to prevent. Therefore, since the same reasons, strengthened by new events and by the hoped for agreements militate now, now is the only opportunity to aid with energy a revolution which is taking form by itself, as well as through the cruelty and stupidity of its enemies. Hence, disdainfully heedless of sympathies which are not needed, and with the approval of reason and honor, those who support the present revolution with all their energy and aid it with all their ability may be proud of their work.

*   *   *

AMERICA

And why not recall, for the glory of those who have known how to conquer in spite of them, the confused origins, stained with blood, of our America, even though one, for whom the light of our glory, the glory of our independence, molests in his function of compromising and cheapening it, may attach the fault of inopportune old age to the faithful record, more than ever necessary today? North America was born of the plough, Spanish [America] of the bloodhound *(perro de presa)*. A fanatical war cast out of their ethereal palaces the moors debilitated by wealth, and the excess soldiery, brought up on crude wine and hate for heretics, cast themselves with cuirass and arquebus upon the Indian with his breastplate of cotton. The ships arrived full of armed cavaliers, of disinherited second sons, rebel junior officers, and hungry lawyers and clergy. They bring culverins, shields, lances, thigh-armor, casques, backpieces, helmets, and dogs. They carry the war *(ponen el espada)* to the four winds, declare the King's ownership of the land, and sack the temples of gold. Cortes entices Moctezuma to the palace which he owes to the latter's generosity or prudence, and makes him prisoner in his own palace. The naively trusting Anacaona invites Ovando to a fiesta to see the garden of his country, its joyful dances, and its maidens; the soldiers of Ovando draw out the swords concealed under their garments, and the land of Anacaona is theirs. The conquistador advances in America between the divisions and jealousies of the Indian peoples; between the Aztecs and the Tlaxcaltecas Cortes reaches the canoe of Cuauhtemoc; between the Quiches and the Zutujiles Alvarado conquers in Guatemala; between the Tunjas and the Bogotaes Quesada in Colombia; between those of Atahualpa and those of Huascar Pizarro passes in Peru; on the breast of the last valorous Indian they plant the red standard of the Holy Office. They steal the women.

*   *   *

And all this poison we have changed into a vital element *(trocado en savia)!* Never was a people more precocious, generous and firm born out of such difficulty and suffering. We were the sewer *(sentina)* and we are coming to be the crucible. We have built upon the hydras. We have cast out the javelins of Alvarado with our railroads. In the plazas where heretics were burned, we have built libraries. We now have as many schools as we previously had familiars of the Holy Office. If we have left anything undone, it is because we have lacked time to do it, busy as we have been with extirpating from our blood the impurities bequeathed us by our fathers. Of the religious and immoral missions, only the bare walls remain, where the owl peers and the lizard sadly crawls. Among the divided races, the ruins of the convents, and the horses of the barbarians, the new American has opened a path,

From a speech before the Hispanic American Literary Society of New York, December 19, 1889, honoring the delegates to the First Interamerican Conference. *José Martí: Prosas.* Selección, prólogo y notas de Andrés Iduarte. Washington: Pan American Union, 1950. Pp. 65, 68–70. Reprinted by permission.

inviting the youth of the world to pitch their tents in his camp. This handful of apostles has triumphed.

*   *   *

Our America, capable and tireless, conquers all, raising its banner higher each day.

*   *   *

From that angry and agitated America, which burst forth with thorns on her brow and [with] words flowing like lava . . . once the evil gag was broken, we have come by main force *(a pujo de brazo)* to [be] the present day America, heroic and hard working, frank and vigilant, with Bolívar on one hand and Herbert Spencer on the other; an America without childish suspicions *(suspicacias),* nor naive trusts, which welcomes all races to the prosperity of its home, because it knows that the America of the defense of Buenos Aires and the resistance of Callao is also the America of the Cerro de las Campanas and of the New Troy.

MY RACE

The term racist is coming to be confused, and it is necessary to clarify it. Man has no special right because he belongs to one race or another: speak of man and you have spoken of all his rights. The Negro, as Negro, is neither inferior nor superior to any other man. It is a sin of redundance for the white to say "my race"; it is a sin of redundance for the Negro to say "my race." Everything which divides men, everything which specifies, separates, or groups them is a sin against humanity. To what intelligent white does it occur to be proud of being white? And what do Negroes think of the white who is proud of being so and also believes he has special rights because of it? What are whites to think of the Negro who is vain concerning his color? To insist upon the divisions of race, upon the racial differences of a people naturally divided, is to make more difficult both public and private welfare, which lie in bringing closely together the factors which have to live in common. When one says that there is no original sin in the Negro, nor any virus which inhibits him from developing completely his human soul, one speaks only the truth; and it must be said and demonstrated, because the injustice of this world is great, as is the ignorance of those who pass for learned. Some, in good faith, even believe the Negro incapable of the intelligence and spirit

(From *La Cuestión racial.* Biblioteca Popular Martiana No. 4. La Habana: Lex, 1959. Pp. 25–29. Originally published in *La Patria,* New York, April 16, 1893).

(corazón) of the white. If this defense of nature is called racism, it does not matter if it is so called, because it is nothing more than natural decorum and a voice which cries out from man's breast for the peace and life of the country. If it is claimed that the condition of slavery does not prove inferiority in the enslaved race, since the white Gauls, with blue eyes and golden hair, were sold as servants, with yokes on their necks, in the Roman markets, that is good racism, because it is pure justice and helps to eliminate prejudice from the ignorant white. But here justifiable racism ends, with the right of the Negro to maintain and prove that his color does not deprive him of any of the abilities and rights of the human species.

What right has the white racist, who believes his race has superior privileges, to complain of the Negro racist who also sees some special [right] in his race? The Negro racist who sees in race a special character, what right has he to complain of the white racist? The white man who believes himself superior to the black man because of race admits the idea of race, authorizing and provoking the Negro racist. The black man who proclaims his race, when perchance what he [really] proclaims in this erroneous form is the spiritual identity of all the races, authorizes and provokes the white racist. Peace demands the common natural rights; differentiating rights, contrary to nature, are the enemies of peace. The white who isolates himself [also] isolates the black. The Negro who isolates himself provokes the white to do the same.

In Cuba there is no fear whatever of a war of the races. A Cuban is more than white, more than mulatto, more than Negro. On the battlefields, dying for Cuba, the souls of whites and blacks have risen together through the air. In the daily life of defense, of loyalty, of brotherhood, and of shrewd planning a black always stood beside each white. Like the whites, Negroes divided themselves according to their characters, [whether] timid or brave, self-denying or egotistical, into the several parties in which men are grouped. Political parties are aggregates of preoccupations, aspirations, interests, and characters. [Within them] essential similarity is searched out and established above the differences of detail, and the fundamental element of the analagous characters is fused in the parties, even though they differ in the incidental or in what is irrelevant to the common aspiration. . . . The affinity of character is more powerful among men than the affinity of color. The Negroes, distributed among the diverse or hostile specialties of the human spirit, can never write, nor will they wish to write against the whites, scattered among the same specializations. Negroes are too tired of slavery to enter voluntarily into the slavery of color. . . . Both racists would be equally blameworthy: the white racist and the black racist. Many whites, as well as many blacks, have already forgotten their color. Whites and Negroes work together for intellectual achievement, the propagation of morality, the triumph of creative work, and sublime charity.

JOSÉ ENRIQUE RODÓ   211

Cuba will never have race warfare. The Republic cannot turn back. . . .
The civil rights, whether those granted astutely by the Spanish government
or those originating in custom prior to the independence of the Island, cannot
now be denied, neither by the Spaniard who will maintain them while he
remains in Cuba in order to continue dividing the Cuban Negro from the
white Cuban, nor by independence, which could not deny under freedom the
rights which the Spaniard recognized under servitude.

2. Did the United States Represent the Materialistic Caliban, and Latin America the Idealistic Ariel?

JOSÉ ENRIQUE RODÓ

This question was first presented in compelling literary expression by the
Uruguayan writer José Enrique Rodó (1872–1917). His biography is unimportant: "he was born in Montevideo of good family, he studied, read
and wrote, was briefly professor of literature and twice member of Parliament. Most European of Latin American thinkers, he went to Europe only
during the World War, poorly supported by a journal at home, and after
eight months' wandering, died there." [1] Reading his classic *Ariel* (1900)
today one wonders how it ever could have influenced Latin American intellectuals and others in the dramatic way it undoubtedly did. For Rodó *Ariel*
"represents the noblest, most wingéd part of the spirit of man, all that rises
above irrationality and sensualism into disinterested action, the play of intelligence, culture and spirituality." [2] Many readers in Spanish America
felt that they represented these ideals, and that the United States was the epitome of materialism, a kind of Caliban that symbolizes mankind's primitive
urges as did the character in Shakespeare's *The Tempest*. As we read today
this conversation in which "the master" discusses democracy "as the enthronement of Caliban," Rodó seem to embody the spirit of a Hispanic
elitist, with no apparent concern for the masses. But this is hindsight, a truth
that we perceive as a result of the pressures of the times in which we live.
    Although *Ariel* was not primarily an attack upon United States material-
ism, and in fact is an example of moderation, other Latin Americans showed
no such restraint in interpreting Rodó's message. The Mexican Carlos
Pereyra, the Argentine Manuel Ugarte, and the Venezuelan Rufino Blanco
Fombona all gave Rodó's message an anti-American twist. *Ariel* has come
to be looked upon as a symbol for all who would exalt the "spiritual" qualities of Latin Americans and depreciate the "money-grubbing Yankees." But
today one Peruvian sociologist interprets *Ariel* as representative of the atti-

[1] William Rex Crawford, *A Century of Latin-American Thought,* rev. ed. (New
York: Praeger, 1966), p. 80.
[2] Ibid., p. 81.

tude of Latin American "intellectuals" who cannot achieve for their countries what they desire and are confronted "by the successes of the United States and by the profound inroads into their world of American economic and political power." And he quotes the Mexican philosopher José Vasconcelos, who wrote a whole book, *Raza Cósmica,* exalting the value of the racially mixed society developing in Latin America but also stated: "Let us admit that it was our misfortune not to have developed the cohesion of that extraordinary breed to the North, which we cover with insult because it has beaten us at every game in the secular struggle." [3] An experienced American observer states that "Rodó still touches chords of sympathy and desire in Latin America" because some there still believe that they represent Ariel and that the United States is Caliban.[4]

Yet Rodó's true message was not this: Rodó used Ariel as a symbol not of Latin American reality but of the qualities to which Latin America and the United States as well should aspire. Rodó stressed that the youths to whom he addressed himself must be patient and not expect results even in their lifetime; he portrayed Latin America as languishing in a relatively primitive condition. If Rodó had believed that Latin America had already achieved spiritual eminence he would not have felt the need to admonish its youth. He was not trying to assert Latin America's superiority to the United States in a defiant posture; his purpose was to exhort, not to extol.[5] Nor did Rodó identify the United States with Caliban, but felt that it, too, could and should aspire to a greater idealism even as he exhorted the youth of Latin America to do.

However we may interpret Rodó's message today, we should remember that *Ariel* was written and published during the years when United States power was being exerted ever increasingly in Latin America and at a time when an American businessman such as George Crichfield declared Spanish America so backward and so inefficient that "the whole world would be benefitted by the United States taking possession of "all those unfortunate nations" (Reading 4).

Often you will have heard attributed to two main causes that torrent of the spirit of utility which gives its note to the moral physiognomy of the present century, with its neglect of the aesthetic and disinterested view of life. The revelations of natural science, whose interpreters, favourable or the reverse, agree in destroying all ideality for its base, are one; the other is the universal diffusion and triumph of democratic ideas. I propose to speak to you exclusively of this latter cause; because I trust that your first initiation in the

[3] César Graña, "Cultural Nationalism: The Idea of Historical Destiny in Spanish America," *Social Research,* 30 (Spring 1963), p. 52.
[4] Kalman Silvert, *The Conflict Society: Reaction and Revolution in Latin America,* rev. ed. (New York: American Universities Field Staff, 1966), pp. 139–142.
[5] Richard Stillinger, "Ariel: Source and Symbol of Misunderstanding." Mr. Stillinger's paper, prepared as a term paper at Columbia University, has been very helpful in the preparation of this section.
From *Ariel* by José Enrique Rodó, trans. F. J. Simpson (Boston: Houghton Mifflin Company, 1922), pp. 60–148, passim. Reprinted by permission.

revelations of Science has been so directed as to preserve you from the danger of a vulgar interpretation. Upon democracy weighs the accusation of guiding humanity, by making it mediocre, to a Holy Empire of Utilitarianism. This accusation is reflected with vibrant intensity in the pages — for me always full of a suggestive charm — of the most amiable among the masters of the Modern Spirit: the seductive pages of Renan, to whose authority you have often heard me refer and of whom I may often speak again. Read Renan, those of you who have not done so already, and you will have to love him as I do. No one as he, among the moderns, appears to me such a master "of that art of teaching with Grace" which Anatole France considers divine. No one so well as he has succeeded in combining irony with pity; even in the rigour of the analysis he can put the unction of the priest. And even when he teaches us to doubt, his exquisite gentleness sheds a balsam over the doubt itself. His thoughts ring in our minds with echoes ineffable, so vague as to remind one of sacred music. His infinite comprehension makes critics class him among those dilettantes of a light scepticism who wear the gown of the philosopher like the domino of a mask; but, once you penetrate his spirit, you will see that the vulgar tolerance of the mere sceptic differs from his as the hospitality of a worldly *salon* from the real spirit of charity.

This master holds, then, that high preoccupation with the ideal interests of our race is irreconcilable with the spirit of democracy. He believes that the conception of life in a society where that spirit dominates will gradually come to seek only material welfare, as the good most attainable for the greatest number. According to him, democracy is the enthronement of Caliban. Ariel can but be vanquished by its triumph. Many others who most care for aesthetic culture and select spirit are of a like mind. Thus Bourget thinks that universal triumph of democratic institutions will make civilization lose in profundity what it gains in extension. He sees its necessary end in the empire of individual mediocrity. "Who says democracy voices the evolution of individual tendencies and the devolution of culture." These judgments have a lively interest for us Americans who love the cause and consequence of that Revolution which in our America is entwined with the glory of its origin, and believe instinctively in the possibility of a noble and rare individual life which need never sacrifice its dignity to the caprices of the rabble. To confront the problem one must first recognize that if democracy does not uplift its spirit by a strong ideal interest which it shares with its preoccupation by material interests, it does lead, and fatally, to the favouring of mediocrity, and lacks, more than any other social system, barriers within which it may safely seek the higher culture. Abandoned to itself, without the constant rectification of some active moral sanction which shall purify and guide its motives to the dignifying of life — democracy will, gradually, extinguish the idea of any superiority which may not be turned into a more efficient training for the war of interests. It is then the most ignoble form of the brutalities of power. Spiritual preference, exaltation of life by unselfish motive, good taste and art and manners, and the admiration of all that is worthy and of good repute, will then alike vanish unprotected when social equality has destroyed all grades of excellence without replacing them with others that shall also rule by moral influence and the light of reason.

Any equality of conditions in the order of society, like homogeneity in nature, is but an unstable equilibrium. From that moment when democracy shall have worked its perfect work of negation by the levelling of unjust superiorities, the equality so won should be but a starting-point. Its affirmation remains; and the affirmation of democracy and its glory consist in arousing in itself by fit incentives the revelation and the mastery of the true superiorities of men.

With relation to the conditions of the life of America, that duty of attaining the true conception of our social state is doubly needful. Our democracies grow rapidly by the continual addition of a vast cosmopolitan multitude, by a stream of immigration which is merged with a nucleus already too weak to make active effort at assimilation and so contain the human flood by those dikes which an ancient solidity of social structure can alone provide, a secured political order, and the elements of a culture that has become deeply rooted. This rapid growth exposes our future to the dangers of a democratic degeneration which smothers under the blind force of the mass all idea of quality, deprives the social consciousness of all just notion of order, and, yielding its class organization to the rough hands of chance, causes the triumph of only the most ignoble, unjustifiable supremacies. . . .

The utilitarian conception as the idea of human destiny, and equality at the mediocre as the norm of social proportion, make up the formula which in Europe they call the spirit of Americanism. It is impossible to think on either of these as inspirations for human conduct or society, while contrasting them with those which are opposed to them, without at once conjuring up by association a vision of that formidable and fruitful democracy there in the North, with its manifestations of prosperity and power, as a dazzling example in favour of the efficacy of democratic institutions and the correct aim of its ideas. If one could say of utilitarianism that it is the word of the English spirit, the United States may be considered the incarnation of that word. Its Evangel is spread on every side to teach the material miracles of its triumph. And Spanish America is not wholly to be entitled, in its relation to the United States, as a nation of Gentiles. The mighty confederation is realizing over us a sort of moral conquest. Admiration for its greatness, its strength, is a sentiment that is growing rapidly in the minds of our governing classes, and even more, perhaps, among the multitude, easily impressed with victory or success. And from admiring it is easy to pass to imitating. Admiration and belief are already for the psychologist but the passive mood of imitation. "The imitative tendency of our moral nature," says Bagehot, "has its seat in that part of the soul where lives belief." Common sense and experience would suffice of themselves to show this natural relation. We imitate him in whose superiority and prestige we believe. So it happens that the vision of a voluntarily delatinized America, without compulsion or conquest, and re-generate in the manner of its Northern archetype, floats already through the dreams of many who are sincerely interested in our future, satisfies them with suggestive parallels they find at every step, and appears in constant move-ments for reform or innovation. We have our *mania for the North*. It is nec-essary to oppose to it those bounds which both sentiment and reason indicate.

Not that I would make of those limits an absolute negation. I well under-stand that enlightenment, inspiration, great lessons lie in the example of the strong; nor do I fail to realize that intelligent attention to the claims of the material and the study of the useful, directed abroad, is of especially use-ful result in the case of people in the formative stage, whose nationality is still in the mould. . . .

Still, the dispassionate study of that civilization which some would offer to us as a model, affords a reason no less potent than those which are based only on the indignity and unworthiness of mere imitation to temper the enthusiasm of those who propose it as our model. . . . And now I come to the very theme of my discourse, and the relation to it of this spirit of imita-tion. Any severe judgment formed upon our neighbours of the North should begin, like the courteous fencer, by lowering a rapier in salute to them. Easy is this for me. Failure to recognize their faults does not seem to me so insen-sate as to deny their qualities. Born — to employ Baudelaire's paradox — with the innate experience of liberty, they have kept themselves faithful to the law of their birth; and have developed, with the precision and certainty of a mathematical progression, the fundamental principles of their organization. This gives to their history a unity which, even if it has excluded the acquire-ment of different aptitudes or merits, has at least the intellectual beauty of being logical. The traces of its progress will never be expunged from the annals of human right, because they have been the first to evoke our modern ideal of liberty and to convert it from the uncertainty of experiment and the visions of Utopia into imperishable bronze and living reality. For they have shown by their example the possibility of extending the immovable authority of a republic over an immense national commonwealth, and, with their fed-eral organization, have revealed — as de Tocqueville felicitously put it — the manner in which the brilliancy and power of great states may be combined with the felicity and peace of little ones. . . .

Theirs are many of the most daring deeds for which the perspective of time shall distinguish this century; theirs is the glory of having revealed completely the greatness and dignity of labour, thereby accentuating the firmest note of moral beauty in all our civilization; the blest force which antiquity abandoned to the abjection of slavery, and which to-day we identify with the highest expression of human dignity, based on the consciousness and the exertion of its own merit. Strong, tenacious of purpose, holding inaction as opprobrious, they have placed in the hands of the mechanic of their shops and the farmer of their fields the mystic key of Hercules, and have given to human genius a new and unwonted beauty, girding it with the leathern apron of the hand-worker. Each one of these presses on to conquer life as his Puritan ancestors did the wilderness. Persistent followers of that creed of individual energy which makes of every man the artificer of his destiny, they have modelled their commonwealth on a kind of imaginary population of Crusoes, who, as soon as they have roughly attended to their training in the art of taking care of themselves, will turn to the making of themselves into a stable State. And, never sacrificing to this their conception of the sovereign Individual, they yet have known how at the same time to make of their association the most admirable instrument of their grandeur and empire; they have got from the sum of their energies, as devoted to research, industry, philanthropy, results that are the more marvellous in that they were secured with the most absolute integrity of their personal liberty.

They have a sleepless and insatiable instinct of curiosity, an impatient eagerness for the light; and, carrying a fondness for public education almost to the point of monomania, have made the common school the surest prop of their prosperity, believing that the mind of the child should be the most cherished of their precious things. Their culture, while far from being spiritual or refined, has an admirable efficiency so far as it is directed to practical ends and their immediate realization. And, while they have not added to the acquisitions of science a single general law, one new principle, they have done wonders in its application to new inventions and made giant strides in its service to utilities; in the steam boiler, the electric dynamo, are now billions of invisible slaves who centuple for their Aladdin the power of the magic lamp. The growth of their greatness and power will astonish future generations. By their marvellous gift for improvisation they have found a spur to time, so that in a few years they conjure, as it were from a desert, the fruitage hitherto the work of centuries.

And that Puritan liberty which gave them light in the past unites with that light a piety which still endures. Beside the factory and the school it has erected churches whence ascend the prayers of millions of free consciences. They have been able to save from the shipwreck of all the idealities that which is the highest of all, and kept alive the tradition of a religious sentiment which, if it does not uplift on wings of the highest idealism, spirituality, at least maintains over the utilitarian stampede some rein of the moral sense. Also, they have known how to maintain a certain primitive robustness even amidst the refinements of a highly civilized life; they hold to the pagan cult of health, sanity, and strength; they preserve in strong muscles the instrument of a strong will; obliged by their insatiable ambition to employ all human energies, they fit the torso of the athlete over the heart of the free man. And from all this springs a dominant note of optimism, confidence, faith, which makes them face the future with a proud and stubborn assurance; the note of "Excelsior" and the "Psalm of Life," which their poets have opposed as a balsam to melancholy or bitterness of spirit.

Thus it is that their Titanic greatness impresses even those made most distrustful by their exaggerations of character and the recent violences of their history; and I, who do not love them, as you see, admire them still. I admire them, first, for their formidable power of *desire;* I bow before that *"school of will and work"* — which Philarete Chasles tells us they have inherited from their forebears.

In the beginning was Action. With these famous words of Faust the future historian of the great Republic may begin; the Genesis, not yet concluded, of their national existence. Their genius may be defined as the universe of the *Dynamists:* force in movement. Above all, it has the capacity, the enthusiasm, the fortunate vocation, for doing things; volition is the chisel which has shapen this people from hard rock. Their characteristic points are manifestations of the will-power, originality, and audacity. Their history is above all a very paroxysm of virile activity. Their typical figure should be entitled, not Superman, but He who wants. And if anything saves them collectively from vulgarity, it is that extraordinary *verve* of energy which they always show and which lends a certain epic character to even the struggles of self-interest and the material life. . . .

North American life, indeed, describes that vicious circle which Pascal remarked in the ceaseless seeking for well-being when it has no object outside of oneself. Its prosperity is as immense as its incapability of satisfying even a mediocre view of human destiny. Titanic in its enormous concentration of human will-power, in its unprecedented triumph in all spheres of material aggrandizement, its civilization yet produces as a whole a singular impression of insufficiency, of emptiness. And if man's spirit demands, with all the reason that thirty centuries of growth under classic and under Christian influence have conferred upon it, *what* are in this new world the dirigent principles, — the ideal substratum, the ulterior end of all this concernment with the positive interests that so informs that mighty multitude, — he will only be met, as a definite formula, by that same exclusive interest in material triumphs. Orphaned of the profound tradition that attended his birth, the

North American has not yet replaced the inspiring ideality of his past with any high unselfish conception of the future. He lives for the immediate reality of the present, and for this subordinates all his activities in the egoism of material well-being, albeit both individual and collective. Of all his aggregation of the elements of wealth and power, one might say, what Bourget said of the intelligence of his character the Marquis Norbert, "a mountain of wood to which they have not yet known how to set fire." The vital spark is lacking to throw up that flame of the ideal, restless, life-giving, from that mountain of dead wood. Not even the selfishness of patriotism, for want of higher impulses, nor the pride of race, both of which transfigured and exalted in ancient days even the prosaic hardness of the life of Rome, can light a glimmer of ideality or beauty in a people where a cosmopolite confusion and the atomism of a badly understood democracy impede the formation of a veritable national conscience. . . .

Sensibility, intelligence, manners — each is marked in that enormous people by a radical unaptness for selection; and this, with the mechanical ordering of their material activities, makes a chaos of all that pertains to the realm of the ideal. It were easy to follow this unaptness from its most obvious manifestations to the more intimate and essential ones. Prodigal of riches — for meanness is not his fault — the North American has learned only to acquire by them the satisfaction of his vanity and material luxury, but not the chosen note of good taste. In such a surrounding true art can only exist as the rebellion of an individual. Emerson, Poe, are as estrays of a fauna expelled from their true habitat by some geological catastrophe. In "Outre Mer" Bourget speaks of the solemn tone in which the North American utters the word Art, when he, a self-made man, has achieved riches which he now desires to crown with all the human refinements; but he never has felt the divine frenzy of poem or picture; he would buy but to add to his collection a new toy, to satisfy at once his vanity and his acquisitive instinct. That in it which is disinterested, chosen, rare, he ignores, despite the munificence with which he scatters his individual fortune to found schools of art, form popular taste, build splendid museums, patronize huge expositions, and deck his cities with monuments and his streets with bronze and marble. And if one had to characterize his taste, in a word, it would be that which in itself involves the negation of great art; strained brutality of effect, insensibility to soft tones or an exquisite style, the cult of bigness, and that sensationalism which excludes all noble serenity as incompatible with the hurry of his hectic life.

The ideal of beauty does not appeal to the descendants of the austere Puritan, nor even a passionate worship of the truth; they care little for any thinking that has no immediate practical object — it seems to them idle and fruitless; even to science they bring no selfless interest for discovery, nor do they seem capable of loving its truths only because they are true; investigation is merely the necessary antecedent of practical application. Their praiseworthy efforts to extend the benefits of popular education are inspired with the noble motive of communicating the rudiments of knowledge to the masses; but it does not appear that they also concern themselves over-much with that higher education which shall rise above the general mediocrity. And so the outcome is that of all their struggle with ignorance the only gain has been a sort of universal semiculture and a profound indifference to the higher. . . . As fast as the general ignorance decreases, so, in the air of that giant democracy, decreases the higher learning and vanishes genius itself. This is why the story of their intellectual activity is of a retrogression in brilliance and originality. For while at the era of their Independence and Constitution many famous names illustrate their history in thought as well as in action, a half-century later de Tocqueville could say of them, the Gods are disappearing. And, when he wrote his master work, there still radiated from Boston, the Puritan home, the city of learning and tradition, a glorious pleiad which holds in the intellectual story of our century a universal fame. Who since has picked up the heritage of Emerson, Channing, Poe? The levelling by the middle classes tends ever, pressing with its desolating task, to plane down what little remains of *intelligentsia:* the flowers are mown by the machine when the weeds remain.

Long since their books have ceased to soar on wings beyond the common vision. To-day the most actual example of what Americans like best in literature must be sought in the gray pages of magazines or periodicals which seldom remind one that that mode of publication was employed in the immortal "Federalist.". . .

As fast as the utilitarian genius of that nation takes on a more defined character, franker, narrower yet, with the intoxication of material prosperity, so increases the impatience of its sons to spread it abroad by propaganda, and think it predestined for all humanity. To-day they openly aspire to the primacy of the world's civilization, the direction of its ideas, and think themselves the forerunners of all culture that is to prevail. The colloquial phrase, ironically quoted by Laboulaye, "America can beat the world," is taken seriously by almost any virile Westerner. At the bottom of their open rivalry with Europe lies a contempt for it that is almost naïve, and the profound conviction that within a brief period they are destined to eclipse its glory and do away with its spiritual superiority; thus once more fulfilling, in the progress of civilization, the hard law of the ancient mysteries, whereby the initiated shall put to death the initiator. It were useless to seek to convince them that, although their services to inventions and material advance have been doubtless great, even rising to the measure of a universal human obligation, they do not of themselves suffice to alter the axis of the earth. It were useless to seek to convince them that the fires lit upon European altars, the work done by peoples living these three thousand years gone by about the shores of the Mediterranean, though rising to glorious genius when bound with the olive and the palm of Athens, a work still being carried on and in whose traditions and teachings we South Americans live, makes a sum which cannot be equalled by any equation of Washington plus Edison. Would they even revise the Book of Genesis, to put themselves upon the front page? . . .

All history shows a definite relation of growth between the progress of utilitarian activity and the ideal. And just as the former can be turned into a shelter and protection for the latter, so the ideas of the mind often give rise to utilitarian results, above all when these latter are not sought directly. For instance, Bagehot remarks that the immense positive benefits of navigation might never have been attained for humanity if in earliest times there had not been dreamers, apparently idle — and certainly misunderstood by their contemporaries — who were interested solely in the contemplation of the movements of the stars.

This law of harmony bids us also respect the arm that labours arduously in what seems a barren and prosaic soil. The work of North American positivism will also at the end serve the cause of Ariel. That which this people of Cyclops have achieved for the direct purpose of material advantage, with all their sense for what is useful and their admirable faculty of mechanical invention, will be converted by other peoples, or later, even by themselves, to a wealth of material for the higher selection. Thus that most precious and fundamental invention of the alphabet, which gives the wings of immortality to the spoken word, originated in Phœnician shops, the discovery of merchants who only desired to keep their accounts. Using it for purposes merely mercenary, they never dreamed that the genius of a superior race would transfigure and transform it to a means of perpetuating the light and the learning of their own being. The relation between material good and good that is intellectual or moral is thus only a new aspect of that modern doctrine which we call the transformation of energy: material well-being may be transformed into spiritual superiority.

But North American life does not as yet offer us any new example of this indisputable relation, nor even dimly suggest it as the triumph of the generation to come. . . .

Already there exist, in our Latin America, cities whose material grandeur and apparent civilization place them in the first rank; but one may fear lest a touch of thought upon their exterior, so sumptuous, may make the shining vessel ring hollow within; lest our cities too — though they had their Moreno, their Rivadavia, their Sarmiento, cities which gave initiative to an immortal revolution that, like a stone cast on water, spread the glory of their heroes and the words of their tribunes in ever-widening circles over a vast continent — may end like Tyre or Sidon, or as Carthage ended.

It is your generation that must prevent this; the youth which is of to-day, blood and muscle and nerve of the future. I speak to you, seeing in you those who are destined to guide the others in coming battles for a spiritual cause. The perseverance of your strength must be in you as your certainty of victory. . . .

Can you not picture to yourselves the America we others dream of? Hospitable to things of the spirit, and not only to the immigrant throngs; thoughtful, without sacrificing its energy of action; serene and strong and withal full of generous enthusiasm; resplendent with the charm of morning calm like the smile of a waking infant, yet with the light of awakening thought. Think on her at least; the honor of your future history depends on your keeping constantly before your eyes the vision of that America, radiant above the realities of the present like the rose window above the dark nave of a cathedral. . . . In dark hours of discouragement may it [the statue of Ariel] rekindle in your conscience the warmth of the ideal, return to your hearts the glow of a perishing hope. And Ariel, first enthroned behind the bastion of your inner life, may sally thence to the attack and conquering of other souls. I see the bright spirit smiling back upon you in future times, even though your own still works in shadow. I have faith in your will and in your strength, even more in those to whom you shall transfer your life, transmit your work. I dream in rapture of that day when realities shall convince the world that the Cordillera which soars above the continent of the Americas has been carved to be the pedestal of this statue, the altar of the cult of Ariel.

3. Ode to Roosevelt

RUBÉN DARÍO

By the turn of the century Rubén Darío (1867–1916) was the undisputed master of *modernismo,* the new literary movement engulfing Latin America. In his lifetime he was recognized as the greatest Hispanic poet produced by the New World, and to this day his work continues to exert a profound influence on Spanish American letters.

Born in Nicaragua, he traveled, lived, and wrote in Central America, Chile, Argentina, Spain and France. He was residing in Europe and serving as Nicaragua's diplomatic representative when Theodore Roosevelt ordered the invasion of Panama in 1903. His poem, "To Roosevelt," was an outspoken political denunciation of the "Big Stick" policy, but it is interesting to note that the pressures of Darío's diplomatic position later impelled him to recant. In 1906 he wrote "Salute to the Eagle," a poem calling for hemispheric solidarity that he dedicated to the Pan-American Congress meeting in Rio de Janeiro.

To Roosevelt[1]

The voice that would reach you, Hunter, must speak
in Biblical tones, or in the poetry of Walt Whitman.
You are primitive and modern, simple and complex;
you are one part George Washington and one part Nimrod.[2]
   You are the United States,
future invader of our naïve America
with its Indian blood, an America
that still prays to Christ and still speaks Spanish.

You are a strong, proud model of your race;
you are cultured and able; you oppose Tolstoy.[3]
You are an Alexander-Nebuchadnezzar,

From *Selected Poems of Rubén Darío,* trans. by Lysander Kemp (Austin: University of Texas Press, 1965), pp. 69–70. Reprinted by permission.

[1] Theodore Roosevelt (1858–1919), president of the United States from 1901–1909.

[2] Mythical king of Chaldea whom the Bible calls "a mighty hunter before the Lord." (Genesis X, 8–10.)

[3] Leo Tolstoy (1828–1910).

breaking horses and murdering tigers.
(You are a Professor of Energy,
as the current lunatics say.)

You think that life is a fire,
that progress is an irruption,
that the future is wherever
your bullet strikes.
          No.

The United States is grand and powerful.
Whenever it trembles, a profound shudder
runs down the enormous backbone of the Andes.
If it shouts, the sound is like the roar of a lion.
And Hugo[4] said to Grant: "The stars are yours."

(The dawning sun of the Argentine barely shines;
the star of Chile is rising . . .) A wealthy country,
joining the cult of Mammon[5] to the cult of Hercules;
while Liberty, lighting the path
to easy conquest, raises her torch in New York.

But our own America, which has had poets
since the ancient times of Nezahualcóyotl;[6]
which preserved the footprints of great Bacchus,[7]
and learned the Panic alphabet once,
and consulted the stars; which also knew Atlantis[8]
(whose name comes ringing down to us in Plato)
and has lived, since the earliest moments of its life,
in light, in fire, in fragrance, and in love—
the America of Moctezuma and Atahualpa,
the aromatic America of Columbus,
Catholic America, Spanish America,
the America where noble Cuauhtémoc[9] said:
"I am not on a bed of roses"—our America,

[4] When General Ulysses S. Grant visited Paris in 1877, Victor Hugo wrote several articles criticizing him. Probably a reference to the North American flag.

[5] God of wealth in Phoenician mythology.

[6] Mexican king, poet, and philosopher of the 16th century.

[7] Roman god of wine.

[8] In the Greek legend, the large island in the western sea; a continent that the ancients believed had existed in the Atlantic, east of Gibraltar.

[9] Nephew of Moctezuma and last emperor of the Aztecs, whom the conquerors tortured by applying fire to his feet.

trembling with hurricanes, trembling with Love:
O men with Saxon eyes and barbarous souls,
our America lives. And dreams. And loves.
And it is the daughter of the Sun. Be careful.
Long live Spanish America!
A thousand cubs of the Spanish lion are roaming free.
Roosevelt, you must become, by God's own will,
the deadly Rifleman and the dreadful Hunter
before you can clutch us in your iron claws.

And though you have everything, you are lacking one thing:
  God!

Translated by Lysander Kemp

4. *The United States Is Honor Bound to Maintain Law and Order in South America*

GEORGE W. CRICHFIELD

Mr. Crichfield expressed in what may seem to be an exaggerated way the feeling of those who looked upon Latin Americans as "a lesser breed" who must be kept in order for their own good. If only the United States would take charge of those countries, the trains would run on time!

Our people believe in justice, and in the liberty which carries the torch of civilization over the earth. They have always earnestly desired to see stable republics established in South America. They do not believe in monarchies. They believe in "a government of the people, by the people, and for the people." Our people enthusiastically upheld President Monroe when he declared that European monarchies should not extend their territory on American soil, and each succeeding administration, without exception, has striven

From *American Supremacy: The Rise and Progress of the Latin American Republics and Their Relations to the United States under the Monroe Doctrine* by George W. Crichfield (New York: Brentano's, 1908), 1, pp. 7–544; 2, pp. 635–644, passim.

to aid in the establishment, maintenance, and development of decent republican governments in these countries.

When our State Department has seen revolutions, anarchy, and crime rampant in South America, foreigners being looted, robbed, and murdered (Americans suffering worse than any other class), infamy, perfidy, intrigue, and scoundrelism covering Spanish America as with a pall — it has not shut its eyes to the facts. On the contrary, no father ever watched over his wayward offspring with more care, sorrow, and anxiety than has the beneficent government of the United States observed these countries, studying by what means it could bring order out of chaos, decency out of crime.

For three quarters of a century this has been our policy, followed with patience and a spirit of philanthropy to which history affords no parallel. As one bandit government after another has appeared on the horizon of South

America, our government has counselled it to exercise moderation, to walk in the paths of civilization, to respect the lives and property of foreigners; and we have stood between these so-called "governments" and the civilized powers of Europe.

In spite of all that our country has done for them, the incontestable fact remains that Venezuela, Colombia, Ecuador, Bolivia, Santo Domingo, Hayti, and practically all of Central America are in a worse condition to-day, politically, socially, commercially, and deeper in barbarism, than they were three quarters of a century ago. Dilettante philosophers, reactionists who are against every policy which has made the United States the peerless giant which it is, will go on shouting in behalf of our "poor oppressed Sister Republics." On such people the facts stated in the following pages will have no effect. But Americans — the hardy, brainy, practical race which has founded the Great Republic, before the tremendous power of whose solemn and deliberate judgment governments must stand or fall — that innumerable army of men who have made and who constitute "God's country" — men who hate brigand governments (all the more if they assume the name of Republics), who love justice and truth, and hate wickedness whatever may be its form — should know these Spanish-Indian-Negro countries as they actually are. If they could see Americans and American enterprises wiped off the face of the earth by the aggregations calling themselves Republics, it would not be long before the machinery of the government of the United States would be diverted towards bringing about a most thorough renovation in their conditions.

To many people it may seem impossible that in this day and age, and in the Western hemisphere, there could exist such conditions of semi-barbarism in Colombia, Venezuela, Santo Domingo, and Central America as are here disclosed. To know a country thoroughly one must have lived in it and done business in it. Distinguished writers have written admirable descriptive works of South America — of landscapes, of cities and rivers and lakes, of mountains and llanos, with a coloring of individual incident and interesting anecdote; they are admirable productions of scholarly men. One may describe a landscape from the window of a Pullman car, but one cannot in such a manner apprehend the social and political problems of the peoples through whose country the railroad passes. However brilliant a traveller may be, however acute his power of observation, it is not possible that he can probe into the depths and analyze the character and capabilities of a people, except by long and varied intercourse with them. . . .

It will be found that practically all Latin Americans exhibit the following peculiarities to a degree greater than that possessed by any other people with which I am familiar: (1) a lack of thoroughness, exactness, definiteness of aim; (2) inability to apply themselves persistently and continually to the mastery of a subject; (3) carelessness and lack of foresight; (4) contempt for the drudgery of ordinary work and a disposition to shirk it; (5) a desire to make a great display, to pretend to be what in fact they are not; (6) satisfaction with the outward appearance of knowledge, with no real desire to get at the heart of any proposition; (7) lack of initiative, invention, creative energy; (8) possession of a multitude of impracticable theories and ideas which are a nuisance, but of which it is impossible to rid them; (9) complete absence of a sense of responsibility; (10) ignorance of the most elementary methods of doing things; (11) a disposition to talk, rather than to act; (12) a disposition to do work in the showiest manner possible, but to produce what is really shoddy and worthless; (13) a disposition to make money by intrigue rather than in legitimate business; (14) a very scant respect for the property or personal rights of others, particularly foreigners; (15) absolute indolence and lack of genuine ambition, and opposition to progress.

All of these will be recognized as characteristics of large sections of our own country; and indeed they cannot be set down as the exclusive peculiarities of any people, or as all of them applying to any one section of any people. Yet in their entirety they come nearer applying to the Latin Americans than to any European race. . . .

NATIONAL INGRATITUDE

The United States has befriended the Latin-American countries in ten thousand ways; it has defended them against civilized powers for eighty years; it has submitted to outrages committed on its flag and on the persons and property of its citizens, outwardly without protest; it has declared in the presence of the world, untruthfully, but nevertheless declared it, that these countries are civilized republics, and their courts worthy the same consideration as are the courts of England or our own; it has called them "Sister Republics," and stood with its army and navy ready to defend them, at the grave risk, on more than one occasion, of having a war on its hands with the whole civilized world. In view of all this, it might reasonably be inferred that Americans are popular in South America; but it is not so. Americans are robbed more than are either Germans or Englishmen; more outrages are committed against Americans than against any other class of foreigners.

If ingratitude is the index of a criminal, then these fighting, quarrelling, intriguing, murdering communities should be classed as criminals. . . .

LATIN AMERICAN TYPES

The military Jefe is the most noted Latin-American type which impresses itself upon a visitor. The Jefe may be colonel, general, comandante, or any of the other numerous military grades. As a rule, he is a man without conscience, of unbridled ambition, cruel and relentless, and a dangerous citizen generally.

Closely allied with the military Jefe is the civil politician. This man can write pronunciamentoes, and hair-raising essays on liberty and patriotism. He also fixes up the decretas for the military Jefe to sign. A considerable portion of the graft is allotted to this type of politician. He is merely a schemer for the Jefe with his army of macheteros.

The doctors of Latin America are as numerous as the generals. They are a much more amiable class of men. While their pretensions to learning are exaggerated and amusing, nevertheless, they are a respectable element of society. Ignoring their idiosyncracies and pretensions of refinement and culture, we may sincerely like and admire these men, most of whom are very decent fellows and a large number of whom are first-class gentlemen of a high type.

Throughout Mexico, Argentina, and Chili there are enormous plantations or tracts of land called *haciendas,* the owner of which is known as a *hacendado.* This man is easily, in my opinion, the highest type of Latin-American gentleman. He has not the literary ability or the refinement and culture of the doctors, but he is an all-round man of affairs, a good business man, and really forms the backbone of the nation. It is the hacendado who gives to Mexico, Chili, and Argentina their stability and higher governmental excellence. The hacendado is usually the supporter of the government, unless it be in fact very vicious, because it is to his interest to maintain the established order of things. He does not want his property overrun by revolutionary hordes, and he knows that it is better to submit to the exactions of a corrupt government than to run the risk of losing all by siding with anarchy. These great plantations are not cultivated thoroughly, and enormous tracts of land lie fallow or in their primeval condition. No opportunity is afforded to the small man to become a landed proprietor, and this constitutes the real element of weakness in the hacienda system. The inconceivable strength of the United

States is due to the fact that we have millions of home owners. A comparatively poor man with us can own his own house and farm. Not so in the countries mentioned. A landed proprietor there is necessarily a man of wealth. The coffee plantations of Venezuela and Colombia afford a somewhat similar system to that of the great landed estates in the other countries mentioned, but owing to the frequent uprisings and the despoliation by predatory bands, these plantations are usually run down and neglected.

There are many special types in Central and South America which are very interesting to a foreign observer. They may be briefly mentioned. The *arierro,* or mule-driver, is a picturesque fellow. He directs the burros in their never-ending work of transporting the products of Latin America. These burro trains by the hundreds can be found in all parts of Latin America, each animal carrying loads of two hundred or two hundred and fifty pounds, over mountains and valleys, wading rivers, climbing where it would seem to be impossible for an animal to step, going on journeys for days or even weeks. The arierro is utterly oblivious to the suffering of his beasts. He is ordinarily not a bad fellow, but is entirely indifferent to pain, and ignorant with regard to every subject except the matter in hand. The *gaucho,* or cow-boy, of the great interior plains of Argentina, Brazil, and Southern Venezuela is a most daring rider, an excellent shot, and makes one of the hardiest soldiers in the world. He loves ornaments in dress, is disposed to drink a great deal of bad liquor and indulge in gambling, and is generally a citizen with whom one must be careful in dealing. . . . The beggar is another distinctive type in Latin America which impresses itself upon the visitor with a vividness and distinctiveness which can never be obliterated. One day a week, usually Saturday, is set apart particularly for the beggars, in which they make their rounds of all the houses and streets, soliciting alms. The utter hopelessness of this type is pitiable and pathetic. They live in indescribable squalor and misery, diseased, deformed, helpless, and hopeless. There are hundreds of thousands of all ages and both sexes belonging to this type in Latin America. The enormous percentage of dire helplessness is one of the saddest features which an observer encounters in every Latin-American country. . . .

PROTECTION OF CIVILIZED MEN IN AMERICA

The United States is in honor bound to maintain law and order in South America, and we may just as well take complete control of several of the countries, and establish decent governments while we are about it. Peru, Chili, and Argentina are already fairly responsible governments. We ought not to interfere with them so long as they conduct themselves in a reasonably satisfactory manner. Mexico is an excellent government, and worthy of our best friendship. A stricter surveillance should be exercised over Costa Rica, Brazil,

Uruguay, and Paraguay. These governments are not as advanced or as worthy of recognition as those named, but they are not wholly bad. There are evidences of genuine efforts at improvement, and some regard for the amenities of civilization and international rights, and a rather more decent spirit towards foreigners. Whether they will ever amount to anything or not, time alone will tell. They should be kept under the strictest friendly supervision by the United States. No marked internal or external policy should be permitted without our consent. They should be held under a quasi-protectorate, yet with such a minimum of interference with their affairs as would secure perfect security for life and property, and a reasonable measure of material and intellectual progress. . . .

THE DICTATORSHIPS SHOULD BE PLACED UNDER A CIVILIZED GOVERNMENT

Now, what shall be said of Venezuela, Colombia, Ecuador, Bolivia, Santo Domingo, and Haiti, and the rest of Central America?

They have sinned away their day of grace. They are semibarbarous centres of rapine in an age which boasts of enlightenment. They are a reproach to the civilization of the twentieth century.

It is a waste of time to argue in connection with these States about sovereign rights. The United States should take immediate possession and jurisdiction of each and every one of them, without waiting for a pretext. It should govern them precisely the same way as it governs other territory of the United States. The century of intrigue and bloodshed and bad faith in these countries should be brought to a close, and a new era ushered in more in harmony with the sentiments of the age. With the United States in control of South America, I venture to predict that within ten years we could take a Pullman car at Maracaibo and go straight through to Buenos Ayres without change, and in ten years longer it might be that we could step into another car and go to New York. Under the present régime such conditions would not be brought about in ten thousand years.

There are doubtless many persons who would concede that this ought to be done and yet hesitate to commit the United States to such a policy on account of the apparent magnitude of the task. Our people have not yet got over the idea that the taking of Porto Rico and the Philippines under our wing was a mighty feat, and the ravings of the "antis" have rather accentuated that belief. As a matter of fact, the Philippines and Porto Rico are only specks in the ocean in comparison with the immensity of England's colonial possessions.

If the United States were to take possession of the whole of the Western Hemisphere, from the Rio Grande to Cape Horn, the total area of its territory would be only about equal to that of the British Empire, and its population not more than one third as great.

What Englishmen can do Americans can do. The United States, with vastly greater territory and population, is as truly a breeding-place of creative energy, of originating and productive enterprise, as England or any other country. . . .

No very great argument should be required to show the incomparable benefit to the United States as a nation in controlling these great territories. It is a curious thing that the English, who are in all ordinary business matters extremely slow and conservative in comparison with Americans, should in this one matter so completely outstrip us in foresight and in a true apprehension of the right policy to pursue. If we are to become a great manufacturing nation, we must have outlets for our goods, and those outlets must be in countries where there is money to pay for them and the disposition to buy them. To develop the continent of South America properly will require twice as many tons of steel rails as it has required to develop the United States, for it is twice as large. It will require as much mining machinery, for the natural mineral resources of South America are unquestionably as great and as valuable as those of North America. The people who are now scantily clothed would, under proper conditions, be large consumers of our manufactured products. The manufactured production of the United States is now running parallel with the domestic consumption, and in a short time will overleap it. We must have markets, vast markets; for our productive capacity is great. If our workingmen are to be kept employed, if the prosperity of the United States is to continue, we must look ahead, and provide ourselves for outlets of our products. It has been truly said that when we export a million dollars' worth of goods, at least $800,000 of money has been paid to our own people for the labor of their production. I am aware that every effort of far-seeing statesmen to establish our future commercial prosperity on a sound basis calls forth protest from a certain class of mugwumps, who join the words "commercialism," "militarism," and "imperialism" as though they constitute a trinity of horrors. . . .

IMPORTANCE OF CIVILIZED CONTROL

It seems unnecessary to emphasize the beneficent effects upon the people of those South American countries which would result from placing them under the American flag. One immediate and very important consequence would be that a man could go to sleep at night without fear of being assassinated. No one, unless he has slept for some years with one eye open and an automatic revolver within reach, can appreciate the delight of unmolested sleep.

Another blessing scarcely less appreciable would be the privilege of working and reaping the results of one's efforts. To-day, in South America, military Jefes will not work, nor will they let any one else work. The enormity of this wrong can be only partially appreciated by those people in the United States who have personally observed the tyranny of the labor boss as displayed in its unvarnished ugliness in certain localities.

As fully explained in another chapter, the great majority of the people of South America are good people — incapable of self-government, but fully capable of marvellous development under decent conditions. To those who wish to live in peace and accumulate a little property against old age or death, the American flag would be a beacon of hope. Rascals, intriguers, and the semi-bandit governing class are the only people whose liberties would in any wise be curtailed by the control of the United States.

Do I need to multiply examples in order to prove my contention? Is there any American so blind that he cannot to some extent perceive the blessings that have accrued to each successive territory which has come under the beneficent control of the United States? Look at that magnificent State, Texas, and that incomparable garden of the world, rich and beautiful California, and the rest of the splendid commonwealths which have been created out of the territory wrested from Mexico.

Suppose that territory had remained in the exclusive control of Mexico and Mexicans, and that the enterprise and capital of Americans had never entered it. Does any sane man believe it would ever have attained a fraction of its present prosperity? Even the progress of Mexico itself is due mainly not to internal activity, but to the stimulus of external enterprise exercised within its borders. Nor can any fault-finder truthfully assert that the rule of the United States in Porto Rico and the Philippines is any less promising. The mediæval systems of a century are not to be swept away in a moment, and the complete regeneration of a people is a question of time; but already much has been accomplished in both those colonies. Never before were they so well governed, never were they so clean, never was education so well looked after, public improvements so actively pushed, happiness and security of the people so thoroughly safeguarded, or such contentment and evidences of future prosperity as at the present time.

Size, distance, or inaccessibility of these countries constitutes no valid objection against this program. The world is apparently destined to be divided up among five or six great powers. The time has passed when we can permit the famines and pestilences and revolutions which grow out of barbaric or semi-barbaric conditions to destroy millions. With the world under the control of half a dozen civilized powers, wars would be unknown, and the chief function of the military would be its police duties. On this hemisphere the power which controls should be the United States. . . .

What shall be the final destiny of these countries no man can tell. What part of the United States is to take in the mighty onward march of affairs is likewise shrouded in the future. But any reasonable man must see clearly that the present condition of anarchy cannot continue indefinitely in Spanish America. It is not they alone who suffer, but the whole world; and not they alone, but the whole world, would be benefited by the United States taking possession of them.

Eva Perón—
Argentine Feminist

Eva Duarte de Perón (1919–1952) has been described as "the most powerful woman in Latin American history."[1] Born in a provincial town in the interior of Argentina, she made her way to Buenos Aires in the 1930's and became a film and radio actress. In 1943 she met Juan Perón, an ambitious army officer and member of the military junta that had recently come to power. First as his mistress and later his wife, Eva was crucial to maintaining the support of laborers for Perón's regime (1946–1955). She spearheaded the movement for women's suffrage, organized a women's division of the Peronist party, established a monopoly on social welfare services through the Eva Perón Foundation, and acted as mediator between labor unions and the government. Eva never held elective office, and a veto by Perón's military supporters prevented her candidacy for the vice-presidency in 1951. Her death from cancer a year later was a devastating blow to the popularity of her husband, who was overthrown by a military coup on September 20, 1955.

Controversial in her lifetime, Evita (as she preferred to be called) was even more controversial after her death. In their recent biography Nicholas Fraser and Marysa Navarro observe that no historical figure in modern times has inspired such complicated myths.[2] For some Perón was a saint—a tireless unselfish worker for the poor; for others she was a whore—a cheap actress who manipulated Juan Perón and amassed enormous personal wealth. Evita's autobiography, *La Razón de mi Vida* (translated into English as *My Mission in Life*) did much to fuel these myths. Ghostwritten by Raul Mende, a speech writer for Juan Perón, the book sold 150,000 copies on the first day

---

[1] June E. Hahner, *Women in Latin American History* (Los Angeles: UCLA, 1978), p.90.
[2] Nicholas Fraser and Marysa Navarro, *Eva Perón* (New York: Norton, 1985), Foreword.

of its publication in October 1951 and was later made required reading in the Argentine public schools. The narrative takes the form of a long conversation by turns intimate and rhetorical. It repeats all the themes in Evita's speeches but contains almost nothing about her life before Perón and presents a distorted account of her work—for example the assertion that she did not interfere in government affairs was an obvious lie. Hailed by some as the sincere testimony of a seeker of social justice and national regeneration, it was branded by others as the propaganda of a cunning, ambitious woman. In the view of Fraser and Navarro, the autobiography develops two myths: the myth of Perón, "the generous, good, hard-working, self-sacrificing, fatherly male" and the myth of Evita, "incarnation of every feminine virtue, all love, humility and even more self-sacrifice"[3] (Reading 1)

Even today, biographers of Evita face a difficult challenge. There are still no accessible archives in Argentina that deal with the Perón era. The contemporary press was highly partisan, and although there have been many renderings of her life, most of these are openly propagandistic. These difficulties have led some to conclude that the accumulation of lies about Evita has made her real story irretrievable.

The Woman with the Whip, published in English in 1952 just after Evita's death, and in 1955 in Spanish in Argentina, was the first book-length biography of this elusive woman. The author was Mary Main, an Anglo-Argentine historical novelist who wrote under the pseudonym María Flores. Main revisited Buenos Aires in 1950 when Evita's power was at its height. Her informants were members of the opposition, and the result is a compendium of the most virulent anti-Peronist gossip mingled with genuine insights into the careers of the Peróns (Reading 2). A more objective biography is that previously mentioned by Fraser and Navarro who purposely set out to distinguish wherever possible between myths and truths in order to present and judge Eva Perón as a human being. They conducted interviews with more than 100 people between 1972 and 1978 to supplement the available written records. The *Library Journal* has called their book "the first convincingly researched and historically accurate account"[4] (Reading 3). Another excellent sketch of Evita is included in Richard Bourne's *Political Leaders of Latin America* published in 1969. Bourne is a British journalist who spent several months in Brazil, Chile, Argentina, and Paraguay in 1967 to gather material on six individuals whom he regarded as representative leaders of twentieth century Latin America: Che Guevara, Alfredo Stroessner, Eduardo Frei Montalva, Carlos Lacerda, Juscelino Kubitschek and Evita Perón. Bourne included Evita because her career demonstrated "the cross currents that flavor mass politics in a relatively advanced Latin American country"

[3] Fraser and Navarro, p. 140.
[4] *Library Journal,* 106 (May 1, 1981), 968.

and because her work continues to have an impact. "Though she died as long ago as 1952, her legend interwoven with that of her husband, contributes to the enduring stalemate in Argentine politics. As long as the Peronists manage to get about 30% of the poll in anything like a free election, and as long as other sectors of political life—especially the military—fear them above all, Argentina seems condemned to insecure civilian government or army rule" (Readings 4 and 6).

Nancy Hollander's essay, "Women: The Forgotten Half of Argentine History," makes clear that the struggle by Argentine women for greater economic and social equality began in the early decades of the twentieth century long before Eva Perón came on the scene. Hollander reviews these efforts and points out that President Juan Perón was well aware of the political significance of women. (Reading 5)

Even in death Evita continues to exercise a powerful hold over the minds of the Argentines. Within three years after Juan Perón fled Argentina, anti-Peronists had torn down her monuments and burned her pictures, books and personal papers. Her embalmed body, which had been kept in the Confederation of Labor headquarters awaiting the completion of a multi-million dollar mausoleum, mysteriously disappeared—beginning a sixteen year odyssey that would take it across five countries on two continents. In the meantime, a cult of "Saint Evita" flourished in Argentina. Posters of an ethereal Evita appeared on the walls of towns throughout the country. Terrorists killed in her name. In 1970, former president General Pedro Aramburu, who had assumed power soon after Juan Perón was overthrown, was kidnapped and murdered in an unsuccessful effort to force him to confess where Evita's body had been taken. Finally in 1976 the army revealed that the body was hidden in a grave marked by the name of another woman in Milan, Italy.[5]

On November 17, 1974 a chartered aircraft brought Evita back to Buenos Aires, and in 1976 her body was finally returned to her family. It now lies in the Duarte family tomb in the Recoleta Cemetery near Palermo Park where many illustrious Argentines are buried. The outwardly unimpressive tomb is more than it appears to be. The government paid for its installation. It is said to be proof against the most ingenious grave-robbers and capable of withstanding a nuclear bomb attack. As Fraser and Navarro assert, these elaborate protections reflect a fear: "a fear that the body will disappear from the tomb and that the woman, or rather the myth of the woman will reappear."[6]

---

[5] John Barnes, *Evita-First Lady* (New York: Grove Press, 1978), p. 3. See also V. S. Naipaul, "The Corpse at the Iron Door," *New York Review of Books*, XIX (August 10, 1972), pp. 3–8.

[6] Fraser and Navarro, p. 192.

"I am nothing more than a humble woman of a great people."
Eva Perón

1. My Mission in Life

EVA PERÓN

Eva Perón's autobiography is divided into three parts: "The Causes of My Mission," "The Workers and My Mission," and "Women and My Mission." In the sections reprinted here, Evita reveals much about her life and feelings. She declares that she is not a feminist who wants to behave like a man, but she protests the absence of women from centers of power, and while she speaks of the sanctity of motherhood and the home, goes on to propose salaries for housewives. Finally, she claims that all her actions are founded on love and praise for Perón. It is clear that Evita regarded herself as the link between her husband and the people.

PREFACE

This book has sprung from my innermost heart. However much I speak in its pages of my feelings, of my thoughts and of my own life, in all that I have written the least observant of my readers will find nothing else but the figure, the soul and the life of General Perón and my profound love for him and for his cause.

Many will reproach me for thinking only of him while having written all this; I confess in advance that it is true, absolutely true.

And I have my reasons, my powerful reasons, which nobody will be able to dispute or doubt: I was not, nor am I, anything more than a humble woman . . . a sparrow in an immense flock of sparrows. . . . But Perón was and is a gigantic condor that flies high and sure among the summits and near to God.

If it had not been for him who came down to my level and taught me to fly in another fashion, I would never have known what a condor is like, nor ever have been able to contemplate the marvelous and magnificent immenseness of my people.

That is why neither my life nor my heart belongs to me, and nothing of all that I am or have is mine. All that I am, all that I have, all that I think and all that I feel, belongs to Perón.

From *My Mission in Life* by Eva Perón, translated by Ethel Cherry, (Garden City: Doubleday and Co., 1952) Preface, pp. 3–9, 181–197, 211–213. Reprinted by permission.

But I do not forget, nor will I ever forget, that I was a sparrow, nor that I still am one. If I fly higher, it is through him. If I walk among the peaks, it is through him. If sometimes I almost touch the sky with my wings, it is through him. If I see clearly what my people are, and love them and feel their affection caressing my name, it is solely through him.

That is why I dedicate to him, wholly, this song which, like that of the sparrow, has no beauty, but is humble and sincere, and contains all the love of my heart.

A CASE OF CHANCE?

Many persons cannot understand the circumstances which have made my life what it is.

I myself have often pondered on all this that is now my life.

Some of my contemporaries attribute it all to chance—that strange and inexplicable thing that does not explain anything, anyway.

No. It is not chance that has brought me to this position, to this life I lead.

Obviously it would all be absurd if my sharpest-tongued critics were right when they say thoughtless that I, "a superficial woman, uninstructed, common, unacquainted with the interests of her country, remote from the sorrows of her people, indifferent to social justice and with nothing serious in her head, suddenly became a fanatic in the struggle for the cause of the people, and, making that cause hers, decided to live a life of incomprehensible sacrifice."

I would like to make myself clear about this.

That is why I have decided to write these notes.

But I do not do so to contradict anyone or to prove anyone wrong.

Rather I would wish my fellow citizens, men and women, to know how I feel and think.

I want them to share in the great things I experience in my heart.

Surely many of the things I shall say here are teachings I received freely from Perón and which I have not the right to keep secret.

A GREAT FEELING

I have to look back on the course of my life to find the earliest reason for all that is happening to me now.

Perhaps I am wrong in saying "the earliest *reason*," since the truth is that all my life I have been prone to be driven and guided by my feelings.

Even today, in this rush of things that I must perform, I let myself be guided very often—in fact almost always—primarily by what I feel.

Reason, with me, often has to give way to emotion; and so, to explain the life I lead today, that is to say, what I am doing now out of motives that spring from the bottom of my heart, I have to go back and search through my earliest years for the first feelings that make sense, or at least explain, what to those severe critics is "an incomprehensible sacrifice," but which to me is neither sacrifice nor incomprehensible.

I have discovered a fundamental feeling in my heart which completely governs my spirit and my life. That feeling is my *indignation when confronted with injustice*.

Ever since I can remember, all injustice has hurt my soul as though something were stabbing it. Memories of injustices against which I rebelled at every age still rankle.

I remember very well how sad I was for many days when I first realized that there were poor and rich in the world; and the strange thing is that the fact of the existence of the poor did not hurt me so much as the knowledge that, at the same time, the rich existed.

THE CAUSE OF THE "INCOMPREHENSIBLE SACRIFICE"

The subject of the rich and the poor has been, ever since, the subject of my musings. I think I never mentioned it to other people, not even to my mother, but I thought about it often.

I still needed, however, to take a step forward along the path of my discoveries.

I knew that there were poor and that there were rich; and I knew that the poor were more numerous than the rich, and were to be found everywhere.

I had yet to learn the third dimension of injustice.

Until I was eleven years old I believed that there were poor just as there was grass, and that there were rich just as there were trees.

One day I heard for the first time, from the lips of a workingman, that there were poor because the rich were too rich; and that revelation made a strong impression on me.

I connected that opinion with all the things I had thought of on the subject . . . and, almost instantaneously, I realized that the man was right. Even more than through the power of reason, I felt that it was true.

Furthermore, although so young, I had already come to believe more in what the poor said than in the words of the rich, because the former seemed to me more sincere, franker, and also better. With this step I had come to know the third dimension of social injustice.

This third step in the discovery of life and its social problems is, indubitably, taken by many people. The majority of men and women know that there are poor because there are rich, but they learn it unconsciously, and perhaps because of that it seems natural and logical to them.

I admit I learned it almost at one blow, and that I learned it through suffering; and I declare that it never seemed to me either logical or natural.

I felt, even then, in my innermost heart, something which I now recognize as a feeling of indignation. I did not understand why if there were poor people there must also be rich ones, nor why the latter's eagerness for riches must be the cause of the poverty of so many people.

Never since then have I been able to think of this injustice without indignation, and thinking about it always produced a stifling feeling, as though, being unable to remedy the evil that I witnessed, I had not sufficient air to breathe.

I think now that many people become accustomed to social injustice in the first years of their lives. Even the poor think the misery they endure is natural and logical. They learn to tolerate what they see or suffer, just as it is possible to acquire a tolerance for a powerful poison.

I cannot accustom myself to poison, and never, since I was eleven years old, have I been able to accustom myself to social injustice.

This is, perhaps, the only inexplicable thing of my life; certainly it is the only thing which manifested itself in me without any apparent cause.

I think that, just as some persons have a special tendency to feel beauty differently and more intensely than do people in general, and therefore become poets or painters or musicians, I have a special inherent tendency to feel injustice with unusual and painful intensity.

Can a painter say why he sees and feels color? Can a poet explain why he is a poet?

Perhaps that is why I can never say *why* I feel pained by injustice, and why I have never been able to accept it as a natural thing, as the majority of men accept it.

Still, even if I cannot understand it myself, it is certain that my feeling of indignation at social injustice is the force which has led me by the hand, since my earliest recollections, to this day . . . and that it is the final cause explaining how a woman who in some people's eyes sometimes seems "superficial, common and indifferent," can decide to live a life of "incomprehensible sacrifice."

WOMEN AND MY MISSION

My work in the woman's movement began and grew, just like my work of social service and my trade-union activities, little by little, and more by force of circumstances than through any decisions of mine.

This may not be what many imagine to be the case, but it is the truth.

It would be more romantic or more poetic or more literary, and more like fiction, if I said, for example, that all I do now I had felt intuitively . . . as a vocation or a special decree of fate.

But such is not the case.

All I brought by way of preparation to the scene of these struggles were those same *feelings* which had made me think of the problem of the rich and the poor.

But nothing more.

I never imagined it would fall to my lot someday to lead a woman's movement in my country, and still less a political movement.

Circumstances showed the way.

Ah! But I did not remain in my comfortable position of Eva Perón. The path which opened up before my eyes was the path I took if by it I could help Perón's cause a little—the cause of the people.

I imagine many other women have seen the paths I pursue long before I did.

The only difference between them and me is that they stayed behind and I started. Actually, I should confess that if I girded myself for a struggle it was not for myself but for him . . . for Perón!

He encouraged me to rise.

He took me out of "the flock of sparrows."

He taught me my first steps in all my undertakings.

Afterward I never lacked the powerful and extraordinary stimulus of his love.

I realize, above all, that I began my work in a woman's movement because Perón's cause demanded it.

It all began little by little.

Before I realized it I was already heading a woman's political movement . . . and, with it, had to accept the spiritual leadership of the women of my country.

This caused me to meditate on woman's problems. And, more than that, to feel them, and to feel them in the light of the doctrine with which Perón was beginning to build a New Argentina.

I remember with what extraordinary fondness, as friend and master, General Perón explained to me innumerable women's problems in my country and in the world.

In these conversations I again became aware of the kindliness of his nature.

Millions of men have faced, as he has faced, the ever more acute problem of woman's role in humanity in this afflicted century; but I think very few of them have stopped, like Perón, to penetrate it to its depths.

In this, as in everything, he showed me the way.

The world's feminists will say that to start a woman's movement in this way is hardly feministic . . . to start by recognizing to a certain extent the superiority of a man!

However, I am not interested in criticisms.

Also, recognizing Perón's superiority is a different matter.

Besides . . . it is my intention to write the truth.

FROM THE SUBLIME TO THE RIDICULOUS

I confess I was a little afraid the day I found myself facing the possibility of starting on the "feminist" path.

What could I, a humble woman of the people, do where other women, more prepared than I, had categorically failed?

Be ridiculous? Join the nucleus of women with a grudge against woman and against man, as has happened to innumerable feminist leaders?

I was not an old maid, nor even ugly enough for such a post . . . which, from the time of the English suffragettes down to today, generally belongs, almost exclusively, to women of this type . . . women whose first impulse undoubtedly had been to be like men.

And that is how they guided the movements they led!

They seemed to be dominated by indignation at not having been born men, more than by the pride of being women.

They thought, too, that it was a misfortune to be a woman. They were resentful of women who did not want to stop being women. They were resentful of men because they would not let them be like them; the "feminists," the immense majority of feminists in the world, as far as I could see, continued to be a strange species of woman . . . which never seemed to me to be entirely womanly!

And I did not feel very much inclined to be like them.

One day the General gave me the explanation I needed.

"Don't you see that they have missed the way? They want to be men. It is as though to save the workers I had tried to make oligarchs of them. I would have remained without workers. And I do not think I should have managed to improve the oligarchy at all. Don't you see that this class of 'feminists' detests womanhood? Some of them do not even use makeup . . . because that, according to them, is womanly. Don't you see they want to be men? And if what the world requires is a woman's political and social movement . . . how little will the world gain if the women want to save it by imitating men! We have done too many strange things and made such a mess of everything that I do not know if the world can be arranged anew. Perhaps woman can save us, on condition that she does not imitate us."

I well remember that lesson of the General's.

His ideas never seemed to me so clear and bright.

That is how I felt.

I felt that the woman's movement in my country and all over the world had to fulfill a sublime mission . . . and everything I knew about feminism seemed to me ridiculous. For, not led by women but by those who aspired to be men, it ceased to be womanly and was nothing! Feminism had taken the step from the sublime to the ridiculous.

And that is the step I always try to avoid taking!

I WOULD LIKE TO SHOW THEM A WAY

The first thing I had to do in my country's woman's movement was to solve the old problem of woman's political rights.

For a century—the dark and painful century of selfish oligarchy and those who sold their country—politicians of every party had often promised woman the vote. Promises which were never made good, like all those they made to the people.

Perhaps that was lucky.

If women had begun to vote in the days of the oligarchy, the disillusion would have been too great . . . as great as the deceit of those elections in which all misconduct, all fraud and all lies were normal!

It was better for us to have no rights then. Now we have an advantage over men. We have not been mocked! We have not joined any strange political confabulation! The struggle for ambition has not touched us. And, above all, we are born to civic life under Perón's banner, whose elections are a model of integrity and honesty, as is admitted by even his most venomous adversaries, who surrender to the truth only when it is impossible to invent one more lie.

Today the Argentine woman may vote. I am not going to repeat the expression used by a politician who, on offering his fellow citizens an electoral law, stated too solemnly:

"Let the people know how to vote!"

No. I think the people always knew *how* to vote. The trouble is that it was not always possible for them to vote. The same things happens with woman.

And she will know how to vote. Although it is not fundamental in the feminist movement, the vote is its most powerful instrument, and with it we women of all the world have to win all our rights . . . or, rather, the great right of being simply *women,* and thus being able to fulfill, totally and absolutely, the mission that, as women, we have to perform for humanity.

What I think we cannot ever forget is a thing Perón always repeats to the men: that the vote, that is to say, "politics," is not an end but a means.

I think that men, in their great majority, above all in the old political parties, never understood this properly. That is why they always failed. Our destiny as women depends on our not falling into the same error.

But I do not want to linger longer on this matter of woman's political rights.

I am more interested at present in woman herself.

I would like to show her a way.

HOME OR THE FACTORY?

Every day thousands of women forsake the feminine camp and begin to live like men.

They work like them. They prefer, like them, the street to the home. They are not resigned to being either mothers or wives.

They substitute for men everywhere.

Is this "feminism"? I think, rather, that it must be the "masculinization" of our sex.

And I wonder if all this change has solved our problem.

But no. All the old ills continue rampant, and new ones, too, appear. The number of young women who look down upon the occupation of homemaking increases every day.

And yet that is what we were born for.

We feel that we are born for the home, and the home is too great a burden for our shoulders.

Then we give up the home . . . go out to find a solution . . . feel that the answer lies in obtaining economic independence and working somewhere. But that work makes us equal to men and—no! We are not like them! They can live alone; we cannot. We feel the need of company, of complete company. We feel the need of giving more than receiving. Can't we work for anything else than earning wages like men?

And, on the other hand, if we give up the work which makes us independent so as to form a home . . . we burn our boats once and for all.

No profession in the world has less chance of a comeback than our profession as women.

Even if we are chosen by a good man, our home will not always be what we dreamed of when we were single.

The entire nation ends at the door of our home, and other laws and other rights begin . . . the law and the rights of man—who very often is only a master, and also, at times, a dictator.

And nobody can interfere there.

The mother of a family is left out of all security measures. She is the only worker in the world without a salary, or a guarantee, or limited working hours, or free Sundays, or holidays, or any rest, or indemnity for dismissal, or strikes of any kind. All that, we learned as girls, belongs to the sphere of love . . . but the trouble is that after marriage, love often flies out of the window, and then everything becomes "forced labor" . . . obligations without any rights! Free service in exchange for pain and sacrifice!

I do not say it is always like this. I should have no right to say anything, since *my* home is happy . . . if I did not see the suffering every day of so many women who live like that . . . with no outlook, with no rights, with no hope.

That is why every day there are fewer women to make homes.

Real homes, united and happy! And the world really needs more homes every day, and for them more women willing properly to fulfill their destiny and their mission. That is why the first objective of a feminine movement which wishes to improve things for women—which does not aim at changing them into men—should be the home.

We were born to make homes. Not for the street. Common sense shows us the answer. We must have in the home that which we go out to seek: our small economic independence—which would save us from becoming women with no outlook, with no rights and with no hope!

AN IDEA

For in reality the same thing must happen with women as with men, families and nations: as long as they are not economically independent, no one concedes them any rights.

I imagine many persons will see too material an outlook in this very personal opinion, very much my own.

And this is not so. I believe in spiritual values. Also, this is what Perón's justicialist doctrine teaches us. That is just why—because I believe in the spirit—I consider it urgent to reconcile in woman her need to be a wife and mother with the other needs which as a worthy human being she also carries in her innermost heart.

And the first thing in solving the problem, I think, would be the small economic independence of which I have spoken.

If we do not find an answer to our dilemma, an inconceivable thing will soon happen in the world. Only the less capable women will be willing to form a real home (not half a home, or half a marriage) . . . those who cannot find any other "economic" way to sustain their minimum rights except by marriage and the home.

The status of mother of a family will come down to a ridiculous level. It will be said—and it is already being said—that only fools burn their boats by getting married, building a home, burdening themselves with children.

And can that not happen in the world?

It is the moral values which have been shattered by this disastrous state of affairs; and it will not be the men who will restore them to their old prestige, nor will it be the masculine women either. No. Will it, perhaps, be the mothers?

I do not know how to prove this, but I feel it is the absolute truth.

But how can one reconcile all these things?

To me it seems very simple, and I do not know if it not too simple and, perhaps, impracticable; although I have often noticed how things we consider too simple are often the key to success, the secret of victory.

I think one should commence by fixing a small monthly allowance for every woman who gets married, from the day of her marriage.

A salary paid to the mothers by all the nation and which comes out of all the earnings of all the workers in the country, including the women.

Nobody will say that it is not just for us to pay for the work which, even if it is not seen, demands the efforts of millions and millions of women whose time, whose lives, are spent on this monotonous but heavy task of cleaning the house, looking after clothes, laying the table, bringing up children, etc.

That allowance could be, for a start, half the average national salary, and thus the woman, housekeeper, mistress of the home, would have an income of her own apart from what the man wishes to give her.

Later increases for each child could be added to this basic salary, an increase in case of widowhood, lost if she joins the ranks of the workers—in a word, in all the ways likely to be of most help so that the original purpose shall not be lost sight of.

I only suggest the idea. If it is suitable, it would have to be given shape and converted into actual fact.

I know that for us, the women of my country, the problem is not serious or urgent.

That is why I do not yet wish to carry this idea into the field of action. It would be better for everyone to think it over. When the time comes, the idea should be ripe.

I offer this solution so that the woman who starts a home shall not feel herself below the woman who earns her living in a factory or in an office.

But it does not solve entirely the old problem. A better use of progress and of the technique of running a home must be added.

And to attain this, it is necessary to raise woman's general level of culture. Economic independence and technical progress should be used in behalf of her rights and of her freedom, without losing sight of her marvelous status as a woman: the one thing which cannot and should not be lost sight of unless one does not want to lose everything.

All this reminds me a little of Perón's basic program in his struggle for the freedom of the workers.

He used to say it was necessary to raise the level of social culture, dignify work and humanize capital.

I, imitating him always, suggest that to save woman, and at the same time the home, it is necessary also to raise the level of woman's culture, dignify her work and humanize her economy by giving her a certain minimum material independence.

Only thus can woman prepare herself to be a wife and mother, just as she prepares herself to be a shorthand-typist.

In this way many women would be saved from the delinquency and prostitution which are the fruits of their economic slavery.

In this way the prestige of the home would be saved and kept really sacred as the foundation stone of humanity.

I know my solution is more a remedy than a solution. I know it is only a beginning, a gesture. I think a great deal more will still have to be done.

Because it is not a matter of trying to return to the home a prestige it is losing, but of giving it an entirely new one.

I have had to create many institutions where children were to be looked after, trying to substitute something for which there is no substitute: a mother and a home. But I dream of the day when institutions will no longer be necessary, when woman will be what she ought to be—queen and mistress of a worthy family, free from the pressures of economic needs.

To bring about that day, and that justicialism in all its aspects may be a reality everywhere, the woman's movement of every country and of the whole world must unite. A woman's movement organized in a world without social justice would be of no value to us.

It would be like a great workers' movement in a world without work. It would be no good whatever!

THE GREAT ABSENCE

I think the feminist movement organized as a vital force in each country and in all the world should and would do great good to all humanity.

I do not know where I once read that in this world of ours the great need is for love.

I would modify this a bit and say that rather does the world today suffer from a great absence: that of woman.

Everything, absolutely everything in this contemporary world, has been made according to man's measure.

We are absent from governments.

We are absent from parliaments.

From international organizations.

We are in neither the Vatican nor the Kremlin.

Nor in the high commands of the imperialists.

Nor in the commissions of atomic energy.

Nor in the great business combines.

Nor in Freemasonry, nor in other secret societies.

We are absent from all the great centers constituting a power in the world.

And yet we have always been present in the time of suffering, and in all humanity's bitter hours.

It would seem as though our calling were not substantially that of creating, but rather that of sacrifice.

Our symbol should be the Mother of Christ at the foot of the Cross.

And yet our highest mission is nothing but to create.

I cannot understand, then, why we are not in those places where an attempt is being made to create man's happiness.

Haven't we, by any chance, a common destiny with man? Shouldn't we perhaps share in creating the happiness of the family?

Perhaps man has failed in his attempts thus far to make mankind happy, precisely *because* he has not invited us to join his great social organizations.

To solve the serious problems of the world, man has created an almost unlimited series of doctrines.

He has created a doctrine for each century.

And after this has been tried and has failed, he has tried another, and so on.

He has been inspired by each doctrine as though it were a definite solution. The doctrine has been more important to him than man or humanity.

And the reason is this: man has no *personal* stake in humanity, as women have.

To man humanity is a social, economic and political problem.

To us humanity is a problem of creation . . . just as every woman and every man represents our suffering and our sacrifice.

Man accepts too easily the destruction of another man or of a woman, of an aged person or a child.

He does not know what it costs to create them!

We do!

That is why we, the women of all the earth, have, in addition to our creative calling, another and allied calling, that of instinctive preservation; in other words, the sublime calling of peace.

By this I do not mean to say that we should prefer "peace at any price."

No. We know there are more important motives than peace, but they are less important to us than they are to man.

We do not understand waging war for imperialism, and still less for economic superiority; we do not understand war as a means of conquest.

Although we do know that there are wars of justice, we think that, up to the present, men have fought very little for that justice.

When man gives us a place in his supreme decisions, the hour will have come to assert our opinion, less from the head perhaps than from the heart.

But is it not our hearts that have to suffer the consequences of the errors of the "brains" of men?

I do not despise man or his intelligence, but if in many parts of the world we have created happy homes together, why cannot we create a happy humanity together?

That ought to be our objective.

Nothing more than to win the right to create—together with man—something better than we now have.

LIKE ANY OTHER WOMAN

All I wanted to say is now said.

I am nothing more than a humble woman of a great people . . . like all the peoples of the earth!

A woman like whom there are thousands and thousands in the world. God chose me from among so many and put me in this position close to the Leader of a new world: Perón.

Why was I chosen and not another?

I do not know.

But what I did and what I do is what any woman would do, out of the immense number of women of this people of ours, or of any people in the world, who know how to fulfill their destiny as women, silently, in the fruitful solitude of the home.

I feel nothing more than the humble representative of all the women of the people.

I feel, like them, that I am the head of a home, much larger, it is true, than those they have made, but in the final count a home: the prosperous home of this country of mine which Perón is leading toward its very highest destinies.

Thanks to him, the "home," which at first was poor and dismantled, is now just, free and sovereign!

He did it all!

His wonderful hands converted each hope of our people into thousands of realities.

Now we live happily, with that happiness of a home, sprinkled with work and even a little bitterness . . . which form a little part of the fabric of happiness.

In this great home of the nation I am like a woman of any of the countless homes of my people.

Like her I am, after all, a woman.

I like the same things that she does: jewels and furs, dresses and shoes . . . but, like her, I prefer everyone in the home to be better off than I am. Like her, like all of her prototypes, I would like to be free to go out and enjoy myself . . . but I am tied, like her, to the duties of the home which no one else is obliged to do in my place.

Like all of them, I get up early thinking of my husband and of my children . . . and thinking of them I go about all day and a good deal of the night. . . . When I go to bed, tired, my dreams are lost in wonderful schemes, and I try to fall asleep before the spell is broken.

Like all of them, I awake startled by the slightest noise, because, like all of them, I am also frightened . . .

Like them I always like to appear smiling and attractive to my husband and my children, always serene and strong so as to inspire them with faith and hope . . . and, like them, I am also at times overcome by difficulties, and like them, I shut myself up and cry and cry!

Like all of them I prefer my smallest and weakest children . . . and love those who have least best . . .

Like all women of all the homes of my people, my joyful days are those when all the children, happy and affectionate, are gathered round the head of the house.

Like them, I know that the children of this great house which is the nation need me and my husband . . . and I try to see that they are not disappointed.

I like, as they do, preparing agreeable surprises and enjoying the surprise of my husband and my children afterward.

Like them, I hide my disappointments and troubles, and often appear bright and happy to my family, while hiding the grief which makes my heart bleed with a smile and with my words.

I hear, as they do, as do all the mothers in all the homes of my people, the advice of visitors and of friends: "But why do you take things so seriously?" "Don't worry so much!" "Enjoy yourself a bit more! Why do you want more than all the pretty things you have in your wardrobe?"

The thing is that, like them, I like looking nice more among my own than before strangers . . . and that is why I wear my best finery when I attend to the *descamisados.*

Very often I think, as they do, of going on holidays, of traveling, of knowing the world . . . but I am prevented by the thought: "If I go, who will do my work?" And I stay!

For I really feel myself the mother of my people!

And I honestly think that I am.

Do I not suffer with it? Do I not rejoice in its joys? Do not its sorrows hurt me? Do I not feel my blood rise when they are insulted or criticized?

My loves are their loves.

That is why I love Perón now in a different way from before: before I loved him for himself . . . now I also love him because my people love him!

For all these reasons, because I feel myself one of so many women of the people building up the happiness of their homes, and because I have reached that happiness, I desire it for all and every one of these women of my people.

I want them to be as happy in their homes as I am in this great home which is my country.

When destiny once more chooses a woman for this highest national home, I want any woman of my people to be able to fill, better than I do, this mission that I perform as best I can.

Until the last day of my life I want to fulfill the great task of opening new horizons and paths for my *descamisados,* for my workers, for my women.

I know that, like any woman of the people, I am stronger than I appear to be, and my health is better than the doctors think.

Like her, like all of them, I am ready to go on struggling so that there will always be happiness in my great home.

I do not aspire to any honor that is not that happiness!

That is my vocation and my destiny.

That is my mission.

Like any woman of my people, I want to perform it well and to the end.

Perhaps someday when I am gone for good, someone will say of me what so many children of the people are wont to say when their mothers have gone, also for good:

Only now do we realize that she loved us so much!

2. *The Woman with the Whip*

María Flores

The Woman with the Whip was the first hostile account of Evita to be published in Argentina. In it Mary Main, writing as María Flores, argued that poverty and illegitimacy taught Evita to hate the world and to hate men, and that everything she achieved was the result of a single-minded quest for revenge. Main also suggested that Evita tolerated Perón because he was soft enough to pander to her drive for power, but that she had not loved him because she was strong and he was weak. This interpretation was picked up subsequently by other writers who disliked Evita; it formed the basis for the title character in the 1978 musical, *EVITA.* In the section reprinted here. Main discusses Evita's contribution to *Peronismo* and her transformation from being the "wife of the president" to "servant of the people."

From *The Woman with the Whip* by María Flores (Garden City, N.Y.: Doubleday, 1952), 238–247. Reprinted by permission.

Eva's only religion was *Peronismo* and its only tenet was faith in Perón. Whatever her personal feeling for him may once have been, it became lost in this extension of her fantasy; whatever her manner towards him in private, and she used her tongue just as roughly on him as on anyone, in public she never faltered in proclaiming her faith. There is no doubt that she saw him and herself canonized after death; but there was evidence in her speech and writing of more. She was building a myth around Perón—and in building it around Perón she was building it around herself—in which he was not only the wise and benign ruler but the semi-divine king.

"I sometimes think," she said, "that President Perón has ceased to be man like other men—that he is, rather, an ideal incarnate. For this our party may cherish him as our leader without fearing that he will disappear on that unhappy day when Perón in person is no longer here. Perón will always stand before the people as an ideal, a flag, a beacon, a very star to point the way through night to final victory."

"I cannot conceive of Heaven without General Perón," she said on more than one occasion; and, "But when we think that San Martín had his betrayers and Christ himself was denied, why should it not be so for Perón?"

"I see him [Perón] sometimes conceive an idea that to me seems too close to the clouds . . . and then I see how that same idea begins to take form . . . and little by little his marvelous hands begin to convert it into reality." The points of suspension are her own. She used the word "marvelous" repeatedly in reference to Perón; she wrote of the day she met him as her "marvelous day," of his "marvelous humility" in stooping to her, and of his "marvelous ways" and his "marvelous heart."

The humble role she allotted to herself in this theocracy seemed in such direct contradiction to reality that it has been dismissed by many as propaganda and totally insincere; those who surrounded her closely certainly made full use of its publicity value. But to Eva herself it was more. It was an essential part of the fantasy with which she deluded and tried to reassure herself, and did not, in fact, contradict her inordinate ambition which, always overstepping what might have been the satisfactions of reality, had reached the limit of human aggrandizement. The next step was divinity, and by elevating her husband and humbling herself she had by no means renounced her own claims. She had been raised in the Roman Catholic religion whose God and whose saints preached and practiced humility; humility was the hallmark of the divine. And it is significant that it was not before God and the Church that she prostrated herself, but before Perón and the people. She referred to herself with an almost psychopathic insistence as a bridge over which the people must pass to reach Perón—and this is reminiscent of the part the Virgin plays in the Catholic religion. She prostrated herself before

Perón—figuratively, of course—in an ecstasy. "I acknowledge," she wrote, "that I no longer exist in myself and that he [Perón] lives in my soul, lord of all my words and feelings, absolute master of my heart and life." She referred to herself as "a sort of slave" to Perón and as his shadow. "I know there is a great difference [between Perón and herself]. Where he gives a masterly lesson I barely stammer. When he can settle a problem in four words, it takes me sometimes a week. Where he decides I barely suggest. What he sees clearly I barely discern. He is the guide and I am only the shadow in his superior presence."

Her speeches and writings were repetitious to a tedious degree—or, perhaps, to a hypnotic one. She used the word "heart" so insistently—she was, in her speeches, forever opening up or giving away or leaving behind her heart—that Tristan, in the scathing cartoons he did for *Vanguardia,* made a pinchushiony little heart her motif; he has, of course, long since disappeared. But such persistent use of the words "heart," "abnegation" and "humility" cannot be dismissed altogether as the dramatics of demagogy or as the extravagance natural to the Spanish language, and there was a morbid note in her prostration that should yield study for the psychologists one day.

Perón himself has given no indication that his ambition exceeds his human nature nor, in spite of the freedom he allowed her and his remarkable loyalty to her person, that he thought of his wife as other than human; indeed there was sometimes a hint of patronage in his attitude towards her. He lent himself to her deification of himself since it suited his design admirably. In public he was the indulgent husband of a beautiful and talented wife; it was in private that he sometimes showed signs of being a little bit in awe of her. Eva was at times possessed of an incontrollable temper when "the lord of all her words and feelings" was as likely to come in for his share of abuse as anyone. When there was a witness to such scenes Perón shrugged his shoulders and explained apologetically, "My wife is so upset today." His attitude had the hallmarks of a henpecked husband. But along with this hint of timidity, and not at all discordant with it, was his obvious pride in her boldness and aggressiveness. When the Foundation was inaugurated he boasted, "Soon my wife will be handling more money than I do!" And when he once showed a favored guest her array of clothes and furs he said, with a smirk, "Not bad for a shirtless one, eh?" He has told how, when an elaborate buffet meal was prepared for Eva and a large party in the government house in Tucumán, she called in the little urchins from the plaza to stuff themselves, and he added with evident glee, "You can imagine the sensation that caused!"

But it is evident that he took her on his own evaluation and not on hers; she was a woman and not a saint to him, and *Peronismo* was no religion. At a dinner given in 1951 to British diplomats Eva broke out suddenly into one of her declamatory eulogies of *Peronismo* usually reserved for the mob in the Plaza de Mayo—that she should do this, almost mechanically as if a button had been pressed, it was said, on such an inappropriate occasion, shows the hold her "religion" had on her—and Perón shrugged his shoulders and grinned and made some apologetic remark about never being able to trust a woman at the dinner table, so that his guests laughed uneasily and Eva, disconcerted for once, was stopped short. It was Eva, not Perón, who had the fanaticism of a Hitler.

Only on very few occasions did Perón thwart Eva; he vetoed a grant of fourteen million dollars that both the Senate and the Chamber of Deputies had voted to the Foundation, and gave no public explanation of his veto; on occasion he censored her speeches before they appeared in print; it is said that he scolded her sometimes for interrupting some serious discussion. If he did not speak of her in public so gushingly as she spoke of him yet his tribute to her was always warm. "You see the extraordinary influence of the president of the Eva Perón Foundation—why is it? Because she dresses well and is pretty? No. She is loved and respected and honored by all the humble because she cannot eat or sleep or live for doing good."

Perón had not changed greatly during his first six-year term. He had grown somewhat fleshier and flabbier; he had, in some photographs, the rather dissipated look of an elderly and out-of-date actor, but possibly this was due to the suntan make-up he used to cover a scar or skin eruption on his cheek; in person he appeared larger, healthier and more genial than those by whom he is surrounded. In the past Eva had some hand in grooming him for public appearances; she insisted that he should have his teeth straightened while she was in Europe so that his smile became more expansive and dazzling than before; it was she who suggested that he should wear a white jacket to his uniform even in winter so that in the poorly printed photographs of the Argentine press his figure should be clearly distinguishable; later, as he withdrew a little and she came forward in the public eye, he gave up this device, and she seemed to have lost her concern in his appearance. He was as industrious, if not as energetic, as his wife and his working day started at 6 A.M.; but his has been the more phlegmatic nature, and until her final illness he showed little sign of strain, unless his chain-smoking were the result of fatigue.

By 1951 Eva's schedule had become so exacting that the time she could spend with her husband had been reduced to a minimum and must have been absorbed by the necessary discussion of their policy. They could have had no time at all for private life. She herself admitted that there were days when she scarcely saw him and sometimes she got home in the early hours when it was time for him to get up and leave for the office; and she added coyly that he scolded her on those occasions. They no longer spent rural weekends in the San Vicente house; at one time she had shocked the more matronly Argentine ladies by her casual appearance in slacks on such occasions. They were no longer to be seen driving along the waterfront on hot evenings as they had once done. They did not have time now for those little democratic acts they had performed together which had done much to popularize them in early days; when the census was taken in 1947 Perón and Eva appeared in half a dozen workmen's homes and, while Perón took down the statistics, Eva distributed gifts among the goggling womenfolk and children; they appeared less frequently at sports events, the more popular of which they had once made a point of attending together. Yet before the world they continued to present an astonishingly united front; there appeared to be no change in their relationship, certainly no weakening of it, and their most bitter enemies were hard put to discover any slip in their sentimental duologue.

But Eva had changed and the change was profound.

The magnificently flamboyant creature of the middle of the decade, the Doña María Eva Duarte de Perón, had become the brusque, businesslike Eva Perón, as beautiful as and more elegant than she had ever been, in her severe tailor-made costumes with her diamond orchid almost as large as a real one in her lapel, her pale hair strained back into a heavy knot on her nape, her thinness accentuating her high round cheekbones and her youthful and rather bulging forehead. She could still look like a little girl at times, but she had lost all the fullness, all the softness of her womanhood; she had the perfect gloss of enamel. She was darting, brilliant, brittle as a dragonfly. She excited amazement and admiration and envy, but she no longer excited desire. When she was not smiling, and in public she wore an almost ceaselessly radiant smile, her mouth was arrogant, even a little cynical; she met strangers with a cold, distrustful, estimating stare but, once assured of their friendliness, melted to a sudden warmth that seemed to be sincere and even in its insincerity had a touch of pathos in it. She was still capable of moments of refreshing candor and would admit quite freely that she was what she called a "repentant brunette." Her complexion was exceedingly pale; it has often been described as having a greenish tinge; it was that matte white complexion that even under a photographer's cruel lights will show no flaw. She appeared to be utterly sure of herself and poised, but her hands betrayed her emotion and her true character; they were not the soft, white hands of a cocotte or the slender, limp hands of the visionary and saint; they were strong, dramatic, vulgar hands and the gestures she made with them were the strong, graphic gestures a countrywoman would use to punctuate her gossiping; they had none of the self-conscious elegance of affected gesturing. She would cross her arms over her chest like a washerwoman, wag a forefinger to emphasize an argument, brush aside all other arguments with a sweep of both hands, catch suddenly at her throat or at her diamond orchid as if a secret fear had caught at her heart, or spread out her fingertips on the table or balustrade before her to show her impatience with the slowness of the proceedings. Her hands were forceful, vulgar, impatient and, it is said, they were always cold.

Only for very formal occasions did she dress herself in her full magnificence now, in those long wide skirts that she had begun to favor for gala affairs soon after her return from Paris and which made it necessary for her to stand a step or two ahead of the men with whom she was photographed—and she was almost always the only woman in the group. In this formal attire she often posed before a tapestry that hangs on the Residency wall and which made a somber and regal background to her pale beauty; she was more frequently photographed at her desk, at the microphone or with a group of union officers or government officials. There were very few informal pictures taken of her; there were very few informal moments in her life. For all the magnificence of her surroundings she was living a life of extreme austerity; she ate strictly according to her diet, drank sparingly, smoked not at all in public—Perón carried carmine-tipped cigarettes for her use in private. She had no purely social engagements, no pleasures beyond her work. She lived a dedicated life; but she was dedicated to a fantasy.

The voice with which she had harangued the mob was almost as harsh and ugly as the overstrained voices of the newsboys who used to cry the evening papers on the corners of Calle Corrientes; with almost every sentence her voice rose to the pitch of hysteria; she spoke rapidly, furiously, as if, it has been said, she were always defending something. Perhaps it was herself she felt called upon to defend, for throughout her book there is an angry, explanatory note. There was in her speeches and her writings an endless repetition of the same emotional phrases; she dealt in abstracts and used no facts or figures to substantiate her arguments. In arguing that the syndicalization of unions is necessary to the Peronista state she explained, "This is true, firstly because Perón says so, and secondly, because it is the truth." She used the same arguments that an ignorant mother uses to quiet the importunities of her child. She claimed proudly that she acted and spoke from the heart, which is to say that she acted and spoke under emotional compulsion. But emotional as her speeches continued to be, their violence had already begun to abate; she was less of a virago and more of the prophetess. She had begun to prepare for her final metamorphosis.

Eva had no intimate friends; she had enemies, disciples, lovers, protégés, but no friends. She had women who played the part of confidante in matters such as clothes and jewelry, but she treated them as ladies-in-waiting rather than as intimates and her confidence in them did not last. When she first came into power her confidential secretary was Isabel Ernst, Mercante's friend, who was always at her elbow to guide her in her official acts; but Eva drove the young woman so ruthlessly, often in the press of work not giving her time to eat, that Ernst became ill and had to retire. One of Eva's first and closest friends was the wife of Alberto Dodero, the shipping magnate, who, for a while, went everywhere with Eva. But Eva expected her companions to be at her beck and call at any moment of the day, she allowed them no life of their own, and Mrs. Dodero, who was an American and had been in show business herself, was not ready to surrender her independence; and they quarreled and parted. For a while Eva had the Señora Largomarsino de Guardo to dance attendance on her, but the two ladies fell out on the European trip and on her return Eva switched her patronage to Hector Campora's shy, pretty wife. Eva was too demanding to allow friendship to survive, and she could no more tolerate a woman's competition in what social life she led than she could tolerate the rivalry of any man in her political life.

Eva carried her family along with her into affluence; she had to do so to assure their loyalty but she did not allow any of them to rival her. Their photographs were seldom seen in the press and their names seldom appeared. Her brother Juancito was the only one she allowed a measure of publicity and for whom she seemed to have had some affection or respect; it is said that he was able to quiet her in her tantrums and that he used no gentle methods to accomplish this. Among many notorious reputations in Buenos Aires his has been conspicuous; there are endless stories of his dealings on the black market and of his brawls with women in public places. So sinister did his reputation become that, so the story goes, the father of one aspiring young actress, seeing that his daughter had caught Juancito's eye, whisked her out of the country overnight. Yet Juancito Duarte continued as close as ever to the Presidency. Eva's eldest sister Elisa became something of a political boss in Junín, but since Eva never returned to the scene of her bitter childhood Elisa's activities in no way trespassed on her own. Blanca was made Inspector of Schools, no very exalted post under the circumstances, and gossip has it that Eva set a watch on her sister to make sure that she left for work by 7 A.M. but that the less energetic Blanca slipped home again to bed.

Eva's mother, the redoubtable Doña Juana, lived modestly in the apartment in Calle Posadas where Eva used to live. A policeman guarded the door but there was no other sign of her residence. Sometimes she returned to Junín for a visit to old friends and while she was there she occupied a house that was no more spacious and very little more up-to-date than the one she occupied when Eva was a child. She liked the comforts and indulgences of a woman growing old and spent her money on massage, beauty treatments and at the roulette tables in Mar del Plata. It is said that she suffered from insomnia and that she used to beg her daughter to allow her enough money to settle her old bones abroad before the crash, but that Eva, infuriated by such croaking, refused. It seems that Doña Juana also consulted the occult sciences and it is probable that the old lady lived in mortal fear of retribution falling on the family.

By the beginning of 1951 Eva Perón had reached what was to be the zenith of her career, although at the time the potentialities of her influence seemed alarmingly unlimited. She was thirty-one and in those thirty-one years she had achieved a world-wide notoriety, she had been decorated by a dozen different nations, had had ships, schools, parks, subway stations, housing projects and a star named after her, she had the title of First Samaritan and was called the Lady of Hope and the Standard Bearer of the Workers—and now it seemed that she was to have the added authority of an official status in the government. But her ambition had outgrown the honors of this world and she was losing touch with reality. The one man with whom she had achieved a close and lasting relationship had become a symbol in her life of fantasy. All the honor and the glory enclosed an emptiness in which she lived alone.

3. *The Gift of Giving*

NICOLAS FRASER AND MARYSA NAVARRO

Nicolas Fraser is a British journalist. Marysa Navarro is a professor of history at Dartmouth College who has published numerous articles about Evita and Peronism. Their effort to delve beneath the myths in judging her as a human being is demonstrated in this section of their book. It describes Evita's work with the Eva Perón Foundation, and evaluates the overall contribution made by the Foundation to social welfare in Argentina.

People who wanted things from Evita came to see her; the procedure was almost as simple as that. In the beginning, they had come without warning

From *Eva Perón* by Nicholas Fraser and Marysa Navarro (New York: Norton, 1980), pp. 122–131, passim. Reprinted by permission.

and simply waited for her, but slowly, under the pressures imposed by thousands of supplicants, a crude system of sorting came into operation. People who wanted things were encouraged by means of radio, newspapers or through the local bureaucracy, first to write to her, saying what they needed. They would receive an invitation card from her giving the time and the place of the meeting. In principle, Evita's afternoons were set aside for 'direct help,' the name she gave to her ritual of seeing people who requested her assistance, but in practice these afternoons began earlier and ended later, until the rest of the day's business—the visits of dignitaries, union officials, foreigners—became part of this central and engulfing feature of her day. . . . The antechamber where the poor waited was heavy with the smells of poverty. The poor who came there had not been selected for the spectacular nature of their ailments or financial problems, they were simply part of the great number of Argentines who lived in tenements, shanty towns or remote villages, in the slums outside the city or in the provinces beyond the slums. Evita was conscious of the violence done to Argentine sensibilities by the presence of the poor in this government building, with its velvet drapes and wood panelling, and that is partly why they were encouraged to come here and to see her, instead of being dealt with by social workers. But she did not use them as stage props or allegorical figures in a didactic play. On the contrary, it is said by those who worked with her that she, who could be arrogant and rude with those who threatened her as rivals or intellectual superiors, was with these petitioners unfailingly gentle and courteous, attending to them not as a bureaucrat, but as an individual who had chosen such work because she enjoyed it. Her jewellery made her seem glamorous and almost ethereal, but when she spoke, smiled, asked questions or made jokes, she appeared to them not as the wife of the President, but as the Evita who declared herself a 'woman of the people,' unlike them in circumstances and power but ineffably still of them and with them.

> Her voice rises as she rebuts a complaint about a benefit concert [a correspondent of the *New York Times* reported]. She calls peremptorily for the head of the General Labour Confederation. She sends a publicist away glowing with the idea that he'd make a fine counsellor of the embassy in Washington. And she pats the Governor of Buenos Aires and guides him back to an impatient circle by the window, where small talk is running thin.
>
> She parries a question about her personal reaction to her work. 'All these people, you see?' she says. 'I am nothing—my work is everything.' She is off an another swing. When she returns there is a little more fencing and she extends a soft, warm hand, smiling superbly; 'Time is my greatest enemy,' she says.

Meanwhile the other room overflows with children. They squirm and giggle, scramble on the floor and wail. At about 6:15, a premature murmur goes around, *'Ya viene!'* (Here she comes!) Presently, the Señora steps in briskly. She sits beneath a huge oil painting of 'Amalia', a melancholy lady in a black mantilla . . . Other pictures in the red-damasked room are of the Peróns or Christ. Four secretaries surround the table. The synchronization is like that of an operating room. One shoves a pencil into her hand, another readies a pad of clothing tickets, a third holds up a phone . . .

The first supplicant is a shapeless woman with a toil-worn face. The First Lady turns her brown eyes to her; clusters of black crystals tinkle at the brim of her open-crown straw hat.

'I live in one room,' the woman says. 'I want a house to live in.'

'How many children do you have?'

'Eight.'

The *presidenta* murmurs to one of her secretaries. 'We can provide a wooden house,' she begins. The woman asks questions. Evita is dictating. 'Clothing for nine . . . a large bed, complete . . .' She turns for a brief aside to a visiting ambassador. Then she takes the slip from the secretary's pad and signs E.P. The woman shuffles out, with the slip.

The fifty-peso notes which Evita handed to those who saw her have been depicted as the purest form of wastage, a foolish hail of devalued pesos spattered over all comers, and while there is some truth in this, they were on occasions also a useful gift since often the supplicants needed money to get home. Sometimes the crisp pile beneath her blotter would be exhausted, and then she would turn to the ambassadors, ministers and civil servants around her and say, 'Señores, the people need your money. There's a tray. Please put some of what you have in your wallets. The government is giving you lots of money and you can afford to put some of it there. When this habit of hers became widely known, those who came to see her would make a point of emptying their wallets beforehand.

In many ways the Foundation completely changed Evita. her work acquired the importance and the sanctity of a 'mission' and this new Evita was as different from the star who had toured Europe as that star had been from the young radio actress from Junín. She now dressed not in frills but in black suits, all similarly cut like a uniform. Rather than piling her hair high, she wore it swept back, and the effect, though never unbecoming or undistinguished, was one of austerity and efficiency, and made her look far older than she was. She still wore her hats, but there were fewer of these, and less jewellery, only the odd spray of ruby orchids or a sapphire and diamond Peronist emblem. This was as much of a costume as the earlier dress, but it was now the costume of seriousness and dedication. A Peronist propaganda photograph widely reproduced and undoubtedly faked, depicts her smiling as usual and waving her hand from the back of her limousine, while a clock in the background stands at four a.m. But this was indeed the way her 'days' frequently ended; and often she made her limousine available to those who came to see her and had to wait until it had returned.

The more of this 'direct aid' she performed, the more she began, in her speeches and in conversations, to adopt a raucously outraged attitude towards the existence of poverty. She spoke of her rage against poverty as a wound affecting her, and her language was violent. 'Sometimes I have wished my insults were slaps or lashes,' she said in her memoirs; 'I've wanted to hit people in the face and make them see, if only for a day, what I see each day I help people.' Both the ferocity and the lack of regard for herself which she showed in the last years of her life came from her days and nights with the poor. She became passionate, a real fanatic, an obsessive.

Those who worked with her were expected to behave as she did, to be continually available and to be beyond suspicion of corruption. Evita might treat the poor as equals, using such terms of endearment as *abuelito* ('Grandpa'), but she required a deference, even a reverence, from those around her, which sometimes had its comic side. Arturo Jauretche found amid 'the cries of babies, the bureaucrats watching those who were waiting and the aureole of sanctity that emanated from Evita' an aging neighbourhood tough who had once worked for the Radicals and was now carrying a large pile of rubber teats. When Jauretche smiled, 'he replied with his seasoned, bar-room voice; "so what am I supposed to do, doctor, if this woman is a saint?"' But there were many who would treat the question of Evita's sanctity not with irony or as a half-truth, but as a possibility to be seriously considered. For Father Hernán Benítez, who frequently attended these sessions, it was not the transfer of objects, whether blankets, sewing machines, cooking pots or slips of denominated paper, that constituted the real importance of Evita's work, but the gestures that went with these gifts. 'I saw her kiss the leprous,' he said, 'I saw her kiss those who were suffering from tuberculosis or cancer. I saw her distribute love, a love that rescues charity, removing that burden of injury to the poor which the exercise of charity implies. I saw her embrace people who were in rags and cover herself with lice.' Father Benítez was unable to consider Evita to be potentially a saint since she had never renounced the riches or honours of the world, but he did feel she had attained a state of quasi-sanctity because she had been 'faithful to her people. Faithful because she loved the poor and condemned the rich. Not because they were rich (for she was too), but because they had remained enemies of the poor (which she was not).'

In 1950, José María Castiñeira de Dios, a young Catholic poet, had watched Evita at her work:

> There were human beings in that room with dirty clothes and they smelt very bad. Evita would place her fingers into their suppurating wounds for she was able to see the pain of all these people and feel it herself. She could touch the most terrible things with a Christian attitude that amazed me, kissing and letting herself be kissed. There was a girl whose lip was half eaten away with syphilis and when I saw that Evita was about to kiss her and tried to stop her, she said to me, 'Do you know what it will mean when I kiss her?'

People around Evita were usually upset by such gestures, but she hated to be interrupted. When her maid was worried after she had kissed a man suffering from syphilis and tried to dab her face with alcohol, Evita took the bottle from her and smashed it against the wall. Perón and Evita were once walking off the gangplank of a yacht when a man came up to Perón and kissed him and Perón told him not to be a pig ('the cry,' he says, 'came from my heart because being kissed by a man, I don't know . . . it disgusts me). But Evita went to him, apologized on Perón's behalf and kissed the man to make him feel better. 'She even allowed herself to be kissed by lepers,' Perón observed, seemingly bemused. . . .

Argentina, though secular in many respects, was essentially a Catholic country, and when Evita touched the leprous or the syphilitic she ceased to be the President's wife and acquired some of the characteristics of saints as depicted in Catholicism. Whether she actually saw herself this way or not, it was effective, a transformation of an essentially secular role by the surrounding religious emotion. This beautiful woman loved the poor and gave up her life to them. She would see them, she would kiss them, and all the cameras and lights did not alter the simplicity of this religious tableau. Questions of why she did this, to whom the goods really belonged, and in whose name they were really being distributed were waived in the intensity of this ritual, performed five days a week for some years. Many of those who experienced these days were not as restrained as Benítez or Castiñeira de Dios; they were sure that Evita was a saint. . . .

In Argentina, as elsewhere, there had been a great difference between the quality of medical care in private hospitals and that in public hospitals; one standard for those who were able to pay and another, greatly inferior, for those who could not. Evita decided to improve vastly the standards of free care and made her hospitals competitive with the best international standards of medical care. She built twelve hospitals, the two main ones, named after Perón and herself, in Buenos Aires. It is probably that for the money that was spent she could have produced more institutions more cheaply, but she chose instead to make a showcase of public care, as a propaganda statement, and also prescriptively: in the sense that the poor should have the same as rich people. The hospitals had marble foyers and staircases, large windows, rooms where patients could watch movies, wards which contained only three beds. The surgical equipment, imported from the United States, was the best available at the time, and the staff was highly paid, so that the best doctors in the country worked there. The 'Policlínico Presidente Perón' serviced the poor neighbourhood in which it was located, but it also became a medical centre and teaching hospital training Evita's nurses and caring for people from remote parts of the country who would be flown in on aircraft provided by the Foundation. All medical supplies were provided free of charge by the Foundation, including drugs for out-patients. In 1951, the 'Presidente Perón' was able to equip a hospital train and send it throughout the country to provide free X-rays, free inoculations and free drugs. In the early 1950s, the Foundation sent the hospital's staff to give medical care after earthquakes in Peru, Colombia, Ecuador, and as far away as Turkey.

Under the auspices of the Foundation, Evita built 1,000 schools in the poorest areas of the country and handed these over to the State to operate. She had created the Peronist Decalogue of Old People's Rights in August 1948, she had sponsored univefsal pension schemes before the State assumed this responsibility, and now the Foundation built and operated four nursing homes, one of them with its own workshop and stable, more a village than a home. In five months and twenty days of 1949, working in twenty-four-hour shifts, the Foundation turned a four block site of Belgrano, a northern suburb of Buenos Aires, in the 'Amanda Allen Children's City,' named after a nineteenth-century Argentine pioneer of health care. It was indeed a city, with streets built to scale, a church, a functioning petrol station, a bank that issued scrip, pharmacies, supermarkets and a town hall that displayed a number of portraits of Perón and Evita in addition to the paraphernalia of government. A slogan of the 'New Argentina' was that children were 'the only privileged ones', and while the regime never imposed this vision on the entire country, it did become a reality with the Children's City. To the dormitories capable of holding four hundred and fifty children came children from the poorest, most problem-stricken families with whom the Foundation workers came into contact. There they were clothed, taught to look after themselves and educated. By the time they left the home they were supposed to be capable of attending public schools without falling behind. The children's toys and clothes were ordered from the best shops in Buenos Aires; there were even dance and music teachers on the staff. Often Evita would arrive without warning in the middle of the night and walk through the dormitories to see if everything was as it was supposed to be.

In addition to the Children's City, the Foundation subsidized a city for university students nearby with a complete replica of the Casa Rosada, including, of course, the photographs of Perón and Evita and the propagandist statements about the 'New Argentina'. In Buenos Aires there were three transit homes where single women with children might find temporary refuge, while the Foundation looked on their behalf for permanent housing and work, and, in Avenida Mayo, a huge building was made into a home for girls who had come to the city looking for work. The latter contained two restaurants, and shops where the girls could buy things at subsidized prices. 'The salon,' an English visitor noted, 'might well have been a reception room in the Casa Rosada. It was lit by eight or nine chandeliers of crystal peardrops; thrown across the grand piano in Edwardian style was a most exquisitely embroidered mantilla, a museum piece, given to Evita in Spain; the Louis XV chairs were covered with the palest silk brocade on which there was not the slightest mark; on the mantelpiece and on tables stood Dresden figurines and in the corner huge Sèvres urns. At each end of the salon were oil paintings, large as the wall would allow, one of Eva and one of Perón.'

Evita's social works have been persistently criticized for being wasteful, ill-conceived and unrelated to people's needs. The conservative military government that succeeded Perón concluded that the institutions of the Foundation were 'disproportinate to the aims, culture and customs of those who were going to use them' and, though in a quite unspecified way, 'liable to encourage customs bringing about moral and family deviations.' However, although the Foundation adopted 'luxury' as a matter of policy, it did function better than many more rational and more frugal institutions. For the first time, there was no inequality in Argentine health care.

Allegations of waste are difficult to substantiate if a high proportion of whatever the money is spent on is actually delivered. Evita's hosptials were expensive, but they worked and they lasted; so would most of her other works had they been permitted to. Many of the objectives of the Foundation (obsessive tidiness in the homes and hospitals, an addiction to decoration) reflected her great concern with appearances, but many of the things that she made available—pots and pans, beds, houses, sewing machines, footballs— had meaning and usefulness because Evita was aware exactly what difference it made to the life of a poor family to have these things. The work of the Foundation was deeply practical and personal, far more so than it might have been had it been bureaucratically exercised.

As propaganda, of course, the Foundation was extraordinarily successful. Nobody who came into contact with any of Evita's works was allowed to forget how grateful they should be for what they received. Perón's sayings were on each wall of each hospital or home and Evita's initials were painted on every iron bedstead, embroidered on each tablecloth or football shirt and stamped on each vial of vaccine used by the Foundation. The Foundation had begun as a response to poverty, but it was now a blueprint of Evita's version of the 'New Argentina,' a benign but authoritarian system in which the entire Argentine people were the children and Perón and Evita the smiling parents.

4. *Eva in Decline*

RICHARD BOURNE

Eva was at the height of her power in 1951 when the decision of the generals not to let her run for vice-president, as well as the rapid decline of her health due to cancer, brought about her premature death in August 1952 at age 33. British journalist Richard Bourne outlines the developments that led to her fall and discusses the fate of Peronism without her.

EVA IN DECLINE AND PERONISM WITHOUT HER

Ever since Eva had been just Perón's mistress she had been an object of annoyance among some of the officers. The growth of her own power as wife of the President, her demagogy about the oligarchy, and the arrival of the CGT as a privileged group which might challenge the armed forces all combined to intensify hostility in the latter. This feeling had been shown, for instance, in her 1947 trip to Europe when the navy had refused to take her in a vessel of the fleet and she had been forced to fly out by Aerolíneas Argentinas, allegedly at her own expense. But it came to a head in 1951 in the peculiar sequence of events by which Eva was asked to accept nomination as vice-President and then refused. In July the parallel esteem in which the two Peróns were held had been shown when Congress had approved the conversion of two Federal territories, La Pampa and the Chaco, into provinces with the names of Eva Perón and Presidente Perón respectively. On 22

From *Political Leaders of Latin America* by Richard Bourne (Middlesex, England: Penguin 1969) pp. 258–262. Reprinted by permission.

August an open council of justicialism, called by the CGT with at least a quarter of a million workers present after a spate of Perón posters had appeared on Argentine streets, asked the two of them to accept nomination as President and vice-President respectively. It seems likely that if Eva had not actually suggested the idea she had done nothing to discourage it. She was not present at the assembly but was called to appear before it. In what at first appeared to be a rhetorical exchange with the audience she initially asked for four days in which to consider the offer, then until the following day, then a couple of hours, before she accepted nomination. But a large number of officers on whom Perón depended in the armed forces were totally opposed to making Eva vice-President, and hence, in the event of the President's death, their own Commander-in-Chief. Not only was there a class and policy bias against her, but the possibility of being commanded by a woman challenged all their conservatism. On 31 August Eva, who may also have been thinking of her own ill health, announced on the radio that she would renounce the nomination. It was an effective performance. 'I do not renounce my work, I'm only refusing the honours,' she said. 'All I ask is that history records that there was at the side of General Perón a woman who brought to him the hopes and necessities of the people and that this woman was called Evita.' At once the CGT suggested that the 31st be celebrated every year as the 'Day of the Renunciation'. On 28 September the army irritation with the Peróns found vent in an attempted uprising, led by General Benjamín Menéndez. Although she was already sick Eva that night made a dramatic popular appeal for loyalty.

Rumours that Eva was suffering from cancer spread round Buenos Aires, but the régime was extremely secretive about her illness. Undoubtedly the disease was responsible for the increasingly erratic nature of her working life in her last couple of years. In November 1951 Eva went into the Policlínica Presidente Perón in Avellaneda for a four-hour operation in which the American cancer specialist, George Pack, took part. Pack's role, which was partially paid for in the form of pedigree bulls, was hidden from Eva. She voted in hospital for the Presidential elections of 11 November. Although she was allowed out in early December, the operation had failed in its object. The last months of her life must have been painful, though public deification reached new heights. On 17 October Eva, who had had the saintly title 'Capitana' attached to her, had been the beneficiary of a mass meeting at which Perón had said she was 'not only the standard bearer of our movement, but one of the greatest women of humanity'. She was given the Peronist medal, and 18 October was named Saint Evita Day. In December La Razón de mi Vida, the statement of faith edited on her behalf, became an instant best-seller. Early in 1952 Congress in extraordinary session gave her the unprecedented title of

Spiritual Chief of the Nation. Her last public speech was on 1 May. On 4 June, when Perón assumed the Presidency for the second time, she courageously stood in the open coach between the Congress and the Casa Rosada. But she collapsed in the Casa Rosada during the swearing-in ceremony. In July national life was overshadowed by the final stages of her illness. Prayers were said for her in the churches and people came to Buenos Aires from distant provinces to accompany her last struggle. On 26 July, with Perón, the Duartes and Padre Benítez, her confessor, at her side, she entered a coma and died.

Official mourning was taken to unusual lengths. Her body was embalmed and lay in state on the first floor of the Ministry of Labour and Welfare. Vast crowds queued up to pay their last respects, and sandwiches were distributed by the Foundation. The coffin was taken to Congress and the CGT. Perón occupied symbolically the deceased's office at the Ministry for several days, memorials were planned, a record of her voice was released, the CGT organized a torchlight procession with Perón on 26 August, and 17 October was consecrated as her day.

The Peronist régime survived Eva's death by three years. Her disappearance removed a lot of its glamour, genuine or manufactured, and the ageing Perón, with his youthful mistresses, offered uninspired leadership. After the alleged suicide of Juan Duarte in 1953 the Duartes lost any influence. The closing stages of Perón's rule were marked by changes of policy on foreign private investment and Church matters which offended both nationalist and Roman Catholic opinion. During the period of a wage freeze, from 1952 to 1954, the régime passed Law 14222, specifically designed to attract foreign capital. In late 1954 Perón became involved in a battle with the Church which, though it was a logical extension of Peronist social policy, had the effect of destroying the tacit Roman Catholic support the régime had always enjoyed, and it developed political overtones. The quarrel arose when Congress passed a law giving illegitimate children full rights. This was followed in December 1954 by decrees abolishing religious education in schools and legalizing prostitution, and a bill legalizing divorce.

In the New Year most Christian festivals lost their status as public holidays, and in May Congress passed a bill to disestablish the Church. Purges and public insults to church leaders led to the deportation of the Auxiliary Bishop of Buenos Aires in June 1955 and to Perón's excommunication. After a failed *coup* in that month, to which Perón skilfully reacted, rioting continued in Buenos Aires and the CGT offered to distribute arms to the workers. After four days of confusion a military rising in September, which began in the staunchly Catholic city of Córdoba, forced Perón into exile. Had Eva lived it is possible that his policy would have stayed more nationalist, more pro-labour, and the offensive against the Church would have been reduced. In the course of this revolution her body, which was supposed by some to have had miraculous powers, was removed from its resting place in the CGT and disappeared mysteriously. Different rumours suggested that it had been thrown into the river Plate or buried secretly outside Buenos Aires. But the only effect of that attempt to bury the legend of Evita was to add an extra twist of romance.

5. Women: The Forgotten Half of Argentine History

NANCY CARO HOLLANDER

Professor Nancy Caro Hollander received her graduate training in Latin American history at the University of California, Los Angeles. During 1971–1972 she served as Chairwoman of the Women's Studies Program at San Diego State College and now is teaching Latin American history at California State College, Domínguez Hills.

The present selection is a part of the paper she delivered at the 1971 annual meeting of the American Historical Association.

The level of civilization of a people can be judged by the social position of its women. DOMINGO FAUSTINO SARMIENTO

Although one would never know it by perusing the majority of books on Argentine history, women make up approximately one-half of that nation's population. Yet the history of Argentine women parallels the history of women in most countries to the extent that it is largely unwritten. This essay is an attempt to redress this injustice and to demonstrate the contributions of the masses of Argentine women to their country's economic and political life.

Nancy Caro Hollander, "Women: The Forgotten Half of Argentine History", in, *Female and Male in Latin America: Essays* edited by Ann Pescatello. (Pittsburgh: Pittsburgh University Press. 1973). Reprinted by permission.

. . . Within this context it evaluates the political mobilization of women within the Peronist movement of 1945–55. In order to appreciate why women became one of the major pillars of support for Peronism, it is necessary to examine the historical experience of women as the most exploited group within the Argentine working class.

Contrary to the generally accepted notion that Argentine women have never been in the mainstream of public employment, since the development of an urban, industrial base in the late nineteenth century women filled the factories and sweatshops as a source of super-exploitable labor. . . .

Employers hired women to work in hazardous, unhealthy conditions and at low wages, paying them on the average half of what male workers earned for the same job. This fact made women workers very appealing to employers, and by 1887, according to the census of Buenos Aires, 39% of the paid work force of that city was composed of women.

In 1904, Dr. Juan Bialet Masse, an investigator for the National Labor Department, traveled the entire expanse of Argentina gathering data with respect to the condition of the working class in each province. He published a three-volume study which documented that the majority of Argentine people suffered from a miserable standard of living and low paying, unsteady jobs. However, he concluded that in every province it was women who suffered from the most intense discrimination and exploitation. In Mendoza, as elsewhere, he reported that upon questioning employers about their preference for hiring women workers, they replied that besides being cheaper labor, women were more subordinate and had lower rates of absence from work than men. . . .

Official government investigations continued to detail the long hours, filthy conditions and low pay that characterized the work of women. Perhaps the most vivid description was provided in 1913 by Carolina Muzzili, a militant feminist and inspector for the National Labor Department. She visited dozens of factories and commercial establishments, issuing questionnaires to women workers which provided her with testimony as to the brutalizing effects of work conditions on their minds and bodies. Muzzili's report pointed out that in the laundry industry, for example, women worked from 11 to 12 hours daily, often without any rest breaks. Her indignation led her to compute the rate of profit made by one employer who consistently overworked his female employees. She concluded that while the worker was paid only 2.60 pesos a day, the employer took 7.30 pesos a day in profits from each worker. All investigations of the National Labor Department revealed the fact that women were paid on the average of one-half the wages earned by men for the same job and that minors were paid yet one-half the wages paid to women. Moreover, most women, shortly after beginning to work, acquired the chronic diseases typical of damp and dirty conditions, such as menstrual irregularities, rheumatism, sciatica and TB.

By 1914, according to the national census of that year, there were 714,893 women working in industrial, commercial and professional positions. That figure represented 22% of the total paid work force 14 years of age and older. The director of the census commented that, "we should applaud the increasing proportion of women working because the degree of independence that women have reached in society, the various ways in which they apply their intelligence and energy and are thus surrounded by respect and consideration, are eloquent indications of the general culture and progress of our society."

This comment serves to highlight the contradiction of women's situation as of that year in Argentina. While it was true that the number of women who were wage earners increased yearly, this fact alone did not define the degree to which women were able to achieve any qualitative change from their traditional secondary status in Argentine society. Women were still subject to the control of their fathers and husbands due to their total juridical dependency on men inherited from Spanish legal tradition. Women's husbands still maintained the right to dispose of their earnings because legally the adult married woman was reduced to the status of a minor. Furthermore, women still did not have the right to vote or to be elected to public office. These restrictions on women underscored legally the idealized image of women in Argentine culture which remained that of the housewife-mother: the lovely decoration, weak, not very intelligent and totally dependent on the male for her source of identification and status. Paradoxically enough, often the very men who spoke of women as the "weaker sex" in need of male protection found no inconsistency in their positions as the owners of industry in which women of the working class were so exploited.

It was to the above inequities that the Argentine feminist movement, emerging in the early twentieth century, addressed itself. The movement was composed of a variety of organizations and ideologies, all of which dealt with the civil, economic and political rights of Argentine women. . . .

The efforts of these militant women and sympathetic individuals in Congress were responsible for changes in the laws during the 1920's regarding women. In 1924 protective legislation for working women (law 11.317) was passed, specifying that industrial and commercial establishments could employ women for only eight hours a day or 48 hours a week. Night work was forbidden, as was work in certain factories or jobs considered dangerous. Special rules regarding maternity were established, as well as the requirement that factories with more than 50 female workers provide rooms in which nursing mothers could care for their infants. A series of penal regulations was set up to enforce the law.

This legislation affected working women who during the 1920's made up approximately 18.4% of the paid work force of Buenos Aires in industry, commerce and communications. It did not affect the thousands of women working in the agricultural sector where families were generally hired as a unit and the wages paid to the husband for his own labor plus that of his wife and children. Nor did it affect the serf-like conditions of thousands of women who worked in rural and urban areas as domestic servants. The legislation, even for the women that it covered, did not address itself to the issue of unequal wages paid to women. In fact, the difference between the wages paid to women and men for the same work *increased* during the 1920's.

On September 22, 1926, the Congress passed historic legislation which potentially affected the lives of all Argentine women by substantially changing their civil status. Undoubtedly influenced by progressive legislative changes regarding women in other countries in the post World War One period, the Argentine Congress voted women their long fought for right to equal civil status with men. The legislation affected mainly the adult married woman who had traditionally been reduced to the legal status of a minor upon marriage. Now she could exercise any profession or job without permission from her husband and could dispose of her earnings at her own discretion; she could enter into any civil or commercial agreement without her husband's authorization; and she had authority over her children and their goods in case of legal separation, whether or not she remarried. Article 6 of the law, however, perpetuated the dominance of the husband in marriage because it claimed that he was the official administrator of conjugal property and income and was under no automatic obligation to share this authority unless the wife demanded it through legal process. Obviously many women continued in the same submissive position within the family due both to the force of custom and because they were unaware that the law provided them with a procedure to claim equal authority in marriage. . . .

During the thirties and early forties, women were increasingly employed in the public work force, especially in the capital city. During this period, many people migrated to Buenos Aires from the interior of Argentina in search of work opportunities, and these migrations were composed of approximately twice as many women as men. Women came to represent roughly one-quarter of the paid work force in Buenos Aires. More strikingly, they represented 33 per cent of all industrial workers in that city, and in such industries as textiles, tobacco and clothing they made up the overwhelming majority.

. . . The increasing public employment of women elicited interesting responses from political economists and intellectuals which revealed Argentine attitudes toward women in general. In an almost hysterical fashion, many viewed the process with alarm and detailed the tragic consequences for Argentina of this change in the traditional role of women. Indeed, many insisted that it was because women were working outside the home that Argentina was suffering from a series of crises such as a declining birth rate, the decreasing moral significance of the family, the increasing unemployment rate among men due to "unfair" competition of cheap female labor and the consequent decline in the dominant position of the father within the family structure. . . .

In contrast to the above arguments, one of the main feminist organizations active during the 1930's, the Argentine Association for Women's Suffrage, argued that women should be paid equal wages for equal work with men. This was necessary because of a rising cost of living and family responsibilities which weighed as heavily on the woman as on the man. It would eliminate the competition between male and female workers and thus improve the conditions for both sexes. According to its founder, Carmela Horne de Burmeister, the organization had branches in many provinces and a membership of 80,000 in 1932. The women campaigned for women's suffrage, workers' housing projects, reduced prices for prime necessities, maternity homes and benefits and day nurseries for the children of working mothers.

In the environment of the thirties and early forties, however, there was little chance that these demands would be realized. In fact, at the same time that the role of women in the work force was being attacked by the intellectuals, women's recently won equal civil rights were being attacked by the conservative Justo government. In 1935 a reform of the civil code was proposed. Article 333 aimed at revising the legislative gains made in 1926 by once again reducing the married woman to the status of a minor. At a time when a large percentage of women were earning their own wages, Article 333 proposed that the married woman would not be able to work, spend her earnings, administer her property or be a member of a commercial or civil organization without the authority of her husband.

A campaign was launched against this reactionary measure and a feminist organization called the Argentine Union of Women was founded in 1936. Its president was Victoria Ocampo, an important figure in the literary world, and its vice president was Maria Rosa Oliver, a prominent writer and political activist. The women in the organization delivered public lectures, sponsored radio discussions and printed and distributed thousands of leaflets demanding equal political and economic rights for women, but especially urging the rejection of the proposed legislative reform. Angered by the attempts to reduce the status of women in Argentina, Victoria Ocampo delivered a speech on radio in which she argued that the feminist movement should begin to speak of "women's liberation" instead of "women's emancipation," because the term referred better to the reality of the master-slave relationship between men and women.

The anti-feminist sentiments of the regimes of the 1930's continued unabated after the GOU [Group of United Officers] army coup of 1943. General Ramírez encouraged industry, commerce and the government to stop hiring female workers; in fact, no woman was supposed to be appointed to any position in the government above the rank of clerk. He tried to halt the influence of the feminist movement and actually disbanded the Committee for Victory, a women's fund raising society working for the victory of the Allies with a membership of 50,000. When Paris was liberated from the Nazis, many Argentines celebrated with demonstrations in Buenos Aires. President Farrell not only claimed that the demonstrations involved "outside elements" of extremist ideologies, but he noted with special disapproval the leading role of women in starting some of the impromptu demonstrations.

However, at the same time that the GOU presidents were attempting to reinforce the notion that women's place was in the home, Juan Domingo Perón, who had become Secretary of the Department of Labor and Welfare, began to implement policies and to make public statements which indicated his departure from the mainstream of official attitudes toward women.

On the 3rd of October, 1944, Perón presided over the inauguration of Argentina's first special Women's Division of Labor and Assistance which he created in the Department of Labor and Welfare. He delivered a speech in which he declared that the establishment of this Division was the most agreeable task that he had yet performed because he recognized the contributions that women had made to the greatness of Argentina. Perón asserted that because "more than 900,000 Argentine women are part of the paid work force in all kinds of jobs and professions . . . it is our duty to morally and materially dignify their efforts." He went on to say that in Argentina women's participation in the paid work force was encouraged rather than restricted and that this special Division dealing with the rights and needs of women workers was a social necessity. He called for the improvement and implementation of existing protective legislation and a law establishing women's right to equal pay for equal work.

Less than one year later, on July 26, 1945, Perón, in his capacity as vice president of Argentina, delivered a speech at a Congressional meeting attended by thousands of women, in which he urged the adoption of legislation giving women the right to vote. He pledged his profound support for women's equal political rights and his intention to work increasingly toward that goal.

After his election to the presidency in 1946, Perón submitted to Congress his first five-year plan in which he included a proposal for women's suffrage.

It is not within the scope of this essay to review the various interpretations of the significance of Peronism as an historical phenomenon in Argentina. Suffice it to say that Peronism, contrary to the traditional interpretation, was not a fascist movement. It represented a bourgeois nationalist movement in an underdeveloped country with a colonial export economy. It was a coalition of class forces which included the new industrialists who had developed as a result of the depression and the Second World War and the working class, especially the previously unorganized workers who had migrated to

Buenos Aires during the thirties and early forties. The populist character of the movement was reflected in the fact that its ideology stressed the equality and dignity of the working class and the necessity of industrialization to ensure that equality.

Within this context, the women's movement became more nationalistic and popularly based than the previous feminist movements described above. Any analysis of Perón's appeal to the newly arrived "cabecitas negras" from the interior of Argentina to Buenos Aires would apply especially to the women who made up a good percentage of these migrants. These women represented the most exploited and marginal group of people in society. Not only had they never before been mobilized politically, but they suffered from a sense of uprootedness, isolation, loneliness and alienation that made them most accessible to a political movement that actually improved their economic and political situation and offered them a charismatic leader — indeed, a charismatic couple — with which they could identify.

It is difficult to evaluate the factors which influenced Perón to view women as he did; and it is almost impossible to know the degree to which he sincerely wished to aid women or to appeal to them in order to gain an added organized source of political support. The point I wish to stress here is that this aspect of the Peronist movement is ignored by most historians. Moreover, the historians who stress the change in the status of women which occurred during the Perón years attribute this change to the influence and actions of Eva Perón. Even official Peronist literature, when referring to the role of women within the movement, account for their participation because of the sudden historical appearance of Eva Perón. While not denying the important role that Eva Perón would play in the Peronist feminist movement, it is my contention that the mobilization of women during the Perón years flowed organically from their objective situation in Argentine society and from Perón's awareness of their growing importance in the work force, as well as his desire to deflect the influence on women of traditional Marxist and feminist leadership.

Though by no means revolutionary, Perón's policies with respect to women were historically progressive. He came to power in Argentina supporting women's suffrage. In contrast, Mexico, which had had a social revolution in 1910, did not give women the right to vote until 1953, and Chile, which has had the longest history of stable parliamentary government in Latin America, did not legalize women's suffrage until 1949. Moreover, the Peronist movement institutionalized the political mobilization of women by establishing the Peronist Feminist Party in 1949, while official ideology eulogized women as equal partners in the struggle to build an industrialized country with a just distribution of the wealth.

Perón, because of post-war prosperity and protective measures for Argentine industry, was able to institute government social security programs which improved the standard of living for the working class in general and for working women in particular. That his policies had a direct impact on women is proven by the fact that by 1949, women, including female minors, made up 45% of the industrial workers in Buenos Aires. This figure represents a 62.5% increase over that of 1939, while for the same period the number of men employed in industry had increased only 23%. The percentage of salaried employees represented by women had risen from 13% in 1939 to 28% in 1949.

The working conditions and wages of this increasing number of working women were improved through protective legislation passed by the Department of Labor. In January of 1944, minimum wages were established for piece work done in the home. On September 28, 1945, decree 23.372 fixed the minimum wage in the food industry and gave women a minimum wage of 20% below that of men. While not giving women equal pay, the measure improved the traditional situation in which women were generally paid 40% of what male workers earned.

In 1949, women working in the textile industry were given the right to equal wages with men, a situation which affected more than 15,000 women workers. It is not possible to document whether in fact this last measure was actualized. According to a questionnaire sponsored by the International Labor Organization in 1959, women workers generally earned from 7% to 15% less than men in Argentina. While by no means equitable, the differential in wages according to sex in Argentina is one of the lowest in the non-Socialist world.

The number of women pursuing university educations and professional careers rose dramatically during the Perón years. While from 1931 to 1940 the increase in the percentage of women attending the university over the previous decade was 68.52%, from 1941 to 1950 there was a 139.51% increase and from 1951 to 1960 a 153.62% increase. At the same time, the increase in the percentage of men attending university from 1941 to 1950 was 74.04% and from 1951 to 1960, 44.27%. However, women tended to prepare for careers traditionally defined as women's professions, including medicine, philosophy, education and law.

In 1954, the Congress passed a new family code. It included the right of divorce, a reform fought for by feminist organizations for decades. In 1955, after Perón's fall, the divorce law was abolished.

The most dramatic change that women experienced during Perón's regime was the conquest of suffrage and the right to be elected to public office. Although there had been numerous attempts in previous years to win Congressional approval of women's suffrage, it was not until September 23, 1947, with pressure from the Executive and the mobilization of women by Eva

Perón, that Congress approved the bill legalizing the vote for women. On that date there were mass demonstrations in Buenos Aires in celebration of the event. Women from all social classes, including workers who left their jobs to join the demonstrations, filled the streets in jubilation and listened to Eva Perón speak to them about the significance of that day for women and for Argentina. She described the struggles that they had had to wage with the representatives of the oligarchy in Congress for the passage of the law. She asserted that the vote which women had won was a new tool in their hands. "But our hands are not new in struggle, in work and in the repeated miracle of creation," she said, urging women to use the vote with the same consciousness that they had demonstrated historically in fighting and working by the sides of their men to build a great Argentina.

The election of 1951 reflected the impact that the conquest of suffrage had had on women. 90.32% of the registered female voters voted in comparison to only 86.08% of the registered male voters. In the Buenos Aires area, 93.87% of the women voted while only 91.45% of the men voted. The majority of women everywhere voted the Peronist ticket; the percentage of women's votes going to Perón ranged from 83% to 53%. Perhaps the most significant fact of all marking a new departure in Argentine history was the number of women Peronist candidates elected to the national and provincial Congresses. In the national Congress, seven female Senators and 24 female Deputies were elected. No other country in the Americas could boast of such a high number of elected female representatives.

On April 25, 1953, the Deputies of the national Congress elected Delfina Deglinomini de Parodi as its vice president, an event which symbolized the rising status of women during this period. She was the first woman in Argentina and one of the first women in the world to occupy such a high position. According to her, the change in the status of women under Perón was "the revolution in the revolution."

The political organization of the masses of women began with the campaign for women's suffrage. Women Peronists who were organizing women in the poor neighborhoods formed women's centers that eventually developed into the "unidades basicas" (literally, basic units, these centers were defined as the basic organizational structure of the Peronist movement), which were organized by women for women all over the country. Their functions, among others, were to affiliate women to the Peronist movement by way of lectures and conferences, to offer new work skills and to provide doctors and lawyers to help women with medical and legal problems. According to women involved in the establishment of these centers, they were in every neighborhood and were always open so that women had a place to be together to develop their own political thought and practice without the influence of men.

On July 26, 1949, under the leadership of Eva Perón, the Peronist Feminist Party was inaugurated. This was also a departure in Argentina with respect to the political organization of women because the forms traditionally used by other political parties were women's "committees" and women's "auxiliaries." In the case of the Peronist movement, the official interpretation was that it was composed equally of three branches: the Peronist Men's Party, the Peronist Feminist Party and the General Federation of Workers. Thus the feminist branch of the party had equal importance with the men's branch. Eva Perón, in her speech inaugurating the first national assembly of the Peronist Feminist Party, asserted that its aspirations and its program were based on the Peronist doctrine of economic liberation, political sovereignty and social justice. She congratulated women on not being mere spectators of history. In spite of having suffered double exploitation, both in the home and on the job, she said, women were joining with equal commitment the struggle of the working class. Thus she linked the women's movement ideologically to the struggle of the workers for a strong Argentina independent of the control of the oligarchy and foreign capitalist powers.

The program of the Peronist Feminist Party stated that the Peronist movement gave women full equality with men and that the Feminist Party functioned to affiliate women to struggle for the conquests of Peronism and the liberation of women. "The Peronist Feminist Party opens its doors to all women of the people, and especially to the humble women who have been forgotten by the poets and by the politicians," the program stated. And quoting Eva Perón, it asserted that women had their own separate branch in the party because "just as only the workers could wage their own struggle for liberation, so too could only women be the salvation of women."

Perhaps it is Eva Perón herself who provides the best synthesis of the progressive and conservative tendencies in Peronism with respect to the image of women. Born an illegal child to a lower class family in Los Toldos, she suffered the stigma of such status in a society dominated by bourgeois morality. In 1935, when she was in her teens, like millions of other women suffering from the depression and seeking jobs in Argentina's capital city, Eva moved to Buenos Aires. She was motivated by the desire to be an actress, one of the few supposedly glamorous alternatives to domestic or factory work available to young women. Condemned to a life of poverty and marginality, she was able to achieve some success only through her relations with prominent men in the theatre. It was through a network of such relations that she eventually met Colonel Juan Perón in the early 1940's. She was a young woman of 25, with little education and no political experience. Thus her political ideology developed mainly as a result of her relationship with Perón. However, it is generally acknowledged that Eva, for all the limitations of her political analyses, felt much more authentically in touch with the working class than did Perón. Indeed, she viewed herself as the link between Perón and the people, and she once said, "The people can be sure that between them and their government, there could never be a separation. Because in this case in order to divorce himself from his people, the President would have to first divorce his own wife!"

According to one author, Perón's approach was a paternalistic one. "Thus with all his welfare work in the balance in his favor, Perón was still part of a system through which he was trying to achieve more power. But Eva came from 'nowhere,' with no institutional ties to this system, and all resolute to destroy it." In this regard, a telling difference between the two came in 1951 when, in reaction to an attempted military coup against Perón, Eva wanted to pass out guns to the workers to defend the regime while Perón feared to do so.

Eva Perón had the dynamic energy and anger that came from being lower class and a woman in Argentine society. She once said that "I remember very well that I was sad for days when I found out that the world had both poor and rich people; and the strange thing is that it wasn't the existence of the poor people that hurt me as much as knowing that at the same time there existed the rich." This statement reflects in a sense the ambivalence of the lower class toward bourgeois society. Eva Perón's public image reflected that ambivalence. At first, as the President's wife, she wanted to be accepted by the women and men of the oligarchy, and so she dressed in elaborate, very expensive clothing and was referred to officially as Señora Doña María Eva Duarte de Perón. But as she became more directly involved in political activity and took on her own militant political identity, her image changed. She began to dress in plain, unadorned clothing and was referred to simply as Evita. In fact, she became known as "comrade Evita" throughout Argentina, and she often asserted that her name had transformed itself into "a battle cry for all the women of the world."

As the head of the Peronist Feminist Party and the Eva Perón Foundation and with her influence in the General Federation of Workers, Evita had perhaps as much power as any woman in the world, and she used it. But for all her power and strength, she constantly emphasized publicly that all of her actions were founded on her love and admiration for Perón. She praised Perón as the savior of Argentina to whom all workers and women should look for leadership in what she perceived as the revolutionary movement to make Argentina economically strong and politically sovereign. Furthermore, at the same time that she urged women to struggle autonomously for their own political development, she reinforced the traditional view of the role of women within the home as the mainstay of the society. "The home," she said, reflecting the general assumptions of Peronist ideology, "is the sanctuary of motherhood and the pivot of society. It is the appropriate sphere in which women, for the good of the country and of her own children, fulfills her patriotic duty daily. . . ."

Not only did Evita represent the progressive and conservative aspects of the Peronist movement with respect to women, but she also symbolized the contradictions of Peronism with respect to its bourgeois class content and the aspirations of the working class that supported it. "The virtues and the defects of Eva Perón," writes Juan José Sebreli, "are those of the Argentine woman of her era with its immense possibilities and its limitations, and all women of Argentina should view themselves through her mirror. Not completely class conscious, her passionate, spontaneous, anarchistic conception at once reflected and stimulated the spontaneity of the Argentine working class. The workers saw themselves reflected in Eva Perón because they lacked ideological tools . . . and because they did not have an authentic class-based party, nor a coherent, revolutionary ideology. . . ."

Because the Peronist movement did not challenge the basic socio-economic structure of Argentina which had traditionally been controlled by the oligarchy and foreign interests, no sustained economic growth could take place from the early 1950's on. Thus whatever advances women (and the working class in general) made under Perón were curtailed, especially after the 1955 coup which removed him from power. The present position of women in Argentina — increasing unemployment among female workers, lack of opportunities for women college graduates and no female representatives in Congress — must be seen within the legacy of Peronism: several decades of economic stagnation, a constant rising cost of living and continual political instability.

6. The Peronist Phenomenon and the Significance of Eva

RICHARD BOURNE

Evita's political influence extended far beyond the woman's movement. Here Richard Bourne assesses her role in Peronism and suggests why the movement won few followers outside of Argentina.

The Peronist movement is an unusual phenomenon. Its fascist associations and *petit bourgeois* supporters mix strangely with its role as a working-class party. But it is as Argentina's biggest working-class party, which has survived the exile of Perón and suppression and divisions among the subordinates he left, not to mention free competition with Socialists and Communists, that it has a lasting significance. Compared with the state-approved syndicalism of Franco's Spain or Mussolini's Italy it is quite apparent that the Peronist trade unions of Argentina are much more responsive to the needs of members. Where the trade-union wing of Justicialism is concerned, nothing could have been better than the disappearance of the Peróns, with the belief that the conditions of the working class had been depressed under succeeding governments to nourish it instead. . . .

As a personal movement Peronism was in a central Latin American political tradition: personalities appear to offer more tangible protection that institutions or ideas and provide a simpler focus for human emotions. In Argentina, where the strongest base for the Peronistas lay among the unstructured *petit bourgeoisie* and the unorganized workers, such a personal appeal could have its greatest strength. But the oddity about Peronism, at least during Eva's life, was that it was a two-headed personal movement. In theory this could have been confusing but in practice it was on the whole an advantage. This was because Eva, in her rhetoric, always boosted Perón and offered herself as a humble intermediary between the *descamisados* and their leader. Without Eva the adulation for Perón would almost certainly have

From *Political Leaders of Latin America* by Richard Bourne (Middlesex, England: Penguin, 1969), pp. 264–270, passim. Reprinted by permission.

existed, but it might not have reached such phenomenal heights. She also, as Compañera Evita in her plain dresses, offered workers and women a human bond with what might otherwise have been a distant leader. As the glamorous wife of the President, dressed in the most expensive Paris dresses and with costly jewellery, she also offered ordinary people a colourful fantasy for their own escapist dreams which reinforced the Compañera Evita. In her skilful play on the class and anti-foreign phobias of Peronists and her highly dramatic stance as Perón's wife it is hard to resist the notion that she was fulfilling some of her ambitions as an actress. The striving for popular effect was blatant near the end of her life, when she sponsored her own sainthood, a move which was perhaps particularly popular among the Catholic *petit bourgeois*. The whole campaign would have seemed odious in a more advanced Catholic country, and in fact it gravely affronted pious middle- and upper-class Argentines. But it undoubtedly hit a chord among unsophisticated people brought up on the saintly legends and miraculous interventions of folk Catholicism.

The real relationship between Eva and Juan Domingo Perón was a fruitful ground for speculation. Her public appearance was so aggressive that he was often supposed to be henpecked. But even if, as seems likely, Eva's influence was responsible for policy taking turns that it otherwise would not have done, the pair preserved an outward unity. One of the few occasions in which they appeared to clash—over a grant of 70m. pesos to the Social Aid Foundation from the Chamber of Deputies which President Perón vetoed in 1949—seems to have been as much a calculated gesture to indicate the Fund's independence as a genuine disagreement. 'I am content with the veto,' Eva said at the time. 'It shows the unlimited faith of President Perón in the spiritual force of the Foundation.' Eva's power in the Peronist movement and the country at large was as far reaching as it was ill defined. Cabinet ministers had reason to be as frightened of her as of her husband. In May 1950 Dr Oscar Ivanisevich, then Minister of Education, was forced to resign after operating on her for acute appendicitis. It was said that Eva had had a blazing row with him and had accused him of exaggerating her illness, which he may already have suspected was cancer, in order to remove her from political activity. One of the weapons of the régime against dissent was the law of disrespect *(de-sacato)* under which public criticism of heads of state was illegal. Eva was sensitive on this score. When in 1949 a photograph from a magazine of 1941 which showed the actress Eva Franco with her husband and daughter was reprinted with the wrong caption that this was Eva Duarte the reaction was vindictive. Eva's old friend of her filming days, Kartulovich, was accused of distributing the photo and was summarily deported to Chile, where he continued to protest his innocence. Grudge-bearing and a lack of humor were part of Eva's reputation.

THE SIGNIFICANCE OF EVA

As a Latin American personality possibly Eva's most revolutionary significance was that she was a woman. The fact that a woman was so obviously playing a leading role in one of the area's biggest countries opened up new horizons for women in every field. She deliberately set herself to shatter the conservative protectionism which had cooped up her sex in her own country, which had wasted the potential of wealthier women and denied rights to hardworking poorer women like her own mother. As a crusade Eva's feminism was logically entwined with an attack on the oligarchy and a drive for industrialization and labour benefits: for the countryside, to the traditional eye of the rural landowners, was a man's world, and increasing industrialization must call on female labour which must itself get near to equal rights if male labour was not to suffer. The virulent dislike of Eva among wealthy women, though it focused on superficialities like her opulent jewellery and her decolleté dresses, testified, along with the latent hostility to her in the officer class, to the revolutionary nature of her role. Women had been important, even in politics in Argentina, before. Encarnación Rosas, wife of the nineteenth-century dictator Manuel Rosas, had been one. But as the protagonist of a new sort of woman, free to pursue any occupation she might fancy in a mass society, Latin America had never seen another Eva.

In conjunction with Perón she was also responsible for giving a new dimension to the continent's tradition of military authoritarianism. This was to frighten the rich and their officer relations outside Argentina. The archetypical military *caudillo* was not interested in class differences in any positive way, though he might have to take them, as he took geographical rivalries, into tactical account. His prime purpose was to get and hold personal power. Having succeeded in this it was only by chance that the *caudillo* altered class relationships.

The triumph of the Peróns—and in this Eva was as much the evangelist as Juan—lay in the creation of a movement based on class antagonism by a military leader which would be sufficiently tough to survive the effective demise of the leader. The easy equation of the Latin American officer class with political and social conservatism, good for many countries for much of the time—and an explanation for the enduring rift between Argentine voters and the military, following Perón's exile—fell down at this point. Had the GOU officers in 1943 realized that they were subscribing to the Peronist launching pad they might have acted differently; but their crude form of fascism, influenced by foreign models and the wave of Catholic thought that was seeking routes to class reconciliation instead of warfare, temporarily undercut their social prejudices. For if Argentina was to be the strong united state they desired it must be more economically advanced and independent than at present and its labour force must work and be disciplined. Yet Perón, in the secretariat of labour and welfare, could have told them that it was not enough to intervene in unions and remove existing leaders. Simple repression could offer peace only in the short term. To provide for the future it would be necessary to establish a new labour leadership and to enable it to show sufficient results to outbid alternative leaders. This was what happened and Eva urged Perón to this end. The evolution of Peronism to a point at which the labour tail seemed frequently to be wagging the military dog reflected the fact that Perón's strength in the armed forces preceded his strength with labour, and that the ethic of authoritarian officers was obedience whereas the ethic of militant trade unionism must inspire disobedience. In Spain, where General Franco came to power after victory in civil war, it would have been unthinkable for the Falange to become so class-conscious and powerful. In Argentina, where the colonel came to power as a result of a street demonstration in which no troops were involved—where the demonstrators could tip the balance in an internal Service power struggle—subsequent developments were likely. He became President after elections which showed support far beyond the armed forces. Eva, by her strong identification with the labour wing of Peronism, discouraged any retreat from the 'Day of the *Descamisados*'.

Eva, along with Perón, was responsible for giving the movement the heady but blurred class-consciousness that distinguished it. Her attacks on the oligarchy and British and American capitalism were demagogic. But they made it possible for anyone who agreed, *petit bourgeois* or unionized or non-unionized workers, to include themselves among the deprived *descamisados*. If Argentina in the early forties had had a stronger industrial and trade-union system it might have fathered a more purely working-class party, and it would have been less easy for the Peróns to have inserted their own concoction. But for much longer the rural sector would predominate in economic status, although it employed a diminishing proportion of the labour force, and, for obvious reasons, it would have been quite impossible for the Peróns to have based their strength on the organization of rural workers. The populist appeal of the Peróns, a combination of glamour, nationalism and labour benefits, was not so different from what other Latin American politicans had tried or would try though without the fascist-military trappings. It corresponded to a social reality in which a relatively small élite, associated with foreign economic imperialism, seemed the most important fact to the bulk of the population, and other social gradations counted for little. Where institutions catering for the majority of the population were absent the personal appeal of Eva and Juan Domingo Perón could burgeon largely unopposed.

Peronism, like Haya de la Torre's theories of Indo America which had originated in Peru in the thirties, and Castro's Marxist variation of the late fifties, aspired to be an original Latin American contribution to politics. As has been seen it had borrowed from foreign models, but a desire to differentiate itself, not only from the North American capitalism of the western hemisphere but also from Stalinist Communism, was inherent in the movement. Independence and originality in dealings with the rest of the world have always been attractive to Latin Americans but, although the Peróns certainly aroused interest outside Argentina, there were two basic limits to their influence. First, Eva and her colonel were not themselves transferable. Second, whatever might be claimed for Justicialism, the movement owed so much to the nationalism of one country that dealings with others were bound to have an air of chauvinism that would be unacceptable. Hence although the Peróns could command attention and their specifics, such as the expropriation of foreign railways and other utilities, would reinforce trends elsewhere, their movement had the look of a blind alley for future generations of Latin Americans. The example of a colonel who had set up a following on the basis of social discontent might inspire or frighten officers but there was a clear boundary to his social revolution: the privileges of the armed forces, the ultimate arbiter of power in so many countries, would not be disturbed. However disappointing this might have been to Eva, it was a constraint she and the *descamisados* had had to accept from the moment they started to worship their Leader. Hence the example of the Cuban Revolution, which began with the destruction of Cuba's professional army, was to prove so much more exciting.

SECTION VIII

Fidel Castro and the Cuban Revolution

The Cuban Revolution easily qualifies as the most dramatic event of twentieth-century Latin American history. It brought to power in 1959 an intensely anti-American political leader of indisputable charisma, Fidel Castro Ruz, whose personality has shaped the course of Cuban development for thirty years. Castro's programs transformed Cuba into a modern Soviet-style society, in which the credos of American progressive thought and democratic ideals were spurned in favor of Marxist guidelines modified by Cuban ideas. For the first time a small Caribbean nation reared in the shadow of American power had successfully challenged American hegemony.[1]

Since the overthrow of Paraguay's Alfredo Stroessner in February 1989, Fidel Castro stands as the most durable Latin American president of our time. Now in his sixties, Castro dominates Cuba as firmly as he did in 1959, although his image as a social revolutionary is increasingly coming under challenge. The materials in this section were chosen to provide insight into the revolutionary program and personal charisma that have endured for more than three decades.

BACKGROUND

Cuba represents the most serious challenge to U.S. policy in the Caribbean. Many nations have sought to dominate the island, but after 1900, United States influence became increasingly powerful. How Fidel Castro managed to triumph in 1959 and escape from the orbit of Uncle Sam remains a fascinating

---

[1] Lester D. Langley, *The United States and the Caribbean in the Twentieth Century*, rev. ed. (Athens, Ga; University of Georgia Press, 1985), p. 211.

story, some of it still shrouded in mystery. One of the best explanations was written by the British author Hugh Thomas, whose monumental study of Cuba's history, *Cuba: the Pursuit of Freedom* (New York: Harper & Row, 1971) has been called "the single most important book in English on the subject."[2] In the article reprinted here, Thomas argues that although United States control of many aspects of the Cuban economy contributed to the climate for change, a stagnant economy heavily based on the sugar industry coupled with ineffective institutions, such as the army, the church, and the civil service, accounted for Castro's rise to power (Reading 1).

THE FIRST FIFTEEN YEARS

From the beginning, Castro has conducted Cuban domestic and foreign policies with frequent public speeches. Often addressing crowds as large as one million, he has in addition skillfully employed television to carry his face, voice, and message beyond the meeting plaza to Cubans in their homes. These speeches, averaging more than two hours apiece in length (the longest one on record lasted around nine hours), are unquestionably the most important political documents of the revolution. They are regularly reprinted in the weekly English language edition of *Granma,* the official organ of the Cuban Communist Party and Havana's one morning newspaper. "The Second Declaration of Havana," delivered on February 4, 1962, in response to Cuba's expulsion from the Organization of American States, marked a significant turning point in Cuban policy toward the rest of the hemisphere. By articulating a call for change, reform, and revolution in other Latin lands, Castro offered an alternative to the Alliance for Progress, which had been endorsed by the United States as the best way to promote democracy and economic justice in Latin America (Reading 2).

   Interviews and oral histories are another major source of information about revolutionary Cuba; they provide a format that lends itself well to the style of Fidel Castro. Several book-length interviews have been published in recent years that offer revealing personal portraits of the *Jefe Máximo.* One of the best is that written by Lee Lockwood based on the interviews he conducted with Fidel in 1965 and 1966, and illustrated with his striking photographs of all aspects of Cuban life. Lockwood probed Castro on a wide range of subjects, including U.S.-Cuban relations, Cuban-Soviet relations, land reform, industrialization, education, censorship, and human rights (Reading 3). Another example of this genre is *With Fidel: A Portrait of Castro and Cuba* (New York: Ballantine, 1975), by Frank Mankiewicz and Kirby Jones. In thirteen hours of interviews with Mankiewicz and Jones, Castro

---

[2] James Nelson Goodsell, *Fidel Castro's Personal Revolution in Cuba: 1959–1973* (New York: Knopf, 1975), p. 345.

discusses foreign policy, the armed forces, the relationship between the Communist Party and the state, and the missile crisis.

By the 1970's, the Revolution seemed to be achieving permanence, and the first scholarly syntheses of the changes that had occurred in Cuba began to appear. Lowry Nelson in 1972 published *Cuba: The Measure of a Revolution* (Minneapolis, University of Minnesota Press, 1972), which surveys the impact of the revolution on agriculture, economic diversification, labor, education, religion, and social services. A sociologist who did extensive field work in Cuba in the 1940s, Nelson could judge Castro's influence from a unique perspective. He concluded that the regime had been a tragedy for Cuba and its people. Less pessimistic assessments made during this decade include Jorge I. Dominguez, *Cuba: Order and Revolution* (Cambridge, MA: Harvard U. Press, 1978), and Carmelo Mesa-Lago, *Cuba in the 1970s: Pragmatism and Institutionalization* (rev. ed. Albuquerque: University of New Mexico Press, 1979).

THE INSTITUTIONALIZED REVOLUTION

Since 1976, Cubans have been ruled according to a constitution that provides for elected municipal, provincial, and national assemblies. Institutionalization has continued through the 1980s, with the Communist Party and the military assuming more dominant roles. Nevertheless, Castro remains firmly at the head of the revolution, holding the offices of President of the Council of State, First Secretary of the Communist Party and Head of Government. Tad Szulc discusses his principal achievements and setbacks during the last fifteen years in *Fidel: A Critical Portrait* (New York: Morrow, 1986). In the view of Szulc, Castro at the age of sixty has few fresh ideas for his aging revolution, and in spite of the fact that he is still enormously popular, he is a lonely man searching for an elusive future (Reading 4). To historian Jaime Suchlicki, Castro is less enigmatic. Suchlicki writes that Castro is as combative and anti-American as he was thirty years ago. He is "less concerned about whether the Cubans eat better and more concerned about his position in history and his position in the world" (Reading 5). As these two readings suggest, where is still no unanimity of opinion on the bearded revolutionary who has had so much impact on Cuba and the Americas.[3]

---

[3] Goodsell, p. 13.

Fidel Castro

1. The Castro Revolution Was the Culmination of a Long Series of Thwarted Revolutions

HUGH THOMAS

Professor Hugh Thomas, the British historian at the University of Reading, here gives a carefully argued explanation of the coming of Castro.

The present Cuban explanation of events is that Cuba, previously a semi-colonialist society, was so severely exploited by U.S. and Cuban capitalists that the condition of the working class eventually became intolerable, the tension being especially sharpened under the tyrant Batista (1952–58); Castro's 26th of July Movement and the Communist Party therefore formed the elite which led the masses towards a coherent realization of their misery and the country towards the "objective conditions" for revolution. Yet this explanation is also inadequate. Cuba, although a poor country in many respects, was certainly among the richer countries of Latin America. Per capita income reached a figure of $341 at its highest level in 1947. The average daily salary about the same time for the best-paid sugar worker was $3.25, which probably would have given him an annual wage (with a six-day week for the five-month sugar harvest) of nearly $500. This is a small wage, but in many countries in Latin America it would be considered high. Wages apart, however, the general availability of consumer goods, the social services per head, the labour laws, the communications system, literacy rates, all normal criteria indicate that Cuba was among the leading nations of Latin America — to be ranked in terms of development below only Argentina and Uruguay, and perhaps on a level with Chile. Certainly, Cuba had had for two generations before the revolution the highest standard of living of any tropical area in the world. It does not therefore seem to be poverty, any more than North American foolishness, that caused the revolution to take the turn it did.

The difficulty of explaining what happened in Cuba in Marxist terms has

From "The Origins of the Cuban Revolution" by Hugh Thomas, *The World Today,* 19 (October 1963), pp. 448–460, passim. Reprinted by permission.

led some people to another extreme: they have seen the whole series of events as dictated by the whims of one man. The trouble with this argument is that it really credits Castro with greater powers than any man can singly possess. Instead of describing a monster, this argument creates a god.

The origins of the revolution seem more likely to be found in the fact that Cuban society was not so much underdeveloped as stagnant: semideveloped perhaps, with some of the characteristics of advanced countries when they enter decline. Cuba was not a country in the depths of poverty, but one extraordinarily frustrated, where opportunities existed for economic and social progress but where these were wasted — and the fact of the waste was evident. The undoubted advances whetted the imagination of the working class, but did not satisfy it. The case of the well-paid sugar worker symbolizes the situation; getting $3.25 a day for the five months of the harvest, afterwards he could expect to earn nothing. Unused to saving, and perhaps incapable of doing so since he had to pay off debts incurred during the previous dead season, his life collapsed. For half the year he was comparatively well off, able to choose between a quite wide selection of consumer goods; for the rest of the year he lived in resentment, possibly more extreme than if he had been unemployed all the time, as a large fraction (around one-fifth) of his colleagues in the trade were. About 500,000 persons were in this frustrating position, nearly one-third of the total labour force of about 1.7 million. Nearly all of them were in debt throughout their lives — being disposed for that reason alone to hope for a violent upturn in society, which might declare a moratorium on, or even an annulment of, debts. The key to Cuban society before the revolution is, in fact, the sugar industry. . . .

In addition to being the world's largest producer of sugar, Cuba was, for about a century, the major single source of sugar for the United States, and for a time after the Civil War her sole source of sugar. For most of this century up to 1960, Cuba supplied between 40 and 60 per cent of U.S. sugar, with a drop towards 30 per cent and for a time 25 per cent during the 1930's depression. After this unstable period, Cuba secured a part of the U.S. market by a specific quota, allocated annually according to the U.S. Secretary for Agriculture's estimate of U.S. sugar needs. . . . The quota was a great advantage but also a great bondage, and therefore there is a certain logic in the Cuban Revolutionary Government's criticism of its existence in early 1960 and denunciation of its disappearance in August of the same year. The tragedy of the Cuban sugar industry in the years before the revolution is that it was hard to see how, even with the most effective methods of production, it could expand its share of the world market, or its own production. Both U.S. and world markets were quota-controlled and tariff-protected to the point where expansion was almost forbidden.

One should note, however, that a large percentage of Cuban sugar mills

were in fact U.S.-owned. . . . Of course, it was natural for Cubans to denounce the high percentage of foreign ownership, throughout this long period, of
the staple product of the country, especially when other sections of the commanding heights of industry were also U.S.-owned; these included almost all
public utilities in Havana, railways, and banks, which had been largely U.S.-
and Canadian-owned since the bank crash in the 1920's. However, there were
some advantages in this: foreign ownership could help to keep the door open
to new ideas in technology and research; some of the best schools in Cuba
seem to have been run by Americans, some being financed as a public obligation, others privately; American firms were also probably less given to tax
evasion than Cuban. The overall effect of U.S. ownership of such prosperity as
there was in Cuba was that Americans could not avoid being blamed when
things went wrong with the economy; and the economy had been in crisis for
as long as anyone could remember.

In fact, Cuban sugar before the revolution was going through the classic
experience of a great industry in decline. Cuban sugar-growers never sought
to make the best use of their ground, the yield per acre, for instance, being far
below that of Puerto Rico or Hawaii. Irrigation was not only rare but not
apparently even planned, though it was obvious that it gave a higher yield.
There was very little research as to the type of cane best suited for Cuban
conditions: the agricultural research center at Sagua la Grande was hardly
able to carry on, since even the meagre ear-marked funds often "disappeared"
before they got there. Further, the industry was hamstrung by bureaucratic
control. . . .

The country was also at the mercy of world sugar demand. Changes of a
percentage of a cent in the world market price of sugar not only meant the
creation or ruin of fortunes in Cuba, but also indicated whether ordinary life
was intolerable or acceptable. . . . For example, in 1950 under the impact of
post-Korean rearmament, the whole of Cuba's molasses from the 1951 harvest
was sold at 20 cents a gallon, instead of 5 cents a gallon a year earlier. . . .

Credit was almost impossible to obtain unless the proposed project was in
some way connected with sugar, yet investment in new industries (perhaps
making use of sugar by-products) and diversification of agriculture were the
only way forward. This blockage could be observed throughout the economy.
Education, health, social services of all kinds, public services, commerce,
departments of agriculture other than sugar, trade unions, all gave the impression of being not only incapable of development, but also afraid of it. The
Cuban educational system had deteriorated between 1925 and 1959. A smaller
proportion of school-age children were enrolled in Cuban schools in 1950
than in 1925. . . .

Other Latin American economies were, and are, as unstable and as unbalanced as that of Cuba: and the central cause of the trouble, the monocrop,

appears elsewhere. At the same time, none of the countries whose economies are to a lesser or greater extent monocultures actually depends on sugar, whose price has always been highly volatile. . . .

The institutions of Cuba in 1958–59 were amazingly weak. The large middle and upper class had failed to create any effective defence against the demands of what may be taken to be the majority when those demands came at last to be clearly expressed, as they did in January 1959, by a group self-confessedly middle class in origin. Perhaps the first and strongest factor working in favour of the revolution was the absence of any regionally based obstacles. . . .

To the absence of a regional restraining force was added the weakness of two other traditional conservative forces — the Church and the regular army. The Cuban Church has never really found an identity. Churches are few in Cuba. The Church played no part in the development of the Cuban spirit of independence, which instead was nurtured by freemasonry and rationalism. Few priests before 1898 were Cuban born, and even after 1900 the majority continued to come from Spain. Church and State had been separated in the Constitution of 1901, State subsidies also disappearing. Later on, the Church made something of a comeback, a large number of Catholic schools being founded in the 1930's; in 1946 a Catholic university was also founded. In the 1950's this educational emphasis led to the appearance of almost radical Catholic groups which opposed Batista. In Oriente, there was, in the early stages, some degree of relationship between the 26th of July Movement and the Church — chiefly since it was widely known that the intervention of the Archbishop of Santiago had helped save Castro's life after the Moncada attack in 1953. The leading Catholic and conservative newspaper, the *Diario de la Marina,* was, on the other hand, among the first to suggest that the 26th of July Movement was communist.

After Castro got to power, the Church made no serious move to gather middle-class opposition, and it was only in 1960, when it was too late, that a series of sporadic pastoral letters appeared denouncing communism. All church schools and convents were closed by the end of 1961, and most foreign priests and secular clergy (i.e., the majority) were expelled. Since then there has been a surprising calm in the relations between Church and State, presumably by mutual consent; the Church in Cuba has, in short, never been a serious factor in the situation.

The regular army, the second traditional opponent of revolutionary regimes, was even less of an obstacle. By early 1959 it had in fact ceased to exist — not simply due to its demoralization in 1957 and 1958, when fighting Castro in the Sierra, but also to the repeated divisions which had weakened its esprit de corps during preceding years. . . .

The trade unions also could offer no serious opposition to the revolution;

yet the revolution destroyed them, or anyway converted them into departments of the Ministry of Labour. Cuban labour began to be effectively organized under the shadow of the depression and the Machado dictatorship. Batista enabled the communists to form and dominate a congress of unions in the late 1930's — in return for communist electoral support for himself. Between 1938 and 1947 the unions were, if not structurally, at least in effect a section of the Ministry of Labour. The rather cynical alliance of Batista and the communists (till 1944) was responsible for some enlightened labour legislation: a minimum wage; minimum vacation of one month; 44-hour week and 48-hour-week pay; nine days of annual sick leave; security of tenure except on proof of one of fourteen specific causes of dismissal, and so on — all admirable measures in themselves, enshrined in the 1940 Constitution, and all in effect till 1959. These measures were in fact so favourable to labour in the 1940's and early 1950's as undeniably to hinder the economic development of Cuba; labour opposition to mechanization, for example, seems to have been a serious handicap. The general impression to be gained from the labour scene just before Batista's second coup was less that of solid benefits won by a progressive working class than of a number of isolated redoubts, held with great difficulty and with continuous casualties, in a predominantly hostile territory. . . .

It was equally hopeless to expect the civil service to be a restraining factor in the revolution, although, with nearly 200,000 employees, it was the second largest source of employment, ranking after the sugar workers. Despite the passage of numerous laws, starting in 1908 under the Magoon administration, no Government was able to depend on a reliable civil service. With the exception of the National Bank, during the short period from its inception in 1949 to the Batista coup, all departments of state were regarded as the legitimate spoils of political victors. Of course, in this Cuba was no different from other countries. But in few countries of a comparable degree of wealth was the absence of an administrative career in government so conspicuous. In some Ministries, employees never seem to have appeared except to collect pay; the absence of responsibility was possibly most marked in the Ministry of Education. Also, since the salary scale was low, there was every incentive for employees of all grades to dip their hands in the government till, as their political masters did. Since governmental and nongovernmental pension funds, which were lodged in the Treasury, had been used by the Grau Government to help pay other lavish but unspecified government expenses, it was very difficult after 1947 to allow any employee to retire. Many people thought that in fact 30,000 to 40,000 government employees were really pensioners. Thus government employment was a kind of social assistance.

The scandal of the old bureaucracy is certainly a reason why, after the victory of the 26th of July Movement in 1959, the idea of a total break with the past seemed so attractive. The word government had been debased for so long; not only the old bureaucracy but the old political parties were widely and with justice regarded as organizations for the private distribution of public funds. Who in 1959, even after seven years of Batista, had really forgotten the scandal of Grau's schoolteachers; or of Grau's Minister of Education, Alemán, who had arrived suddenly one day in Miami with, was it $10 million, or was it $20 million in cash in a suitcase? In what way was Batista's cheating in the State lottery worse than Prío's? It was all very well to return to the Constitution of 1940: but how far had it worked between 1940 and 1952? It had in many instances merely laid down general principles; the subsequent legislation had never been carried out to implement it. . . .

Some of the best-intentioned sections of the Constitution were in fact a little absurd, such as the provision in Article 52 that the annual salary of a primary schoolteacher should never be less than a millionth part of the national budget. At the same time, not many people, even sincere democrats, could summon up enthusiasm for the 1940 Constitution, since it had been established with the backing of Batista and the communists. And at a deeper level, there was a genuine doubt among many in Cuba in 1958–59 about the structure of previous Cuban Constitutions ever since independence. Batista's police were certainly bloody, but the old days of gangsterism under the democratic rule of Grau were hardly better. There was a time, for instance, in 1947, when three separate political gangster groups were fighting each other in the streets of Havana, each being separately backed by different divisions of the police, whose chiefs had been specifically appointed by the President to balance them off.

Although Castro did not come to power with a real party organization, or even a real political plan, he nevertheless did have behind him a real revolutionary tradition, a tradition which was firmly rooted in the previous sixty years of Cuban politics, almost the whole of which had been passed in perpetual crisis. . . . All the time between 1902 and 1959, Cubans were trying to prove themselves worthy of the heroic figures of the War of Independence — Martí, Gómez, or Maceo. Efforts were made, understandably, necessarily perhaps, by Castro to make himself, Camilo Cienfuegos, and others the equals of the past. The men of 1959 were undoubtedly in many cases the real sons of the men who made the revolution in 1933. Castro was to do the things that many people had been talking about before. Many moderately middle-class Cubans suspected, without much economic knowledge, that the only way out of the chronic sugar crisis, the only way to diversify agriculture, was to embark on very radical measures; to nationalize American property and to force a break in commercial relations with the United States.

Amateur Marxism was a strong force on the left wing of the *Ortodoxo* Party in the early 1950's, though it is now proving an illusion to suppose that even Marxist-Leninism can bring a swift diversification of agriculture. One can see how the illusion nevertheless became widespread, how anyone who seemed likely to realize it was certain of backing, regardless of whether he trampled on formal democracy. There can be only one reason why the moderates in the Cuban Cabinet of 1959 — the admirable professional and liberal persons who now perhaps back Manuel Ray and argue that Castro has betrayed the revolution — failed to unite and resist Castro, backed by the considerable strength of the Cuban middle class: the reason is surely that they half felt all the time that, given the betrayal of so many previous revolutions, Castro was right. Many moderates after all did stay in Cuba, and many are still there.

What of the communists? They have never dictated events, but merely profited from opportunities offered to them. . . . The communists got 117,000 votes in the presidential elections of 1944, but they were by that time in a curious position, being less a party of revolution than one which had a great deal to lose, almost conservative in their reactions in fact. Thereafter their influence waned, throughout the intermediate period between then and the Castro civil war, until mid-1958 when, after some difficulty, they established a working alliance with Castro, whom they had previously dismissed as a *putschista*. Since then, they have, of course, come into their own in many respects, if not quite absolutely; but their role in the origins of the Cuban revolution seems to have been small.

To sum up: the origins of the Cuban revolution must be sought in the state of the Cuban sugar industry. Similar conditions may exist in other countries of Latin America, in respect of other crops; these have hitherto been less pronounced. Even though other revolutions in the area may in fact be equally due, they have been hindered by the strength of institutions or regional habits, which in Cuba, for historical reasons, were especially weak. Finally, the Cuban revolution of 1959, far from being an isolated event, was the culmination of a long series of thwarted revolutions.

2. The Duty of a Revolutionary is to Make the Revolution: The Second Declaration of Havana

FIDEL CASTRO

In this speech delivered in Havana on February 4, 1962 Castro sets forth one of his most provocative themes—"the necessity for revolutionaries to create conditions for struggle themselves and not to wait for material conditions to sweep them into power." Although his approach is Marxist-Leninist, his language is restrained. The declaration marked a turning point in Cuban policy toward the rest of the hemisphere, and while parts of it were directed to internal issues, it has come to be studied primarily for its importance in foreign relations.

On May 18, 1895, on the eve of his death from a Spanish bullet through his heart, José Martí, apostle of our independence, said in an unfinished letter to his friend Manuel Mercado: "Now I am able to write . . . I am in danger each day now of giving my life for my country and for my obligation . . . to prevent before it's too late—through achieving Cuba's independence—the United States from extending its control over the Antilles and consequently falling with that much more force upon our countries of America. Whatever I have done till now, and whatever I shall do, has been with that aim. . . .

"The people most vitally concerned with preventing the imperialist annexation of Cuba, which would make Cuba the starting point of that course—which must be blocked and which we are blocking with our blood—of annexation of our American nations to the violent and brutal North which despises them, are being hindered by lesser and public commitments from the open and avowed espousal of this sacrifice, which is being made for our and their benefit.

"I have lived inside the monster and know its guts; and my sling is the sling of David."

In 1895, Martí already pointed out the danger hovering over America and called imperialism by its name: imperialism. He pointed out to the people of Latin America that more than anyone, they had a stake in seeing that Cuba

From *Fidel Castro Speaks*, edited by Martin Kenner and James Petras (New York: Grove Press, 1969), pp. 93–117 passim. Reprinted by permission.

did not succumb to the greed of the Yankee, scornful of the peoples of Latin America. And with his own blood, shed for Cuba and America, he wrote the words which posthumously, in homage to his memory, the people of Cuba place at the head of this declaration.

HUMILIATION

Sixty-seven years have passed. Puerto Rico was converted into a colony and is still a colony saturated with military bases. Cuba also fell into the clutches of imperialism. Their troops occupied our territory. The Platt Amendment was imposed on our first constitution, as a humiliating clause which sanctioned the odious right of foreign intervention. Our riches passed into their hands, our history was falsified, our government and our politics were entirely molded in the interests of the overseers; the nation was subjected to sixty years of political, economic, and cultural suffocation.

But Cuba rose, Cuba was able to redeem itself from the bastard guardianship. Cuba broke the chains which tied its fortunes to those of the imperialist oppressor, redeemed its riches, reclaimed its culture, and unfurled its banner as the Free Territory of America.

Now the United States will never again be able to use Cuba's strength against America, but conversely, dominating the majority of the other Latin American states, the United States is attempting to use the strength of America against Cuba.

What is the history of Cuba but the history of Latin America? And what is the history of Latin America but the history of Asia, Africa, and Oceania? And what is the history of all these peoples but the history of the most pitiless and cruel exploitation by imperialism throughout the world?

At the end of the last and the beginning of the present century, a handful of economically developed nations had finished partioning the world among themselves, subjecting to its economic and political domination two-thirds of humanity, which was thus forced to work for the ruling classes of the economically advanced capitalist countries.

*   *   *   *

U.S. POLICY

North American imperialism's declared policy of sending soldiers to fight against the revolutionary movement of any country in Latin America, that is, to kill workers, students, peasants, Latin American men and women, has no other objective than the continued maintenance of its monopolistic interests and the privileges of the traitorous oligarchies which support it.

It can now be clearly seen that the military pacts signed by the government of the United States with Latin American governments—often secret pacts and always behind the backs of the people—invoking hypothetical foreign dangers which did not exist, had the sole and exclusive object of preventing the struggle of the people; they were pacts against the people, against the only danger—the internal danger of the liberation movements that would imperil Yankee interests. It was not without reason that the people asked themselves: Why so many military agreements? Why the shipments of arms which, even though technically outmoded for modern war, are nevertheless efficient for smashing strikes, repressing popular demonstrations, staining the land with blood? Why the military missions, the pact of Rio de Janeiro and the thousand and one international conferences?

Since the end of World War II, the nations of Latin America have been impoverished more and more, their exports have less and less value, their imports cost more, the per capita income falls, the awful rate of infant mortality does not decrease, the number of illiterates is higher, the people lack jobs, land, adequate housing, schools, hospitals, means of communication, and means of life. On the other hand, North American investments exceed ten billion dollars. Latin America, moreover, provides cheap raw materials, and is the buyer of expensive finished articles. The United States trades with Latin America like the first Spanish conquerors, who bartered mirrors and trinkets for gold and silver. To guard that torrent of riches, to gain ever more control of Latin America's resources and to exploit its suffering peoples—that is what is hidden behind the military pacts, the military missions, and Washington's diplomatic lobbying. . . .

This policy of gradual strangulation of the sovereignty of the Latin American nations, and of a free hand to intervene in their internal affairs culminated in the recent meeting of foreign ministers at Punta del Este. . . .

Behind closed doors, in repugnant and unlawful meetings, the Yankee minister of colonies dedicated entire days to beating down the resistance and scruples of some ministers, bringing into play the millions of the Yankee treasury in an undisguised buying and selling of votes. A handful of representatives of the oligarchies (of countries which together barely add up to a third of the continent's population) imposed agreements that served up to the Yankee master on a silver platter, the head of a principle which cost the blood of all our countries since the wars of independence. The Pyrrhic character of such sad and fraudulent deeds of imperialism, their moral failure, the broken unanimity, and the universal scandal do not diminish the grave danger which agreements imposed at such a price have brought so close to the peoples of Latin America. At that evil conclave Cuba's thundering voice was raised without weakness or fear, to indict, before all the peoples of America and the world, the monstrous attempt, and to defend with a virility and dignity which will be clear in the annals of history, not only Cuba's rights but the deserted rights of all our sister nations of the American Continent. The word of Cuba could find no echo in that house-broken majority, but neither could it find a refutation; only impotent silence greeted its demolishing arguments and the clearness and courage of its words. But Cuba did not speak for the ministers, Cuba spoke for the people and for history, where its words will be echoed and answered.

At Punta del Este a great ideological battle unfolded between the Cuban Revolution and Yankee imperialism. Who did they represent there, for whom did each speak? Cuba represented the people; the United States represented the monopolies. Cuba spoke for America's exploited masses; the United States for the exploiting, oligarchical, and imperialist interests; Cuba for sovereignty; the United States for intervention; Cuba for the nationalization of foreign enterprises; the United States for new investments of foreign capital. Cuba for culture; the United States for ignorance. Cuba for agrarian reform; the United States for great landed estates. Cuba for the industrialization of America; the United States for underdevelopment. Cuba for creative work; the United States for sabotage and counter-revolutionary terror practiced by its agents—the destruction of sugar-cane fields and factories, the bombing by their pirate planes of the labor of a peaceful people. Cuba for the murdered teachers; the United States for the assassins. Cuba for bread; the United States for hunger. Cuba for equality; the United States for privilege and discrimination. Cuba for the truth; the United States for lies. Cuba for liberation; the United States for oppression. Cuba for the bright future of humanity; the United States for the past without hope. Cuba for the heroes who fell at Girón to save the country from foreign domination; the United States for mercenaries and traitors who serve the foreigner against their country. Cuba for peace among peoples; the United States for aggression and war. Cuba for socialism; the United States for capitalism. . . .

The agreements obtained by the United States through methods so shameful that the entire world criticizes them, do not diminish but increase the morality and justice of Cuba's stand, which exposes the sell-out and treason of the oligarchies to the national interests and shows the people the road to liberation. It reveals the corruption of the exploiting classes for whom their representatives spoke at Punta del Este. The OAS was revealed for what it really is—a Yankee Ministry of Colonies, a military alliance, an apparatus of repression against the liberation movements of the Latin American peoples.[1]

Cuba has lived three years of the Revolution under the incessant harassment of Yankee intervention in our internal affairs. Pirate airplanes coming from the United States, dropping incendiaries, have burned millions of *arrobas* of sugar cane; acts of international sabotage perpetrated by Yankee agents, like the explosion of the ship *La Coubre*, have cost dozens of Cuban lives; thousands of North American weapons have been dropped by para-chute by the U.S. military services into our territory to promote subversion; hundreds of tons of explosive materials and bombs have been secretly landed on our coast from North American launches to promote sabotage and ter-rorism; a Cuban worker was tortured on the naval base of Guantanamo and deprived of his life with no due process before or any explanation later; our sugar quota was abruptly cut and an embargo proclaimed on parts and raw materials for factories and North American construction machinery in order to ruin our economy. Cuban ports and installations have been surprise-attacked by armed ships and bombers from bases prepared by the United States. Mercenary troops, organized and trained in countries of Central America by the same government, have in a warlike manner invaded our territories, escorted by ships of the Yankee fleet and with aerial support from foreign bases, causing much loss of life as well as material wealth; counter-revolutionary Cubans are being trained in the U.S. army and new plans of aggression against Cuba are being made. All this has been going on inces-santly for three years, before the eyes of the whole continent—and the OAS was not aware of it.

The ministers meet in Punta del Este and do not even admonish the U.S. government nor the governments who are material accomplices to these aggressions. They expel Cuba, the Latin American victim, the aggrieved nation.

The United States has military pacts with nations of all the continents; military blocs with whatever fascist, militarist, and reactionary government there is in the world: NATO, SEATO and CENTO, to which we now have to add the OAS; it intervenes in Laos, in Viet Nam, in Korea, in Formosa, in Berlin. It openly sends ships to Santo Domingo in order to impose its law, its will, and announces its proposal to use its NATO allies to block commerce with Cuba. And the OAS is not aware! The ministers meet and expel Cuba, which has no military pacts with any country. Thus the government that organizes subversion throughout the world and forges military alliances on four continents, forces the expulsion of Cuba, accusing her of no less than subversion and having ties beyond the continent.

CUBA'S RECORD

Cuba, the Latin American nation which has made landowners of more than 100,000 small farmers, provided year-round employment on state farms and co-operatives to all agricultural workers, transformed forts into schools, given 70,000 scholarships to university, secondary, and technological stu-dents, created lecture halls for the entire child population, totally liquidated illiteracy, quadrupled medical services, nationalized foreign interests, suppressed the abusive system which turned housing into a means of exploiting people, virtually eliminated unemployment, suppressed discrimination due to race or sex, ridded itself of gambling, vice, and administrative corruption, armed the people, made the enjoyment of human rights a living reality by freeing man and woman from exploitation, lack of culture, and social inequality, which has liberated itself from all foreign tutelage, acquired full sovereignty, and established the foundations for the development of its economy in order to no longer be a country producing only one crop and exporting only raw materials, is expelled from the Organization of American States by governments which have not achieved for their people one of these objectives. How will they be able to justify their conduct before the peoples of the Americas and the world? How will they be able to deny that in their concept the policy of land, of bread, of work, of health, of liberty, of equality, of culture, of accelerated development of the economy, of national dignity, of full self-determination and sovereignty, is incompatible with the hemisphere?

The people think very differently, the people think that the only thing incompatible with the destiny of Latin America is misery, feudal exploitation, illiteracy, starvation wages, unemployment, the policy of repression against the masses of workers, peasants, and students, discrimination against women, Negroes, Indians, mestizos, oppression by the oligarchies, the plundering of their wealth by the Yankee monopolists, the moral stagnation of their intellectuals and artists, the ruin of the small producers by foreign competition, economic underdevelopment, peoples without roads, without hospitals, without housing, without schools, without industries, the submission to imperialism, the renunciation of national sovereignty, and the betrayal of the country. . . .

How can the imperialists make understood their conduct and condemnatory attitude toward Cuba? With what words and what arguments are they going to speak to those whom, all the while exploiting, they ignored for so long?

THE IMPERIALIST RECORD

Those who study the problems of America are accustomed to ask: what country has concentrated upon—for the purpose of remedying—the situation of the idle, the poor, the Indians, the Blacks, and the helpless infants, this immense number of infants—thirty million in 1950 (which will be fifty million in eight more years). Yes, what country?

Thirty-two million Indians—like the Andes mountains—form the backbone of the entire American continent. It is clear that for those who considered the Indian more as a thing than a person, this mass of humanity does not count, did not count and, they thought, never would count. Of course, since they were considered a brute labor force, they had to be used like a yoke of oxen or a tractor.

How—under what oath—could anyone believe in any benefit, in any "Alliance for Progress" with imperialism, when under its saintly protection, its killings, its persecutions, the natives of the South of the continent, like those of Patagonia, still live under strips of canvas as did their ancestors at the time the discoverers came almost 500 years ago? Where are those great races which populated northern Argentina, Paraguay, and Bolivia, such as the Guarani who were savagely decimated, hunted like animals, and buried in the depths of the jungle? Where is that reservoir of indigenous stock—whose extinction is continually hastened—which could have served as a base for a great American civilization? Across the Paraguayan swamps and desolate Bolivian highlands, deeper into itself, America has driven these primitive, melancholy races, brutalized by alcohol and narcotics to which they became addicted in order at least to survive in the subhuman conditions—not only of nutrition—in which they live. Where does a chain of hands stretch out almost in vain, yet still stretching out across centuries, over the Andean peaks and slopes, along great rivers and in the shadowy forests, uniting their miseries with those of others who are slowly perishing. Where do hands stretch out to Brazilian tribes and those of the North of the continent and the coasts, until in the most incredible and wild confines of the Amazon jungle or mountain ranges of Perija, Venezuela's hundred thousand indigent are reached, then to the isolated Vapicharnas, who await their end, now almost definitively lost to the human race, in the hot regions of the Guianas? Yes, all these thirty-two million Indians, who extend from the United States border to the limits of the Southern hemisphere, and the forty-five million mestizos, who for the most part differ little from the Indians; all these natives, this formidable reservoir of labor, whose rights have been tramped on, yes, what can imperialism offer them? How can these people, ignored so long, be made to believe in any benefit to come from such bloodstained hands?

Entire tribes which live unclothed; others which are supposed to be cannibalistic; others whose members die like flies upon their first contact with the conquering civilization; others which are banished, that is, thrown off their lands, pushed to the point of squatting in the jungles, mountains, or most distant reaches of the prairies where not even the smallest particle of culture, light, bread, nor anything penetrates.

In what "alliance"—other than one for their own more rapid extermination—are these native races going to believe, these races who have been flogged for centuries, shot so their lands could be taken, beaten to death by the thousands for not working faster in their exploited labor for imperialism?

"ALLIANCE" FOR BLACKS?

And to the Black? What "alliance" can the system of lynching and brutal exclusion of the Black offer to the fifteen million Negroes and fourteen million mulattoes of Latin America, who know with horror and rage that their brothers in the North cannot ride in the same vehicles as their white compatriots, nor attend the same schools, nor even die in the same hospitals?

How are these disinherited racial groups going to believe in this imperialism, in its benefits or in any "alliance" with it which is not for lynching and exploiting them as slaves? Those masses who have not been permitted even modestly to enjoy any cultural, social, or professional benefits, who—even when they are in the majority or number millions—are persecuted by the imperialists in Ku Klux Klan costumes, are ghettoed in the most unsanitary neighborhoods, in the least comfortable tenements built expressly for them, are shoved into the most menial occupations, the hardest labor and the least lucrative professions. They cannot presume to reach the universities, advanced academies and private schools.

What "Alliance for Progress" can serve as encouragement to those 107 million men and women of our America, the backbone of labor in the cities and fields, whose dark skin—black, mestizo, mulatto, Indian—inspires scorn in the new colonialists? How are they—who with bitter impotence have seen how in Panama there is one wage scale for Yankees and another for Panamanians, who are regarded as an inferior race—going to put any trust in the supposed Alliance? . . .

What can the workers hope for, with their starvation wages, the hardest jobs, the most miserable conditions, lack of nutrition, illness, and all the evils which foster misery?

What words can be said, what benefits can the imperialists offer to the copper, tin, iron, coal miners who cough up their lungs for the profits of merciless foreign masters, and to the fathers and sons of the lumberjacks and rubber-planation workers, to the harvesters of the fruit plantations, to the workers in the coffee and sugar mills, to the peons on the pampas and plains who forfeit their health and lives to amass the fortunes of the exploiters?

What can those vast masses—who produce the wealth, who create the values, who aid in bringing forth a new world in all places—expect? What can they expect from imperialism, that greedy mouth, that greedy hand, with no other face than misery, but the most absolute destitution and death, cold and unrecorded in the end?

What can this class, which has changed the course of history, which in other places has revolutionized the world, which is the vanguard of all the humble and exploited, what can it expect from imperialism, its most irreconcilable enemy?

And to teachers, professors, professionals, intellectuals, poets and artists, what can imperialism offer? What kind of benefits, what chance for a better and more equitable life, what purpose, what inducement, what desire to excel, to gain mastery beyond the first simple steps, can it offer to those who devotedly care for the generations of children and young people on whom imperialism will later gorge itself? What can it offer to these people who live on degrading wages in most countries, who almost everywhere suffer restrictions on their right of political and social expression, whose economic future doesn't exceed the bare limits of their shaky resources and compensation, who are buried in a gray life without prospects which ends with a pension that does not even meet half the cost of living? What "benefits" or "alliances" can imperialism offer them? . . .

If imperialism provides sources of aid to the professions, arts, and publications, it is always well understood that their products must reflect its interests, aims and "nothingness." On the other hand, the novels which attempt to reflect the reality of the world of imperialism's rapacious deeds; the poems aspiring to protest against its enslavement, its interference in life, in thought, in the very bodies of nations and peoples; and the militant arts which in their expression try to capture the forms and content of imperialism's aggression and the constant pressure on every progressive living and breathing thing and on all that is revolutionary, which teaches, which—full of light and conscience, of clarity and beauty—tries to guide men and peoples to better destinies, to the highest summits of life and justice—all these meet imperialism's severest censure. They run into obstacles, condemnation, and McCarthyite persecution. Its presses are closed to them; their names are barred from its columns of print and a campaign of the most atrocious silence is imposed against them—which is another contradiction of imperialism. For it is then that the writer, poet, painter, sculptor, the creator in any material, the scientist, begins truly to live in the tongue of the people, in the heart of millions of men throughout the world. Imperialism puts everything backward, deforms it, diverts it into its own channels for profit, to multiply its dollars; buying words or paintings or stutterings or turning into silence the expression of revolutionists, of progressive men, of those who struggle for the people and their needs.

We cannot forget, in this sad picture, the underprivileged children, the neglected, the futureless children of America.

America, a continent with a high birth rate, also has a high death rate. The mortality of children under a year old in eleven countries a few years ago was over 125 per thousand, and in seventeen others it stood at ninety children per thousand. In 102 nations of the world, on the other hand, the rate is fifty-one.

In Latin America, then, there die, sadly neglected, seventy-four out of a thousand in the first year after birth. In some Latin America countries that rate reaches 300 per thousand; thousands and thousands of children up to seven years old die of incredible diseases in America; diarrheas, pneumonias, malnutrition, hunger. Thousands and thousands are sick without hospital treatment, medicines; thousands and thousands walking about, victims of endemic cretinism, malaria, trachoma, and other diseases caused by contamination, lack of water and other necessities. Diseases of this nature are common among those Latin American countries where thousands and thousands of children are in agony, children of outcasts, children of the poor and of the petty bourgeoisie with a hard life and precarious means. The statistics, which would be redundant here, are blood-curdling. Any official publication of the international organizations gathers them by the hundreds. . . .

The Duty of Revolutionaries

The duty of every revolutionary is to make the revolution. It is known that the revolution will triumph in America and throughout the world, but it is not for revolutionaries to sit in the doorways of their houses waiting for the corpse of imperialism to pass by. The role of Job doesn't suit a revolutionary. Each year that the liberation of America is speeded up will mean the lives of millions of children saved, millions of intelligences saved for culture, an infinite quantity of pain spared the people. Even if the Yankee imperialists prepare a bloody drama for America, they will not succeed in crushing the peoples' struggles, they will only arouse universal hatred against themselves. And such a drama will also mark the death of their greedy and carnivorous system.

Unity

No nation in Latin America is weak—because each forms part of a family of 200 million brothers, who suffer the same miseries, who harbor the same sentiments, who have the same enemy, who dream about the same better future and who count upon the solidarity of all honest men and women throughout the world.

Great as was the epic of Latin American Independence, heroic as was that struggle, today's generation of Latin Americans is called upon to engage in an epic which is even greater and more decisive for humanity. For that struggle was for liberation from Spanish colonial power, from a decadent Spain invaded by the armies of Napoleon. Today the call for struggle is for liberation from the most powerful world imperialist center, from the strongest force of world imperialism and to render humanity a greater service than that rendered by our predecessors.

But this struggle, to a greater extent than the earlier one, will be waged by the masses, will be carried out by the people; the people are going to play a much more important role now than then, the leaders are less important and will be less important in this struggle than in the one before.

This epic before us is going to be written by the hungry Indian masses, the peasants without land, the exploited workers. It is going to be written by the progressive masses, the honest and brilliant intellectuals, who so greatly abound in our suffering Latin American countries. Struggles of masses and ideas. An epic which will be carried forward by our people, despised and maltreated by imperialism, our people, unreckoned with till today, who are now beginning to shake off their slumber. Imperialism considered us a weak and submissive flock; and now it begins to be terrified of that flock; a gigantic flock of 200 million Latin Americans in whom Yankee monopoly capitalism now sees its gravediggers.

This toiling humanity, inhumanly exploited, these paupers, controlled by the whip and overseer, have not been reckoned with or have been little reckoned with. From the dawn of independence their fate has been the same: Indians, gauchos, mestizos, zambos, quadroons, whites without property or income, all this human mass which formed the ranks of the "nation," which never reaped any benefits, which fell by the millions, which was cut into bits, which won independence from the mother country for the bourgeoisie, which was shut out from its share of the rewards, which continued to die of hunger, curable diseases and neglect, because for them there were never enough essentials of life—ordinary bread, a hospital bed, the medicine which cures, the hand which aids—their fate has been all the same.

But now from one end of the continent to the other they are signaling with clarity that the hour has come—the hour of their redemption. Now this anonymous mass, this America of color, somber, taciturn America, which all over the continent sings with the same sadness and disillusionment, now this mass is beginning to enter conclusively into its own history, is beginning to write it with its own blood, is beginning to suffer and die for it. . . .

Because now in the fields and mountains of America, on its slopes and prairies and in its jungles, in the wilderness or in the traffic of cities, this world is beginning with full cause to erupt. Anxious hands are stretched forth, ready to die for what is theirs, to win those rights which were laughed at by one and all for 500 years. Yes, now history will have to take the poor of America into account, the exploited and spurned of Latin America, who have decided to begin writing history for themselves for all time. Already they can be seen on the roads, on foot, day after day, in endless marches of hundreds of kilometers to the governmental "eminences," to obtain their rights.

Already they can be seen armed with stones, sticks, machetes, in one direction and another, each day, occupying lands, sinking hooks into the land which belongs to them and defending it with their lives. They can be seen carrying signs, slogans, flags; letting them flap in the mountain or prairie winds. And the wave of anger, of demands for justice, of claims for rights, which is beginning to sweep the lands of Latin America, will not stop. That wave will swell with every passing day. For that wave is composed of the greatest number, the majorities in every respect, those whose labor amasses the wealth and turns the wheels of history. Now, they are awakening from the long, brutalizing sleep to which they had been subjected.

For this great humanity has said, "enough!" and has begun to march. And their giant march will not be halted until they conquer true independence— for which they have vainly died more than once. Today, however, those who die will die like the Cubans at Playa Giron. They will die for their own true and never-to-be-surrendered independence.

Patria o Muerte! Venceremos!

THE PEOPLE OF CUBA
Havana, Cuba
Free Territory of America
February 4, 1962

3. *A North American Journalist Interviews Castro*

LEE LOCKWOOD

Lee Lockwood was in Havana when Castro came to power on January 1, 1959 and experienced first hand the national euphoria at the overthrow of Batista. On later trips to the island he was struck by the fact that the Cubans were enthusiastic in their support of Castro in spite of the image presented in the U.S. press of a country whose political regime maintained itself in power through terror and oppression. In 1965 and 1966 Lockwood conducted a series of interviews with Castro that became the basis of his book, *Castro's Cuba, Cuba's Fidel.* His purpose was to provide Castro with a forum to state his views "because while our government and our press attack him virulently and unceasingly, we are allowed to hear nothing from the man himself. Whether one agrees or disagrees with another, the best way to begin understanding him is by listening to what he has to say." Reproduced here are Lockwood's introduction and the portions of the interviews that concern education, political indoctrination, censorship, and personal power.

INTRODUCTION

It was my extremely good fortune to be in Cuba on the very day the Cuban Revolution took power. I can take no credit for this; it came about solely through the insistence of a friend and fellow journalist, Bob Henriques. In late December, 1958, we were together at Cape Canaveral (now Cape Kennedy), Florida, when he received an assignment from his editor to proceed immediately to Cuba. There were reports on the wires of heavy fighting around Santa Clara, and the editor correctly surmised that a "big story" might be about to break. I personally did not think so, but my friend argued with me so long and insistently that at last, with great reluctance, I agreed to accompany him to Havana.

So it was that my first visit to Cuba began, quite by accident, on New Year's Eve of 1958. In the early hours of the following morning dictator Fulgencio Batista fled to Santo Domingo, and Cuba unexpectedly found itself in the hands of Fidel Castro's rebel army. The city of Havana, which had exhibited its opposition to Batista by passing a sober and uncelebrant New Year's, erupted in joyous pandemonium which lasted for eight days. Mingled with the sounds of rejoicing the reports of firearms were frequently heard as the vanguard of Castro's rebel army, aided by the citizenry of Havana (nearly everybody seemed to have a gun or rifle), went about cleaning up pro-Batista pockets of resistance, sometimes in extended pitched battles. After three tumultuous days in Havana my friend and I commandeered a car, and after an arduous and dangerous journey down island, caught up with Fidel Castro in the town of Ciego de Avila, several hundred miles eastward. From there we followed him down the central highway on the remainder of his slow, triumphal progress from the Sierra Maestra to Havana.

No one who was in Cuba then, whether Cuban or foreigner, and regardless of his present opinion of Castro, could ever forget the spirit of exaltation and hope that permeated the island during the first days of the Revolution. The central highway was a 500-mile-long parade route lined an entire day in advance with Cubans waiting to catch a glimpse of Fidel as he passed. In each provincial capital Castro made a speech that lasted four, five, even six hours; some of them did not begin until after midnight, yet hundreds of thousands of *cubanos* listened to the end, cheering with delirium. During a speech in Santa Clara somebody released a flock of white pigeons; one spiraled upward through the spotlight beams to the high balcony where Castro was standing, lit upon his shoulder and perched there comfortably

From *Castro's Cuba, Cuba's Fidel* by Lee Lockwood (New York: Vintage, 1969), pp. xii–xix; 107–117, 147–151. Reprinted by permission.

while he spoke. Days later, entering Havana, Fidel addressed a crowd of 500,000 gathered in front of the Presidential Palace. Then he walked down the stairs, and, completely unescorted, passed through the entire assemblage, which chanted his name, *"Fi-del! Fi-del!"*—parting before him and closing behind him, like Moses passing through the Red Sea. It was a fabulous time, one of those rare, magical moments of history when cynics are transformed into romantics and romantics into fanatics, and everything seems possible. For Cubans, and for much of the onlooking world, Fidel Castro seemed a modern incarnation of the legendary savior-hero, a bearded Parsifal who had brought miraculous deliverance to an ailing Cuba.

It all seems a very long time ago—much longer than the seven years that have transpired since Fidel Castro came to power. Since that day almost everybody and everything Cuban have undergone great change, Castro himself not least of all. In retrospect, it is now clear that the true Cuban Revolution began *after* January, 1959, and that it is still going on. Like all revolutions, it has sacrificed the well-being of the few for that of the many and has brought with it violent controversy and division. Many thousands of those who jammed the sun-swept plaza in Havana that January afternoon, and cheered Fidel as he passed through them with the fever of prophecy in his eyes, now loiter in exile on the stoops of Manhattan and in the dark poolhalls of Miami's Flagler Street, embittered, dreaming with diminishing hope of the day when the United States will send its marines to liquidate Castro and restore them to their homeland. For the millions who remained in Cuba, those first euphoric days are an ever more distant memory, bearing scant relation to the years of economic hardships and political crises through which they have since struggled, or to the overwhelming sense of pressure beneath which they are now laboring to construct a Communist society within ninety miles of the American mainland.

In this process, the United States has played a significant and shameful role. Almost from the moment that Castro acceded to power, the U.S. government has done everything within its means, short of full-scale armed invasion (if one excludes the Bay of Pigs), to bring down his regime and replace it with a reactionary one representing the *status quo ante*. Except for differences of degree, the United States' policy toward Cuba has changed hardly at all through the administrations of Presidents Eisenhower, Kennedy and Johnson. Indeed, our policy of blockade, embargo, and infiltration has become so much a routine that the American public has largely forgotten Cuba. At this point in history, of course, Castro has his own very good tactical reasons for wishing to keep tensions with the United States tightly strung. But the fact is that neither the government nor the people of the United States have made more than a token effort to understand Cuba in terms of her cultural heritage, her ethnic temperament, and her national aspirations, all of which differ markedly from our own. We show little comprehension of what a revolution entails or of the forces that produce it. We are surprised that Cubans do not seem eager to adopt for themselves our political institutions (which we regard as sacred), and that they are outraged when we tell them that Cuba lies within "the United States' sphere of influence" and therefore must "sever its links with the international Communist movement," as was announced in a State Department White Paper on Cuba published a few days before the Bay of Pigs invasion.

I made three more journalistic trips to Cuba in 1959 and 1960. Then came the Bay of Pigs and the missile crisis, and nearly four years passed before I was again able to obtain a visa, in 1964, when Castro briefly opened the doors to the American press to cover the 26th of July celebration in Santiago de Cuba. After almost four weeks of traveling in every province of the island, including an exciting and hectic seven-day, cross-country trip taken in the company of Castro himself (it was unforeseen and came about through the slenderest of coincidences), I returned to my country amazed at the contradictions between the beliefs about Cuba popularly held in the United States (and reinforced by the reporting of the U.S. press) and what I had actually seen with my own eyes. There had been considerable changes during the four years, of course, not all of them salutary. But I could find little evidence of the standard image of Cuba so luridly painted by American newspapers, magazines, and television: a Cuba whose economy was crumbling, whose populace was in tatters and near starvation, and whose political regime had lost its popular support and maintained itself in power through terror and oppression and with the aid of Russian soldiers. Instead, I found that in spite of the American blockade, nearly everyone was working and had money; that in spite of rationing, people were well clothed and more than adequately fed (especially in the interior); that there were few Russian soldiers to be seen anywhere, and that, contrary to all pronouncements by the U.S. State Department, Castro still enjoyed the support—the enthusiastic and affectionate support—of a great majority of Cubans.

These preliminary revelations, together with my personal fascination with the singular character of Fidel Castro, were what prompted me to attempt this book-length study. Taking advantage of Fidel's offhand invitation to "come back whenever you like," I returned to Cuba in May, 1965, and stayed three and a half months. During that time I traveled widely, without supervision or restriction, photographing freely and talking with hundreds of Cubans. I also made three separate trips with Castro. A promised interview with him, which almost did not take place, materialized suddenly at the last moment and grew into a marathon seven-day conversation in a secluded house on the Isle of Pines. I finally left Cuba at the end of August, returning for three weeks in October to cover the exodus of refugees from Camarioca (for *Life* magazine) and returning again in May, 1966. On both of these occasions I spent several hours with Castro and was able to make corrections of and additions to the original interview.

Of all the political leaders of the contemporary world, Fidel Castro is one of the most influential and easily the most interesting. Few would question this assertion, I think. Yet, inevitably, there will be many who criticize this book because it grants Castro so much space in which to set forth his views. (The interview, edited to less than half its original length, fills three chapters of the book.) However, I have provided Castro with such a forum precisely because, while our government and our press attack him virulently and unceasingly, we are allowed to hear nothing from the man himself. Officially, we don't like Fidel Castro; therefore, the entire American public must close its eyes and hold its ears (as if by so doing we could make him go away). Yet if he really is our enemy, as dangerous to us as we are told, then it seems obvious that we ought to know as much about him as possible. And if he is not—then that fact should be made known. Whether one agrees or disagrees with another, the best way to begin understanding him is by listening to what he has to say.

Finally, this book has an intentionally limited scope. It is neither a political analysis nor a sociological study of the Cuban Revolution, nor a psychological examination of its leader. All three kinds of studies are badly needed and other people should write them. This book is intended as an introduction to both Fidel Castro and revolutionary Cuba, nothing more. The title, *Castro's Cuba, Cuba's Fidel*, is meant to suggest that the focus is on both phenomena simultaneously—upon the interrelationship between the man and the society which he leads, an interrelationship so close as to border upon identity. To borrow a term from photography, the effect striven for is something like that of an intentional double exposure on one piece of film; that is, a double portrait of Cuba and Castro together, with Fidel's great image superimposed upon the foreground. Since contemporary Cuban society is dominated in every conceivable way by Castro's mind and personality, I believe that this is an accurate working image for an introduction to the Cuban Revolution.

LEE LOCKWOOD

New York City
July 26, 1966

Lockwood's Interview with Castro

EDUCATION

LOCKWOOD: You seem to have awakened a great interest in education. It seems that there is hardly anyone in Cuba these days under the age of seventy who is not studying something.

CASTRO: That is true, an extraordinary interest has been awakened. If you remember that our population is some seven-and-a-half million inhabitants, about 30 percent of the population is studying, that is, some two-and-one-half million people. That includes one million adults.

LOCKWOOD: One of the first big programs that you created was the system for training student-teachers in Minas del Frío[1] and elsewhere. How has that worked out—are you satisfied with the results?

CASTRO: Yes, it has been a great success. Before, it was very difficult to get teachers who would go to teach in the mountains. Now, students from every province and from all the towns of the country go into that school, and when they graduate they begin to teach in the mountains. At present we have some fifteen thousand young people[2] studying to be teachers. In 1965, the first thousand graduated; beginning in 1968, four thousand per year will graduate; and between 1970 and 1980, we will graduate a total of fifty thousand teachers. And we have this well organized. During their last two years of school the students study and teach. By 1968, practically all the primary schools in Havana will be staffed by students from the Teachers' Institute, and the present teachers, through advanced training courses, will go on to teach in the secondary schools. This program is progressing very well.

LOCKWOOD: I've seen some of the young teachers in action—they have a great deal of enthusiasm.

CASTRO: Terrific spirit! Really, great teachers have developed. We also have about ten thousand[3] workers studying in the agricultural technology insti-

---

[1] *Minas del Frio* ("The Mines of the Cold") is a school camp for student-teachers located in Oriente Province high in the Sierra Maestra Mountains. It is the first stage in Cuba's unique crash program to acquire a corps of trained teachers for the rural area schools.

[2] By 1968, the figure had risen to twenty-nine thousand.

[3] Fifty thousand in 1968.

tutes, workers from the countryside who have been outstanding in their work. We send them first to elementary school courses until they reach the level of the eighth grade, and afterward they study for two years in agricultural technology centers. When they finish and go back to work, they will have a level of preparation that will allow them to matriculate in the university through correspondence courses.

Really, it would be worth the trouble if all these things that are being done today in Cuba, which in our judgment are the only way in the long run to resolve the problems of the country, could be compared with what is being done elsewhere. Is anything similar being carried out in other Latin American countries?

We stand ready to show these things to everybody who might come to Cuba in good faith, to make an objective appraisal. We would show them everything, in order that they should see both good and bad, what would please them and what would displease them, things that are going well and things that are not. We are sure that the balance is very positive. The years we are now going through are the most difficult, and they are already being left behind. Within four or five years the position of Cuba will be incomparable; it will be superior to that of any other country in Latin America.

LOCKWOOD: Is it true that a young man cannot enter the university unless he is a revolutionary?

CASTRO: Well, there is no regulation, but there is a policy that is applied through the students' organizations, by means of agreements that are discussed and adopted in public general assemblies, in which the mass of all the students of a department participate. It is required at least that one not be *counter*revolutionary.

To train a university-educated technician costs thousands upon thousands of pesos. Who pays for that? The people. Should we then train technicians who later on are going to leave to work in the United States? I don't believe that is right. The country, in making this expenditure, has the right to the guarantee that it is training technicians who are going to serve the country. The future intellectuals of the country are being educated in the university, and without any hesitation we must try to see that those intellectuals are revolutionaries.

LOCKWOOD: How can you expect a young man of sixteen or seventeen to have made up his mind politically? Even you yourself, in fact, were not a revolutionary when you entered the university.

CASTRO: True, I was not a revolutionary; hardly anybody was. I was one of the privileged when I went to the university.

LOCKWOOD: But isn't that a rather early age at which to expect a young man to have formed himself politically?

CASTRO: No, at seventeen a boy can be politically developed. However, that wasn't the real problem. The problem was that, on account of compulsory military service, some persons from bourgeois families who had already left school and who were not seventeen, but twenty-five, twenty-seven, or thirty, tried to enroll in the university to avoid fulfilling this obligation, since university students are exempted.

LOCKWOOD: But that was before. I am asking about now—why is it not possible now to allow young men to enter the university even if they have a questioning attitude about political and social matters?

CASTRO: We have to insist on certain intellectual requirements; that is, a good record in studies, high motivation, and good conduct. Even a questioning attitude about political and social matters could not be a good reason to prevent young people from going into the university. If that young person has "human sensibility," science and truth will convert him into a revolutionary.

LOCKWOOD: What does it mean that a student must have a record of "good conduct"?

CASTRO: Good conduct means his behavior as a student and as a citizen.

LOCKWOOD: In his private life too?

CASTRO: Academic and civil. But a boy doesn't have to be necessarily a Marxist-Leninist in order to study at the university. For example, a Catholic boy can enroll, a Protestant boy can enroll.

LOCKWOOD: Can he be neutral to the Revolution and still be accepted?

CASTRO: It is enough if he is an honorable individual who is willing to study in order to live and work in the country and who embodies the necessary requirements of capability and motivation. You must not forget that in a revolution there are hardly any neutrals.[1]

POLITICAL INDOCTRINATION

LOCKWOOD: To what extent does the curriculum in Cuban schools include political indoctrination?

CASTRO: What you call political indoctrination would perhaps be more correctly called social education. After all, do not forget that those children are being educated to live in a Communist society. From an early age they must be discouraged from every egotistical feeling in the enjoyment of material things, such as the sense of individual property, and be encouraged toward the greatest possible common effort and a spirit of cooperation. Therefore, they must receive not only instruction of a scientific kind but also education for social life and a broad general culture.

---

[1] This last sentence was added later by Castro. At the same time, he deleted the first sentence of his original reply; "It doesn't matter whether he is neutral toward the Revolution."

LOCKWOOD: Is this "culture" to which they are exposed selected from a political point of view?

CASTRO: Of course some knowledge is of a universal kind, while other subjects that are taught may be influenced by a definite conception. For instance, history cannot be taught as a simple repetition of events that have occurred without any interrelationship, in an accidental way. We have a scientific conception of history and of the development of human society, and of course in some subjects there is and will be influences from our philosophy.

LOCKWOOD: A Marxist influence?

CASTRO: Yes.

LOCKWOOD: What about in the arts? Is there an attempt to teach the history of art and literature and their criticism from the Marxist point of view?

CASTRO: We have very few qualified people as yet who could even try to give a Marxist interpretation of the problems of art.

Concerning art criticism . . . I think that that too is a complex problem. I have the intention of calling together a group of outstanding students in the humanities faculty of the university who are totally lacking in prejudice and put them to thoroughly studying the problems of culture and art, so that we might one day have a team capable of correctly approaching these problems. We don't suppose that all the political leaders should have an encyclopedic knowledge and be in a position to speak the last word on matters of culture and of art. I would not consider myself sufficiently skilled to make decisions in that realm without professional advice from really qualified people in whose sound and revolutionary judgment I could trust.

As a revolutionary, it is my understanding that one of our fundamental concerns must be that all the manifestations of culture be placed at the service of man, developing in him all the most positive feelings. For me, art is not an end in itself. Man is its end; making man happier, making man better. I do not conceive of any manifestations of culture, of science, of art, as purposes in themselves. I think that the purpose of science and culture is man.

LOCKWOOD: Those words "happier," "better," can be interpreted very broadly—

CASTRO: They *should* be interpreted in a broad sense. I don't think there has ever existed a society in which all the manifestations of culture have not been at the service of some cause or concept. Our duty is to see that the whole is at the service of the kind of man we wish to create.

But doesn't this mean that perhaps every work must have a political content in itself? No, that is not necessary. I believe that the content of any artistic work of any kind—its very quality for its own sake, without its necessarily having to carry a message—can give rise to a beneficial and noble feeling in the human being.

CENSORSHIP

LOCKWOOD: Is there any attempt to exert control over the production of art in Cuba? For example, of literature?

CASTRO: All manifestations of art have different characteristics. For example, movies are different from painting; movies are a modern industry requiring a lot of resources. It is not the same thing to make a film as it is to paint a picture or write a book. But if you ask whether there is control—no.

LOCKWOOD: One thing that is surprising is the amount of creative freedom given to your artists, the painters and sculptors, as compared with other Socialist countries. However, this liberalism seems to apply to a lesser extent to literature.

CASTRO: Because literature involves the publication of books. It is principally an economic problem. The resources that are available are not sufficient for all the needs for the printing of textbooks, for example, schoolbooks, reference works, books of a general nature. That is, we cannot waste paper. That is one of the limiting factors. This doesn't mean that the political factor doesn't have its influence too. A book that we did not believe to be of some value wouldn't have a chance of being published.

LOCKWOOD: In other words, an author who wrote a novel that contained counterrevolutionary sentiments couldn't possibly get it published?

CASTRO: At present, no. The day will come when all the resources will be available, that is, when such a book would not be published to the detriment of a textbook or of a book having universal value in world literature. Then there will be resources to publish books on the basis of a broader criterion, and one will be able to argue whatever one wishes about any theme. I, especially, am a partisan of the widest possible discussion in the intellectual realm.

Why? Because I believe in the free man, I believe in the well-educated man, I believe in the man able to think, in the man who acts always out of conviction, without fear of any kind. And I believe that ideas must be able to defend themselves. I am opposed to the blacklists of books, prohibited films and all such things. What is my personal ideal of the kind of people that we wish to have in the future? People sufficiently cultivated and educated to be capable of making a correct judgment about anything without fear of coming into contact with ideas that could confound or deflect them. For example, how do we think of ourselves? We think that we could read any book or see any film, about any theme, without changing our fundamental beliefs; and if there is in a book a solid argument about something that could be useful, that could be positive, that we are capable of analyzing and evaluating it.

May all the men and women of our country be like that in the future! That is the kind of man we wish to shape. If we did not think like that, we would be men with no faith in our own convictions, in our own philosophy.

LOCKWOOD: But such an atmosphere is not possible at the present time?

CASTRO: It would be an illusion to think so. First on account of the economic problems involved, and second because of the struggle in which we are engaged.

LOCKWOOD: Is it also in the name of that "struggle" that the Cuban press writes so one-sidedly about the United States?

CASTRO: I am not going to tell you that we don't do that. It's true, everything that we say about the United States refers essentially to the worst aspects, and it is very rare that things in any way favorable to the United States will be published here. We simply have a similar attitude to the attitude of your country. I mean that we always try to create the worst opinion of everything there is in the United States, as a response to what they have always done with us. The only difference is that we do not write falsehoods about the United States. I told you that we emphasize the worst things, that we omit things that could be viewed as positive, but we do not invent any lies.

LOCKWOOD: But it amounts to the same thing. By emphasizing only our bad qualities, you create a distortion that is the equivalent of a lie.

CASTRO: That depends on what you mean by "lie." I agree that it is a distortion. A lie is simply the willful invention of facts that do not exist. There is a difference between a distortion and a lie, although unquestionably they have some effects of a similar kind.

This is not ideal. But it is the result of realities that have not been imposed by us. In a world of peace, in which genuine trust and respect among peoples existed, this wouldn't happen. And we are not responsible for this situation.

LOCKWOOD: But if you persist in promoting these distortions, which encourage only hostile feelings in your citizens, how can you ever expect to have peace?

CASTRO: Again, we are not the ones responsible. It is the United States who cut all relations with Cuba.

LOCKWOOD: I don't think that has anything to do with the question.

CASTRO: I am simply fulfilling my duty of speaking to you with complete frankness when I tell you how things are from our side. I have the honesty to speak like this—how many leaders of the United States would speak in the same terms?

LOCKWOOD: You are most frank. But I would like to insist on this point a bit longer. In my personal opinion, you have more to gain by keeping your society open to knowledge of all kinds about the United States than by persisting in painting a distorted image of us. For example, in recent years there has been an increasing effort on the part of our government to support the Negroes' fight for civil rights and strong legislation has been passed. This is something which could also be covered by the Cuban press, besides the fact that there are Negroes rioting in California, or that the Ku Klux Klan is marching in Georgia and Alabama, which is the only kind of thing you ever publish here.

CASTRO: It is my understanding that news of that legislation was published here, although naturally we have a substantially different point of view about it than you do. We believe that the problem of discrimination has an economic content and basis appropriate to a class society in which man is exploited by man.

This is clearly a difficult, complex problem. We ourselves went through the experience of discrimination. Discrimination disappeared when class privileges disappeared, and it has not cost the Revolution much effort to resolve that problem. I don't believe it could have been done in the United States. It would be a little absurd to speak at this moment of a revolution there. Perhaps there will never even be a revolution in the United States, in the classic sense of the word, but rather evolutionary changes. I am sure, for example, that within five hundred years North American society will bear no similarity to the present one. Probably by that time they won't have problems of discrimination.

LOCKWOOD: But why not speak of the evolutionary changes in the United States too? Why not tell the Cuban people the whole story?

CASTRO: Because altogether there have not been any evolutionary changes in a positive sense in the United States. But rather, politically speaking, a true regression. From our general point of view the policy of the United States, above all her foreign policy, has advanced more and more toward an ultra-reactionary position.

LOCKWOOD: We were not talking about United States foreign policy.

CASTRO: In reality that is what affects us most.

LOCKWOOD: Since we're on the subject, it also seems to me that anybody who has a point of view substantially different from the governmental line about almost anything has very little opportunity to express himself in the press here. In fact, there is extremely little criticism of any kind in the Cuban press. It seems to be an arm of the government.

CASTRO: Well, what you say is true. There is very little criticism. An enemy of Socialism cannot write in our newspapers—but we don't deny it, and we don't go around proclaiming a hypothetical freedom of the press where it actually doesn't exist, the way you people do. Furthermore, I admit that our press is deficient in this respect. I don't believe that this lack of criticism is a healthy thing. Rather, criticism is a very useful and positive instrument, and I think that all of us must learn to make use of it.

LOCKWOOD: Don't you think that there are Cuban writers who would make use of that instrument if there existed an atmosphere in which their statements would be taken as constructive criticism?

CASTRO: Criticism, yes—but not work in the service of the enemy or of the counterrevolution.

LOCKWOOD: But who is to decide at any given point which criticism is constructive and which is counterrevolutionary?

CASTRO: Well, we are in the midst of a struggle, a more or less open war, and when, for example, the United States has been faced with such situations, what they have done is to repress without consideration all those who opposed the interests of the country while it was at war. When you were at war against the Nazis, you had such a policy.

LOCKWOOD: But you haven't answered the question. Who is to decide?

CASTRO: Under such circumstances, the party decides, the political power, the revolutionary power. Naturally, when we no longer live under these circumstances, the causes that require severe measures will actually disappear.

LOCKWOOD: But in the meantime there is almost no criticism of any kind in your society, either in the press or in the literature, radio and television, or in any of the other organs of communication in Cuba.

CASTRO: Certainly there is a minimum of criticism. And there is something more: we have to pay attention to the training of the journalistic cadres, because millions of people read what they say and write. If we are going to have a people of wide culture, then the men who have daily contact with them must have a wide culture too, to be really qualified for the social functions which they perform. We believe that journalism in its different forms has an extraordinary importance in modern life.

Not that I would tell you we delude ourselves that under the present circumstances journalism can have any other function more important than that of contributing to the political and revolutionary goals of our country. We have a goal, a program, an objective to fulfill, and that objective essentially controls the activity of all the journalists. I would say that it essentially controls the labor of all the intellectual workers. I am not going to deny it.

LOCKWOOD: But isn't there a certain danger inherent in suppressing all forms of criticism—?

CASTRO: I agree! I do not say at all that the absence of criticism can be useful. On the contrary, it could even be harmful.

LOCKWOOD: What do you think has been responsible for the growth of this atmosphere?

CASTRO: I believe various circumstances, but fundamentally the situation of emergency and strain under which the country has been living, required to survive by the skin of its teeth. Almost all activities have had to be subordinated to the need for survival.

LOCKWOOD: One thing which may have influenced this atmosphere of inhibition is your own strong personal position against "counter-revolutionary" attitudes. Isn't it possible, once this climate has been established, that an intellectual may come to fear that any critical idea may be interpreted by the government as counterrevolutionary? That is, perhaps the strong position you have always taken has shut off a line of communication between you and people of intelligence who are in a position to see that something is wrong or who may have a better idea. By stifling critical comment, don't you make it unlikely that you will hear any ideas but your own?

CASTRO: I confess that those are themes which we have to pay attention to in the near future. Because other things have been occupying our attention, we have not been able to concern ourselves with such obvious deficiencies as these.

LOCKWOOD: This lack of a critical perspective seems to apply in education as well. In my visits to schools in various parts of the country I found generally that the children are being taught to accept concepts at face value rather than to question them. Don't you feel that this is potentially dangerous to the intellectual future of your country?

CASTRO: I think that the education of students depends very much upon the level of training and capability of the teacher. That is, it is not a question of policy. The child must be taught to think; to develop his intelligence must be the essential objective of teaching.

Anyway, I am going to concern myself with the observations you have made. One of our fundamental concerns has been the training of a corps of teachers on the highest pedagogical level. It must never be forgotten that the conditions under which we have lived are not normal ones; they are conditions of violent class struggle, clashes of ideas, of judgments, of feelings. All this can contribute to the creation of a certain environment, a certain atmosphere of inhibition. . . . However, this was not what we were most concerned about in these first days. What concerned us much more was to open a school in a place where there was no teacher, to teach the ABC's, to teach reading and writing. In that first stage we were concerned with the elemental things in education, and many things had to be improvised because we lacked skilled personnel.

I think it is logical that we should make sure that the children now in elementary school and who are going to be the future intellectuals, the future citizens of our country, should not be educated in a dogmatic way, but should develop their capacity to think and to judge for themselves.

LOCKWOOD: I've also noticed in the classrooms a tendency to approach facts dogmatically. For example, we were talking before about how the Cuban press purposely does not paint a well-rounded picture of the United States. Well, the interpretations and the "facts" about the United States which are presented to the students in their classes are precisely those printed in the newspapers, repeated without clarification. What is going to happen when all of these young boys and girls who have been receiving this one-sided picture all through school, perhaps ever since the first grade, become adults?

CASTRO: Without doubt they will have a very bad opinion of the United States and about everything it represents, in the same way that in the United States children are educated with a very bad opinion of Communism. It is lamentable, but it is a reality.

LOCKWOOD: Someday the United States and Cuba are going to have friendly relations again. When that happens, won't you have to deal with the legacy of this bad feeling with which you are indoctrinating your youth?

CASTRO: This is not an easy question to reply to. Besides, nobody has ever before posed this question. Actually this is the first time that I have heard it posed by a North American. Nor have we posed it to ourselves; it can be said that we have never been consciously concerned about that problem.

Perhaps that is due partly to our great pessimism about whether the American people really have much opportunity to express their own opinions, or to change a situation. It is possible that even we ourselves have not fully understood how deeply the feeling of solidarity with the Negroes has penetrated the hearts of the North American people. That is, we have no faith at all in the government of the United States, and that could also have led us toward a certain degree of underestimation of the people of the United States. But this is not the result of a deliberate policy.

Maybe when you publish your book many of those who work in our press will also meditate on those questions. I, for my part, in conversations with them, can express those concerns and ask them to meditate a little on these themes. That for the sake of something you say which I think is true: that someday—which I do not at all believe will be immediate, but rather a great deal of time will pass—it will have to happen that better relations exist between our two peoples.

LOCKWOOD: It seems to me that we should try to lessen that time as much as possible, rather than to prolong it for unnecessary reasons.

CASTRO: I think that is reasonable. Let's go to lunch. . . .

PERSONAL POWER

LOCKWOOD: It is a commonly held view in my country that you are a dictator with absolute power, that the Cuban people have no voice in their government, and that there is no sign that this is going to change.

CASTRO: I think we have to state the ideas a little more precisely. We are Marxists and look upon the state as an instrument of the ruling class to exercise power. What you people call "representative democracy" is, in our opinion, the dictatorship of the capitalists, and the North American state is an instrument of that class domination, from the domestic point of view as well as from the international point of view.

I believe that these are not simply theoretical positions. The ruling classes exercise power through the state and through all the means that they can depend on to defend their system. They depend not only on the state, its administration, and its armed forces for this purpose, but on all the rest of the instruments at the service of the system: the dominant political parties, which are completely controlled by those classes and take turns in power, and all the media of communication—the press, radio, television, newspapers, magazines, movies, publishing houses, technical and scientific societies, public education, the universities. All those media are at the service of a system that is under the control of the wealthy of the United States.

Naturally, you might tell me that in the United States it is possible to publish a book that is against the government or to write some critical articles. This doesn't at all threaten the security of the system. Anything that might threaten the system would be repressed, as has been proven. Even activities that constitute no danger at all to the United States have been persecuted; various personalities who were characterized, not by Marxist, but by progressive thought—in the movies, in television, in the universities, and in other intellectual media—have been investigated, have been imprisoned, have suffered persecution, have been required to appear before the Committee on so-called Un-American Affairs, with all the consequences that this implies. So, a real intellectual terror exists in the United States. The people who have the courage to express progressive opinions are few, out of fear of bringing down those consequences upon themselves. Criticisms are made in the United States, yes, but *within* the system, not against it. The system is something untouchable, sacred, against which only genuine exceptions dare to express themselves.

So I ask myself whether that isn't really a class dictatorship, the imposition of a system by all material and moral means? In the United States the people vote every four years for one of the candidates that the two parties choose, but that doesn't imply any change.

On the other hand, we think of the revolutionary state as an instrument of the power of the workers and peasants, that is, of the manual and intellectual workers, directed by a party that is composed of the best men from among them. We organize our party with the participation of the workers of all the centers of labor, who express their opinions in a completely free way, in assemblies, proposing and supporting those whom they believe should be members of the party or opposing those whom they believe should not be.

Our party is the representative of the workers and peasants, of the working class, in the same way that the Congress of the United States is the representative of the capitalists. So that our system is a class system too, in a period of transition. Ultimately, we will go even a little further and proclaim the nonnecessity of the sate, the disappearance of the state with the disappearance of social class. When Communism is a reality, that instrument will no longer be necessary as a coercive force by which one class maintains its domination over another, since neither exploiters nor exploited will exist. As Engels said, "The government over the people will be replaced by the administration of things and by the conduct of the processes of production."

You ask about power concentrated in one person. The truth is that, although I perform certain functions inherent to the offices that I hold within the state and the party, my authority to make decisions is really less than that of the President of the United States. If we are going to speak about personal power, in no other country in the world, not even under absolute monarchies, has there ever been such a high degree of power concentrated in one person as is concentrated in the President of the United States. That officeholder whom you call President can even take the country into a thermonuclear war without having to consult the Congress. There is no case like it in history. He intervened in Vietnam on his own decision. He intervened in Santo Domingo on his own decision.[5] Thus, that functionary you call President is the most complete expression of the dictatorship of a class which on occasions exercises itself by conceding really absolute powers to one man.

Why don't you North Americans think a little about these questions, instead of accepting as an irrefutable truth your definition of democracy? Why don't you analyze the realities and the meaning of the words a little, instead of repeating them mechanically?

We honestly consider our system infinitely more democratic than that of the United States, because it is the genuine expression of the will of the vast majority of the country, made up not of the rich but of the poor.

LOCKWOOD: How do the majority express this "will"?

CASTRO: By struggling and fighting against oppression. They revealed it in the Sierra Maestra by defeating the well-equipped army of Batista. They revealed it at Playa Girón [6] by destroying the mercenary invaders. They revealed it in the Escambray in wiping out the counterrevolutionary bands. They reveal it constantly, in every public demonstration that the Revolution organizes with

---

[5] Castro is referring to President Lyndon B. Johnson.
[6] The Bay of Pigs.

the multitudinous support of the masses. They have revealed it with their firm support of the Revolutionary Government in the face of the economic blockade, and by the fact that there are hundreds of thousands of men ready to die defending their Revolution.

LOCKWOOD: But if Cuba is not a dictatorship, in what way are your people able to effectively influence the leadership?

CASTRO: I believe that there is a mutual influence of the people over the leaders and of the leaders over the people. The first and most important thing is to have a genuine affection and respect for the people. The people can feel that and it wins them over. Sometimes the leaders have to take responsibilities on their own; sometimes they have to walk at the head of the people. The important thing is the identification of the leaders with the necessities, the aspirations and the feelings of the people. There are many ways of establishing this identification. The best way of all is to maintain the most immediate contact possible with the masses.

LOCKWOOD: Che Guevara, in his book *Socialism and Man in Cuba,* characterizes the manner of communication between the leaders of the Revolution and the people as "almost intuitive." Do you agree that there is this intuitive element in your leadership of the people?

CASTRO: At certain moments, under certain circumstances, when there is a great sense of confidence between the leaders and the masses, yes. Especially in such a convulsive process as a revolution, the intuitive element can be necessary at the beginning, but not later on, when the revolution advances and is consolidated, because in such a process millions of men raise their political culture and their revolutionary conscience; thousands of capable men arise from the masses to take on the tasks of organization, of administration and of policy-making; and all this creates a developed culture, a powerful and organized force. Individual men begin to have less importance to the degree that the whole social task becomes more and more a collective undertaking, the work of millions of persons and the responsibility of tens of thousands of men.

LOCKWOOD: But do you feel that a kind of intuitive communication between yourself and the masses during these first years has kept you from making bad mistakes?

CASTRO: I don't know how a leader can arise or how a revolution can be led without a great sensitivity for understanding the problems of the people and without the ability, too, of formulating the means of confronting and resolving those problems. A revolution is not an easy process. It is hard, difficult. Great errors can cost the life of the revolution. Not only the leadership of the revolution, but its very life.

There must be not only intuition, an emotional communication of the leaders with the people, but there are other requisites. One has to find

solutions, one has to put them into operation, one has to go forward, o
to choose the path correctly, the way of doing what has to be done.
leaders in a revolutionary process are not infallible receptacles of what th
people think. One must find out how the people think and sometimes combat
certain opinions, certain ideas, certain points of view which, in the judgment
of the leaders, are mistaken. One cannot conceive of the leader as a simple
carrier of ideas, a simple collector of opinions and impressions. He has to be
also a creator of opinions, a creator of points of view; he has to *influence the
masses.*

LOCKWOOD: Can you cite an example from your own experience when the
leadership was in error about something and was so informed by the Cuban
people?

CASTRO: Well, certain omissions or problems, rather than mistakes. For
example, I remember visiting some regions of the Sierra Maestra where the
peasants talked to me about the lack of credit. Also problems of the lack of
roads, of medical services, a certain negligence on the part of the administrative leaders in certain regions. Cases like that occur often. But some
particular error about which the leadership was informed by the people?
Doubtless there must have been such mistakes, but offhand I don't recall any.

LOCKWOOD: Che Guevara, in the same book, says that whenever revolutionary leaders are mistaken, the fact manifests itself in a reduction of the spirit
of labor on the part of the workers, and in this way the leaders become aware
that something is wrong. He gives the example of Aníbal Escalante.

CASTRO: Good. The example of Aníbal Escalante is a good example. Although, rather than an error, it could be considered as a wrong that developed in the course of the process, because at the beginning our movement
was one force among many forces. It is true that ours was the most influential. A whole period of unification passed, of overcoming reservations and
distrust, and in that period of union not everything was done in a harmonious
way.

When you began to talk about this theme I thought you were referring to
concrete mistakes of an administrative kind, but I see from the example you
gave that you meant political mistakes that could affect the general course of
the Revolution.

LOCKWOOD: But wasn't the problem created by Escalante potentially of great
practical importance—?

CASTRO: Potentially it was important, because sectarianism was discouraging
the masses and alienating them from the leadership. It was provoking discontent, encouraging opportunism, and creating a whole series of similar problems. And we had to overcome the problem without creating another kind of
sectarianism, without making divisions in the ranks of the Revolution. There
have been sectarianisms of different kinds which achieved greater or lesser

ave actually always fought against all forms of sec-
where they exist or what part or organization they come
are all damaging.

scalante is an example, indeed, of mistakes, of wrongs
course of a revolution which sometimes are not the
t simply phenomena that appear and must be rectified.
Often there are currents that get out of hand for which you cannot hold
anybody in particular responsible.[7]

4. *Castro at the Age of Sixty*

TAD SZULC

Castro has been the subject of large numbers of biographies from the earliest
days of the guerrilla struggle. Whether panegyrics, polemics, or scholarly
studies, these books tend to exalt or excoriate the Cuban leader. Tad Szulc is an
anthoritative and well-connected journalist who had his first conversations with
Castro in 1959 when he was the *New York Times* correspondent in Havana. His
biography, *Fidel: A Critical Portrait* was completed in 1986 with the collabora-
tion of Cuban officials, and is one of the most detailed works available in
English. Szulc conceals neither his own liberal, anti-communist viewpoint nor
his overall admiration for the genius and character of his charismatic subject. In
the section reproduced below, he surveys developments in Cuba between 1976
and 1986 and paints a vivid portrait of Castro at the age of sixty.

The first great milestones in Fidel Castro's revolution were the victory in 1959
and the creation of the new Communist party in 1965 as the ruling political

[7] Aníbal Escalante was Secretary of the Partido Socialista Popular (PSP), Cuba's pre-revolution-
ary, Stalinist-oriented Communist Party. When Fidel formally espoused Communism, he gave
Escalante the job of constructing the nation-wide party apparatus for a new Communist government. Soon, however, Castro feared that he was creating his own power base. On March 26, 1962
he denounced Escalante in a four-hour television address and ordered him into exile. Returning
to Cuba in 1964 Escalante lived as a private citizen. In 1968 he was again denounced by Castro
for taking Moscow's side in the ideological polemic between Cuba and the USSR. A trial
followed in which Escalante and his collaborators received prison sentences. The case is
important because it demonstrates the tension between old and new Communists in Cuba which
was resolved in favor of the new.
From *Fidel: A Critical Portrait* by Ted Szulc (New York: William Morrow, 1986), pp. 642–653.
Reprinted by permission.

body in Cuba. The next milestone was the "institutionalization of the Revolution," as Castro called it, through the promulgation of a new Cuban constitution on February 24, 1976. Over the past seventeen years, the "Fundamental Law," drafted immediately by the first revolutionary government, and literally thousands of laws and regulations formed the juridical framework of the Cuban state, though no doubt ever existed as to where actual power reposed.

Nevertheless, laws had to be refined, revised, and codified, and, as much as anything else, full legitimacy had to be granted to the socialist character of Cuba and its Communist objectives. Consequently, in October 1974, Blas Roca, secretary general of the old Communist party and a member of the Politburo of the new party, was named chairman of a commission charged with the task of drafting the new constitution. The draft was published six months later, then it was submitted for discussion to millions of Cubans in party and military organizations, labor unions, and youth and women's groups. Clearly, no basic changes resulted from these discussions, which Castro regarded as "direct democracy," but—quite surprising to the regime—people wanted that democracy to be even more direct.

An innovation in the constitutional draft was the creation of a type of local self-government called "Popular Power" (no such governmental structure exists in other Communist countries) capped by a National Assembly with legislative functions described as the "supreme organ of state power." A profound division developed, however, over the method of selecting deputies to the National Assembly. Some advocated direct elections and some favored choice by municipal Popular Power assemblies. In the first instance, voters would at least potentially have a voice in the formulation of main national policies, and the decision-making process would have to be made reasonably visible to the public. In the second instance, membership in the National Assembly could be determined through political manipulation on the local level with candidates nominated from the municipal assemblies or by party and government officials. Inasmuch as the draft also provided for National Assembly deputies "to explain the policy of the state and periodically render account to [the electors]," direct elections could have been disastrous for the central government. So bitter was the internal dispute over this point that the constitution, on which a popular referendum was held on February 15, 1976, failed to spell out the method of election. Only *after* 97.7 percent of the voters had approved the charter, did the Central Preparatory Commission, headed by Fidel Castro, insert the provision that "the National Assembly . . . is composed of deputies elected by the Municipal Assemblies." This was the end of the first and last major attempt to democratize Cuban Marxism.

The constitutional referendum was preceded in December 1975 by the first Congress of the Cuban Communist Party, chaired by Castro and attended by Mikhail Suslov, the chief Soviet Communist ideologue and one of the most powerful members of the Politburo. Castro's report to the Congress was a 248-page document (in book form) chronicling the history of Cuba, the *Fidelista* revolutionary movement, its transformation into socialism, the first ten years of the Communist party, the achievements of the revolution, and the Cuban struggle against "imperialism" and in support of "liberation movements." Although Cuban troops were fighting in Angola even as Castro addressed the Congress, his report made no mention of it; he simply alluded to "the recent constitution of the independent republic of Angola, under the direction of the MPLA, in the midst of strong and heroic struggle against imperialism." The Angolan war was not yet a public event as far as Cuban opinion was concerned.

The constitution itself defined Cuba as a "socialist state of workers and peasants and all other manual and intellectual workers," and the Communist party was "the highest leading force of the society and of the state, which organizes and guides the common effort toward the goals of the construction of socialism and the progress toward a Communist society." First, it hailed José Martí, who "led us to the people's revolutionary victory," then Fidel Castro, under whose leadership the "triumphant revolution" was to be carried forward.

Thus enshrined in the constitutional text, Castro was in effect named Leader for Life as a law; the corollary was that it would be unconstitutional (and not just "counterrevolutionary") to challenge him. Pursuant to constitutional provisions, the National Assembly then elected a thirty-one-member Council of State with Fidel Castro as president and Raúl Castro as first vice-president. As president of the council, Castro became "the Head of State and Head of Government." Total power was therefore legally vested in him as President of Cuba and chairman of the Council of Ministers as well as first secretary of the Communist party and military Commander in Chief.

There was no specific succession procedure, but Raúl was the first vice-president of both the Council of State and Council of Ministers, the second secretary of the Communist party (no other Communist party in the world has such a post), and defense minister; the rank of General of the Army was also created for him. Succession was thus automatically resolved, and Fidel remarked once in absolute seriousness, "The creation of the institutions has assured the continuity of the Revolution" after his death. He added straight-facedly that he was not really needed anymore, explaining over the years that Raúl was his successor (automatically) because he had the leadership qualities, not because he was his brother. The faithful Dorticós was demoted from the presidency of Cuba to a ministerial post (he later committed suicide).

The 1976 constitution and the Cuban Communist party's First Congress established the permanent character of the Cuban revolutionary state, ruling out any basic structural or ideological changes in the future—barring cataclysms. As time went on, normal societal requirements would be reflected, but the existing structure or philosophy of the state would never be affected. In this sense, the future of Cuba was set in granite. By 1986, after two more quinquennial Communist party congresses, everything remained the same, with Fidel Castro the only and final authority and arbiter of every decision taken in Cuba. The National Assembly held its two annual sessions as prescribed by the constitution, but each session lasted only two or three days.

The decade between 1976 and 1986, the year when Fidel Castro celebrated his sixtieth birthday and the twenty-seventh anniversary of his revolution, was devoted to immense activity in foreign policy and to continually frustrated efforts to energize and organize the Cuban economy and improve the quality of life of the island's ten million citizens after basic needs of health and education had been met equitably. Internationally, Castro scored more successes than defeats, remaining as defiant as ever and gaining a considerable degree of world acceptability and respectability. In fact, his only defeats since the 1970s, when Allende was overthrown in Chile, were the electoral ouster of his friend Prime Minister Michael Manley in Jamaica, and the American invasion of Grenada, where Castro had had great hopes of expanding Cuban influence in the eastern Caribbean.

Grenada was a bitter blow to Castro because his combat platoons and armed workers there hardly resisted the American invasion and were quickly defeated. Castro demoted his military commander and his ambassador in Angola to lowly occupations. At the Havana airport, when the bodies of dead Cubans arrived from Grenada, Fidel stood alone for a long moment of meditation, his shoulders hunched.

With the United States, there were gains and losses. Negotiations with the Carter administration led to the establishment of diplomatic "interests sections" by the Cubans in Washington and by the Americans in Havana in 1977. These "sections," euphemisms for embassies in the absence of actual diplomatic relations, provided instant channels of communication between the two governments. The Carter and Reagan administrations kept the chief of the Cuban interests section at arms' length, but Castro made a point of giving quasi-ambassadorial treatment to the senior American diplomat in Havana, inviting him to palace receptions. When he was informed in 1985 that a new chief of the American interests section had been appointed, he showed great curiosity, asking visiting Americans and diplomats what sort of person the new *Americano* was. Talks with the United States in 1978 led to an agreement that allowed exiles on the mainland to visit their families in Cuba. Tens of thousands took advantage of this agreement (it was suspended in 1985 when Castro became annoyed with the Reagan administration over the establishment of the antiregime Radio Martí operated by the Voice of America). Political negotiations with the Carter administration, personally orchestrated by Castro, fizzled out, and in 1980 the exodus of over 120,000 Cubans to Florida in small boats from the port of Mariel put an end to the diplomatic contacts. Castro encouraged their departure out of anger over an unguarded remark by President Carter that the United States awaited Cuban political refugees with "open arms."

Castro's great moment in the international sun came when he was elected chairman of the Nonaligned Movement for 1979–1982, assuming the formal Third World leadership to which he had so long aspired. He hosted the Nonaligned Movement's summit conference in Havana in September 1979, at which ninety-two heads of state or their representatives were present—from the Communist octogenarian Marshal Tito of Yugoslavia to the deeply religious Islamic president of Pakistan, Mohammad Zia ul-Haq, and Prime Minister Indira Gandhi of India—and he succeeded at all times in keeping the spotlight on himself. Events were going his way everywhere. In March of 1979, a pro-Cuban regime was established on the tiny island of Grenada in the eastern Caribbean by his friend Maurice Bishop, a leftist lawyer and politician of vast personal appeal. In July the *Sandinista* Liberation Front rebels ousted the Somoza dictatorship in Nicaragua; Castro knew Carlos Fonseca, the founder of the *Sandinista* movement who was killed in 1966, well and he provided considerable assistance to the rebels after forcing them to unite in a common front. Now Cuba had revolutionary allies in Central America and on the outer fringes of the Caribbean, just a hop away from strategic Venezuela.

In October Fidel Castro returned to New York for the first time in nineteen years to address the United Nations General Assembly as chairman of the Nonaligned Movement. It was a moment of vindication he savored: In 1960 he had sought refuge in a hotel in Harlem, and now he was spending three days in New York at the twelve-story midtown building belonging to the Cuban mission to the United Nations (complete with living quarters and a school) that Cuba had just purchased for $2.1 million. The Cuban mission employed the third largest number of officials after the United States and the Soviet Union. Reminiscing about this latest visit to New York and the reception he had held at the Cuban mission, Fidel told me with immense satisfaction, "that first time in 1960, we lived on chicken . . . this time I brought my own lobsters, my own rum . . ." In his two-hour speech at the General Assembly on October 12, Castro—acting as spokesman for the destitute Third World—urged the United States and other "wealthy imperialists" to grant the underdeveloped nations $300 billion over ten years. "If there are no resources for development, there will be no peace," he said, "and the future will be apocalyptic." The fate of the Third World, including its gigantic debt to the industrial nations, became the centerpiece of Castro's foreign policy in the Eighties: He fervently championed it at the 1982 Nonaligned Movement's summit meeteing in New Delhi, and in an extraordinary antidebt offensive he mounted in Havana in 1985.

Economic issues were one aspect of Castro's ever-growing "internationalism." Another was military participation in revolutionary confrontations across the globe. From the initial involvement in Angola in 1975, Castro moved on to Ethiopia in 1978, dispatching nearly twenty thousand combat troops to assist the new Marxist regime of Lieutenant Colonel Mengistu Haile Mariam repulse an attack by Somalia on the contested Ogaden region. As it had done in Angola, the Soviet Union provided arms and advisers; this was the second Soviet-Cuban joint military venture. In Third World policies, Castro and the Russians were totally on the same wavelength. When the Soviet Union invaded Afghanistan in December 1979 to save "socialism" in an Asian rerun of applying the Brezhnev Doctrine to Czechoslovakia, Castro stood foursquare behind this action. He rationalized it even though the fierce Afghan resistance to the Russians created great embarrassment for Castro as the Nonaligned Movement's chairman, especially with Moslem nations. But he could also rationalize switching Cuba's early support for the Eritrean secession movement from Ethiopia to the other side once President Mengistu became his ally. Again Castro's activities threatened to create a Soviet-American confrontation. The presence of Soviet-supported Cuban forces in the crucial Horn of Africa nearly led the Carter administration to break off Strategic Arms Limitation Talks with the Soviet Union. Fidel was always in the limelight.

Castro has never made a secret of his support for the *Sandinista* movement before or after its triumph. He has given Nicaragua, his revolutionary junior partner, maximal support in military advisers and civilian technicians. The Cubans had trained the *Sandinistas* in military camps in Pinar del Río and on the Isle of Youth, and it was Fidel who took it upon himself in 1978 to bring together rival factions among Nicaraguan rebels. Unless they were united, he told them at a secret meeting in Havana, Cuba would not supply arms to them in their "final offensive" year. Since the *Sandinista* victory in 1979, Castro continues to stage-manage the Nicaraguan revolution from Havana; Nicaraguan President Daniel Ortega Saavedra is a very frequent guest in Cuba, sometimes publicly, sometimes secretly.

Castro fully supports the leftist guerrillas in El Salvador (he also supports the M-19 guerrillas in Colombia), but he knows that Cuba cannot protect the two Central American countries from a direct United States attack (and he realizes that the Soviet Union would not commit itself to a military defense of Nicaragua as it is committed to do in Cuba). He believes that political settlements are possible both in Nicaragua and El Salvador because endless stalemate is the alternative. But he is also aware that in a total crisis, the United States might try to annihilate him. His concern is heightened by early Reagan administration threats to go "to the source" of Central American upheavals, which it believes is Cuba—and by the invasion of Grenada in 1983.

Early in 1984, in a conversation about possible American military action in Central America and beyond, Castro told me: "We have no means to be able to decide militarily the events there. All our means are defensive. We have no fleet and no air force capable of neutralizing or breaking a blockade by the United States. It's not a question of options, it's a practical question. . . . Besides, from a political viewpoint it would be improper for us to attempt a military participation under such circumstances because it would be justification before American public opinion for a United States agression." Replying to my question whether he was concerned about an American invasion, Castro said: "We have made great efforts to strengthen our defenses. After Grenada, we have made even greater efforts. We are increasing considerably our defense and resistance capability, including the preparation of the people for a prolonged, indefinite war. If the United States deterrent, as the Reagan government has said, is the nuclear force, our deterrent is to make it impossible for this country to be occupied, for an occupation army to be able to maintain itself in our country. First, it would be necessary to fight very hard to occupy our country. But the occupation of our country would not be the end, but the beginning of a much harder and much more difficult war, in which we would be victorious sooner or later at an enormous cost."

Castro still believes that the Salvador civil war can be settled politically by negotiation, and he does not hide the Cuban support for the leftist guerrillas there. Just as he knew most of the Nicaraguan leaders prior to the 1979 victory, he is acquainted with the Salvadoran guerrilla leaders, having tried hard to impose unity on their factions. During a conversation with me early in 1984, he indicated that these leaders had been visiting him in Havana, saying that "I haven't spoken in many months with the principal leaders of the revolutionary movement in El Salvador because all of them are now inside their country, and it's not possible to have any direct contact with them."

In Castro's Third World vision and policies, doctors and teachers are as important as combat troops, and he takes immense pride in explaining that

Cuba is the only developing nation willing and ready to help others. He says that the new Cuban generation has an internationalist spirit not found elsewhere. In a conversation about this internationalism, he told me: "Look—when after the triumph of the revolution in Nicaragua we were asked for teachers, there were twenty-nine thousand volunteers. . . . In the beginning, we had no doctors to send to the interior of our country. Today, we have doctors in more than twenty-five countries of the Third World—more than fifteen hundred doctors working in the Third World. And there will be more because we are graduating two thousand doctors annually. It is a new culture, a new morality. . . . It is amazing: You go to our universities, and one hundred percent volunteer for any task. When we needed volunteers to go to Angola, three hundred thousand of them responded. When we needed volunteers for Ethiopia, more than three hundred thousand responded. They were civilian reservists. Now, hundreds of thousands of Cubans have fulfilled internationalist missions. People ask why there are two thousand Cuban teachers in Nicaragua, but who else will do the work that Cubans perform there? How many [people] in Latin America are prepared to go where our teachers go to live with the poorest families, to eat what the poorest families eat themselves, to teach there? You won't find such people. . . . We have more people disposed to go to any place in the world as doctors, as teachers, as technicians, and as workers than the Peace Corps of the United States and all the churches together—and we are a country of only ten million inhabitants."

Since 1985, Castro has devoted an astounding amount of time to the problem of the Third World's debt to the banks and governments of industrialized countries, arguing that the destitute debtors cannot pay what they owe without destroying their economies, and predicting dire consequences if efforts are made to collect the money. In 1986 Latin America alone owed more than $350 billion (much of this to United States banks), and the Third World total debt stood near $750 billion. In speeches, interviews, and at conferences he had sponsored in Havana, Castro turned the debt issue into a powerful political instrument in battling "imperialism," but his efforts have had the positive impact of calling international attention to the gravity of the crisis. Staying excellently informed about all Latin American developments, he was, in effect, repeating in 1985 and later exactly what he had done in 1959: warn the industrialized countries of the north that an explosion was in the offing if they did not decisively attack the roots of hemispheric problems. In 1961, President Kennedy took up Castro's challenge by launching the Alliance for Progress; in the late 1980s the "rich" governments would do well to listen again to this Cuban Cassandra.

At home, however, Castro is much less bold and imaginative. He stubbornly refuses to relax the harsh standards of totally centralized planning (even when most of the Communist world has discovered the merits of relative decentralization). Because of his orthodox ideological inflexibility, Castro sees heresy in any attempt to experiment with market forces. Even though the Soviet Union has begun to establish joint industrial production ventures with Western capital, and in 1979 China embarked on a market-economy policy—including allowing private retail stores—Castro will not be budged. The chronic and alarmingly deficient performance of the Cuban economy seems to strengthen his resolve to be faithful to orthodoxy. In June 1986—sounding as he did during the "revolutionary offensive" in 1968— Castro denounced "certain concepts [proposed] by persons, supposedly very Marxist and very versed in Marxism, but really with a capitalist or petit-bourgeois soul." Ideological and political controls over what must be the world's most indoctrinated society tend to tighten rather than relax after the twenty-seven years of revolution.

Even some of Castro's close associates are at a loss to understand the reasons for his new hard-line attitude during the mid-1980s. After the Mariel exodus of 120,000 Cubans in 1980, Castro appeared to have concluded that the nation required a certain relaxation of tensions—the Mariel experience was a trauma because the regime was taken aback by this manifestation of internal resentments—and must be allowed a degree of consumer freedom. Accordingly, many food items were released from rationing and made available at "free stores" for extremely high prices, and uncontrolled farmers' markets were authorized to sell produce in the cities. It was far from a bonanza because foodstuffs remained in short supply as a result of inadequate production, but it seemed a small step toward a liberalization of the economy within Marxism.

As preparations were made during 1985 for the Third Congress of the Communist party, many senior economic planners hoped for still more liberalization and a new policy of decentralization. There was talk about allowing private owners operating through cooperatives to take the government out of the business of running taxis all over Cuba, and about ending clothes and footwear rationing, which had created a state monopoly over shoddy products at an immense cost to the treasury (Cuban women increasingly preferred to have private seamstresses make their dresses). Ideas also circulated about abandoning the ideologically designed youth work brigades whose weekend activities cost more in blankets, boots, mosquito netting, food, and transportation than they brought in farm production. But Castro evidently would have none of it, reemerging as the fierce apostle of the pure revolution while the economy kept deteriorating.

Presumably because Fidel was unable to formulate an economic plan for the next quinquennial party Congress—in part because he was busy presiding over international conferences on Third World debt—the Congress was postponed to February 1986. But even then Castro was still not ready to deal with the key issues, so the most important work of the Congress was postponed till the end of 1986. According to Castro, the most significant achievement of the first part of the Congress was to rejuvenate the leadership. Even this, however, was an illusion. The Politburo contained the same old faces, although several cosmetic changes were made. The new Central Committee was an assemblage of middle-aged men and women drawn from the bureaucracy, party organizations, the armed forces, and Security Services. In a nation where more than half the population was born after the revolution, only 9 percent of the Central Committee membership were under thirty-five; more than 50 percent were over the age of forty-six. Only 18.2 percent were women. And 78.1 percent had a university education, all of which suggests that the party created a new ruling elite, heavy on bureaucrats and administrators (27.5 percent) and full-time party officials (27.1 percent). Twenty percent of the seats went to the armed forces and Interior Ministry Security Services.

In 1986, Fidel Castro imposed an ossification of the regime and society under the guise of keeping the revolutionary fires burning. Almost immediately after the first session of the party Congress ended, Castro ordered the closing of the farmers' markets on the grounds of illicit enrichment and corruption. It was strangely reminiscent of his discovery in 1968 that privately owned hot dog stands were hotbeds of counterrevolution. At the same time, Castro moved even further ahead with the militarization of the Cuban society through the expansion of the Territorial Troop Militias, a highly trained reserve organization exceeding one million people—10 percent of the population. The Militias' 340-page illustrated *Basic Manual* is must reading in Cuba (though it sells for one peso in bookstores), and exercises and maneuvers are conducted continuously in "defense zones" into which the island has been divided. The ever-present threat of invasion by the United States has always justified a high degree of preparedness in Cuba, especially after the Grenada incident, but militarization in the mid-1980s is as much as anything, a political move to strengthen the cohesion of the revolutionary society under Castro's extremely strict leadership.

Castro's revolution was again in trouble with the Soviets in the mid-1980s, chiefly because of Cuba's economic waste and inability to meet its sugar delivery commitments. Soviet emissaries had warned him frankly that this state of affairs could not continue indefinitely, and when the 1985 trade agreement was finally signed in the middle of the year, the communiqué published in the Cuban press said the accord had been reached after "long and difficult negotiations," a most unusual phrase. In fact, Castro had to take the unprecedented step in 1985 and 1986 to purchase for cash sugar from the

Dominican Republic to keep going the shipments to the Soviet Union. However, he was able to pay the very low world price in dollars to the Dominicans while being credited by the Soviets for this sugar at a very high, subsidized price.

Politically, Castro shows total deference to the Russians. He dutifully attended the Soviet Communist Party Congress in 1986, holding his first meeting with Gorbachev since the latter became the top Kremlin leader. Then, he found it necessary to visit North Korea to meet Kim il-Sung, the senior Communist dictator in the world who presides over the most repressive Communist society anywhere. His Moscow and Pyongyang speeches sounded like carbon copies of every communist speech delivered that year in the Soviet sphere of influence. Fidel seemed to join the ranks of the great conformists.

Who is Fidel Castro at the age of sixty? In the immediate sense, he is the undisputed and still enormously popular (and even loved) leader of an extremely volatile nation, which he has led for more than a quarter-century to a place in the sun in world affairs and toward what he has called "a life of decency." A grandfather himself, he sees to it that in Cuba all children are healthy and clean and well educated. In 1985 the national goal was a ninth-grade education for every Cuban. None of this was true a generation or so ago. It is a great accomplishment in any society, underdeveloped or industrial. No Third World country approaches Cuban standards in the area of that decent life. None has a higher doctor-population ratio than Cuba or a greater longevity expectation at birth.

But there are other aspects to Castro, and disturbing ones when one takes his intelligence and experience into account. Since around 1980 his behavior suggests that he has few fresh ideas for his aging revolution. Curiously, this man of astonishing daring and imagination and romanticism is allowing—or forcing—his beloved social and human experiment to be locked into obsolete ideological orthodoxy and deadening bureaucratization. His sallies against "bourgeois" tendencies sound quaintly antiquated, if not slightly caricatural, in a world that has changed so much since such expressions were still in vogue. Considering the extent to which national creativeness has been blunted (one hopes not buried) in the name of conformism, Castro faces the danger that his revolution may be decaying.

In the physical sense, much of the early revolutionary construction is already decaying: the paint is peeling off and windows are broken at the great and admirable Camilo Cienfuegos school complex at the foot of the Sierra Maestra, and masses of costly imported equipment are destroyed by the Caribbean weather because the regime remains unable to solve the problem of unloading ships and loading trucks. These are obvious examples: There are others. Mismanagement discourages work and production, and resulting shortages aggravate the problem of low productivity and high absenteeism. It becomes a vicious circle. Bureaucratic corruption and black marketeering in the streets are reemerging like a cancer on the body of the revolution that was born so pure, and Fidel Castro inveighs in rage against "vile money." Young people drink too much because there is little else to do in their spare time, and they are not touched by the mystical magic of the revolution as their fathers and mothers were when Fidel Castro was an obsessed young rebel.

He is furious over the immense rate of absenteeism among Cuban workers, low productivity, shoddy quality of industrial goods (in the province of Havana in 1985, one half of the soft drink and beer bottles produced in the first six months were unusable and had to be destroyed), and the shocking waste of materials and resources in industrial plants, farms, and government offices. At the Third Congress of the Communist party in 1986, Fidel lectured and chastised his fellow citizens in a speech lasting five hours and forty minutes. However, he rejects any suggestion that it is the over-centralized system of government and management that is at fault, allows no basic structural changes, and resents outside criticism as "counterrevolutionary." Again, such absolutism in a man who does understand the workings of Cuban society is perplexing, and raises the question of whether he has lost contact with his people on this small island.

Does Fidel Castro have doubts and fears, and can he share them with another human being? Celia Sánchez died of cancer in January 1980, and her passing was not only a personal and emotional tragedy for Fidel, but it deprived him of a safe haven—the opportunity occasionally to be himself as Fidel and not as Commander in Chief. Watching him, almost motionless, hour after hour, listening to hundreds of speeches at the conferences on external debt he had organized in Havana during 1985, it seemed as if Castro was seeking refuge in this environment from pressures elsewhere; perhaps it was an illusion. Still, in a variety of surroundings, Fidel Castro appears a lonely man—frustrated one day, triumphant the next, but lonely, and still searching for something that is impossibly elusive. He might be pondering about the past and the future—and about the verdict of the generations to come. Indeed, he expressed this concern in two sentences at two very crucial moments of his life:

Addressing the judges trying him for the assault on Moncada, the moment of the revolution's birth in 1953, Fidel Castro said: "Condemn me. It does not matter. History will absolve me!"

Speaking about the creative process to Cuban artists and writers in 1961, the year he triumphed at the Bay of Pigs and declared himself a Marxist-Leninist, Fidel Castro said: "Do not fear imaginary judges we have here. . . . Fear other judges who are much more fearsome, fear the judges of posterity, fear the future generations who, in the end, will be responsible for saying the last word!"

5. The Revolution at Thirty: A Political Assessment

JAIME SUCHLICKI

Jaime Suchlicki is a professor of history at the University of Miami Graduate School of International Studies and author of a widely-used textbook entitled, *Cuba: From Colombus to Castro* (rev. ed., New York, 1986). He gave the following assessment of the accomplishments and failures of the Cuban Revolution on January 10, 1989 at a conference sponsored by the Cuban American National Foundation to evaluate Castro's regime on its thirtieth anniversary.

It has been thirty years since Fidel Castro came to power, so I think it is possible now to make an assessment of where the Revolution is, and what are its accomplishments and failures. I would like to divide my talk into four parts: one, the successes and contributions of the Cuban Revolution; two, the failures of the Revolution; three, where Cuba is today; and four, where Cuba is going—and all of that in about twenty minutes.

First of all, the successes and contributions of the Revolution: If we look at the past thirty years the obvious and first thing that comes to mind is the survival of the Cuban Revolution. Fidel Castro has been able to survive six U.S. administrations, the Bay of Pigs, the missile crisis, as well as other crises. So survivability has been one of the characteristics of Fidel Castro and an important element in the Cuban Revolution.

The second contribution or success is the militarization of Cuba. Cuba is today, aside from the United States, probably the most important military power in the Western Hemisphere, with armed forces in excess of 300,000 men, a territorial militia of 500,000 men—armed, well-equipped, and well-trained—and with some 300,000 men that have seen military service in Angola. It is the only army in Latin America—maybe aside from the Salvadoran army—that has had to fight consistently and has seen this kind of military service.

From *The Cuban Revolution at Thirty:* Proceedings from a conference sponsored by the Cuban American National Foundation, January 10, 1989. Occasional Paper #29. Cuban American National Foundation. Washington, D.C. 1989, pp. 1–5. Reprinted by permission.

The projection of military power has also been one of the significant characteristics of the Cuban Revolution. Fidel has projected power in Africa, and is projecting power in Central America. Cuba is a regional power, although we could call it a world power, probably out of proportion to its size, its population and its resources. Cuba flexes its muscles not only in Latin America, but also in Africa and the Middle East, and sits down at conferences with South Africa, the Soviet Union, and the United States. So Cuba and Fidel have achieved world stature.

Finally, perhaps the most significant contribution of Fidel Castro is his commitment to violence; in other words, his contribution to revolutionary theory is the way to power in Latin America and elsewhere is not through the ballot box but through bullets.

So having looked at the contributions of the Cuban Revolution, let's look at the failures of thirty years of Fidel Castro. First of all, he has destroyed Western values, culture, and ideas in Cuba. The things that are dear to the Western world—democracy, human rights, the family, religious freedom, individualism, free enterprise—are non-existent in Cuba. Fidel Castro has eradicated these values and for thirty years has remained a bastion against Western culture and values in Cuba.

A second failure in Cuba today is probably more dependent on the Soviet Union than it was on the United States prior to 1958. Not only is it dependent economically, politically, and militarily on the Soviet Union, but it is more dependent today on the sugar economy than it was prior to 1958. In other words, Cuba has not diversified; it has not moved from monoculture. In fact, it has re-emphasized it.

Third, Fidel has created a society of scarcity and repression. Of all the societies in Latin America, Cuba is probably the most totalitarian and the most repressive. The Cuban people are suffering from scarcity, as most products are rationed today in Cuba. So, economically, the Revolution has not fulfilled its promises of 1959.

Perhaps the most important failure of the Revolution is in the area of the youth. The Cuban Revolution has not captured the imagination of the Cuban youth, and if it did in the beginning, has lost it now. Cuba is characterized now by disillusionment and cynicism. The youth in Cuba are not interested in the slogans of the Revolution. The new generation, the "New Man" Fidel Castro promised in 1959, has not been created.

This is a brief summary of where I see the Revolution after thirty years. Where is Cuba today?

First of all, Fidel Castro is the last Stalinist leader in the communist world. He has returned recently to the failed policies of the past. He is emphasizing again moral incentives. He toyed, for example, in 1979–80 with material incentives. He allowed the opening of the *mercados populares,* or popular markets. He allowed a budding capitalism and free enterprise in Cuba, but then in 1983–84, began to close it down in part because he saw *perestroika* as a threat to his position. Cuba has gone through a period of *perestroika*. But Castro has seen what it can do and doesn't like it. He sees it as a threat to his power, to his control in Cuba, and is not willing to provide that transformation. He has gone back to the ideas of creating a "New Man," that Cubans work best when they are motivated by ideas, ideology, and moral incentives rather than material incentives. So there is this policy of the "rectification of errors" of the past that in a sense maybe is reminiscent of the cultural revolution in China, maybe not as bloody as China, but there is a re-emphasis on the old values, the old ideas he tried to impose in Cuba in the 1960s that did not work.

In Cuba's foreign affairs, there are several elements that have remained consistent over the past thirty years. One is internationalism, Castro's commitment to violent revolution, to supporting revolutionary and terrorist groups in various parts of the world. Internationalism also takes the form of state-to-state relations. We see Fidel Castro as the statesman going to Ecuador for the inauguration of President Borja and meeting with Latin American leaders. On this level, internationalism is seeking acceptability and respectability as a statesman in Latin America. A third level of internationalism is his connections with groups throughout Latin America and other parts of the world—labor groups, student groups, political parties and political organizations.

The next important element in Castro's foreign policy is anti-Americanism. Castro's contribution to history, as he sees it, is his position against the United States, whether it is by supporting revolutionary groups, uniting Latin America on the question of the debt crisis, or creating mischief for the United States in Latin America. What makes Castro tick is his anti-Americanism.

The final element of his foreign policy is his solidarity with the Soviet Union. We have heard significant statements recently about the divisions and the problems between Cuba and the Soviet Union. And there are problems. There have been problems between Cuba and the Soviet Union going back to Khrushchev. These differences included Fidel's apprehension about the limit to Soviet support of Cuba, especially in case of crisis; the limits of Soviet support toward revolutionary regimes like Grenada and Nicaragua; and the insistence of the Soviet Union on economic changes. Yet these differences have to be balanced against the intertwined relationship—at the military, party, and state level—that exists between Cuba and the Soviet Union and has developed over the past thirty years.

Cuba provides the Soviet Union with a military base and a base for espionage at Lourdes. The DGI works very closely with the KGB throughout the world. Cuba votes with the Soviet Union at the United Nations and it receives military and economic aid to the tune of four-and-a-half to five billion dollars a year. This relationship has been cemented over the past thirty years and is not likely to break up or fall apart because of Gorbachev's *perestroika* in the Soviet Union. I see Cuba continuing to be tied to the Soviet Union and as a continuing element in Soviet worldwide interests.

There is also a convergence of Soviet and Cuban views in Central America. It is in Gorbachev's interest to have a relaxation of tensions between Cuba and the United States and between the United States and Nicaragua. The Soviet and Cuban objectives coincide in the consolidation of the Nicaraguan Revolution at a low cost to the Soviet Union.

If Gorbachev is able to prevail on the new U.S. administration to normalize relations with Nicaragua and to normalize relations with Cuba, he would achieve this significant goal. So in this sense we have seen the overtures, mild overtures, of Fidel Castro toward the United States: normalization of immigration agreements, allowing certain religious leaders to visit Cuba. There is an element of tokenism on the part of Cuba toward the United States in the hope of achieving this immediate objective of reducing the cost to the Soviet Union of supporting both Cuba and Nicaragua.

I am doubtful Fidel Castro is willing to provide the meaningful concessions necessary for normalization with the United States. It always puzzles me how we think we can buy Third World leaders like Fidel Castro or Qaddafi. It is misreading the intentions, objectives, and the things that make Fidel Castro tick when we think we can sell him computers and Fruit of the Loom underwear, buy Cuban sugar, and somehow he will become the Tito of the Western Hemisphere, abandoning world revolution and his commitment to the Soviet Union and allies throughout the world. If Fidel Castro had a real commitment to economic development in Cuba and to the Cuban people, he wouldn't have carried out many of the policies and actions he has carried out in the world. Fidel Castro is less concerned about whether the Cubans eat better and more concerned about his position in history and his position in the world.

Fidel Castro hasn't mellowed in thirty years. I don't think there is any indication he has mellowed—read his last speech or his speech commemorating the anniversary of the Revolution. He is as combative and as anti-American as he's always been. To think we can weaken his relationship with the Soviet Union and normalize relations, and Cuba will abandon world revolution and its commitment abroad is an illusion. Every four years I see this illusion emerging in Wasshington and every four years I see it go down the drain.

The only rabbit that Fidel Castro has in his hat now is relations with the United States. Yet he is not willing to provide meaningful concessions—

concessions regarding the Soviet military presence in Cuba, his commitment to revolutionary violence, and internal democratization. Relations with the United States at this point will provide a longer lease on life to his economically disastrous regime. It would give hope to the Cuban people that things are going to get better. It is ironic that when the Cuban economy is at a low point, when our policy of thirty years has been somewhat successful, we are now again talking about normalizing relations with Cuba.

Thank you.

SUGGESTIONS FOR FURTHER READING AND VIEWING

SECTION I
SIMÓN BOLÍVAR—THE LIBERATOR
BOOKS

Belaunde, Victor Andrés. BOLÍVAR AND THE POLITICAL THOUGHT OF THE SPANISH AMERICAN REVOLUTION. Baltimore: 1938. A careful analysis of Bolívar's thought against a background of the revolutionary period as a whole.

Bushnell, David. THE LIBERATOR, SIMÓN BOLÍVAR: MAN AND IMAGE. New York: Knopf, 1970. An excellent collection of writings by and about Bolívar.

————. THE SANTANDER REGIME IN GRAN COLOMBIA. Newark: The University of Delaware Press, 1954. A history of Gran Colombia until the overthrow of Santander in 1827.

Johnson, John J. SIMÓN BOLÍVAR AND SPANISH AMERICAN INDEPENDENCE, 1783–1830 New York: D. Van Nostrand, 1968. An informative biography augmented by selections from key writings by the Liberator.

Lynch, John. THE SPANISH AMERICAN REVOLUTIONS, 1808–1826. 2nd ed. New York: Norton, 1986. The best study of the independence era—well-written and based on thorough research.

Masur, Gerhard. SIMÓN BOLÍVAR. Albuquerque: University of New Mexico Press, 1948. Still considered the best biography in English.

O'Leary, Daniel Florencio. BOLÍVAR AND THE WAR OF INDEPENDENCE. Translated and edited by Robert F. McNerney, Jr. Austin: University of Texas Press, 1970. A valuable set of memoirs concerning events of Bolívar's career, by his Irish-born aide.

Von Hagen, Victor W. THE FOUR SEASONS OF MANUELA. Switzerland: Plata, 1974. Novelistic but fascinating biography of the most influential woman in Bolívar's life.

FILMS AND VIDEOTAPES

SIMÓN BOLÍVAR. (Color, 105 minutes, English soundtrack, 1972) Feature film. Starring Maxmilian Schell and Rosana Schiaffino. Filmed in Venezuela and Spain with the cooperation of the Venezuelan government and the Academia de Historia de Venezuela. Distributor: Films, Inc.

Described in the distributor's catalogue as "a colorful biography of the great nineteenth century Liberator of South America," this film is short on fact and long on fancy, but Schell makes a creditable Bolívar in appearance, energy, and personality.

SECTION II

THE AGE OF CAUDILLOS—JUAN MANUEL DE ROSAS

BOOKS

Bunkley, Allison W. THE LIFE OF SARMIENTO. Princeton, 1952. A scholarly biography that emphasizes the early years of this great educator, president, and writer.

Burgin, Miron. THE ECONOMIC ASPECTS OF ARGENTINE FEDERALISM, 1820–1852. Cambridge, MA: Harvard University Press, 1946. An outstanding study of the economics behind the Rosas regime.

Bushnell, David. REFORM AND REACTION IN THE PLATINE PROVINCES. Gainesville: University of Florida Press, 1983. Discusses the social and political content of the liberal-conservative antagonisms.

Hamill, Hugh M., ed. DICTATORSHIP IN SPANISH AMERICA. New York: Knopf, 1965. Excellent collection of theories and case studies of caudillism.

Lynch, John. ARGENTINE DICTATOR: JUAN MANUEL ROSAS, 1829–1852. New York: Oxford University Press, 1981. Best biography in English.

Rennie, Ysabel F. THE ARGENTINE REPUBLIC. New York: Macmillan, 1945. Old but still usefuly, highly readable survey of Argentina.

Wilgus, Alva Curtis, ed. SOUTH AMERICAN DICTATORS DURING THE FIRST CENTURY OF INDEPENDENCE. 2nd ed. New York: Russell and Russell, 1963. Contains short biographies of the leading caudillos in all the South American republics. Good introductory source.

FILMS AND VIDEOTAPES

CAMILA. (Color, 105 minutes, Spanish sound track, English subtitles, 1984) Argentine feature film. Starring Susu Pecoraro, Imanol Arias and Hector Alferio. Filmed in Argentina and Uruguay by Maria Luisa Bemberger.
Distributors: 16 mm film—European Classics/VHS video—Facets

A romantic drama set in the time of Juan Manuel de Rosas. Tells the story of a beautiful, well-born Buenos Aires woman, Camila O'Gorman, who elopes with a Jesuit priest, Ladislao Gutiérrez in 1847. Provides insight into the tyranny imposed by Rosas and also makes a modern political statement since it was produced in Argentina after the civilian government headed by Raul Alfonsín replaced the military dictatorship. Highly recommended.

SECTION III

NINETEENTH-CENTURY ECONOMIC AFFAIRS

BOOKS

Burns, E. Bradford. A HISTORY OF BRAZIL. 2nd ed. New York: Columbia University Press, 1980. The best general history of Brazil. Good background material on Pedro II and Baron Mauá.

Díaz Alejandro, Carlos. ESSAYS ON ECONOMIC HISTORY OF THE ARGENTINE REPUBLIC. New Haven: Yale University Press, 1970. Particular problems of economic development are treated in detail and with understanding.

Furtado, Celso. THE ECONOMIC DEVELOPMENT OF LATIN AMERICA. Translated by Suzette Macedo. 2nd ed. Cambridge: Cambridge University Press, 1976. Most widely-read economic history of Latin America.

Graham, Richard. BRITAIN AND THE ONSET OF MODERNIZATION IN BRAZIL, 1850–1914. Cambridge: Cambridge University Press, 1968. Describes the English influence on Brazil's transformation into a major exporting nation.

Martín, Luis. THE KINGDOM OF THE SUN: A SHORT HISTORY OF PERU. New York: Charles Scribner's Sons, 1974. The best general history of Peru. Good background for understanding the exploits of Henry Meiggs.

Safford, Frank. THE IDEAL OF THE PRACTICAL: COLOMBIA'S STRUGGLE TO FORM A TECHNICAL ELITE. Austin: The University of Texas Press, 1976. A study of the efforts of the Colombian upper class to use technical education as a way of developing entrepreneurs and an industrious working class.

Scobie, James. ARGENTINA: A CITY AND A NATION. 2nd ed. New York: Oxford Press, 1971. The best general historical survey of Argentina.

Stewart, Watt. HENRY MEIGGS, YANKEE PIZARRO. Duram: Duke University Press, 1951. Biography of the colorful North American entrepreneur.

Williams, John Hoyt. THE RISE AND FALL OF THE PARAGUAYAN REPUBLIC, 1800–1870. Austin: University of Texas Press, 1979. A well-written, well-researched survey of Paraguay's fascinating nineteenth-century history.

FILMS AND VIDEOTAPES

WALKER. (Color, 90 minutes, English sound track, 1987) Feature film made in Nicaragua with the cooperation of the Sandinista government. Starring Ed Harris, Marlee Matlin, Peter Boyle, and Blanca Guerra.
Distributor: VHS video—Facets
  A historical recreation of the effort of William Walker to invade Nicaragua in 1855 and rule the country. The genre is political satire, with many historical anachronisms. The goal of director Alex Cox is to portray the nineteenth-century episode in a way that implies criticism of contemporary U.S. support for the contras.

SECTION IV

AFRICAN SLAVERY IN BRAZIL

BOOKS

Conrad, Robert Edgar. CHILDREN OF GOD'S FIRE: A DOCUMENTARY HISTORY OF BLACK SLAVERY IN BRAZIL. Princeton: Princeton University Press, 1983. A collection of primary sources that cover various aspects of slavery, written in vivid, direct language.

————. THE DESTRUCTION OF BRAZILIAN SLAVERY, 1850–1888. Berkeley: University of California Press, 1973. Deals with the crucial issue of abolition.

Freyre, Gilberto. THE MASTERS AND THE SLAVES, rev. ed. Berkeley: University of California Press, 1989. The classic Brazilian work on slavery and race relations. Difficult reading, but indispensable.

Klein, Herbert S. AFRICAN SLAVERY IN LATIN AMERICA AND THE CARIBBEAN. New York: Oxford University Press, 1986. Most comprehensive recent survey of slavery in all its aspects throughout Latin America.

Pescatello, Ann M., ed. THE AFRICAN IN LATIN AMERICA. New York: Knopf, 1975. Good selection of materials relating to slavery in Brazil and Spanish America.

Queiros Mattoso, Katia M. TO BE A SLAVE IN BRAZIL, 1550–1888. New Brunswick, N.J.: Rutgers University Press, 1986. Very readable account of the experience of slaves based on fundamental research.

Russell-Wood, A.J.R. THE BLACK MAN IN SLAVERY AND FREEDOM IN COLONIAL BRAZIL. New York, St. Martin's Press, 1982. Excellent survey.

Stein, Stanley. VASSOURAS: A BRAZILIAN COFFEE COUNTRY, 1850–1900. Cambridge: Harvard University Press, 1957. Classic study of Brazilian plantation economy.

Toplin, Robert Brent. THE ABOLITION OF SLAVERY IN BRAZIL. New York: Atheneum, 1972. Study of the decline of slavery.

FILMS AND VIDEOTAPES

QUILOMBO. (Color, 114 minutes, Portuguese sound track, English subtitles, 1984) Brazilian feature film. Starring Antonio Pompeo, Zeze Motta, and Toni Tornado. Directed by Carlos Diegues.
Distributors: 16 mm film—New Yorker/VHS video—Facets
   Epic history of Palmares, a fugitive slave settlement in Pernambuco whose existence between 1605 and 1695 was regarded as a threat to Portuguese rule in America. Great heroes, terrible events, and victory of the spirit. A vivid fresco that traces the African roots of Brazilian civilization.

THE LAST SUPPER (Color, 110 minutes, Spanish sound track, English subtitles, 1977) Cuban feature film. Directed by Tomas Gutiérrez Alea.
Distributor: 16 mm film—New Yorker
   Based on an incident from eighteenth-century Cuban history when a pious slaveholder decided to instruct his slaves in Christian humility by inviting them to participate in a reenactment of the Last Supper. Sardonic *tour-de-force*.

THE OTHER FRANCISCO (B&W, 97 minutes, Spanish sound track, English subtitles, 1975) Cuban feature film. Directed by Sergio Giral.
Distributor: 16 mm film—New Yorker
   A vital, impassioned exploration of the roots of black rebellion in Cuba based on a famous Cuban anti-slavery novel of the nineteenth century.

SECTION V

PORFIRO DÍAZ: DICTATOR OF MEXICO

BOOKS

Beals, Carleton. PORFIRIO DÍAZ: DICTATOR OF MEXICO. Westport, CT: Greenwood Press, 1971. Originally written in 1931, this biography is still the best available in English.

Coatsworth, John H. GROWTH AGAINST DEVELOPMENT: THE ECONOMIC IMPACT OF RAILROADS IN PORFIRIAN MEXICO. DeKalb: Northern Illinois University Press, 1981. Study of the impact of railroads in late nineteenth century.

Cockcroft, James D. INTELLECTUAL PRECURSORS OF THE MEXICAN REVOLUTION. Austin: University of Texas Press, 1968. Valuable study of intellectual dissent in the late Porfiriato.

Flandrau, Charles M. VIVA MEXICO! Urbana: University of Illinois Press, 1964. Classic account of life on a coffee plantation in eastern Mexico during the later period of the Porfiriato as seen by a young American.

Knight, Alan. THE MEXICAN REVOLUTION. Cambridge: Cambridge University Press, 1986. Rich and highly readable synthesis of the revolution's first decade.

Meyer, Michael C. and William L. Sherman. THE COURSE OF MEXICAN HISTORY. 2nd ed. New York: Oxford, 1983. Detailed, well-balanced, and up-to-date one-volume survey of Mexican history.

Vanderwood, Paul J. DISORDER AND PROGRESS: BANDITS, POLICE AND MEXICAN DEVELOPMENT. Lincoln: University of Nebraska Press, 1981. Reexamination of the role of the rural police under Díaz.

Womack, John Jr. ZAPATA AND THE MEXICAN REVOLUTION. New York: Knopf, 1968. Excellent study of the agrarian revolution led by the legendary Emiliano Zapata.

FILMS AND VIDEOTAPES

ART AND REVOLUTION IN MEXICO. (Color, 60 minutes, English soundtrack, n.d.) Documentary. Written by Octavio Paz.
Distributor: VHS video—Films for the Humanities
   Shows how art—from the satiric cartoon to the broad-stroked mural—was both the result and the cause of the Revolution of 1910. Features work of Rivera, Orozco, and Siqueiros.

MEMORIAS DE UN MEXICANO. (Color, 45 minutes, English soundtrack, 1971) Mexican-made documentary.
Distributor: VHS video—Madera Cinevideo
   An edited version of a two-hour black and white documentary based on newsreel footage of the Mexican Revolution. Shows key events between 1904–1924. Vivid portraits of Díaz, Madero, Villa, Huerta, Zapata, Carranza and Obregón. Highly recommended.

THE RAGGED REVOLUTION (Color, 37 minutes, English soundtrack, 198?) British-made documentary.
Distributors: 16 mm film—The Cinema Guild/VHA video—The Cinema Guild
   TV documentary that uses newsreel footage to bring events and personalities of the Mexican Revolution to life. Discusses U.S. role and shows the influence of muralists Rivera, Orozco, and Siqueiros.

SECTION VI

CONFLICTING LATIN AND YANKEE ATTITUDES AT THE TURN OF THE TWENTIETH CENTURY

BOOKS

Anderson-Imbert, Enrique. SPANISH-AMERICAN LITERATURE: A HISTORY, 1492–1963. 2 vols. Detroit: Wayne State University Press, 1969. Comprehensive survey of Latin American literary figures in historical context. Very helpful.

Arévalo, José Justo. THE SHARK AND THE SARDINES. New York, 1961. Biting critique of U.S. policy in Latin America by a former Guatemalan president.

Crawford, William R. A CENTURY OF LATIN AMERICAN THOUGHT, Rev. ed. Cambridge: Harvard University Press, 1961. Lively survey of major thinkers in Latin America in the nineteenth and early twentieth centuries.

Crow, John A. THE EPIC OF LATIN AMERICA. 3rd ed. Berkeley: University of California, 1980. A history of Latin America that pays great attention to the role of ideology and literature. Readable but outdated.

Franco, Jean. THE MODERN CULTURE OF LATIN AMERICA: SOCIETY AND THE ARTIST. Rev. ed. Middlesex, England: Penguin, 1970. Excellent survey of Latin American literature and the relationship between writers and their societies.

Johnson, John J. LATIN AMERICA IN CARICATURE. Austin: University of Texas Press, 1980. Analysis of U.S. attitudes and policies toward Latin America through a study of cartoons published in major newspapers from the late nineteenth century to the 1970's.

Langley, Lester D. THE UNITED STATES AND THE CARIBBEAN IN THE TWEN-TIETH CENTURY. Rev. ed. Athens, GA: University of Georgia Press, 1985. Well researched and written comprehensive survey of U.S. relations with the Caribbean nations.

Lizaso, Felix. MARTÍ: MARTYR OF CUBAN INDEPENDENCE. Albuquerque: University of New Mexico Press, 1953. Standard biography of the Cuban patriot.

Rodríguez Monegal, Emir, ed. THE BORZOI ANTHOLOGY OF LATIN AMERICAN LITERATURE FROM THE TIME OF COLUMBUS TO THE TWENTIETH CEN-TURY. 2 vols. New York: Knopf, 1983. An anthology of major works by Spanish-American and Brazilian writers translated into English. Helpful introduction to a vast field.

Munro, Dana Gardner. INTERVENTION AND DOLLAR DIPLOMACY IN THE CA-
RIBBEAN, 1900-1921. Princeton: Princeton University Press, 1964. Scholarly, but sup-
portive of U.S. actions during an aggressive period.

FILMS AND VIDEOTAPES

EL NORTE. (Color, 139 minutes, Spanish sound track. English subtitles, 1984) Feature
film directed by Gregory Nava. Starring David Villalpando and Zaide Silvia Gutiérrez.
Filmed in Guatemala, Mexico, and the United States.
Distributor: VHS video—Facets
    In three parts this film dramatizes the flight of a peasant brother and sister who flee
political repression in Guatemala to enter the U.S. illegally in search of a better life.
Moving portrayal of the clash of cultures and the desperate plight of the refugees.

SECTION VII

EVA PERÓN—ARGENTINE FEMINIST

BOOKS

Alexander, Robert. THE PERÓN ERA. New York: Columbia University Press, 1951.
One of the first analyses of the Perón regime.

Blanksten, George I. PERÓN'S ARGENTINA. Chicago: University of Chicago Press,
1974. A classic work that is still valuable.

Fraser, Nicholas and Marysa Navarro. EVA PERÓN. New York: Norton, 1985. A scholarly and readable biography. Highly recommended.

Hahner, June E. WOMEN IN LATIN AMERICAN HISTORY. Rev. ed. Los Angeles:
UCLA Latin American Center, 1978. A general introduction to the lives and views of
Latin American women from colonial times to the present.

Henderson, James D. and Linda Henderson. TEN NOTABLE WOMEN OF LATIN
AMERICA. Chicago: Nelson-Hall, 1978. Short biographies of prominent women from
colonial times to the present including one of Eva Perón. Good introductory work.

Lavrin, Asunción. LATIN AMERICAN WOMEN: HISTORICAL PERSPECTIVES.
Westport, CT: Greenwood Press, 1978. Important study by major scholar in women's
history.

Page, Joseph. PERÓN: A BIOGRAPHY. New York: Random House, 1983. Well-written,
well-documented biography.

Taylor, J. M. EVA PERÓN: THE MYTHS OF A WOMAN. Chicago: University of
Chicago Press, 1979. An anthropologist examines the good and bad legends inspired by
Eva Perón.

Barnes, John. EVITA—FIRST LADY. New York: Grove Press, 1978. Readable, somewhat sensational biography lacking scholarly footnotes.

FILMS AND VIDEOTAPES

EVA PERÓN. (B&W, 26 minutes, English sound track, 1963) Documentary film. Produced by David L. Wolper for CBS-TV.
Distributors: 16 mm Film—Syracuse University Film Rental; Oregon State University Audiovisual Instruction
   Biography of Eva narrated by Mike Wallace based on newsreel footage. Commentary is violently hostile to Eva and Juan Perón. It concludes that she dominated her husband and was motivated solely by selfish ambition. Useful as an example of this view of the Peróns and the bias in North American TV reporting.

PERÓN AND EVITA. (B&W, 26 minutes, English sound track, 1958) Documentary film. Produced for CBS-TV News "Twentieth Century Series."
Distributors: 16 mm Film—University of Texas at Austin Film Center
   Combines newsreel footage with narration by Walter Cronkite to describe the rise, reign, and fall of Juan Perón. Includes highlights of the careers of both Peróns. Narration is more objective than EVA PERÓN. Highly recommended.

THE OFFICIAL STORY. (Color, 112 minutes. Spanish sound Track, English subtitles, 1985) Argentine feature film. Directed by Luis Puenzo. Starring Norma Aleandro, Hector Alterio, and Amalia Castro.
Distributor: VHS video—Facets
   Tells the story of a schoolteacher who suspects that her adopted five-year old daughter was stolen as an infant from her parents, who were arrested and executed during the "Dirty War" waged by the Argentine military during the 1970's. Academy Award winner for the Best Foreign Language Film in 1986.

SECTION VIII

FIDEL CASTRO AND THE CUBAN REVOLUTION

BOOKS

Bonachea, Rolando E. and Nelson P. Valdés, eds. CUBA IN REVOLUTION. New York: Anchor Books, 1973. An anthology that includes selections on revolutionary war, bureaucracy, economic policy, sugar, labor, education, and culture.

Dominguez, Jorge. CUBA: ORDER AND REVOLUTION. Cambridge: Harvard University Press, 1978. Surveys Cuba in the twentieth century with emphasis on conditions after 1959.

González, Edward. CUBA UNDER CASTRO: THE LIMITS OF CHARISMA. Boston: Houghton Mifflin, 1974. Fine study of Castro's role in the political process, and of revolutionary politics in general.

Goodsell, James Nelson, ed. FIDEL CASTRO'S PERSONAL REVOLUTION. New York: Knopf, 1975. Anthology including essays and excerpts dealing with politics, economic development, culture, and foreign policy.

Mesa-Lago, Carmelo. CUBA IN THE 1970s. Rev. ed. Albuquerque: University of New Mexico Press, 1978. Examines the social and economic policies of the Revolution through the 1970's.

——. THE ECONOMY OF SOCIALIST CUBA: A TWO DECADE APPRAISAL. Albuquerque: University of New Mexico Press, 1981. An analysis of the successes and failures of the economy during the Revolution.

Pérez, Louis A. CUBA: BETWEEN REFORM AND REVOLUTION. New York: Oxford, 1988. Scholarly, well-written one-volume survey from colonial times to the 1980's.

Ruiz, Ramón. CUBA: THE MAKING OF A REVOLUTION. New York: Norton, 1970. Study of nationalism and anti-Americanism, and their impact on the Cuban Revolution and its leaders.

Suchlicki, Jaime. CUBA: FROM COLUMBUS TO CASTRO. 2nd ed. Washington, D.C.: Pergamon-Brassey's International Defense Publishers, 1986. Readable one-volume survey of Cuban history from colonial times to the present.

FILMS AND VIDEOS

CUBA: IN THE SHADOW OF DOUBT. (Color, 28 minutes, English sound track, 1986) Documentary film directed by Jim Bourroughs for broadcasting on Public TV.
Distributors: 16 mm film—Filmakers Library/ VHS video—Filmakers Library
   Examines the origins of the Cuban revolution and its successes and failures in the 1980's. Interviews with Castro, Cuban artists and critics of the Revolution. Contrasts the successes of health, education, and housing with the often repressive political measures implemented by Castro. Highly recommended.

MEMORIES OF UNDERDEVELOPMENT. (B&W, 97 minutes, Spanish sound track, English subtitles, 1968) Cuban feature film. Directed by Tomás Gutierrez Alea.
Distributor: 16 mm film—New Yorker
   Based on Edmundo Desnoes' novel of the same title, this film is the diary of a bourgeois intellectual caught in the middle of the rapidly changing social reality of revolutionary Cuba. A complex and fascinating portrait of an individual alienated from the social process around him.

PORTRAIT OF TERESA. (Color, 103 minutes, Spanish sound track, English subtitles, 1979) Cuban Feature film directed by Pastor Vega.
Distributor: 16 mm film—New Yorker
   Realistic account of a woman in revolutionary Cuba struggling with the overwhelming

demands of family and her job in a textile factory. Shows the disintegration of her marriage with compassion and authenticity, and focuses on the survival of *machismo* and sexism in post-revolutionary Cuban society.

FILM AND VIDEO DISTRIBUTORS

The Cinema Guild
1697 Broadway, Suite 802
New York, NY 10019
(212) 246-5522

European Classics
4818 Yuma NW
Washington D.C. 20016
(202) 363-8800

Facets Multimedia, Inc.
1517 W. Fullerton Ave.
Chicago, IL 60614
(312) 281-9075

Filmakers Library
133 East 58th St., Suite 703A
New York, NY 10022
(212) 808-4980

Films for the Humanities
Box 2053
Princeton, NJ 08540
(609) 452-1128/(800) 257-5126

Films, Inc.
440 Park Avenue South
New York, New York 10016
(212) 889-7910/(800) 223-6249

Madera Cinevideo
620 East Yosemite Ave.
Madera, CA 93638
(800) 624-2204

New Yorker Films
16 W. 61st Street
New York, NY 10023
(212) 247-6110

Oregon State University Audiovisual
   Instruction
133 Gill Coliseum
Corvallis, OR 97331
(503) 754-2911

Syracuse University Film Rental Center
1455 East Colvin Street
Syracuse, New York 13210
(315) 479-6631

University of Texas at Austin Film Library
Box W, Educ. Annex G-5
20th at San Jacinto
Austin, TX 78713-7448
(512) 471-3572